DATE DUE

MAR - 3 1995	
MAR 1 5 1995	
Mar 29/95	
DEC - 9 1996	
SEP 2 2 1998	
APR - 6 2001	
FEB 2 0 2002	
FEB 2 8 2002	

BRODART   Cat. No. 23-221

Women and the Environment

Human Behavior and Environment

ADVANCES IN THEORY AND RESEARCH

Women and the Environment

Edited by

IRWIN ALTMAN
University of Utah
Salt Lake City, Utah

and

ARZA CHURCHMAN
Technion-Israel Institute of Technology
Haifa, Israel

PLENUM PRESS • NEW YORK AND LONDON

Library of Congress Cataloging-in-Publication Data

Women and the environment / edited by Irwin Altman and Arza Churchman.
        p.   cm. -- (Human behavior and environment ; v. 13)
    Includes bibliographical references and index.
    ISBN 0-306-44680-4
    1. Environmental psychology. 2. Women--Psychology.   I. Altman,
Irwin. II. Ts'erts'man, Arzah. III. Series.
BF353.H85 vol. 13
155.6'33--dc20   94-16018
                                                                   CIP

ISBN 0-306-44680-4

©1994 Plenum Press, New York
A Division of Plenum Publishing Corporation
233 Spring Street, New York, N.Y. 10013

Printed in the United States of America

Contributors

IRWIN ALTMAN • Department of Psychology, University of Utah, Salt Lake City, Utah 84112

KATHLEEN CHRISTENSEN • Environmental Psychology Program, Graduate School and University Center, City University of New York, New York, New York 10036

ARZA CHURCHMAN • Faculty of Architecture and Town Planning, Technion-Israel Institute of Technology, Haifa 32000, Israel

ROBERTA M. FELDMAN • School of Architecture, University of Illinois at Chicago, Chicago, Illinois 60607-7024

MELISSA GILBERT • Department of Geography, Georgia State University, Atlanta, Georgia 30303

SUSAN HANSON • Graduate School of Geography, Clark University, Worcester, Massachusetts 01610

LIISA HORELLI • Department of Psychology, University of Helsinki, 00570 Helsinki, Finland

SANDRA C. HOWELL • Department of Architecture, Massachusetts Institute of Technology, Cambridge, Massachusetts 02139

DOREEN MATTINGLY • Graduate School of Geography, Clark University, Worcester, Massachusetts 01610

WILLIAM MICHELSON • Centre for Urban and Community Studies and Department of Sociology, University of Toronto, Toronto M5S 1A1, Ontario, Canada

ELLEN-J. PADER • Department of Landscape Architecture and Regional Planning, University of Massachusetts–Amherst, Amherst, Massachusetts 01003

GERALDINE PRATT • Department of Geography, University of British Columbia, Vancouver V6T 1Z2, British Columbia, Canada

MARSHA RITZDORF • Department of Urban Affairs and Planning, Virginia Polytechnic Institute and State University, Blacksburg, Virginia 24061-0113

LYNDA H. SCHNEEKLOTH • School of Architecture and Planning, State University of New York at Buffalo, Buffalo, New York 14222; and The Caucus Partnership, Buffalo, New York 14222

RACHEL SEBBA • Faculty of Architecture and Town Planning, Technion-Israel Institute of Technology, Haifa 32000, Israel

SUSAN STALL • Department of Sociology, Northeastern Illinois University, Chicago, Illinois 60625

KIRSTI VEPSÄ • Planning and Building Department, Ministry of Environment, Korkeavuorenkatu 21, 00230 Helsinki, Finland

Preface

This thirteenth volume in the series addresses an increasingly salient worldwide research, design, and policy issue—women and physical environments.

We live in an era of worldwide social change. Some nation-states are fracturing or disintegrating, migrations are resulting from political upheavals and economic opportunities, some ethnic and national animosities are resurfacing, and global and national economic systems are under stress. Furthermore, the variability of interpersonal and familial forms is increasing, and cultural subgroups—minorities, women, the physically challenged, gays, and lesbians—are vigorously demanding their rights in societies and are becoming significant economic and political forces.

Although these social-system changes affect many people, their impact on women is especially salient. Women are at the center of most forms of family life. Whether in traditional or contemporary cultures, women's roles in child rearing, home management, and community relations have and will continue to be central, regardless of emerging and changing family structures. And, because of necessity and opportunity, women are increasingly engaged in paid work in and outside the home (women in most cultures have historically always worked, but often not for pay). Their influence in cultures and societies is also mounting in the social, political, and economic spheres. In technological societies, women are playing higher-level roles, though still in small numbers, in economic and policy domains. This trend is likely to accelerate in the twenty-first century.

The present volume addresses selected aspects of these broad-ranging issues, especially in respect to women and the physical environments in which they live and work. In planning this volume, we were guided by the philosophical perspective adopted by the *Psychology of Women Quarterly*, 1990, as follows:

> [This perspective] . . . (c) looks at women within the meaningful contexts of their lives . . . (e) solicits samples other than college sophomores, including diversity in age, ethnic and economic status, relational preferences, and so on; (f) considers sex and gender comparisons in context rather than simply looking for "sex" differences; (g) interprets women's response repertoires . . . in ways that do not blame the victims of violence and injustice; (h) explores alternatives that empower women and minorities; (i) examines the structural and interpersonal hierarchies that render women and other minority groups less powerful; (j) contains implications for social change. . . .

The chapters in this volume attempt to reflect the preceding principles. The women whose lives and environments are described or whose voices are heard are young, middle-aged, and elderly; white, African-American, and Latino/Hispanic; North and Central American and Western European; lower, middle, and upper class; within the labor force and outside of it; urban and suburban; educated and noneducated; and living in a variety of family forms and embedded in a variety of personal, familial, community, and work relationships.

The changing and often enhanced roles of women in public and private life are not without significant barriers in respect to constraints and public policies regarding the environment. It is to these environmental issues regarding women's lives that the present volume is directed. For example, chapters examine environments through the life cycle—children's environments, family home environments, elderly women's living settings. Authors also analyze aspects of women's work and related environments such as homes, communities, public places, and transportation systems. And several chapters address community and public-policy issues associated with homes, large-scale housing, and women's roles in community action and policy formulation. Furthermore, several authors examine legal, legislative, and public-policy barriers to environmental change, as well as provide case examples of successful efforts by women to create positive social change in their home and community environments. Finally, some chapters address philosophy of design and research issues in respect to women and environments.

Taken as a set, the chapters in the volume emphasize simultaneously problems and opportunities, needs for continuity and change, and issues associated with large- and small-scale aspects of women and physical environments. The focus on women and environments makes evident the opportunities and challenges for creating better environments for all persons, families, communities, and societies.

Consistent with other volumes in the series, authors reflect the perspectives of several social-science and environmental-design disciplines, including architecture, anthropology, geography, sociology, psychology, and urban and regional planning. The diversity of disciplines and perspectives attests to the breadth, complexity, and importance of a multidisciplinary approach to understanding women and environments.

The chapters are more or less organized according to an overlapping tripartite schema of physical scale, social-system units, and research/design/policy. Following our introductory chapter, which provides a perspective on the field, William Michelson (Chapter 2) examines a variety of physical evironments involving women and families, including homes, transportation, and work settings.

Chapters 3–6 address directly homes and proximate environments of families and family members. In Chapter 3, Rachel Sebba describes environments and associated social roles of children over time. Then, Ellen Pader (Chapter 4) examines challenges faced by women who moved to a new culture and new configurations of home and community environments. In Chapter 5, Sandra Howell considers varying home environments and environmental challenges of elderly women. In her analysis, Kathleen Christensen (Chapter 6) describes women's use of the home as a workplace, and the challenges of bridging and intermingling family life with the world of public work.

The next cluster of chapters focuses on larger-scale environments and social systems, including communities, neighborhoods, metropolitan areas, and social groups. In Chapter 7, Roberta Feldman and Susan Stall analyze how women in low-cost housing projects can be self-organizing and self-empowering in changing aspects of their community life and environment. Similarly, Liisa Horelli and Kirsti Vepsä (Chapter 8) describe how women are playing an increasing role in housing policy and planning in Scandinavia, especially Finland. Then, Susan Hanson, Geraldine Pratt, Doreen Mattingly, and Melissa Gilbert (Chapter 9) describe variations in work patterns and transportation for men and women in two metropolitan areas. In Chapter 10, Marsha Ritzdorf analyzes a variety of public-policy practices, problems, and challenges in respect to housing and community zoning regulations. Finally, Lynda Schneekloth (Chapter 11) undertakes a wide-ranging and provocative analysis of feminist perspectives on research and environmental design that has implications for all environmental scales and all social-system units.

Research, design, and policy regarding women and the environment is an emerging and challenging topic. We trust that the array of perspectives presented in this volume is a stimulant to innovative work on the myriad issues associated with women and physical environments.

IRWIN ALTMAN
ARZA CHURCHMAN

Historical Note on the Series

This thirteenth volume—a baker's dozen—celebrates the twentieth birthday of the Human Behavior and Environment series. Although the first volume was published in 1976, Jack Wohlwill and I began planning it a couple of years earlier. So this is an occasion worthy of reflection on our work of the past two decades.

In the early 1970s, Seymour Weingarten, then senior editor at Plenum Publishing Corporation, invited us to compile a "handbook" of environment and behavior studies. Jack and I demurred because we did not believe that the field had matured intellectually at the time to warrant a handbook compendium (it was not until 1987 that the *Handbook of Environmental Psychology* was published). As an alternative, we proposed a series of thematic edited volumes that would, over the years, cumulatively reflect the state of research, design, and policy in the interdisciplinary environment and behavior field. Plenum accepted this proposal and the series was launched.

The first two volumes were "samplers" and illustrated the breadth of the field. Thereafter volumes were thematic, organized around topics for which there was a reasonable body of knowledge, a cohort of active researchers and environmental designers, and subjects that were worthy of future study. The topical themes of the volumes in the series are listed in the front of this volume; they include a focus on *people and social actors*, for example, children, the elderly, and women; *places and environmental settings*, such as natural environments, transportation settings, public places, homes, communities, and neighborhoods; *key human issues*, such as culture and environment, and place attachment. In volume 11, senior participants in the field described their personal and professional "intellectual histories," illustrating the diversity of their intellectual origins and paths, the personal and professional underpinnings of their work, and the successes, failures, barriers, and serendipitous events over the course of their careers.

Our goals for each volume have been explicit and consistent. First, we wanted to present readers with representative environmental research, design, and policy analyses for a particular theme. Therefore, authors have been asked to summarize aspects of the "state of the art" of the topic they addressed. Second, we have invited authors to present, reflect on, and synthesize their own work, and to stretch their thinking beyond the normal bounds of their day-to-day efforts. Thus, each chapter has the personal intellectual stamp of its author. Third, we have asked authors to include a final "Future Directions" section in their chapters so that readers might be alerted to promising directions of environmental research, design, or policy formulation.

Fourth, in every volume we have invited participants from a variety of fields and disciplines. The study of human behavior and the physical environment is not "owned" by any discipline but requires the philosophical, theoretical, methodological, and value perspectives of the social sciences, humanities, and environmental-design professions. Fifth, the series has sought to attract new scholars and practitioners to the field by presenting exciting topics, opportunities, and challenges in the emerging field of environment and behavior studies. It is difficult to assess the extent to which we have met our goals, but here are some facts and figures about the series that portray aspects of the field's profile over the past two decades. In round numbers, the 13 volumes in the series include:

- 125 chapters
- 4200 pages of text and indexes
- 160 authors
- Nine coeditors, not counting Jack Wohlwill and Irwin Altman
- Authors from at least two dozen disciplines
- Authors affiliated with disciplinary and interdisciplinary university and college departments and institutes; private consulting, research, design, and policy organizations; and federal, state/province, and city/community governmental agencies.

Underlying these archival facts are personal and professional relationships that have been rewarding, often have been sustained over the years, and, most important, are steeped in intellectual commitment and integrity. Our personal and professional relationships with participants in the series have been enormously gratifying and ultimately are the bedrock that has sustained the series over the years.

First and foremost among these relationships was my association with Jack Wohlwill. In crafting the series and coediting the first seven volumes, he and I became close friends and colleagues. He was innovative, respectful of diverse perspectives, and nurtured authors while simultaneously being rigorous and demanding. Jack was also a wholly reliable and responsible collaborator and editor. Above all he was a man of integrity. His death a few years after withdrawing from the series in order to devote all of his energies to developmental psychology was a loss to the field and to his many colleagues and friends.

Jack Wohlwill and I shared editorial responsibilities with Peter Everett, Amos Rapoport, and M. Powell Lawton on three of the first seven volumes. Thereafter I coedited volumes 8–13 with Carol Werner, Abraham Wandersman, Ervin Zube, Kathleen Christensen, Setha Low, and Arza Churchman, respectively. What a pleasure it has been to share editorial anguishes and pleasures, and frustrations and joys, with these colleagues and friends. Each experience has been a gratifying interplay of stimulation, different perspectives, consistent competence and reliability, and friendships that continue to this day, along with the sharing of purpose and investment in the field. I thank them all for their contributions to the field, to the series, and to my own personal and professional growth.

Needless to say, the 160 authors who have written chapters in the first 13 volumes are the real heroes of this two-decade adventure. Their collective competence and dedication to their work and to the field is extraordinary. And they have been almost universally responsive to our editorial suggestions, have met deadlines (with varying degrees of prodding by us), and have been so responsible and sincere that it has been easy for us, the editors, to create high levels of guilt when they were tardy. The result is that we have rarely failed to meet our publication schedules. It has been a personal, professional, and intellectual pleasure to work with each and every author, and they have contributed enormously to my own education and appreciation of the diversity of the environment and behavior field.

Although coeditors and authors are surely important, the series also depends heavily on Plenum Publishing Corporation and its staff for survival, continuity, and presentation to the world. Seymour Weingarten, the senior editor with whom we collaboratively launched the series, was its spiritual parent. He helped us plan the series, provided freedom and flexibility for us to shape and reshape it, and took the gamble to commit to it and to us. Leonard Pace helped stabilize and establish the series over the course of a few volumes. For most of the life of the series, we have worked closely with Eliot Werner, presently executive editor at Plenum. Our relationship with Eliot has been unique and extraordinary, and he deserves enormous credit for the success of the series. We plan each volume in collaboration with him and rely on his sharp eye and understanding of the field, publishing, and market possibilities for advice. With each contact we have increasingly appreciated Eliot's insight and judgment, and he has shaped constructively our thinking at crucial decision points. Beyond our professional relationship, I have come to appreciate Eliot as a fine human being and friend, and I look forward to our continued association. The series also depends heavily on the production staff at Plenum, especially Robert Freire, who has guided several volumes through the production process with competence, thoroughness, and attention to myriad details.

This historical note is a brief pause to reflect on the Human Behavior and Environment series with an eye toward how it came to be, and how it has evolved over the years. Just as all chapters in every volume end with a section on "Future Directions," so it is that we are only at the barest beginnings of the challenge to understand and create better lives for people in the many environments in which they live, work, and relate to one another. May our research and design efforts prosper and celebrate another anniversary 20 years hence.

IRWIN ALTMAN

Contents

CHAPTER 3

GIRLS AND BOYS AND THE PHYSICAL ENVIRONMENT: AN HISTORICAL PERSPECTIVE   43

RACHEL SEBBA

Chapter 4

Sociospatial Relations of Change: Rural Mexican Women in Urban California   73

ELLEN-J. PADER

Chapter 5

Environment and the Aging Woman: Domains of Choice   105

SANDRA C. HOWELL

Chapter 6

Working at Home: Frameworks of Meaning   133

KATHLEEN CHRISTENSEN

Chapter 7

The Politics of Space Appropriation: A Case Study of Women's Struggles for Homeplace in Chicago Public Housing   167

ROBERTA M. FELDMAN AND SUSAN STALL

Chapter 8

In Search of Supportive Structures
for Everyday Life 201

LIISA HORELLI AND KIRSTI VEPSÄ

Chapter 9

Women, Work, and
Metropolitan Environments 227

SUSAN HANSON, GERALDINE PRATT,
DOREEN MATTINGLY, AND MELISSA GILBERT

CHAPTER 10

A FEMINIST ANALYSIS OF GENDER AND RESIDENTIAL ZONING IN THE UNITED STATES   255

MARSHA RITZDORF

CHAPTER 11

PARTIAL UTOPIAN VISIONS: FEMINIST REFLECTIONS ON THE FIELD   281

LYNDA H. SCHNEEKLOTH

Women and the Environment

1

Women and the Environment

A PERSPECTIVE ON RESEARCH, DESIGN, AND POLICY

ARZA CHURCHMAN and IRWIN ALTMAN

INTRODUCTION

The topic "women and the environment" encompasses far more than the transactions of a particular user group with the physical world of homes, neighborhoods, communities, and regions. It also addresses fundamental questions about the nature of our society, the nature of our environments, the nature of our professions, and the way we study, educate, do research, design, and plan. The present chapter first describes the general history of research, design, and policy with respect to women and the physical environment. We then discuss how the topic may be profitably addressed in terms of several themes: (1) the contextual nature of women's lives, their embeddedness in a variety of social and cultural relationships, and the interpenetration of women's activities with many physical settings; (2) the varied and changing nature of the traditional public/private distinction for women, and historical tradi-

ARZA CHURCHMAN • Faculty of Architecture and Town Planning, Technion-Israel Institute of Technology, Haifa 32000, Israel.   IRWIN ALTMAN • Department of Psychology, University of Utah, Salt Lake City, Utah 84112.
Women and the Environment, edited by Irwin Altman and Arza Churchman. Plenum Press, New York, 1994.

tions and restrictions deriving from this distinction; (3) needs and exemplars of social change in respect to women's environments, with emphasis on sociophysical units of change (e.g., homes, neighborhoods, communities, workplaces, etc.), the domains of needed environmental change (e.g., household activities, services, work, etc.), and the process of change (e.g., social action, policy and politics, and women's participation in environmental decision-making processes).

BACKGROUND

Interest in issues relating to women and the physical environment arose in the 1970s, not long after the emergence of the field of environment/behavior studies (then called man/environment studies). Early in the 1980s, two edited volumes reflected a growing and diverse body of multidisciplinary knowledge on women and environments (Wekerle, Peterson, & Morley, 1980; Stimpson, Dixler, Nelson, & Yatrakis, 1981). Although work up to that point was not voluminous, the issues raised then are valid today and are the focus of much ongoing research. The pace of interest quickened in the ensuing years, with an exponential increase in the number of publications, and with a broadening and deepening of research, design, planning, and policy questions addressed by scholars (Peterson, 1987). Since that time, work has continued to accelerate.

At present there are two major trends in the analysis of women and the physical environment. One line of work examines particular women/environment/social/economic/physical/temporal units. Representative examples include Moser and Peake's (1987) analyses of women, human settlements, and housing in developing countries, Watson's (1988) work on gender and housing in Australia, Christensen's (1988) study of women and home-based work in the United States, Franck and Paxson's (1989) examination of women and urban public space, Franck and Ahrentzen's (1989) investigation of new households and new housing, and Leavitt and Saegert's (1989) study of women housing activists in New York. In addition to housing, attention is also being given to other environmental settings, for example, transportation, neighborhoods, and urban areas (see Churchman, 1991, for a review of some of this literature).

A second major stream of work on women and the environment focuses on environmental design, especially architecture and planning, and on the theoretical and professional implications of women–environment issues. For example, within the planning field, Sandercock and Forsyth (1990) and Milroy (1991) analyzed the implications of feminist research for planning theory, the *Planning Theory Newsletter* (1992) presented a symposium on bridging planning and feminist theory, and Friedmann (1992) included gender equality as a cornerstone of his alternative model of development. Within architecture, Matrix (1984)—the British feminist architectural cooperative and research network—presented a unique approach to designing for and with women. In addition, because of the increasing number of books on the topic, the journal *Design Book Review* (1992) devoted a major portion of one issue to gender and design, including Hayden's (1984) pioneer work and more recent critiques by Sprague (1991), Weisman (1992), and Spaine (1992). A paper by Ahrentzen (1993) also examines the practice and discipline of architecture through a feminist lens. Much of this literature deals with symbolic aspects of the environment, and how a variety of physical environments reflect, symbolize, and affect the role and status of women in society.

The present volume adopts a multifaceted and cross-disciplinary lens to examine women and their environments. In so doing, authors focus on women's behavior, attitudes, and perceptions, and how they interpret, use, cope with, and change their environmental settings. Moreover, authors also consider how women function in environmental settings that vary from microenvironments of homes to macroenvironments of cities and regions, with methodological approaches ranging from narrative and individual case histories to action research to large-scale surveys. Furthermore, chapters in this volume address a range of research, design, and policy issues through empirical, theoretical, and historical analyses of women and environments.

To achieve this multifaceted perspective, each chapter in the present volume focuses on some particular social/economic/physical/temporal environmental setting. In so doing, authors highlight the unique nature of women's functioning and transactions in complex environmental contexts, for example, home-based work amidst family life, transportation in the context of multiple personal and professional responsibilities, living arrangements of elderly women as they are embedded in family and social relationships, health systems, and everyday life, and others.

Environmental implications of women's lives relate to all scales of the environment: from the dwelling to the neighborhood to the settlement and the region, and to the nature of the personal and societal decision-making processes that affect them. Although research, design, and policy issues have been somewhat sensitive to women in respect to small-scale environments, for example, homes, recent analyses have also begun to highlight the more salient issues of urban and regional planning as they apply to women (Sandercock & Forsyth, 1990; Milroy, 1991; Friedmann, 1992).

The present volume does not give voice to all possible "groups" of women. Indeed, taken as a whole, this book exemplifies the fact that women–environment relationships are diverse within and across cultures, and that women's lives and situations are complex, change over the life span, and require a broad-based set of research studies, environmental design perspectives, and public policy initiatives. At the same time, there are some communalities among women's environmental needs, stemming mainly from the internalized, cultural definitions of women's roles and their responsibilities to others, as well as from dramatically changing roles of women in many cultures. We believe that this interplay of common and diverse needs of women in respect to their physical environments can be addressed within the three themes implicit in the chapters of this volume—social and environmental contexts within which women function, changes in the traditional public/private nature of environmental settings, and needed directions of social change.

CONTEXTS OF WOMEN'S LIVES

Women's lives are inherently contextual in respect to the multiplicity of their roles and social relationships, the environmental settings in which they live, the cultural and historical backdrops of their lives, and their varied activities. The fact that all of the chapters in this book present women as part of larger social, historical, and physical contexts is not artificial; it is a result and reflection of the impossibility of separating women from their responsibilities and interconnections with others. One cannot separate the roles of woman-as-person, woman-as-worker, woman-as-user of services, woman-as-community activist (or woman-as-candidate for attorney general) from woman-as-mother, woman-as-daughter, woman-as-wife, woman-as-homemaker. Women's lives are characterized by interdependence to such an extent that one is forced to consider their responsibilities to and for others as significant and critical elements in their environmental transactions. Richter (1990) illustrates this contextual theme by highlighting the permeability and intermeshing of work and home, and the everyday mutual interpenetration of one by the other—even where home and work are physically and geographically separate. In so doing, Richter (1990) suggests that women's boundaries are more permeable than those of men and that women are not able to detach themselves from one setting and domain of their life while in another setting. The result, according to Richter (1990), is considerable stress in women's lives.

The contextual and interpenetrating aspect of women's multiple roles in relationship to the physical environment is highlighted in most chapters in the present volume. Michelson (Chapter 2) illustrates the breadth of social and physical contexts of women's lives in respect to housing, land use, transportation, safety, and time/space qualities of urban settings. And Sebba (Chapter 3) adds to the breadth of contextual factors in her discussion of the sweep of historical and culturally based links of the lives of boys and girls with specific environments and roles.

More specific aspects of cultural, social, and political domains and contexts are reflected in the following:

Pader's (Chapter 4) analysis of how home designs geared to one culture affect the lives of migrating women and families from another culture.

Christensen's (Chapter 6) research on the complexities of home-based work by women, and how the social contexts and expectations of husbands and families and the very design of homes makes it difficult for women to manage multiple roles when work and home are in the same space.

Howell's (Chapter 5) assessment of the changing contexts of personal, work, and interpersonal lives of elderly women, and the relationship of these changes to shifting environmental residential needs.

Hanson, Pratt, Mattingly, and Gilbert's (Chapter 9) work on the challenges faced by women in different types of communities as they attempt to weave together home and work in the context of transportation, job opportunities, family roles, and the place of work in their unique family structures.

Feldman and Stall's (Chapter 7) case studies of how women in a low-cost housing complex struggled with the social, political, and economic system to obtain community services and influence community policies.

Horelli and Vepsä's (Chapter 8) description of Scandinavian women's political and social activism in creating communities appropriate to their changing family and personal/professional needs.

Michelson's (Chapter 2) and other authors' discussion of women's safety in public places.

Ritzdorf's (Chapter 10) analysis of the impact of residential zoning policies on life stresses in new forms of family organization.

Schneekloth's (Chapter 11) discussion of the ways in which we define and generate knowledge, and design environments.

Thus, many chapters in the volume describe how women in contemporary society function within unique and complex configurations of constraints and challenges. Because women's lives are so intertwined with those of others, they are necessarily more temporally constrained in their activities and have fewer degrees of personal freedom. Their schedules are determined, to a large extent, not by choice, but by the temporal schedules of work, school systems, child-care providers, stores and services, transportation networks, and others. Taken together, women are clearly embedded in and inseparable from their physical, social, and temporal contexts—a theme that crops up in almost every chapter in the volume, thereby reflecting the complex, holistic, and transactional quality of women's lives (Altman & Rogoff, 1987).

The breadth of contextual factors in women's lives speaks to the necessity for a holistic analysis that deals with a variety of social processes involving individual actors functioning within their social, environmental, and temporal contexts. A contextual approach highlights the fact of various configurations of particular needs and requirements that, all too often, physical environments do not wholly satisfy (Churchman, 1990). It is critical, therefore, that environmental designers and planners both acknowledge and understand the different social/cultural/ environmental/temporal systems in which women are embedded and that they work toward achieving environments that are congruent with the complex contexts of women's lives. In the public policy area, it becomes clear that one cannot treat issues of housing, child care, employment, transportation, services, and zoning as separate and distinct. For most women, these domains are inextricably linked, and they must therefore be researched, designed, and planned for in an integrated and coordinated way.

THE DISTINCTION BETWEEN PRIVATE AND PUBLIC ENVIRONMENTS

An interesting thread that runs through many of the chapters in the present volume is the distinction between private and public environments in women's lives. This distinction appears at many levels of discourse and at many environmental scales. One level of scale is that of the residential environment and its links to public settings. Pader (Chapter 4) describes the experiences of women who migrated from a Mexican village where private/public distinctions within the home were virtually nonexistent (i.e., where there were no areas off limits to visitors, and where the behavioral distinction between home and street was minimal), to their life in an urban community in the United States, where there was spatial separation between public and private areas inside the home, and a clear boundary between inside and outside the home.

Christensen (Chapter 6) relates the difficulties encountered in some households when the public (work) activity takes place in the private (home) setting, and where nonhousehold members are sometimes present as coworkers or household staff. Establishing and maintaining public/private boundaries in such circumstances is not a simple task and often requires renegotiation of space and social relations in the household.

Howell (Chapter 5) describes the changing life settings of elderly women, how they often must relate to family and friends in their and others' homes in new ways, shifting patterns of life that sometimes involve congregate or health-care settings, the involvement of children or health-care professionals in their day-to-day lives, and the like. Sometimes what is public and what is private becomes quite blurred and changes from what they had previously experienced.

Another level of discourse and of scale is the broader, historical, and cultural association of women with the private sphere and men with the public sphere, with all of its ramifications. Sebba (Chapter 3) traces children's gender differentiation over history and how the physical range and activities of girls' lives were spatially narrowed and essentially limited to the immediate home environment, whereas boys were allowed and encouraged to venture into a range of public spaces.

Ritzdorf (Chapter 10) illustrates how zoning and land-use regulations in the United States are based on the cultural assumption that the physical and geographical separation between private (home) and public (workplace, culture, politics) is the "correct" lifestyle, and how laws and policies regulate and enforce this separation at the community level. The irony is that zoning laws essentially give the public sphere the right to intrude into the private sphere at the most basic level—defining a family, dictating its composition, determining who may or may not live in a home, and what occupations may be pursued there.

Historically, research and policy have been primarily directed at the public sphere, with less explicit attention given to the private domain. By association, women's lives and concerns have been relatively neglected and even made invisible. Today, however, there is a growing tendency to redefine the concepts of public and private life and even to question the need for this distinction (Sandercock & Forsyth, 1990). One aspect of the issue involves the differentiation made by traditional economists between production (in the workplace) and consumption (in the home). More radical contemporary economists view the home as the setting for reproduction (used in the sense of direct nurturing and caring, and social and cultural relations) and as also contributing to the economy even though home work is often unpaid. Recognizing that households are essential reproductive and productive economic units blurs the public/private distinction and reinforces the argument that they should be treated as both production-centered and public (Friedmann, 1992).

Horelli and Vepsä (Chapter 8) also call for an overlap between private and public domains and propose creating "intermediary levels" in the urban environment that integrate selected aspects of dwelling, child care, and work in space and time and that serve as mediating structures between the private and public spheres. They and Michelson (Chapter 2) describe alternative housing arrangements in Scandinavia that reorganize the environment, with cooking, eating, cleaning, leisure, and child care (in different combinations) not defined solely as private matters for each separate household but treated as shared activities involving sets of households. These arrangements also ideally allow for and often consciously break down traditional rigid distinctions between women's and men's roles.

In a somewhat different way, Feldman and Stall (Chapter 7) describe how women in a low-cost housing project waged campaigns to develop communal and shared facilities, protect their neighborhood from large-scale urban development, and essentially extend the concept of "homeplace" into public environments of community facilities, neighborhoods, and regions.

On an ideological level, Schneekloth (Chapter 11) and Feldman and Stall (Chapter 7) give voice to the feminist claim that the personal is also political. That is, the conceptualization of what is private and what is public is a political and value-laden act that has implications for what issues and what groups are considered legitimate parts of political and policy discourse (Ackelsberg, 1988). They call for women to become empowered in order to constructively shape and change their physical and social environments in ways that are congruent with their changing lives and needs.

On a philosophical level, given a transactional approach, one can argue that the distinction between private and public spheres is untenable because individuals and groups function in contexts that are embedded in and inseparable from larger contexts and with all such contexts relevant to people's lives. Thus we must pay attention to the patterns of weaving in and out of various settings that make up our daily lives. Women in particular are involved in a balancing of roles and a merging of role-associated interests and orientations, thereby weaving together social institutions and environments (Lengermann &

Niebrugge-Brantley, 1990). The intermeshing and embeddedness of different domains of life in the contemporary world makes artificial the traditional public/private separation of places and settings.

IMPLEMENTING SOCIAL CHANGE

The broad issue of social change regarding women and the environment involves at least three different facets: the social/physical units in which change can occur, the content or areas of life of change, and the process of change.

SOCIAL/PHYSICAL UNITS OF CHANGE

As discussed in various chapters in this volume, social, political, economic, and environmental changes may take place in the individual (Howell, Chapter 5; Schneekloth, Chapter 11) in the home and household (Sebba, Chapter 3; Pader, Chapter 4; Christensen, Chapter 6), in the community (Michelson, Chapter 2; Feldman and Stall, Chapter 7; Horelli and Vepsä, Chapter 8; Schneekloth, Chapter 11), on the regional level (Hanson et al., Chapter 9; Ritzdorf, Chapter 10), and on the national or international scale (Horelli and Vepsä, Chapter 8).

Clearly, these are not separate and distinct levels, and a change in one is affected by and affects the others. However, there are differences in foci depending upon which level is addressed. Thus change within the individual makes salient variability within cohorts or particular groups of women. For example, Howell (Chapter 5) describes the varied ways in which women at particular stages in their life actively choose or have environments and lifestyles chosen for them, within the opportunities and constraints of their social, environmental, and physical circumstances.

Pader (Chapter 4) discusses the role of women in the home as mediators of the change required by the clash or disequilibrium between the "old ways" of their original life and their new environment and culture. She argues that it is on the level of daily life in its most mundane domestic routines that many of the most important instigations of change and adaptation occur. The examples from Scandinavia (Michelson, Chapter 2; Horelli and Vepsä, Chapter 8), from low-cost housing projects in the United States (Feldman and Stall, Chapter 7), and from zoning in the United States (Ritzdorf, Chapter 10) reflect changes that occur and are needed at the community level but simultaneously involve change at the household level. Interesting recent work has emphasized the importance of the household as a central source and venue of social change. Thus Friedmann (1987) concluded that radical planners could not work with disarticulated individuals but only with families or households within organized political communities.

On the other hand, Sebba (Chapter 3), Michelson (Chapter 2), Ritzdorf (Chapter 10), and Schneekloth (Chapter 11) point to the relative inertia of cultural values that often mitigates against the possibility of rapid and necessary social change—in the form of strong and restrictive norms regarding gender roles, women's responsibilities that are often fixed and rigid, and public policies that work against new family configurations. So, very often there have been changes in homes and family functioning that are not supported by macrolevels of social and cultural contexts.

Once it is understood that women cannot be detached from their social, cultural, political, and physical environmental contexts (in the most inclusive sense), then it becomes clear that changes that take place only within the individual (such as individual empowerment) do not necessarily yield significant changes in the larger or "whole" social system (Sadan & Churchman, 1993). Change must be eventually introduced throughout all levels of systems, including the physical environment.

THE CONTENT OF CHANGE

This issue addresses the areas of life in which change is, or should be, occurring. Molyneux (1985) proposed a useful distinction between practical and strategic gender issues. Practical issues deal with basic survival needs (such as shelter, food, healthy environments, services) and do not challenge existing gender relations. However, strategic issues (such as equality within the law, the right to own property, changing the sexual division of labor within the home and workplace, participation in decision-making processes) are concerned with the systematic disempowerment of women that is encoded in social institutions. It is these domains that call for change.

The women and life circumstances described by Pader (Chapter 4) of women living in a new culture, Howell's (Chapter 5) analyses of elderly women, Christensen's (Chapter 6) studies of home-based work, Feldman and Stall's (Chapter 7) work with women in low-cost housing projects, and Hanson et al.'s (Chapter 9) study of women in different types of communities all involve practical gender issues, such as home management, relationships in families, child rearing, access to basic services, home and work relationships, and the like. Although women in these and other cases may achieve some modest improvements in the practical aspects of their lives, many such changes are often primarily adaptations to circumstances rather than an innovative reorganization or design of new life settings.

On the other hand, strategic interests that transcend everyday practical survival issues often require more macrolevel, societal changes that are difficult to institute because of the inertia and resistance of social, cultural, and political systems. For example, Horelli and Vepsä (Chapter 8) and Michelson (Chapter 2) describe some relatively successful attempts at changing community planning in Scandinavia to reconfigure relationships between households, redefine the activities that distinctively apply to households versus communities, and develop processes for designing alternative models of living. Some success as well as resistance to large-scale environmental and community change is reflected in Feldman and Stall's (Chapter 7) analysis of the difficulties women faced in affecting aspects of urban development that impinged directly on family and community life in low-cost housing projects in the United States. Furthermore, Schneekloth (Chapter 11) reminds us of the utopian underpinnings of the field of environment/behavior studies, of the belief and desire that efforts in such work would create better places for people to live in, and would transform the institutions and places that were oppressive in people's lives. And she also reminds us of the need to make more progress in these directions and of the institutional and social milieu that consciously and unconsciously hampers our progress in instituting change in both practical and strategic domains of life.

From a "political" point of view, the dilemma arises as to whether, in arguing for the amelioration of practical gender issues, one ignores the need for broader strategic change and perhaps even delays or prevents such change (Churchman, 1990). Or, should one focus instead on strategic gender interests and then run the risk of ignoring practical changes in day-to-day life? A possible resolution to this dilemma is to assume that the practical problems of everyday life are socially and environmentally generated and also need to be addressed in anticipation of the time when they are no longer firmly linked to gender but apply equally to women and men alike. Tactically, it may be wise to emphasize the fact that the practical problems of everyday life are, in fact, issues that simultaneously and intrinsically involve men, women, and children, not women alone. As Schneider (1992) reminds us, services that are universal or are important to all people are more durable and are less likely to be cut or ignored, compared with those geared to particular groups (especially when those groups are perceived to be weak and less influential).

The Process of Change

Many of the chapters in the volume illustrate the proactive nature of women's actions in households, immediate proximate environments, and larger community environments, as well as revealing the opportunities and importance and success of such actions. Thus, Feldman and Stall (Chapter 7) reveal how women working together to preserve and improve their residential environment and neighborhood can achieve a significant degree of organization, collective action, and success in creating change. And Schneekloth (Chapter 11) and Ritzdorf (Chapter 10) set forth philosophies, principles, and courses of action necessary to effect change in women's environments. Hanson et al. (Chapter 9) point out that policies should also be sensitive to the local context at a fine spatial scale, not just at general state or national levels. At the same time, they and other authors in the volume point to the realistic barriers to change and the challenges facing women in exerting control over their lives and environments. Many of the chapters vividly present the inevitable frustrations, costs, and energies required of women to maintain, let alone change, the environmental systems within which they function. Too often, the process of change also requires a confrontational or adversarial stance that may have negative or costly consequences or that may create a significant degree of conflict and social upheaval.

In a strategic sense, it is clear that attention to women's needs requires political action and concern with political issues. Horelli and Vepsä (Chapter 8) address this reality quite directly, reflecting the social and political action undertaken by a group of Scandinavian women to influence environmental change (The Research Group for the New Everyday Life, 1991). Women's issues also inevitably lead to concern for environmental sustainability and to the demand for participatory decision-making structures that involve a greater range of citizens. Such processes are discussed in Friedmann's (1992) theoretical treatise, which deals with problems of developing countries but whose principles are also relevant for more technologically developed societies. Thus strategic gender interests have implications for society as a whole and for the environment as a whole.

A FUTURE AGENDA

Schneekloth (Chapter 11) addresses the implications of a feminist stance for basic questions of philosophy of science and for issues unique to the field of environment–behavior studies. She takes on the challenging task of questioning entrenched beliefs about the nature of knowledge and its relationship to power; where and who are knowers and their relationship to that which is "known'" and how the language we use to describe the world and our work structures our practice. (Schneekloth, Chapter 11, this volume)

Schneekloth and others in this volume raise fundamental questions about the ways in which we "know" the world, learn about it systematically, and attempt to change it. Horelli and Vepsä (Chapter 8) and Howell (Chapter 5) argue that we also need to reject traditional simplistic definitions of issues, for example, women's generic social roles, cohort concepts of elderly women's needs, and other perspectives that deemphasize the variability within each gender. Simplistic categorization of issues, in general, is described by Schneekloth (Chapter 11) as having been problematic in the field of environment–behavior studies and results in the submerging of differences between people and the invisibility of certain groups (Franck, 1986). As an example, Schneekloth points to the use of the seemingly innocuous term *users of environments* as implying consumption, passivity, and homogeneity, rather than describing active, producing, and varied individuals in groups.

Taken together, the chapters in this volume provide a road map for the future. They call for approaches to gaining knowledge about women in environments that highlight the contextual nature of women's lives. On a basic level, the chapters convey the broad message that our focus in research, design, and planning should be in terms of person/group/ social/physical/temporal holistic units, regardless of the contextual scale in question and with recognition of the legitimacy of different ways of knowing, thinking, and living. Chapters in this volume also demonstrate the value and power of broad-ranging research methodologies, concepts, and theories—from qualitative case descriptions to traditional quantitative techniques and from broad-ranging philosophical perspectives to precisely defined theoretical orientations. The chapters also emphasize the need for action research, participant involvement in research, environmental design and policy formulation, and the development and fostering of social and political empowerment strategies that permit people to engage larger social and political systems.

Clearly, there is much that we do not yet understand about women and their environments. Many groups of women, as holistic social units, have yet to be listened to, especially nontraditional and minority groups. They deserve to have their voices heard, for their benefit and for the benefit of society at large. In addition, many of the settings that are part of everyday life (such as health, education, recreation, religion, workplaces) have not yet been sufficiently examined through a woman–environment lens. They also need to be heard and attended to. We end with the maxim that one is not called upon to finish the task, but neither is one permitted to abandon it.

REFERENCES

Ackelsberg, M. (1988). Communities, resistance, and women's activism: Some implications for a democratic polity. In A. Bookman & S. Morgen (Eds.), *Women and the politics of empowerment* (pp. 297–313). Philadelphia: Temple University Press.

Ahrentzen, S. (1993). The F word in architecture: Feminist analyses in/of/for architecture. Unpublished manuscript.

Altman, I., & Rogoff, B. (1987). World views in psychology: Trait, interactional, organismic and transactional perspectives. In D. Stokols & I. Altman (Eds.), *Handbook of environmental psychology* (pp. 7–40). New York: Wiley.

Christensen, K. (1988). *Women and home-based work: The unspoken contract.* New York: Henry Holt.

Churchman, A. (1991). *A differentiated perspective on urban quality of life: Women, children and the elderly.* Paper presented at the International Pluridisciplinary MAB UNESCO Symposium on perception and evaluation of the urban environment, Rome, Italy.

Churchman, A. (1990). *Women and urban quality of life.* Paper presented at International Association of Applied Psychology, 21st Congress, Kyoto, Japan.

Design Book Review (1992). Gender and design. 25 (Summer), 7–45.

Franck, K. (1986). *The cost of knowing: A call for examining categories in environmental design research.* Proceedings of the Environmental Design Research Association: EDRA 17 (pp. 47–54). Washington, DC.

Franck, K., & Ahrentzen, S. (Eds.) (1989). *New households, new housing.* New York: Van Nostrand Reinhold.

Franck, K., & Paxson, L. (1989). Women and urban public space: Research, design and policy issues. In I. Altman & E. Zube (Eds.), *Public places and spaces* (pp. 121–146). New York: Plenum Press.

Friedmann, J. (1987). *Planning in the public domain: From knowledge to action.* Princeton: Princeton University Press.

Friedmann, J. (1992). *Empowerment: The politics of alternative development.* Cambridge, England: Blackwell.

Hayden, D. (1984). *Redesigning the American dream.* New York: W. W. Norton.

Leavitt, J., & Saegert, S. (1989). *Housing abandonment in Harlem: The making of community households.* New York: Columbia University Press.

Lengermann, P., & Niebrugge-Brantley, J. (1990). Contemporary feminist theory. In G. Ritzer (Ed.), *Sociological theory* (pp. 400–443). New York: McGraw-Hill.

Matrix. (1984). *Making space. Women and the man-made environment.* London: Pluto Press.

Milroy, B. (1991). Taking stock of planning, space, and gender. *Journal of Planning Literature,* 6 (1), 3–15.

Molyneux, M. (1985). Mobilization without emancipation? Women's interests, state and revolution in Nicaragua. *Feminist Studies*, 11 (2), 227–254.

Moser, C., & Peake, L. (Eds.). (1987). *Women, human settlements and housing.* London: Tavistock.

Peterson, R. (1987). Gender issues in the home and urban environment. In E. Zube & G. Moore (Eds.), *Advances in environment, behavior and design*, Vol. 1 (pp. 187–218). New York: Plenum Press.

Planning Theory Newsletter. (1992). Planning theories, feminist theories: A symposium, 7/8, Summer-Winter, pp. 9–62.

The Research Group for the New Everyday Life. (1991). *The new everyday life-ways and means.* Copenhagen: Nordic Council of Ministers.

Richter, J. (1990). Crossing boundaries between professional and private life. In H. Grossman & N. Chester (Eds.), *The experience and meaning of work in women's lives* (pp. 143 163). Hillsdale, NJ: Lawrence Erlbaum.

Sadan, E., & Churchman, A. (1993). *Empowerment and professional practice.* Proceedings of the Environmental Design Research Association: EDRA 24 (pp. 196–201). Oklahoma City.

Sandercock, L., & Forsyth, A. (1990). *Gender: A new agenda for planning theory.* Berkeley: University of California–Berkeley, Institute of Urban and Regional Development. Working Paper 521.

Schneider, W. (1992). The suburban century begins. *The Atlantic Monthly, 270*(1), 33–44.

Spaine, D. (1992). *Gendered spaces.* Chapel Hill: University of North Carolina Press.

Sprague, J. (1991). *More than housing: Lifeboats for women and children.* Boston: Butterworth-Heinemann.

Stimpston, C., Dixler, E., Nelson, M., & Yatrakis, K. (Eds.). (1981). *Women and the American city.* Chicago: University of Chicago Press.

Watson, S. (1988). *Accommodating inequality. Gender and housing.* North Sydney, Australia: Allen & Unwin.

Weisman, L. (1992). *Discrimination by design: A feminist critique of the man-made environment.* Urbana: University of Illinois Press.

Wekerle, G., Peterson, R., & Morley, D. (Eds.). (1980). *New space for women.* Boulder, CO: Westview Press.

2

Everyday Life in Contextual Perspective

WILLIAM MICHELSON

During roughly the past 15 years, a variety of issues dealing with women's environmental interests, uses, and concerns has been elaborated, conceptualized, and studied empirically, with sensitive and comprehensive reviews integrating this substance at regular intervals (cf. Hapgood & Gedzels, 1974; Palm & Pred, 1974; Hayden, 1980; Saegert, 1980; Wekerle, 1980; Zelinsky, Monk, & Hanson, 1982; McClain, 1984; Wekerle, 1984; Peterson, 1986; Moser, 1987; Peterson, 1987; Andrew & Milroy, 1988; Franck, 1988; Franck & Paxson, 1989). Although reviews are essential to communicate an important set of considerations and their knowledge base to a public that has not as yet fully understood and incorporated them, I shall not attempt one here, at least directly.

Rather, I shall attempt to place 'woman and her urban environment' into a perspective that corresponds to the complex reality that women (and men) actually experience on an everyday basis.

Specific environments are part of a larger mosaic, whereas specific behaviors and activities are also part of a meaningful, repetitive pattern. Most research on women and environment has focused on the "trees," and this chapter aims to identify the "forest." Research and practical

WILLIAM MICHELSON • Centre for Urban and Community Studies and Department of Sociology, University of Toronto, Toronto M5S 1A1, Ontario, Canada.
Women and the Environment, edited by Irwin Altman and Arza Churchman. Plenum Press, New York, 1994.

17

interest in women and environment has strengthened as a function of a complex of changes affecting women's daily lives, and therefore our comprehension must benefit from a more inclusive social ecology.

The trees are still important! A terrible event or place can bring ruin to any otherwise harmonious day (or life). But, in lives that involve regular routines, unwieldy or otherwise stressful daily patterns and mosaics put a negative cast on what might otherwise be tolerable or even pleasurable activities and places. Particular forms of environment and behavior are not lost in this process but are shown to be of greater salience when seen as part of a larger pattern.

Because it is difficult to argue in favor of transcending particular considerations without identifying them clearly and showing the nature of changed conceptualization, this chapter will follow through a series of hopefully logical steps:

1. The argument in favor of viewing contexts less as trees and more as a mosaic comes first. This is followed by a discussion of the accompanying need to view everyday life as a pattern. A basis for integrating these two complexes comes next.
2. At this point, the salience for women of such an integrated approach can be elaborated and understood.
3. Specific aspects of urban environment are then analyzed as to how they may be dealt with more adequately in the interests of women when viewed by this approach.
4. The chapter concludes with a few current policy issues in urban areas that are highly pertinent to women. Future research with a contextual perspective may provide directions to their solution.

CONCEPTUALIZING THE RELATIONSHIPS OF PEOPLE AND EVERYDAY CONTEXTS

CONTEXTS

Contexts are settings external to the individual serving as a basis for behavior. They have objective, physical parameters, but many others as well. Contexts are something to have (economic and political aspects), to see and experience (aesthetic), to use (functional), to leave from and travel to (locational), to retreat to (safety), and to support a diffuse range of human activity and social contact (behavioral and social).

Although environments in many meanings of the word, they vary in the degree of concreteness that they take. For example, a room and a dwelling are both contexts that are imageable environments. Ironically, larger contexts often appear less concrete because they are not immediate and hence as imageable. The land-use patterns of neighborhoods and cities, for example, are not particularly imageable, but they nonetheless serve as important contexts for daily life. Means of transportation are not fixed in place the same way but also play a major part in everyday life.

This chapter is devoted to the relevance of contexts to everyday life. Everyday life has been a relatively neglected aspect in the literature on women's environments, which deals heavily, for example, with such basic questions as women's differential economic and social access to housing, transportation, and support services. Yet, contexts are integral to behavior. All behaviors occur in a context.

The social-science literature typically deals with specific environments and their relationships to targeted and/or outcome behavior. This is a limited view, and there is a need to understand context(s) in light of the pattern of behavior that people need or want to carry out.

For example, what has been noted as the single most valuable formulation on environment and behavior (Zeisel, 1981), Roger Barker's ecological psychology approach, illustrates both the strengths and weaknesses of analyses to date. In his magnum opus (1968), Barker focuses on a form of context he calls the behavior setting (see also Wicker, 1987). Each community is said to consist of a number of such behavior settings. Barker describes in great detail of what a behavior setting consists and the dynamics through which predictable behavior is elicited and maintained. These boil down roughly to the physical parameters, sets of rules (formal and informal), symbols and other props, participants, and behavior. Behavior is regularized in behavior settings because the physical parameters make it possible, the rules and props make it expected, and the participants are attracted or forced to appear. The contributing elements of the behavior setting create an operational setting when they are mutually compatible, in a state of what Barker called *synomorphy*. Two of what seem to be Barker's favorite behavior settings are the drugstore soda fountain and the high-school basketball game, rooted in American small-town life in midcentury.

Barker's formulation was fruitful because it presented a way of understanding how regularities of behavior could be facilitated by context. The spatial dimensions make it possible. Cultural and institutional factors provide orientation and reinforcement. And sufficient numbers of individuals provide motivation and personnel to make it happen. Furthermore, locating and inventorying the settings that have these complementing aspects within a community present a way of understanding the contextual basis for how and why behavior between communities may differ.

Thus, the study of behavior settings in ecological psychology points the way to a view of the role of environments as facilitators of behavior, for individuals and for collectivities—aside from the many other aspects of environment that surely also have validity.

But the strength that follows from the detailing of unambiguous examples of synomorphy suggests the weaknesses of this approach to comprehensive analysis and understanding. First, the spotlight gets fixed on very specific activities. These are typically shared, interpersonal activities requiring specific physical properties. Second, these are behaviors that occur only in a specific place, not which are built up across places such as shopping in one or more districts or involve travel more generally. And third, ecological psychology, by its emphasis, does not address patterns of behavior and their facilitation or constraint by the larger contextual pattern. In sum, the behaviors captured by ecological psychology are relatively microscopic and specific.

Much work in environmental psychology parallels Barker's approach in its focus on specific activities. It provides an empirical and conceptual basis for the design and the related behavioral implications of very specific settings like hospital wards, offices, apartments, schools, playgrounds, submarines, and space stations. This is in fact similar to the growth of fields in the social sciences, where much is known about particular topics like crime, gender relations, factories, Karl Marx, and bureaucratic settings, *but not the general content of everyday behavior.* Emphasis on specific outcome behaviors of specific contexts is necessary but not sufficient for issues that involve a larger, more complex picture of everyday life. For such issues, it will be necessary to deal with contexts in a more integrative conceptual way, which corresponds to a wider consideration of behaviors.

What basis do we have for considering behaviors in a more integrated way and in conjunction with environmental contexts?

EVERYDAY LIFE

Contrasting to a focus on specific behaviors, their causes, and contextual parameters, is one that deals with the pattern of experiences that people have as part of their daily routines. Although often consisting of rather mundane content, it is nonetheless the stuff of life, or, at least, everyday life.

A more integrated conceptual view of behavior has emerged from the results of time-use research methodology. Assessment can and has been made of what people do throughout their days and weeks, in a systematic and detailed way (cf. Michelson, 1987). Thus, the focus is on the person (and/or persons making up a household) and his or her activities over a finite period of time, rather than on what happens in particular behavior settings or on specific issues.

Operationally, studies of time use generally rely on interviews or diaries covering one or more immediate days. Systematic data are recorded by interviewer or subject starting from the beginning of the period or from the time the subject woke up within it. Each episode of significant activity is recorded serially in matrix format and includes most of the following aspects: what the person did, when the episode started and when it was completed (hence its duration), who else was involved, where it took place, what secondary activity might have been occurring simultaneously (e.g., listening to the radio), and the subject's subjective evaluation of this activity.

Analysis of the ensuing data set enables construction of many ways of viewing everyday life in a more integrated way. Let me provide a few examples. Activities are typically coded into categories of considerable detail. A 99-category code is most typical (Szalai, 1972), though schemes vary from about 24 categories to several hundred. It is common to calculate how much time is devoted to each kind of activity across the span of the day (or sometimes the week or even year). This enables the assessment and comparison of how much (or little) time people devote to behaviors that may be of practical or analytic interest: paid employment, commuting, one or more aspects of housework or child care, leisure, sleep, and so forth. The approach and methodology are important here because people are often unaware of the precise dimensions of their activities but can nonetheless record (or reconstruct) them accurately enough to enable the aggregation of discrete episodes by the researchers.

The same kind of aggregation can be done with information about the social and locational dimensions of daily activities. In what kind of social milieu do people spend their time? How much or little contact do people have with their spouses, children, parents, friends, and the like? How much time is spent in what kind of place during the time period in question? How far do people travel, and for what purpose(s)?

Patterns of daily life can be constructed by looking at the various categories on a given dimension of time use. The balance between employment-related activities, household and child-raising activities, recreational activities, and biological necessities, for example, is strategic. So is the kind and balance of contact that people have with others. Another integrating outlook deals with the kind of travel pattern that individuals follow across the day. One that is similarly informative but less common is construction across episodes of an overall scale of evaluation for the period of time in terms of perceived happiness, stress, time pressure, and so forth.

Another kind of aggregate pattern can be computed across the different dimensions of time use measured. For example, where do people see others they consider their friends: at home, in the neighborhood, at or near their places of employment? What kinds of activities are considered stressful and which ones not (and by whom)? For what purposes do people travel by particular modes of transportation and for what distance/duration?

Still another pattern can be computed that details the dynamics of time use across and among the various household members. Who does which household chores? Do spouses complement each other in their activities, or does what one person undertakes have little or no bearing to the situation of the other(s)?

In sum, this view takes behavior as a system of activities, involving several dimensions. In it, people not only experience specific activities (or the inability to perform them) but also the impact of the pattern itself. A given behavior may be relevant not only for its discrete experience but for how it fits into and impacts the greater system of behaviors. The need for a long commute, for example, may be important not only for its expense, hassle, and duration, but also in terms of its interaction with the performance of responsibilities at home and at work, as well as the kind and amount of other activities that can be undertaken in the remaining time available. So behavior is pertinent not only as a delimited event but also as component parts creating a greater whole called everyday life.

Nonetheless, a focus on period-specific patterns of time use does not by itself expand our understanding of environments (cf. Berk & Berk, 1979; McGrath, 1988; Adam, 1990). For this, a conceptual scheme that links time use to appropriate contexts is needed. Let us turn to one.

EVERYDAY LIFE IN CONTEXTUAL PERSPECTIVE

The conceptualization of how behavior is related to specific contexts of a relatively microscopic nature has been a major challenge and preoccupation within environmental psychology and its sibling disciplines. It began with the need to show that environments actually have behavioral implications that are tangible and relevant enough to consider along with economic and locational dimensions of context. The challenge is greater yet, however, when the relationship between environment and behavior involves more macroscopic and integrative but less imageable levels of concern. Fortunately, there is a precedent in the work of Torsten Hagerstrand (cf. Hagerstrand, 1970; Carlstein, 1978; Parkes & Thrift, 1980; Michelson, 1987).

Hagerstrand devised a scheme for comprehending the ways in which macroscopic contexts come to bear on what a person can work into the daily routine: individual activities and combinations. His scheme illuminates the variables of time and space as crucial aspects of people's contexts that create either opportunities or constraints for behaviors and patterns. Although one can demonstrate opportunity, it is of less priority than constraint; having opportunity to do something is no determinant that it will be done, whereas being constrained can eliminate the possibility entirely. Thus, Hagerstrand focused on constraints. His scheme deals primarily with what is difficult or impossible to accomplish on a specific day given the spatial and temporal contexts in which behavior might occur. For example, how does the structure of a particular city constrain everyday behavior?

Time and space work in tandem even though they are separate concepts. Space is taken as the distribution of land uses. How clustered or decentralized are particular locations that people may consider visiting on a given day? Is there much or little difficulty in combining such visits in the course of a day and the time available within it? For a particular individual with a fixed workplace, for example, spatial distribution can make a big difference in what it takes to visit a post office.

But space alone is not sufficient. Temporal considerations make spatial distributions meaningful. It takes time to cover space. How much time it takes depends not only on distance but on the means and speed of transportation available and the route that is feasible. With infinite time and means, it would be possible to get to most places from most others; but for everyday life, time is limited. Everybody has the same allocation of 24 hours. It is a zero-sum game; in the face of heavy demands on limited time, activities are traded off against each other (Staikov, 1973).

Time is very limited. Meeting biological needs takes most people more than a third of the daily time allocation, and full-time employment or education take at least another third. Only a small fraction of the day remains for anything else. And within the constraints of time, the logistical process of getting to and among dispersed land uses becomes highly problematic.

The constraints become most evident and potent according to the priorities people have and hence their prior allocations of time. Most people fit their habitual time schedules around their primary commitments, to their own life and health (i.e., sleep, eating, etc.) and to their employers or family members. How much else you can do, given ambient contexts, is severely restricted once you have taken these primary commitments (and their associated travel-time requirements) from the daily pot of time. But how much you actually can do, of what you might want or need to do, is a function of the time and space dimensions of the particular contexts within which your 24 hours are played.

Hagerstrand points in particular to three kinds of constraints in this regard:

Authority constraints are decisions from external sources that limit access to daily activity. Opening and closing hours for the loci of specific activities are a major form of authority constraint, and these are normally outside the reach of influence by the individual user. But freedom of opportunity for particular activities is very much dependent on whether their hours are restricted to traditional working hours or are extended into the nights and weekends (Melbin, 1978, 1987). Similarly, land-use regulations serve as authority constraints on the spacing of people's homes and nonresidential activities. Although Hagerstrand does not mention it as a de jure authority constraint, the established gender roles within given societies have typically set limits as to where women in particular can't be at certain hours.

Capability constraints are those that deal with how aspects of your context allow you to fit particular activities into the uncommitted portions of the day. Can you physically get to the post office, for example, in the time you have between commitments at home and work, given the locations of all three places and the means of travel available?

Coupling constraints deal with the extent that, given the spatial and temporal dimensions of context, sufficient numbers of interested people can get together for sufficient time to make an activity possible. Shopping opportunities, for example, are necessarily constrained in areas of sparce population (Palm, 1981). Major league sports require catchment areas that provide sufficiently large game attendance.

Thus, Hagerstrand's concepts help us understand what people find difficult or impossible to do in their local contexts, rural and urban alike. They also help in the determination of what would have to be changed to lessen constraint and provide opportunity. Proposed interventions into space and time can be tested to see what impact they make on constraints relevant to people's needs and wants (cf. Lenntorp, 1976). But, most of all, this approach helps us to *comprehend* how the more integrated pattern of people's daily lives interacts with the contexts in which these lives are found. As Mackenzie puts it, "Time and space . . . not only form the context of human environmental relations, but . . . are categories which allow us to collect the multitude of activities which make up people's lives while at the same time retaining the conceptual fluidity to see changes in these lives" (1988, p. 25).

This approach is obviously extremely general, applicable to all people in all places, with the necessary details to be filled in for specific situations. In the next section, I shall turn to why it is particularly germane to the study of women and environment.

THE SALIENCE OF EVERYDAY BEHAVIOR AND ITS CONTEXTUAL PERSPECTIVE FOR THE STUDY OF WOMEN AND ENVIRONMENTS

There are two good reasons why the study of women and environments should expand to include both specific behaviors and the pattern of everyday behavior in its purview. The first is that not only have dramatic changes in various aspects of women's daily routines occurred in recent decades but that these interact systematically to create a changed whole even greater than its parts. Therefore, one must attend to more than isolated parts but rather to the behaviors and contexts constituting the whole. The second is that, even before these changes, women were shortchanged in the creation of environments because only some of their activities were considered—and not the greater whole that they constituted. In essence, recent changes have simply exascerbated the problems arising from an incomplete view of women's environments and behaviors.

The main changes are doubtless familiar. During the past half century, women have undertaken paid employment to a degree that was unprecedented in industrialized nations. This includes not only adult women in general but also a clear majority of women with young children (cf. Hasell & Peatross, 1990; Naesman, 1990). Even in families with children aged 1 and under, the majority of women have paid employment (Williams et al., 1991). This trend varies in degree and timing by country and culture but holds strongly for most nations in Europe and North America. Indeed, the most dramatic changes have occurred in the past 20 years, reflecting in great part changes in the standards and cost of living, as well as increasing education and vocational aspirations by women (cf. Michelson, 1985a).

A concomitant change is the increase in maintenance of households, often with children, by single women. A major factor behind this is an increase in the rate of divorce (Hapgood & Getzels, 1974). But this increase in percentage of households headed by women has been fostered also by delays in the age of first marriage, earlier moves away from the family of procreation not connected to marriage, and extensions to longevity. Hassell and Peatross (1990, p. 5) point out that "in 1983, only 11.7% of all [U.S.] households consisted of a wage-earner father, a homemaker mother, and dependent children."

These changes have been associated with specific problems. Concerns about equity for women in the spheres of employment, economics, and housing are widespread. The availability and quality of child care and similar support services has become an explicit issue (cf. Cook, 1989). The design and location (not to speak of availability) of housing for nontraditional households have received increased attention (Franck & Ahrentzen, 1989). So have local neighborhood design, the form of cities and their centers, transportation, and technology more generally. Safety issues for women can be contextual (street safety, safety in travel, residential safety) and not (sexual harassment at work).

Pursuit of these issues in their own right is surely needed. The particular interface of women and specific situations and contexts is important (cf. Churchman, 1990). Yet, the changes facing women form a more systematic whole. And these are not addressed adequately without recognition of the larger pattern and how the various contexts contribute as well to the whole.

The daily lives of women have changed in terms of the combinations and patterns of activities they carry out as part of everyday life. Among the many women who combine (in various ways) paid employment and domestic responsibilities with a certain number of other necessary and voluntary activities, there are questions not only of the behavioral adequacy of the component contexts, but how they interact with each other within the temporal and spatial framework of the day and in their impact on the individual woman.

The conventional American suburb was designed on the premise that it would primarily serve housewives with young children in terms of everyday behavior. The individual home was thought an oasis, far from conflicting land uses, and surrounded by sufficient grounds to permit safe play by toddlers. The dwelling itself was sufficiently large for multiple uses by family members, not least for entertaining. The woman's place was in the home (cf. Wekerle, 1984), with major responsibility for maintenance of children and dwelling. For the men who did the planning and the greater number commuting to work from suburbs, this situation was thought to foster the ideal domestic picture to which men would periodically return. Ironically, this enshrining of North American women's domestic role in suburban homes took on very different effects when exported to less developed nations, where women's well-defined roles as workers, oriented around their central-city homes, got constrained out of existence by suburbanization (Moser, 1987).

Where this set of objectives broke down was in the degree that it failed to include other behaviors that suburbanites wanted to incorporate into their days, even then but more and more as behavior patterns changed over time in North America. Housewives, for example, contemplated behaviors other than housework and child care, and these were often hard to achieve in an area of low density, separation of land uses, and transportation deficits, particularly in combination with existing responsibilities. The patterns of daily activity that were hard to fulfill under typical suburban spatial patterns in the time available grew with the age of children and the desire for nondomestic activities on the part of women. Thus the problem with suburbs was that the contexts provided adequately for only some, albeit major, behavior needs and not for the larger pattern that women increasingly envisaged. Even before the major changes in employment and domestic status, women were potentially more than housewives in terms of the everyday behavior for which their contexts provided opportunities or constraints.

What has changed so dramatically is not the fact of multiple behaviors but the content, location, and relative balance among multiple daily obligations (cf. Ontario Women's Directorate, 1991). Fortuijn and Karsten (1989, p. 365) refer to women who pursue paid employment, domestic work, and child care on an everyday basis as "combiners," who "have to fit in many different activities in many different locations. They are continually confronted with the limitations imposed by time and space."

Although environmental psychologists and sociologists typically studied the fit of specific contexts to behaviors, it was geographers following Hagerstrand's approach that pioneered the explication of women's more integrative everyday lives in contextual perspective. Palm and Pred (1974) use this scheme to compare the particular constraints entering the daily lives of both full-time housewives and those with outside employment, together with variations reflecting differential family composition and access to transportation.

Their succinct article captures very well the capability constraints encountered by the employed mother who maintains traditional domestic and child-care responsibilities (through choice, coercion, or single parenthood) alongside employment. Assuming school-aged children, she remains at home at least until the children leave for school, requires travel time to the place of employment, must put in a prescribed workday (traditionally, with fixed hours), and must be home again at a time consistent with the afterschool timetable. Shopping, food preparation, housekeeping, and laundry, as well as occasional needs such as medical and dental care, must be fit around all the others, but still have to be done precisely when needed. How hard it is to carry out such an everyday life is in part a function of external contexts: the respective locations of the respective activities, how they are timetabled, what kind of transportation is available.

Among mothers with younger children, some form of child care is necessary to maintain employment, and Palm and Pred note the importance of not just the availability and quality of child care but also that its location and hours are major constraints to the daily program of the employed woman. In other words, child care's value is not just in its presence or absence to enable employment or the excellence of its experience for children, but in how its temporal and spatial dimensions interact with the day's other commitments: affecting them all.

Thus, each of the major daily commitments undertaken by the employed woman interacts within limited time with the others, in a pattern of mutual constraint. Palm and Pred derive from this scheme that the choice of employment among these women may be limited, having to fit within the constraints accompanying other commitments; indeed, subsequent studies have regularly documented ᷱat women typically suboptimize their employment choices, basing them much more than men on convenient locations and hours, as compared to logical career development (e.g., Ericksen, 1977; Hanson & Hanson, 1981; Madden, 1981; Zelinsky, Monk, & Hanson, 1982; Wekerle & Rutherford, 1987).

Moreover, Palm and Pred's explication of the everyday lives of full-time housewives in contextual perspective provides a basis for understanding the flaws in the picture of this earlier pattern as an idyll of leisure. This analysis shows that the woman's role as managing parent and consumer in at least suburban land-use patterns and conventional opening and closing hours requires frequent, often unconnected trips by car. Children need chauffeuring to various activities, and the various commercial, institutional, and support services are just around the corner only on exception. The impact in the daily pattern of women is to break up the day into minor segments, eliminating the chance for the kind of continuity that defines genuine leisure. One study comparing the time use of American women early in the century to those in the mid-60s showed that amount of domestic labor in the days before labor-saving devices was more than matched by the later need for women to drive children all over the landscape (Vanek, 1974).

Thus, the impact of recent changes affecting women is greater than that of the specific situations that women now encounter. Palm and Pred add to more conventional analyses of women and environments by giving a precedent for expanding the focus on contexts to reflect a more systematic and dynamic view of women's behavior, in stasis and change alike.

AN EXPANDED VIEW OF ENVIRONMENTS PERTINENT TO WOMEN

The purpose of this section is not one of discovery but rather of exploration. We all know what housing, land use, transportation, and safety are and that they are important. My aim is to show how the change of paradigm to treat behavior as part of a pattern of everyday life *extends* our understanding of the pertinence of these contexts.

Housing

Franck suggested (1988, p. 293) that "future research on women and housing might do well to consider the temporal dimensions of women's lives along with the spatial dimensions." What kind of advance would this represent?

Housing attributes are increasingly considered as to how they might facilitate certain behaviors desired by women (Hayden, 1980, 1984; Cooper Marcus & Sarkissian, 1986; Peterson, 1987; Wekerle, 1988; Franck & Ahrentzen, 1989; Hasell & Peatross, 1990; Pedersen & Vestbro, 1990). The focus has been on such aspects as (1) making kitchens more open to other household areas and functions to facilitate activity and contact, (2) designing rooms as multifunctional to enable greater adaptability to different household composition, (3) use of materials taking less time to clean, (4) facilitating contact and mutual support with immediate neighbors through immediate access to common facilities, and (5) taking a broader view of housing as more than the sum of private housing units.

The importance of such innovations, however, goes beyond the immediate behavior found within. The specific relationships of environment and behavior might be thought trivial if not rooted in a fuller picture of everyday life. For example (Michelson, 1986), the employed woman spends a significantly smaller number of hours per day at home than the housewife. The people she sees are at or near the job, and she is much less likely to have contact with neighbors. All else equal, a spacious dwelling requiring extensive housekeeping becomes neither necessary for behaviors that occur elsewhere nor desirable for the time required, in view of constraints from external commitments.

The second trend, toward women heading their households, is often linked with that of outside employment by women. In this case, the woman is not only absent from home a major part of the day, but when at home does not have the companionship or whatever assistance and support with domestic and child-care activities another adult might provide (however less than equal these might prove in reality).

For both these examples, two questions arise. What desired activities, made salient by the aggregate pattern of daily activity but absent as a consequence of temporal and spatial constraints could be realized by changes in housing contexts? Second, time needed for which activities is exacerbated by housing contexts and creates constraints on other aspects of daily life? Each question is addressed by using the temporal and spatial perspective in the microcosm of the housing complex.

Some developments in Sweden that I have recently studied shed light on these questions and support the understanding of housing in the context of everyday life. In the archtypical situation of time pressures on women spawned by the combination of employment with housekeeping and child-care responsibilities, with only relatively minor adaptation by male partners, policymakers have set ameliorative objectives to be realized within the context of experimental housing complexes. These complexes are intended to improve upon the great number of housing units built to relieve housing shortages through the mid-1970s, which have objectively high standards in site planning, size per capita, and equipment but are criticized in terms of social considerations.

The single most common objective is to provide a context within which people will spontaneously have the opportunity of social contact with their neighbors. This is to compensate for the degree of local social isolation felt to accompany long days of employment, followed by the need for domestic and child-care activities.

Two very pragmatic objectives usually accompany the goal of enhanced social contact. One is to lessen the amount of housework needed. The other is to make child care easier on the parent(s).

Enhancing social contact exemplifies the use of housing to realize a behavior made hard to achieve in view of more compulsory activities. The housework and child-care goals involve attempts to mitigate time demands found in conventional housing, which prove difficult within the total daily routine.

Some of the innovations in housing context are physical, and some have to do with social organization. Some join the two. In my research, I attempted to gather a small sample of housing complexes with representative approaches to the goals mentioned. One was starkly physical: placing a glass roof over about three blocks of parallel row houses, making what would have been outside space into an indoor streetscape with plazas, institutions and a store. A second involved intensive public use of the ground floor of a renovated high-rise building, in the form of a convenience store, boutique, concierge desk, cafe, library, party room, meeting room, laundry room and adjacent playroom, and sauna; the local municipality manages this space. The third and fourth experimental complexes are what Swedes call collective houses, in which there are both enhanced levels of shared spaces and major resident participation in the management and maintenance of the complex and its programs. One of these is at the scale that some collective house pioneers consider ideal, with 41 households, each in a private apartment scaled down by about 10%; space gained is turned over to shared spaces, which include a dining room in which dinner is served five nights a week by rotating teams, a lounge, playroom, diverse hobby rooms, sauna, day-care center, and decentralized sitting rooms. The second collective house is much larger than normal, with an added segment of persons needing extra care, but also with even more extensive and well-equipped common spaces including a gymnasium. Although municipal support for the service-dependent residents and in-house elementary-school classes enables people to eat lunch collectively in the dining room, resident-organized meals are confined to two dinners a week (on weeknights).

All these approaches follow the assumption that behavior (in this case, neighbor contact) that is constrained by the major demands of the daily life pattern and by conventional residential space (consisting of mostly private dwelling units) can be fostered by provision of unique opportunities, making contact the path of least resistance. In the case of the collective houses, residents have the chance to trade off some conventional time constraints (to buy, prepare, eat, and clean up after dinner) for social contact. Working on house committees is another kind of tradeoff, against higher rents, but again providing the bonus of neighbor contact.

But even without the innovations in social organization inherent in the collective houses, these examples show how space can be allocated and arranged so that people can meet each other spontaneously, despite other pressures on their time. Walking home under the protection of the glass roof, shopping at the convenience store or snacking at the cafe, keeping an eye on toddlers in hallway spaces, weaving on a loom, and playing in the gym all potentially bring neighbors together.

Not all the experimental complexes make the same level of commitment to lessening of household work. Neither the glass roof nor the intensive ground-floor facilities address household work as directly as do the provision of space, facilities, and social organization for the evening meal.

Easier child care is not a major objective within the service-intensive high-rise building. But having a glass roof as protection against extreme cold, wind, precipitation, and darkness gives children a far greater chance for play outside the dwelling unit yearround and is very likely to make child care easier for parents. In the collective houses, the combination of diverse indoor activity spaces and a tight network of mutually cooperating adults gives children a richness of opportunity outside their own apartments and a safety net of continuous supervision by parents throughout the building. Although children are thought to benefit from such specified behavior settings, much added significance comes from how this objective fits into the parents' everyday life patterns.

In the design of our study, each of these four areas was matched to a more conventional housing complex that served as a control. Hence, it was possible to compare not only the impact of different approaches to these objectives with each other but also the outcome of experimental complexes against reasonably similar places that lack the experimental features.

The research was conducted in the winter and spring of 1988. It involved three complementary methods. Systematic observations were made during both winter and summer weather conditions of the areas on the same days and times, charting who participated in what kinds of social contact in common spaces. Questionnaires covering considerable factual material about residents, their residential choices and expectations, and their experiences were gathered from adults in the eight housing complexes. Finally, precoded time-use diaries were completed by both adults and (by and for) children.

Our results (cf. Michelson, 1990, 1991, 1993) provided general confirmation that housing can facilitate behavior that may not occur to the same degree under conventional contextual constraints. But it showed as well that the results vary greatly by the kind of innovations pursued.

For example, the combination of spatial and organizational planning found in the collective houses is most effective in facilitating contact. The collective dinner is a strategic factor, explained directly through temporal and spatial analyses, with degree of contact even a function of the number of nights per week in which dinner is served (see also Woodward, 1989; Woodward, Vestbro, & Grossman, 1989). Neighbor contact is less responsive to physical opportunities in the absence of accompanying social organization. Hence, children are more likely than adults to go "out" under the roof for play than adults; children are expected to go out, whereas adults have no special reason to do so. In the process, the turf gets transferred to the children! The intensive service high-rise example shows that although people can be found in ample contact in the rather specific, commercially oriented activities on the apartment's ground floor, this does not generalize to their more general pattern of interpersonal behavior.

A major lessening of household work was largely confined to the collective house with dinners available on all the weekdays. The data showed that conventional housing, too, can address this goal through such details as more efficient kitchens, household materials, and room designs. But it took systematic application of substituting the collective for the individual to reduce household work appreciably more.

Although child care is also addressed in many ways, the greatest perceived ease of child care was found in the collective houses, with the combination of physical and organizational innovations. There, the combination of diverse behavioral opportunities in a safe milieu of shared supervision achieves the greatest results.

The literature (cf. Michelson 1977) suggests that outcomes like these can be a function of a process of self-selection: specific kinds of people with preexisting behaviors are attracted to particular residential milieus. Our data indicated definite evidence of self-selection, with accompanying expectations of the new environments. But our statistical analyses (Michelson, 1991) indicated that the impact of living with specific physical and social features of housing is essential to the extent that subsequent behaviors materialize, well beyond the impact of persons with expectations and the levels held. Contexts are necessary for the behaviors assessed.

And the significance of these housing contexts and their outcomes are a function of how they redress the constraints of everyday life.

LAND USE AND TEMPORAL AVAILABILITY

Much attention has been given to land use serving as context to women's housing. Observers point to the location of housing in terms of the other amenities and necessities of daily life: jobs, child-care facilities, shopping, social and medical support institutions, recreational facilities, and more (e.g., Peterson, 1986; Franck, 1988; Dyck, 1989; Franck & Paxson, 1989). Where once the North American neighborhood was evaluated as to how well it insulated households from the disturbances and dangers of nonresidential land uses, more recent, feminist scholars have repeatedly stressed the desirability of integrating the kinds of locations that women increasingly have to incorporate into their daily routines (e.g., Hayden, 1980; Churchman, 1990). Wekerle entitled an article "A Woman's Place Is in the City" (1984) in an argument that the very land-use patterns that suburbs were built to replace on behalf of women are now more functional for their needs.

The point here is that this is not a revision of aesthetic judgment, planning standards, or how well an activity can be provided or enjoyed, but rather how well a woman can carry out her everyday life within the context available. When land uses are at low density, segregated, and randomly located, it becomes difficult or impossible for the woman to put together all that's necessary within the limits of available time. The same domestic obligations that made it once seem desirable for women's lives to be oriented around the home environment are still largely in place, even at the same time that paid employment takes out significant amounts of time from the daily supply; thus, localization of the activities and facilities that women need is even more appropriate than before (Franck & Paxson, 1989).

Day care is a representative example of this situation. Dyck (1989), for example, notes that day-care trips fall between the demands of home and job, indeed serving the purpose of making the two reconcilable within the daily routine. My research on employed mothers brought out the stressful nature of this commuting interface. The qualitative structure of women's days is very different from that of their husbands. For the men, only one major time use is perceived as very high in tension— work. Among their wives, who mostly take primary responsibility for household and child-care chores as well, getting everybody up and out in the morning is stressful, as is the job. The trip that links the two is extremely stressful if only because it falls between a rock and a hard place; each commitment is major, and what happens at one end can have negative implications at the other. Day-care trips, predominently carried out by the women, have a bearing on the distance, duration, and ease of what is in any case a stressful trip to and from work. Among our respondents, the location of day-care providers added a conservative 28% to the distance linking home and work for women (Michelson, 1985b). An increasing criterion of the adequacy of such a service or activity is how it fits into the lives of its users, in this case spatially.

Opening and closing hours are a major aspect of the temporal side of access to goods, services, and activities. Day care exemplifies this side as well. The hours of its availability are an explicit constraint on what kind of work a woman (or male parent) can do, other needs or desires that can be incorporated into the routine, and the extent of pressure placed on daily travel (cf. Martensson, 1977). It is not surprising that women with the most demanding jobs (and accompanyingly high pay) attempt to have child care at home by full-time nannies, eliminating the discontinuities of spacing and timing associated with external child-care services.

Indeed, revolutions in accessibility in time are following the trend of change in women's daily lives in such local activities as banking (24-hour ATMs), food shopping, and nonemergency medical care. Again the logic of banking, shopping, or seeing a pediatrician at 10 P.M. is in how it fits into the pattern of everyday life.

TRANSPORTATION

Transportation is the dynamic side of the understanding of how well daily life can be carried out within existent land-use patterns (cf. Matzner & Reusch, 1976). Considerable research has established that women have less access to transportation resources than do men, travel shorter distances even if employed, are much more likely to travel with children, are more exposed to physical danger en route, and experience much more stress while traveling (e.g., Rosenbloom, 1978; Zelinsky, Monk, & Hanson, 1982; Michelson, 1984). Obviously, these findings are highly interrelated!

This situation is ironic in view of the structure of everyday life. Full-time housewives traveled primarily around local areas. With the onset of widespread employment, it is women who have the more numerous constraints on daily activity brought about by the combination of major commitments. Yet, the most flexible means of optimizing choice of activities and minimizing the time between them is characteristically less available to them than to men. The man is more likely to have a driver's license and primary access to the household's first car. Single women (especially single mothers) are more likely to be in marginal financial positions. This leaves many women, as Carp (1974, p. 6) put it, "transportation deprived and transit dependent."

Once again, the seriousness of a transportation situation that primarily reflects an earlier era lies in how transportation interacts with many of the day's other activities—often a major constraint on them. The cost or disagreeable nature of a trip is minor compared to how transportation opportunities and constraints contribute to the shape and pressures of everyday life. Popenoe explicates clearly how decisions concerning the nature and distribution of transportation resources within municipalities impact the life chances of women, among other population groups (1977, 1985).

SAFETY: EXPANDED CONTEXTS

One of the results of the trend in women's lives is that they appear in more locations as a consequence of increased employment and autonomy. Another is that they use public spaces and transportation facilities at different times of day than before. A third is that they are less likely to be accompanied by a spouse. All these are conditions making women more at risk to crime than previously.

It puts the spotlight on areas within cities where women were not customarily found. As job equity increases, women's geographic range will inevitably increase. But will the areas to which they go adapt in the direction of user friendliness with sufficient speed? Or are women placed into added jeopardy of unknown duration?

Public transportation offers less control and protection to women than does the private automobile, yet women are more transit-dependent than men. Now that travel necessarily includes more areas and times of travel, what greater exposure do women have to crime?

The message of this section is that public safety requires increasing attention away from familiar sites of crime and toward increasing numbers of places and times of day when women's newer routines increase their risk of victimization. The study of women and environment requires the discovery of additional contexts than have previously entered public consciousness as pertinent to women.

FUTURE RESEARCH ON POLICY ISSUES

In this section, I shall suggest some contemporary issues that arise in large part from the changing nature of women's lives and the contextual perspectives in which they are found. How can future research based on expanded perspectives on environment and behavior better inform their resolution?

EXTENDED HOURS

An ongoing debate in many jurisdictions focuses on the extent that commercial services can be open all night and on Sundays. When women were predominantly full-time housewives, it was expected that they could and would attend to family needs during the normal hours of employment. This, of course, extended beyond purely commercial services to institutional and medical activities. With paid employment, women have severe capability constraints, if still expected to do this. Opportunities to combine activities in time can be enhanced with the expansion of service hours into the nighttime and throughout the weekend. Melbin called this our last "frontier": an underused resource available for exploitation (1978). My own first experience more than 25 years ago with an all-night supermarket left a feeling of greater personal liberty! Indeed, as noted earlier, some service providers have altered their hours (authority constraints) during recent years. But there is no general consensus or policy on this issue, and political jurisdictions make conflicting laws.

Extended hours are an issue for several reasons. First, religious traditions frown on commercial activity on the sabbath. This point of view is extended to the alleged right of workers to have a day per week when they know all family members can relax together. Whether religious or not, many employees are reluctant to face the prospect of regular Sunday work. Nighttime openings also require employees in what are nontraditional shifts for many. These may differ from the daily patterns of other family members, as might Sunday openings. When relatively few enterprises are open late at night, people think them at risk regarding crime. Furthermore, consumers not used to extended hours are uncertain as to their alleged benefits.

Yet, it is not certain that extended hours are uniformly negative for employees. They may permit members of households to complement each other in such activities as child care and shopping, parents don't necessarily have to work at the same time and seek external child-care services. Many merchants claim greater sales, profits, and need for employees if stores are open when consumers find it more convenient to shop at leisure. This creates additional jobs, some of which are welcomed by groups like students who are occupied other parts of the day and week.

My own hypothesis is that, at the least, extended hours remove constraints within the daily routine and lessen time pressures for the average worker. Research is needed to assess differences among those with and without exposure to nighttime and Sunday hours. This needs to be applied both to those who use the services in question and to those who staff them. Do extended hours add to or take away from the feelings of leisure and liberty of users? How does working unusual hours or days fit into people's lives, in general and with respect to the rest of their households? This issue, like so many others, rests on a factual basis, for which much more needs to be learned. What is clear at the moment is that these aspects of context are highly salient.

Exposure to Dangerous Contexts

Placing everyday life in contextual perspective shows the need to expand environmental perspectives on crime prevention beyond the examination of residential contexts and typical local street scenes (cf. Newman, 1972). It is vital to inventory and understand the situations of risk that are only now opening up as part of changed patterns of daily life, in space and in time. For example, parking lots appear to be emerging as an increasingly dangerous site for women—in apartment complexes, shopping centers, near transportation nodes—not least as women use them more.

Precedents for the exploration of exposure to risky sites and districts lie in epidemiological and equivalent studies that have assessed different daily time and space-use patterns (Armstrong, 1973; Wiley, 1991). What are the odds of pathology that accompany the use of certain places or the choice of specific routes under current conditions? Risk of crime should not be a price of life pattern changes, but rather a target for attention and remediation. Research studies must produce evidence of which contexts are typically dangerous and hence require either more policing or alternative forms of amelioration. It is not a matter of blaming women for the outcomes of their new daily lives any more than the elderly are at fault for wanting to go out after dark. It is again a pragmatic matter of assessing where the problem now lies, so as to do something appropriate.

Workplace Flexibility

Viewing daily life in contextual perspective shows that the impact of paid outside employment is immense, not only in itself, but particularly as it affects most other daily activities. Increasing attention has been paid to how jobs can be made more flexible, so that their greater impact is minimized (cf. Cook, 1989; Ontario Women's Directorate, 1991). Such devices as staggering hours among major employers, providing flexible hours for individual employees, fostering job sharing, and managing home-based work all aim at easing the daily routine. But they do so unequally in view of what typically contributes to constraints in everyday life.

Employment and commuting go hand-in-hand in conventional situations. Home-based work, when feasible, cuts out commuting other than on an occasional basis; but it doesn't necessarily lessen the length of time spent at work that is not available for other purposes. Flexible hours enable a lessening of commuting time and the ability to put work hours more into sync with other commitments. Job sharing, on the other hand, cuts into the hours of work per se, without loss of perks but sacrificing earnings. And staggered hours lessen the load on public infrastructure but don't necessarily address the needs of individual workers. My own previous analyses (Michelson, 1985a), among others (cf. Bohen & Viveros-Long, 1981) suggest that the more time a form of job flexibility gives women to use for other daily commitments, the less stress is encountered in the daily routine. Whether loss of potential income is an acceptable tradeoff for a smoother existence is an additional question.

Much more understanding is needed about how specific conditions of work interact with the other aspects of everyday life.

The Substance of Planning and Planning Research

A final ongoing issue is highlighted by the foregoing discussions. There is ongoing malaise about what it is that planners plan. To what extent is planning restricted in practice not just to physical development but to particular parcels of land at a time? Or does planning expand to capture the greater array of contexts and their interaction as impacting on people's life chances? Do decisions about land use (and the information base bearing upon them) go beyond matters of economics, efficiency, and overt threats to health, welfare, and safety? If expanding to behavior, does the information base for planning extend beyond the immediate impacts of environment and behavior?

The argument of this chapter is that a number of contexts provide opportunities and constraints on the nature and quality of everyday life, particularly as they interact. Although macroscopic contexts are seldom determinative, they are not, on the other hand, neutral or irrelevant. Will this level of consideration continue nearly unheeded, or does a new level of planning need to enhance and expand what pioneer efforts have shown to impact upon people's lives?

And, in any case, who plans time in any serious or empirical way, particularly at a collective and interactive level? We are increasingly told to plan our personal time. Various time-management devices flood the market. But who is concerned with the public impact of authority constraints on time literally every day? This does not mean that such an exercise should be construed as determinative, but the impacts of constraints are real enough. And pragmatic efforts to understand and deal rationally with them should be developed and encouraged.

If dimensions of context such as time and space are as integral and all-pervasive as they are, men and women alike identify with their impact. Making these dimensions and their effects explicit can surely ameliorate situations affecting people of all kinds. Nonetheless, their current application to women and environment is strong and immediate because changes in public contexts have lagged behind the profound changes in the content and pattern of women's everyday lives, a classic cultural lag (Ogburn, 1964). Additions to the paradigms of planning and its research base are urgently required for the contextual perspectives of women's everyday lives, but they pertain to the existence of all.

Acknowledgments

The research on Swedish experimental housing was carried out under a grant from the (Swedish) State Council on Building Research, with subsequent support for analysis from the Humanities and Social Sciences Committee of the University of Toronto Research Board. The study was done in collaboration with Professor Birgit Kranz, Institute for Building Functions Analysis, Department of Architecture, University of Lund, Sweden, to whom I am sincerely grateful for her interest, initiative, and cooperation.

REFERENCES

Adam, B. (1990). *Time and social theory.* Cambridge: Polity.

Andrew, C., & Milroy, B. (1988). *Life spaces: Gender, household, employment.* Vancouver: University of British Columbia Press.

Armstrong, R. (1973). Tracing exposure to specific environments in medical geography. *Geographical Analyses, 2,* 122–132.

Barker, R. (1968). *Ecological psychology.* Stanford: Stanford University Press.

Berk, R., & Berk, S. (1979). *Labor and leisure at home: Content and organization of the household day.* Beverly Hills: Sage.

Bohen, H., & Viveros-Long, A. (1981). *Balancing jobs and family life: Do flexible work schedules help?* Philadelphia: Temple University Press.

Carlstein, T. (1978). A time-geographic approach to time allocation and socio-ecological systems. In W. Michelson (Ed.), *Public policy in temporal perspective* (pp. 69–82). The Hague: Mouton.

Carp, F. (1974). *Employed women as a transportation-deprived and transit-dependent group* (Document no. TLM-4-1-74). Berkeley: Metropolitan Transportation Commission.

Churchman, A. (1990). *Women and urban quality of life.* Paper presented to the 22nd International Congress of Applied Psychology, Kyoto.

Cook, A. (1989). Public policies to help dual-earner families meet the demands of the work world. *Industrial and Labor Relations Review, 42,* 201–215.

Cooper Marcus, C., & Sarkissian, W. (1986). *Housing as if people mattered.* Berkeley: University of California Press.

Dyck, I. (1989). Integrating home and wage workplace: Women's daily lives in a Canadian suburb. *The Canadian Geographer, 33,* 329–341.

Ericksen, J. (1977). An analysis of the journey to work for women. *Social Problems, 24,* 428–435.

Fortuijn, J., & Karsten, L. (1989). Daily activity patterns of working parents in The Netherlands. *Area, 21,* 365–376.

Franck, K. (1988). Women's housing and neighborhood needs. In E. Huttman & W. Van-Vliet (Eds.), *Handbook of housing and the built environment in the United States* (pp. 285–300). Westport: Greenwood Press.

Franck, K., & Ahrentzen, S. (Eds.). (1989) *New households, new housing.* New York: Van Nostrand Reinhold.

Franck, K., & Paxson, L. (1989). Women and urban public space: Research, design, and policy issues. In I. Altman & E. Zube (Eds.), *Public places and spaces* (pp. 122–146). New York: Plenum Press.

Hagerstrand, T. (1970). What about people in regional science? *Papers of the Regional Science Association, 24,* 7–21.

Hanson, S., & Hanson, P. (1981). The impact of married women's employment on household travel patterns: A Swedish example. *Transportation, 10,* 165–183.

Hapgood, K., & Getzels, J. (1974). *Planning, women, and change.* Chicago: American Society of Planning Officials.

Hasell, M., & Peatross, F. (1990). Exploring connections between women's changing roles and house forms. *Environment and Behavior, 22,* 3–26.

Hayden, D. (1980). What would a non-sexist city be like? Speculations on housing, urban design, and human work. *Signs: Journal of Women in Culture and Society, 5,* Supplement, 167–184.

Hayden, D. (1984). *Redesigning the American dream.* New York: Norton.

Lenntorp, B. (1976). *Paths in space-time environments: A time-geographic study of movement possibilities of individuals.* Lund: C. W. K. Gleerup.

Mackenzie, S. (1988). Building women, building cities: Toward gender sensitive theory in the environmental disciplines. In C. Andrew & B. Milroy (Eds.), *Life spaces: Gender, housing, employment* (pp. 13–30). Vancouver: University of British Columbia Press.

Madden, J. (1981). Why women work closer to home. *Urban Studies, 18,* 181–194.

Martensson, S. (1977). Childhood interaction and temporal organization. *Economic Geography, 53,* 99–125.

Matzner, E., & Reusch, G. (Eds.). (1976). *Transport as an instrument for allocating space and time—a social science approach.* Vienna:Institute of Public Finance, Technical University in Vienna.

McClain, J. (1984). *Women and housing: Changing needs and the failure of policy.* Ottawa: Canadian Council on Social Development.

McGrath, J. (Ed.). (1988). *The social psychology of time: New perspectives.* Beverly Hills: Sage.

Melbin, M. (1978). The colonization of time. In T. Carlstein, D. Parkes, & N. Thrift (Eds.), *Human activity and time geography* (pp. 100–113). London: Edward Arnold.

Melbin, M. (1987). *Night as frontier.* New York: Free Press.

Michelson, W. (1977). *Environmental choice, human behavior, and residential satisfaction.* New York: Oxford University Press.

Michelson, W. (1984). *The impact of changing women's roles on transportation needs and usage.* Washington, DC: U.S. Department of Transportation, Urban Mass Transportation Administration.

Michelson, W. (1985a). *From sun to sun: Daily obligations and community structure in the lives of employed women and their families.* Totowa, NJ: Rowman & Allenheld.

Michelson, W. (1985b). Divergent convergence: The daily routines of employed spouses as a public affairs agenda. *Public Affairs Report, 26,* 1–10.

Michelson, W. (1986). *The implications of social change for interpersonal contact and use of place.* Paper presented to 11th World Congress of Sociology, New Delhi.

Michelson, W. (1987). Measuring macroenvironment and behavior. In R. Bechtel, R. Marans, & W. Michelson (Eds.), *Methods in environmental and behavioral research* (pp. 216–243). New York: Van Nostrand Reinhold.

Michelson, W. (1990). Measuring behavioral quality in experimental housing. In Y. Yoshitake, R. Bechtel, T. Takahashi, & M. Asai (Eds.), *Current issues in environment-behavior research* (pp. 173–182). Tokyo: University of Tokyo.

Michelson, W. (1991). Built environment as a mediator of human intentions. In T. Niit, M. Raudsepp, & K. Liik (Eds.), *Environment and social development* (pp. 98–107). Tallinn: Tallinn Pedagogical Institute.

Michelson, W. (1993). The behavioral dynamics of social engineering: Lessons for family housing. In E. Arias (Eds.), *The meaning and use of housing* (pp. 302–305). Aldershot, U.K.: Avebury.

Moser, C. (1987). Women, human settlements, and housing: A conceptual framework for analysis and policy-making. In C. Moser & L. Peake (Eds.), *Women, human settlements and housing* (pp. 12–32). London: Tavistock Publications.

Naesman, E. (1990). *Working mothers and nurturing fathers?* Paper presented at the 12th World Congress of Sociology, Madrid.

Newman, O. (1972). *Defensible space.* New York: Macmillan.

Ogburn, W. (1964). *On culture and social change: Selected papers.* Chicago: University of Chicago Press.

Ontario Women's Directorate. (1991). *Work and family: The crucial balance.* Toronto: Ontario Ministry of Community and Social Services.

Palm, R. (1981). Women in non-metropolitan areas: A time-budget survey. *Environment and Planning A, 13,* 373–378.

Palm, R., Pred, A. (1974). A time-geographic perspective on problems of inequality for women. Berkeley: Institute of Urban and Regional Development, University of California, Working Paper No. 236.

Parkes, D., & Thrift, N. (1980). *Times, spaces, and places*. New York: Wiley.

Pedersen, B., & Vestbro, D. (1990). Develop forms of dwelling. In S. Thiberg (Ed.), *Housing research and design in Sweden* (pp. 201–222). Stockholm: Swedish Council for Building Research.

Peterson, R. (1986). Ten active years: A review of women and environments research. *Women and Environments, 8* (Fall), 9–11.

Peterson, R. (1987). Gender issues in the home and urban environment. In E. H. Zube & G. T. Moore (Eds.), *Advances in environment, behavior, and design* (pp. 187–218). New York: Plenum Press.

Popenoe, D. (1977). *The suburban environment: Sweden and the United States*. Chicago: University of Chicago Press.

Popenoe, D. (1985). *Private pleasure, public plight*. New Brunswick: Trans-Action Books.

Rosenbloom, S. (Ed.), (1978). *Women's travel issues: Research needs and priorities*. Washington, DC: U.S. Department of Transportation.

Saegert, S. (1980). Masculine cities and feminine suburbs: Polarized ideas, contradictory realities. *Signs: Journal of Women in Culture and Society, 5*, Supplement, 96–111.

Staikov, Z. (1973). Modelling and programming of time-budgets. *Society and Leisure, 5*, 31–47.

Szalai, A. (1972). *The use of time*. The Hague: Mouton.

Vanek, J. (1974). Time spent in housework. *Scientific American, 231*, 116–120.

Wekerle, G. (1980). Women in the urban environment. *Signs: Journal of Women in Culture and Society, 5*, Supplement, 185–211.

Wekerle, G. (1984). A women's place is in the city. *Antipode, 16*(5), 11–19.

Wekerle, G. (1988). Canadian women's housing cooperatives: Case studies in physical and social innovation. In C. Andrew & B. Milroy (Eds.), *Life spaces: Gender, household, employment* (pp. 102–140). Vancouver: University of British Columbia Press.

Wekerle, G., & Rutherford, B. (1987). Employed women in the suburbs: Transportation disadvantage in a car-centered environment. *Alternatives, 14*, 49–54.

Wicker, A. (1987). Behavior settings reconsidered: Temporal stages, resources, internal dynamics, context. In D. Stokols & I. Altman (Eds.), *Handbook of environmental psychology* (Vol. 1, pp. 613–653). New York: Wiley Interscience.

Wiley, J. (1991). *Study of children's activity patterns*. Sacramento: California Air Resources Board.

Williams, K., Suls, J., Alliger, G., Learner, S., & Wan, C., (1991). Multiple role juggling and daily mood states in working mothers: An experience sampling study. *Journal of Applied Psychology, 5*, 664–674.

Woodward, A. (1989). Communal housing in Sweden: A remedy for the stress of everyday life? In K. Franck & S. Ahrentzen (Eds.), *New households, new housing* (pp. 71–94). New York: Van Nostrand Reinhold.

Woodward, A., Vestbro, D., & Grossman, M. (1989). *Dan nya generationen kollektivhus*. Stockholm: Byggforskningsraadet.

Zeisel, J. (1981). *Inquiry by design: Tools for environment-behavior research*. Monterey: Brooks/Cole.

Zelinsky, W., Monk, J., & Hanson, S. (1982). Women and geography: A review and prospectus. *Progress in Human Geography, 6*, 317–365.

3

Girls and Boys and the Physical Environment

AN HISTORICAL PERSPECTIVE

RACHEL SEBBA

INTRODUCTION

In the following passage (that looks impressionistic at first glance), Maccoby (1987) summarizes decades of research on the topic of differences between boys and girls in the emotional, social, and cognitive fields and in relation to movement and the physical surroundings, while relating specifically to both the category of sex and that of age:

> A 4-year-old boy would be considered masculine if he enjoyed (and frequently engaged in) rough and tumble play; if he preferred to play with blocks and trucks; and if, during free play periods at nursery school, he tended to play outdoors in company of other boys. A 4-year-old girl would be seen as feminine if she liked to wear dresses, played with dolls and art materials, and didn't get into fights. At age 10, a masculine boy would be one who engaged in active sports, avoided girls, and wasn't particularly diligent about his schoolwork. A feminine girl would be one who had one or two close girlfriends, did not try to join boys' sports play groups, paid attention to the teacher in class, did not brag, liked to baby-sit, and preferred romantic television shows. At age 15, a masculine boy would be one who excelled in

RACHEL SEBBA • Faculty of Architecture and Town Planning, Technion-Israel Institute of Technology, Haifa 32000, Israel.
Women and the Environment, edited by Irwin Altman and Arza Churchman. Plenum Press, New York, 1994.

> spatial-visual tasks, liked and did well at math, was interested in cars and machinery, and knew how to repair mechanical gadgets; a feminine girl would be more interested in English and history than math or science. (p. 227)

Maccoby confirms Rousseau's observations, written about 250 years earlier in his well-known book *Emile*. "Boys," according to Rousseau (1964):

> like movement and noise-drums, tops and hobby-horses; girls prefer decorations that please the eye. Dolls are the favorite amusement of little girls—a taste clearly based on their life work. Girls are generally more docile than boys. (pp. 222–223)

Rousseau's observations were not much of a novelty either; the early thirteenth-century encyclopedist Bartholomaeus Anglicus offered his observations on this subject. Small boys were described by him as:

> living without thought or care, loving only to play, fearing no danger more than being beaten with a rod...wanting everything they see, quick to laughter and quick to tears, resisting their mothers' efforts to wash and comb them and no sooner clean but dirty again. (see McLaughlin, 1974, pp. 136–137)

Little girls, according to Bartholomew, are better disciplined, more careful, more modest and timid, and more graceful.

Comparison of these paragraphs (which were all written by the greatest authorities on the subject of their time) indicates not only the existence of a consistent perception of the personal, social, and psychological characteristics of boys and girls that has been and still is accepted in Western civilization but also extensive preoccupation with the differences between boys and girls for at least 700 years.

The research that has tried to relate to this topic (much of which is summarized in Maccoby & Jacklin, 1974; Jacklin, 1989; Liss, 1983; Halpern, 1986; Maccoby, 1990, and others) consists of diagnosing the differences and of trying to explain them and formulate hypotheses regarding their origins. This chapter is not intended to add observations regarding the nature and size of the differences between boys and girls but rather to illuminate the existing ones and to try and illustrate the relationship between the sex-related characteristics of children and the characteristics of the environment in which they were brought up.

The major argument set forth in this chapter is that the sex-related behavioral patterns of boys and girls, their environmental preferences, their social attitudes and their gender-attributed cognitive abilities are affected by their experience within the physical environment in which they are raised. Furthermore, the chapter argues that this idea was acknowledged by all the cultures that deliberately designed different environments for boys and girls, in order to exercise the potential of the physical environment in molding the child's personality, shaping his/her social behavior and developing his/her abilities.

In order to support these arguments, an attempt is made in this chapter to connect what we know about environmental conditions in which boys and girls were reared and what we know about the influence of the environment on children. The chapter first outlines the main characteristics of boys' and girls' environments in Western culture, from the recorded history of childhood, together with the educational ideas according to which these environments were shaped. The chapter then examines the main variables of those environments in an environmental–developmental model and analyzes their impact on the development and behavior of boys and girls. Some references to children from other cultures are made in this part so as to shed additional light on the data. Finally, the chapter refers to the environmental developmental model of girls and boys today.

The chapter focuses on Western culture and its concept of gender, as interwoven in all our cultural systems, including the spiritual heritage (e.g., religion, philosophy, literature, and the arts) and the cultural mechanisms that control our behavior (e.g., language, dress, inheritance laws, division of labor, family structure, children, education, etc.). Within this culture, the chapter relates to the affluent urban society, whose children were educated according to the theoretical educational guidelines common in their time and never exploited as a source of labor, as were the rural children and the children of the poor classes in the towns (Ariès, 1962; Cunningham, 1991).

EDUCATIONAL ENVIRONMENTS OF BOYS AND GIRLS: A CHRONOLOGICAL REVIEW

> When once it is shown that men and women neither are nor ought to be constituted alike either in character or in temperament, it follows that they ought not to receive the same education.
> —*Rousseau (1749), 1964, p. 219*

Referring to children's lifestyle in Mesopotamia in 1800 B.C., Summerville (1982) reports that the boys in the urban class studied at school during most of the daytime hours, whereas regarding girls we know almost nothing. We can assume that they helped the family's work as soon as they were able.

In Greece (400–600 B.C.), children lived at home with their mother until the age of 7. At that age[1] boys began their education outside the home. Until the age of 16, children's education was the family's responsibility. From the age of 16 to 20, the youth was educated at gymnasiums far away from his home. At 20 there was a division of the education of those intended for the army and those for politics. According to Summerville, the marriage age for men in Greece was about 30 and for women between 16 and 18. A similar age difference was characteristic of European society until the end of the nineteenth century.

From the writings of Plato and from many other sources we learn that the open-air theaters, the Athenian Agora, and the open areas near the temples were part of the legitimate educational environment of the Athenian boys. As to girls' educational environment, Summerville (1982) reports that "the Greeks let girls grow up in a sedentary and secluded home atmosphere" (p. 26) under the supervision of their illiterate mothers, whose "life was one of gossip and working up wool into clothes." "Even the sons of the humbler classes," according to Summerville, "were more likely to be literate than aristocratic women" (p. 29).

In Rome, boys remained at home until the age of 7; after that they became permanent escorts to their fathers. The boy helped him in his work, was his acolyte in religious observances, went along when his father visited friends, and could even attend the Senate if his father was of the Senatorial class. Roman fathers taught their sons to swim and to ride horses, to read and to write, and at the age of 16 the boy received adult clothes and went to live with a respected family for at least a year to polish his social manners. Only boys studied at school. Schooling that began at about the age of 7 included four stages, starting from the school for games (*ludi magistri*) that continued until the age of 12 and ending with the school for professional training that ceased after the youth turned 21 (the age at which, in the Roman's opinion, adolescence ended and the period of youth that continued until the age of 28 began). The girls in Rome were brought up and educated at home.

In the Middle Ages, most children grew up at home until the age of 7. At that age boys began to be distanced from the home. The sons of noblemen, who were designated for knighthood, were moved to the court of another nobleman where they were educated until the age of 15. At this age they left the court where they were raised to search out a master whom they would serve. The sons of the aristocrats of the administration went to a local day school at the age of 7, moved on to

[1]The ages mentioned here are, according to the literature, accepted ages for the stages in a child's education. In reality, there were deviations from these ages (see also Ariès, 1962, pp. 189–240).

grammar school at 10 to 12 and to a far-off university at the age of 16. In the artisan classes, the boys left home at the age of 7 to a secular school. At the age of 10 to 12, if not earlier, they moved to other artisan's homes as apprentices. When they were 18, they were already working at their profession.

The girls of all classes lived in their parents' home until puberty (except some of the aristocratic girls who were sent to be raised in their future husbands' homes and those who were put into nunneries at a very young age). Some of the girls studied at home or in local schools. Their education ended at the age of 12, and most of them could only read. High schools did not accept girls, and the professional guilds were also off limits to them. They were not sent to other families for educational purposes either. After the age of 12, it was unacceptable for a girl to walk in the city alone.

Restricting the space for girls, while systematically enlarging the home range of boys is explained in one of the popular didactic works of the thirteenth century: Philip of Novara (1988) claimed that because preeminent parents were busy doing important things and had no time to educate their children, their sons would be sent to professional teachers specially trained to instruct noble boys in the elements of courtesy as well as to prepare them for one of the two "honorable" professions, "clergy" or "chevalrie." Their daughters, on the other hand, would remain at home and would be indoctrinated from the beginning in the one virtue that is sufficient for them: obedience. According to Philip of Novara, God wished women to remain always in subjection. There was no need to teach them to read and write because many evils came from feminine knowledge of these arts; instruction in sewing and weaving was desirable, however, even for the rich.

Regarding education in the seventeenth century, Ariès (1962) states:

> If schooling in the seventeenth century was not yet the monopoly of one class, it remained the monopoly of one sex. Women were excluded. The result was that in their lives the habits of precocity and brief childhood remained unchanged from the Middle Ages to the seventeenth century. (p. 331)

Regarding education in the eighteenth century, Summerville (1982) pointed out that boys and girls "hardly seemed to belong to the same world" (p. 180). According to Rousseau (1964), the world to which the girls belonged was a "small world." As an excellent diagnostician, Rousseau states clearly that children's development "is common to both sexes—but it is directed to different objects" (p. 221). Since education, according to Rousseau, must begin at a young age, the blockade on the girl's intellectual potential must be started as early as possible:

> Girls . . . should at an early age be inured to constraint. They will all their
> lives be subjected to an unceasing and unyielding constraint, that of conven-
> tion. They must therefore be accustomed to restriction from the first, that it
> may cost them nothing [pp. 223–224]. Do not suffer them [the girls] to be free
> from restraint a single moment of their lives. Accustom them to be called
> away in the middle of their play and return to their work without a murmur.
> (p. 225)

Rousseau, who preceded Piaget by 200 years with his observations
on the connection between cognitive development and the development
of sensory perception, presents the traditional approach of his contem-
poraries and their predecessors. His amazing diagnostic and analytic
abilities are expressed here in the clarity with which he presents the
conditioning process in the girls' education and in the way he presents
the connection between the limits of the physical space and the limits of
the human mind. After stating (in regard to a boy's education) that
"Delicate observation is only possible among persons of wide experience" (p. 213), he argues that the education of girls should (as it in fact
did) remain confined to the home: "Love of home is only learned at
home" (p. 234). The siege on girls' ability of abstraction and on their
artistic skills took the form of a spatial narrowing of the physical range of
their lives. Ariès confirms that, even when school participation was
enlarged and open to boys from all the social classes (at the end of the
eighteenth century and the beginning of the nineteenth century), the
girls stayed at home or studied in the house of a neighbor or relative.

During the nineteenth century the schooling network was significantly broadened, and there was an awareness throughout Europe of
the need to provide children of all classes and of both sexes with equal
education. Dyhouse (1981), relying on the report of the Schools' Inquiry
Commissions from 1867, describes the pattern of education among the
merchant and professional class in Lancashire as fairly typical of the
country as a whole:

> Daughters of these families were commonly taught at home by nursery or
> visiting governess until they were about ten years old. They frequently
> shared lessons with their brothers at this stage. They were then often sent for
> two or three years to local day school. At about twelve . . . they might be
> sent to a select boarding school. Then they either came home for good, or
> were possibly sent for a year to "finishing school." The aims of this kind of
> school was social—not academic. After leaving school daughters of middle
> class families were expected to stay at home. (p. 41)

On the basis of biographical descriptions and classroom drawings
we learn that the few girls who learned in the local day school were
separated from the boys. They learned either in separate schools or were
designated a corner of the classroom.

The vast changes that have taken place since the Industrial Revolution influenced both the child's status and his or her environment. Simultaneously in England, Italy, France, and Russia, authors and intellectuals censured the exploitation of children and the destructive influence of city life on them. The needs of the industrial-technological society demanded the enlargement of the social base of literates and the utilization of the intellectual potential of the entire population. This meant simultaneously separating the children's world from that of the adults and enlarging the framework of schools. This process received significant impetus from the functional division of the city that separated the residential neighborhood from the other urban areas.

The mental and geographical severance of the children's society from that of the adults caused a blurring of two previously more important categories: that of rich and poor and that of boys and girls. The division of the children to subgroups according to age eliminated the fear of boys and girls sitting together in the same class (a fear that according to Ariès prevented girls' acceptance in school from the Middle Ages until the nineteenth century).

The United States was the first country to equalize the education of both sexes in the state schools. Summerville (1982) quotes a French educator who visited the American schools at the beginning of the century:

> The first impression of the stranger is that there are no sexes in the United States. Girls and boys walk to school side by side, they sit on the same benches, they have the same lessons, and go about the streets along. (p. 195)

In Western society today, within the class boundaries set for this discussion, it is hard to point to any overt differences in boys' and girls' opportunities for education or in their environmental conditions. Women's integration in the workforce outside the home and the state's concern for equal opportunities in education have created a situation in which boys and girls are educated until maturity in the same institutions, the same rooms, by the same teachers and are exposed to the same environment and the same games.

Nevertheless, researchers claim that despite formal equality in environmental conditions boys and girls do not have similar experiences. Their main observations are that (1) parents guide boys' and girls' development differently by reinforcing sex-typed activities (Maccoby & Jacklin, 1974; Eisenberg, 1983; Plomin, 1989), by providing their children with different toys and therefore different play experiences (Liss, 1983; Pitcher & Schults, 1983), and by setting different boundaries on the environment for boys and girls (Hart, 1977; Whiting & Edwards, 1988);

and that (2) children on their own initiative organize themselves (from the age of 3–4) in groups of their own sex for games and other joint activities (Lever, 1976, 1978; Pitcher & Schults, 1983; Maccoby & Jacklin, 1987; Maccoby, 1988).

As a result, most researchers conclude that today, as in the past, boys and girls develop different cognitive styles and different patterns of social relationships. These differences occupy many researchers who are busy measuring and trying to explain them.

An historical perspective is offered by Sutton-Smith and Rosenberg (1971). From their analysis of the change in game preferences of American children between 1898 and 1959 they conclude that there is evidence of increasing similarity between the sexes in game preferences and report that a number of studies have demonstrated that differences between the sexes, as measured by checklist preference (of games), have been considerably reduced between 1940 and 1970. A similar conclusion regarding cognitive skills is suggested by Feingold (1988), who claims that gender differences in cognitive abilities (as determined by the Differential Aptitude Tests conducted between 1947 and 1980 and the Scholastic Aptitude Test between 1960 and 1983) diminished sharply over the years surveyed.

The perspective of time can illuminate not only the relative size of the differences but also the direction of their change. Regarding this direction, Sutton-Smith and Rosenberg (1971) remark that the increasing similarity between the sexes is manifested more by changes in girl's play preferences than by changes in those of boys and that this finding is consistent with the other investigations of changes in boy–girl differences.

THE ENVIRONMENTAL MODEL OF THE CHILD AS A MIRROR OF HIS/HER EDUCATION

THE ENVIRONMENT AS AN INDICATOR OF CHILD DEVELOPMENT

Children's education is based on a (overt or covert) developmental model that every society (both at the popular and scientific level) adopts for itself. This model delineates the child's physiological, psychological, and cognitive abilities at each age and offers explanations regarding the factors that affect their development. At the analytical level this model is intended to pinpoint the environmental factors that play a role in human development. At the operational level, it serves as a compass that navigates the choice of timing and means in the educational intervention.

Despite the differences between the models of various cultures, they all share a perception of the child's development as a process characterized by a multistage accumulation of experiences in an ever-expanding physical and social range.

The physical environment experienced by the child has, according to accepted developmental theories, a direct influence on the development of the senses, on perception and on cognition and serves as an intervening factor that facilitates the circumstances for social development (Piaget, 1968; Gibson, 1969; Bower, 1977; Bronfenbrenner & Crouter, 1983, and others). Anthropologists who investigated children's development in different cultures argue that the difference in the physical environment is the imputed factor in observed differences in perceptual ability and in behavioral patterns between different cultural groups (Wagner, 1982). Mead (1952) claims that the physical environment reflects child development more than any other variable. Whiting and Edwards (1988) state in the preface to their analysis of children's development in 12 different communities across the world:

> We have adopted Margaret Mead's classification of age groups, based on her research on childhood in six different societies. Her four age grades are characterized in terms of the **"world"** of the child at each stage: first comes the **lap child** (aged 0–1 year), then the **knee child** (2–3 years)—followed by the **yard child** (4–5 years) and finally the **community or the school-age child** (6–10 years). (p. 4)

THE ENVIRONMENTAL MODEL OF THE CHILD

We will use Mead's analogy between the age of the child and his/her environment as a basis for the construction of a developmental–environmental model in which the environment included within the child's home range serves as a dependent variable. The main independent variables determining the child's environment in such a developmental–environmental model are (1) the child's age and the meaning ascribed to it by his/her parents and educators; (2) the characteristics of the environment, including the dangers and potentials it holds (these include physical and social variables that influence the establishing of the boundaries for the child's movement, the rules concerning setting occupancy, and the design of special environments for children; and (3) the scenario that the parents (and/or society) project for the child's future.

The developmental environmental model associates different stages in children's development with the environment that is considered their legitimate one at those stages. This model can be described by two axes:

(1) a vertical one indicating the child's age and (2) a horizontal one showing his/her home range. The vertical cross-section reflects the significant ages in regard to children's relation with their environment. The horizontal cross-section of such a model displays a map of the child's environment at a given age.

THE MAIN VARIABLES IN THE ENVIRONMENTAL MODELS OF BOYS AND GIRLS

> The power of parents and socializers to mold social behavior lies primarily in the assignment of boys and girls to different settings.
> —*Whiting and Edwards, 1988, p. 35*

From the descriptions available to us of children's lives in Western culture (Ariès, 1962; DeMause, 1974; Summerville, 1982; Shahar, 1992, and others), it seems that the environmental models of boys and of girls differed significantly both in vertical and horizontal cross-sections from the beginning of recorded history until the beginning of the twentieth century. The major differences between the boys' model and the girls' model were:

1. In the vertical cross-section: The childhood of boys lasted longer than the childhood of girls.
2. In the horizontal cross-section: The boys' environment was larger than the girls', from the age of 4 onwards.
3. In a combined cross-section: Changes in the boys' stages of childhood were accompanied by more significant environmental modifications than changes in the girls' stages of childhood. In other words, the environmental model of girls is more continuous in its character than that of boys.
4. In a combined cross-section: The boys were removed from their parents' home only to return to it toward the end of their childhood. The girls lingered at their parents' home until maturity, when they were removed from it forever (see Figure 1).

THE BOYS' ENVIRONMENTAL MODEL

The Home and Its Periphery

> "Joy to Philip! he this day
> Has his long coats cast away,
> And (the childish season gone)
> Puts the manly breeches on ...

Sashes, frock—to those that need 'em,
Philip's limbs have got their freedom.
He can run, or he can ride,
And do twenty things beside
Which his petticoats forbad;
Is he not a happy lad?[2]

On the whole, during the first four years, children of both sexes were raised at home in similar environmental conditions. Barry et al. (1975) reports that similar environmental conditions of babies of both sexes were found in many other societies, because the status of "baby" is generally undifferentiated by sex.

The home was considered the boy's legitimate environment at least until the age of 7, but from the age of 4 onwards the boy started to move outside the home in order to become acquainted with the society beyond his family. Ariès (1962), who illustrates how the status of the child and his/her sex, age, and home range were interrelated, claims that from the sixteenth century until the end of the nineteenth century, the youngest boys were dressed exactly like their sisters. They abandoned their feminine heavy robes around the age of 4, when they began to exceed the orbit of the home. At that stage the boy received his first pair of trousers and his hair was cut for the first time.

First haircut and breeches were often described in the popular literature and art as a joyful moment for the boy but traumatic for his mother, who perceived this moment as "first step toward the inevitable day when she would lose her son forever to the world outside the home" (Paoletti & Kregloh, 1989, p. 33).

At the age of 4, a significant change in the boy's environmental status took place in other cultures as well. Yamamura (1986) points out that at that age the Japanese boy was permitted to wear *hakama* or formal divided skirts. Whiting and Edwards (1988), Rogoff (1981), Barry et al. (1957), and others confirm that factors of language development and social communication, firmness of movement, and environmental awareness allow 4-year-old children to begin enlarging their home range, start learning about the society beyond the family, and behave according to the patterns they begin to discover around them. Read (1968) found that the Noni children do not sleep with their parents beyond the age of 4 or 5 because (according to their words): "From this age they will begin to see things and ask questions" (p. 40). Rogoff et al. (1976) conclude from a comparative study of 13 societies that in the age period centering on 5 to 7 years children become responsible for their

[2]A nursery rhyme that can be found in many children's books (see Robertson, 1974, p. 413).

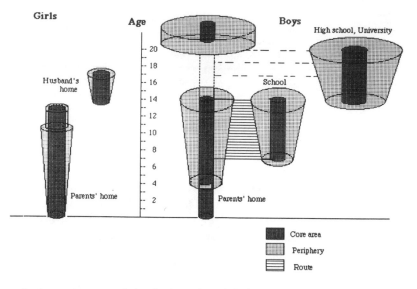

Figure 1. An environmental–developmental model of boys and girls of the higher social class in Europe until the nineteenth century.

own social behavior and become active agents in their own socialization process.

Between the ages of 4 and 7, the boy, in the population we are referring to, began to get used both to his male identity and to the environment near his home. At the age of 7 he was supposed to go to school.

The School

Going to school introduced a significant environmental and social change in the boy's life (see Figure 2). With his departure from home to school, a new focal point was added to his environmental model—a point to which he must go daily, spend time in, and return home from. The boy's home range, after the age of 7, included the home and its periphery, the school, and the route connecting between them.

The school of the past centuries did not resemble the schools we are familiar with today—neither in physical structure, goals, and methods of teaching nor in age of the pupils. Summerville (1982), in his discussion of the school in Rome, claims that the teaching methods were so bad that between the ages of 7 and 12 children didn't even succeed in

Figure 2. A classroom in the nineteenth century—through the eyes of a child. The drawing was made by the painter Gustav Doré, in 1844, when he was 12 years old. The bitter criticism that characterized the pictures of schools drawn by (adult) painters from previous centuries is replaced here by a humorous attitude (which was typical to Doré at this age). The emphasis is on children's activities and positions (and not on their expressions). The classroom itself contains 61 boys, 17 girls, and 6 adults. The girls are sitting at a separate table near the door. They seem to be much more relaxed than the boys, who are busy doing everything possible except learning. The adults in the drawing are whipping the children, threatening them, or pushing them inside.

learning how to read and write. The teachers, who were poor and frustrated, held lessons that bordered on bedlam: They yelled and waited for an excuse to hit their pupils.

When describing the secular school in the Middle Ages, Ariès (1962) notes that children between 10 and 13 sat in the medieval school, next to adolescents between 15 and 20. The various ages remained mixed within each class until the eighteenth century. Illustration of this observation can be found in a fresco painting from 1465 in the church of San Antonio, San Giminiano, Italy (see De Silva et al., 1966, p. 34) titled "St. Augustine at grammar school." The painting portrays a schoolroom full of boys of all ages. The teacher is beating a boy of 3 to 4 on his bare behind while he is being held on a teen-age boy's back. About 100 years later (1556), Peter Breughel the elder painted a schoolroom in Belgium that Von Simonson (1966) described in the following words:

> This nightmarish school room is . . . filled with a bewildering crowd of little figures, most of whom are crowded around the teacher who has stuck the inevitable birch in his hat and is about to spank the bare behind of one of his pupils. All the dwarf-like figures carry a tablet with the alphabet written on it. Not all of them . . . are children; some of the faces are those of old people. Others are grimacing, and they do not all pay attention. Every one of these "pupils" seems undeferred, prematurely old, enslaved, almost insane. (p. 47)

Breughel's painting is not unique in its approach and content. Tens of schoolroom paintings from Holland in the seventeenth century reflect the same critical approach (see Durantini, 1983). In the schoolroom paintings of Richard Brakenburgh, Jan Steen, Adrian van Ostad, Adrian Brouwer, Peter de Bloot, and others, we find children of all ages in all possible situations. The teacher looks either embittered and helpless vis-à-vis the pupils' yells, or appears estranged from what is going on in the room or is trying to put a stop to the pranks or is furiously beating the pupils. The pupils are running wild, upsetting the teacher, mocking the child being beaten, or playing pranks. The situation seems almost impossible for all sides.

When we examine these paintings more closely we learn not only about teaching aids (the whip intended for beatings on the behind and the wooden spoon used for hitting the fingers) but also about the children's affective reactions to the situation. From the wide variety of the children's expressions we can conclude that they could not remain passive subjects in their educational process: They had to react to the prevailing situations at school, to draw on internal sources, to determine ways of behaving, and to activate mental powers that would not have been needed in more comfortable situations.

The Driving Away from Home

After the local school, city boys were sent out from their families to schools far away from their homes.[3] In Rome, 16-year-olds moved in with another family for final training in social behavior. The noble classes of the Middle Ages used to send sons who were destined for the military life for rearing in the households of others at the age of 7. Sons who were destined for monastic life were offered to the church even earlier (see Shahar, 1992; McLaughlin, 1974). The affluent families sent their sons, at least until the end of the nineteenth century, to a far-off boarding school, and merchants and artisans sent their sons to be apprentices in the workshops of other artisans.

Leaving home was almost always accompanied by a crisis, a feeling of estrangement and loneliness. McLaughlin (1974), when referring to the early separation of children from their parents and siblings in the medieval society, quotes the memories of Orderic Vitalis, who was offered by his father to the Norman monastery in the late eleventh century:

> And so, a boy of ten, I crossed the English channel and came to Normandy as an exile, unknown to all, knowing no one. . . . Like Josef in Egypt I heard a language which I could not understand. (p. 129)

The fact that Joseph is mentioned reveals that in the Middle Ages the custom of removing the boy from his home had the status of a myth. Not only Joseph, but also most of the other biblical figures who brought about historical changes (like Abraham, Jacob, Moses, Yiftah, Samuel, Saul, and David) were pushed to leave their father's home during their childhood or adolescence.

The roots of myths are to be found grounded in basic psychological needs. In this respect, Bettelheim (1976), when referring to the removal of boys from home as it is reflected in folk tales and legends, tells us:

> In most stories of two brothers, one . . . rushes out into the world and courts dangers, while the other . . . simply remains home. In many European fairy tales the brother who leaves soon finds himself in a deep, dark forest, where he feels lost, having given up the organization of his life which the parental home provided, and not yet having built up the inner structures which we develop only under the impact of life experiences we have to master more or less on our own. [pp. 93–94] Here, as in many fairy tales, being pushed out of

---

[3]We are dealing here with the removal of boys from their home as part of the educational process and not the sending away of poor boys to work in order to support their families.

the home stands for having to become oneself. Self realization requires leaving the orbit of the home, an excruciatingly painful experience fraught with
many psychological dangers. This developmental process is inescapable; the
pain of it is symbolized by the children's unhappiness about being forced to
leave home. (p. 79)

The necessity for leaving home, in order to fulfill the criteria of
becoming a man, is found in many other cultures as well. Befu (1986),
referring to the sociocultural background of child development in Japan,
remarks that "it used to be said that to become a mature person, a
person has to eat someone else's rice, that is, to be away from home and
living in a setting where it is necessary to defer to others and to endure
psychological and material hardships" (p. 24).

Far from home and from his parent's empathy, the boy develops not
only independent behavioral structures and original thought but also
endurance and perseverance. As a result of dwelling among strangers,
whose motives he is unaware of, the threshold of the boy's social sensitivity rises, along with it his skills as a warrior, and his ability to ignore
the concrete attendance of people and events around him and to concentrate on contemplation that is not connected to the here and now.

Anthropologists who investigated the initiation into manhood in
nonliterate cultures (Van Gennep, 1908; Malinowski, 1927; Whiting et
al., 1958; Mead, 1949) found that boys' rites of passage to a mature stage
involve at least one of the following factors: painful hazing by the adult
males of the society, tests of endurance and manliness, seclusion from
women, a genital operation, or a change of residence that involves separation of the boy from his mother and sisters.

The boy in Western culture was not sent away from home for a short
time but rather for a period that lasted years. Neither was he removed to
the outskirts of the settlement, but rather to an institution or to a household that was considered to be on a higher level than those at home or in
the city. There he was exposed to a different society, with different
traditions, ideas, lifestyle, and manners. Generally, the boy was removed from home when he was already at the age of abstract thought.
At that age he had to accommodate himself to the new environment, to
assimilate the values and the concepts of another culture and integrate
them with those he internalized in the past. After having integrated the
contents and values he had been exposed to, the son returned home,
according to the rule of the patrilocal tradition, not only as an individual
but also as a cultural transmitter. As a man (in his late 20s or early 30s) he
married a girl in her teens only after establishing himself either profes-
sionally or economically.

The Girls' Environmental Model

The girls' environmental model was different from the boys' along the horizontal cross-section (the child's home range in each of the stages of childhood) and along the vertical cross-section (the number and duration of the stages of childhood themselves)

If we consider childhood as a preparation period for adulthood, we find that for centuries, the period of childhood was almost twice as long for boys as for girls. The history of childhood describe two seemingly contradictory attributes of the maturation of girls: On the one hand, the girl matured long before the boy, and on the other, she remained childish even when mature.

Referring to the early maturation of the girl, Ariès (1962) remarks: "It is interesting to note that the attempt to distinguish children [from adults] was generally confined to boys . . . as if childhood separated girls from adult life less than it did for boys" (p. 58).

Despite their early involvement with adults, girls never attained maturity. Whether childhood is defined as a social state of dependence on adults (Plumb, 1976), or as a state of cultural disorientation (Postman, 1982), or as a state of psychological immaturity—the girl remained in it even after she was married and became a mother. Hall (1904) argued that women never really outgrew their adolescence—psychologically and emotionally they could best be understood as having their growth arrested in the adolescent phase.

Summerville (1982) claims (referring to Greece) that the great difference in age and experience between the husband and his wife situated her closer to the world of her children than to that of her husband. Sartre recalls in his biography (*The Words*) how he grew up along with his mother in her childhood room. From Ibsen's *Nora* we learn that society expected the woman to remain immature and actually molded her personality so that she would remain dependent, obedient, and grateful throughout her life. The organization of the environment in which the girl was raised constituted a major instrument in the molding of her personality and in the way she was manipulated to realize the values and knowledge bestowed upon her.

The typical environmental model for girls included two principal stages: The first was in her father's home and the second in her husband's home.

The Father's Home

The home was considered to be the girl's legitimate environment in the first stage of childhood (that usually continued until marriage), from the beginning of the recorded history of childhood until the end of the nineteenth century. The girl grew up at home, studied there, and became integrated in the adults' lives in a natural and gradual manner. The home environment was the legitimate one even for the few girls who went to school. For girls, school was not considered necessary, as it was for boys. In most cases, they went with their brothers and sat on the side or studied in an intimate family framework.

The home as a developmental environment was a limited and narrow milieu, both geographically and socially. It was a comfortable and familiar place, to which the girl was adapted from her first days and it supplied her with the appropriate models for imitation.

A Limited, Comfortable, and Safe Environment. While referring to the education of girls in the late Victorian and Edwardian England, Dyhouse (1981) concludes:

> The Victorians educated boys for the world, girls for the drawing room. "Masculine" characteristics of independence, self-reliance and enterprise were seen to be developed in a public school environment, away from the intimacies and emotional dependence of home. "Femininity," conversely, might best be cultivated in the home. . . . A home education cultivated "feminine" virtues in a number of ways. The daughter was schooled in dependence and protected from undesirable social contacts. (p. 44)

The home was considered the girl's legitimate environment by most human cultures (see Mead, 1949, 1952; Whiting & Edwards, 1988; Benedict, 1946, and others). The Chinese culture went further than others. It was not satisfied with determining rules of behavior and designing clothes that would not be appropriate for walking outside. Rather, it introduced a custom of tieing girls' feet from the age of 4, in a way that limited their mobility and caused them permanent pain that lasted until their physical growth had been completed. The home, as a narrow environment (not connected to communication networks like today) cut the girl off from many kinds of environmental information and did not afford her the experiences that boys were afforded on their way to maturity. The restricted physical environment and the limitations on the girl's movements beyond the orbit of the home prevented her from being exposed to the environmental experiences necessary to develop both geographical and social orientation.

Referring to the connection between the horizons of the environment and the horizons of the mind, Rousseau (1964) was aware, already in the seventeenth century, of the idea that "our first instructors in science are our feet, hands, and eyes" (p. 124). The idea was confirmed by Piaget (1968), Gibson (1969), Bower (1977), and others in their studies on perceptual and cognitive development (see also Bronfenbrenner &

Crouter, 1983), and by anthropologists in cross-cultural research (Wagner, 1982).

Secure within her familiar environment, without leaving the boundaries of home by her own, the girl never experienced a situation of environmental, social, and cognitive disequilibrium and was never stimulated to draw on internal sources to determine ways of performing the activity or to find solutions to unexpected situations. The comfortable environment at home that *"murders,"* according to Gibran (1980), *"the passion of the soul,"* was meant to tranquilize and paralyze her curiosity and her urge to attain and to know more. Returning to Bettelheim's (1976) remarks, quoted above, we can conclude that the girl was that "brother" who remained at home—out of the story, far from the society, and beyond the culture of her period, without a chance to realize her social and intellectual potentialities.

Imitation of Socializing Agents and the Development of Environmental Attentiveness. The girl was supplied at home not only with comfort and security but also with the appropriate socializing agents whom she was expected to imitate. By imitating her mother and the other women in the household, the girl was implementing the simplest and most primordial type of learning. According to Carpenter (1983), Weitzman (1979), Lynn (1969), and others, modeling, as an educational method, supplies direction and expectations for appropriate behaviors and is generally followed by children without direct prompting or reinforcement because it can not be misinterpreted.

With observation of models as the dominant mode of learning, the girl had to increase her attentiveness and sensitivity to the immediate environment. The boy, on the other hand, finding himself in the tough environment of the school or the street, was compelled to filter the contradictory external stimuli, listen to himself, identify his goals, and develop a capability for analytic thought. The girl developed attentiveness to her immediate environment that directly supplied her with clues and directions for correct behavior.

Was this distinction between the cognitive styles of girls and boys clear to educators in previous periods? An answer is to be found with Rousseau (1964), who states: "The world is the women's book. Women observe, men reason" (p. 223). Furthermore, developing the girl's attentiveness to the environment was an educational goal in itself, as postulated by Rousseau: "She must learn to discover their [men's] sentiments by their conversation, by their actions, by their gestures" (p. 223).

We can learn abut society's attitude to the girl's environmental sensitivity from the fairy tale about "the princess and the pea"—here the exaggerated environmental sensitivity of the girl testifies to her being a real princess. If we accept Bettelheim's (1976) argument that fairy tales outline directions for children and help them in their process of maturation, then the message of this type of story to any girl from a good family is that she must sharpen her senses and attend to the stimuli of her environment.

Anthropologists testify to the fact that this type of environmental attentiveness was demanded from girls in other cultures as well, by demanding that they control their movements in their sleep (Benedict, 1946), or by giving them delicate dresses and ornaments that would be ruined if they ran or played freely (Mead, 1953), or by demanding that they observe their mothers and watch over their younger siblings (Barry et al., 1957; Whiting & Edwards, 1988).

The Husband's Home

According to the patrilocal tradition the girl (in Europe, China, Japan, the Arab world, India, and in most of the African cultures) had to move to her husband's home after their marriage. The role that was designated to the girl by society ("To please" men, "to win their love and esteem, to bring them up when young," Rousseau, 1964, p. 220) was to be fulfilled in this new and unfamiliar residence. After growing up in her parents' home with the knowledge that this warm and comfortable nest was temporary, she had to adapt to a new place and a new society. Because the girls of the upper classes were married very young, even before puberty, many of them continued to mature in their husband's home (Summerville, 1982; Shahar, 1992; Marvick, 1974, and others).

The situation of the girl bride in her new house emerges from popular stories and from legends and fairy tales. The latter were addressed to the girls themselves and were intended (according to Bettelheim's conception regarding the meaning and importance of fairy tales[4]) to reflect her inner problems and to reveal the steps required for her development from immaturity to maturity. If we place familiar fairy tales within the atmosphere of the previous centuries (an application not done by Bettelheim himself[5]), we can deduce from them that the above situation

[4]Fairy tales, according to Bettelheim (1976), are future-oriented and directed to help the child to cope with the conditions imposed by society and to assist the child to achieve psychological independence and moral maturity. They are attuned to the child's anxieties and aspirations, give full recognition to his [sic] difficulties, while at the same time suggesting solution to the problems that perturb him and to pressing difficulties.

[5]Bettelheim's (1976) interpretation of the fairy tales themselves relate to the child of our society as a universal child. The only distinction he makes between the girl and the boy refers to their sexual identify (according to the Freudian interpretation). Bettelheim ignores the child's gender identity (that encompasses his or her status in the society and the conditions of life related to it).

(that involved moving to an unknown environment and a strange society, including a mother and sisters-in-law and a repellent husband) was considered an inevitable and most important stage in a girl's life and at the same time extremely difficult to cope with. From the "Beauty and the Beast," "Cinderella," "Goldilocks and the Three Bears," and "Rapunzel," we learn about the loneliness and the fooling of strangeness in the new place. The need to adapt physically to the new environment is communicated in "Goldilocks," "Snow White," and "Cinderella." The suffering from the stepmother or the enchantress (who can be easily converted into mother-in-law[6]) is the main issue in "Snow White," "Cinderella," and "Rapunzel."

Situating the fairy tales within the conditions of life that generated them, we are compelled to deduce that the fairy tales that were addressed to girls were completely different from those that were addressed to boys, and their messages were completely different. During those periods when boys and girls did not belong to the same world the meaning of becoming adult was completely different for each of them. Whereas the boys were encouraged by the boys' legends to enlarge their home range and their horizons before coming back to their "designated kingdom," the girls were prepared by the girls' fairy tales to adapt themselves to the place in which they found themselves after being pushed away from home.

From the various stories that relate to childhood we learn that the girl had to cope not only with the close presence of a man much older than herself, but also with the covert competition from her mother-in-law, under whose supervision the bride was brought up until she matured and succeeded in making contact with her intended husband.

While the boy gradually enlarged his home range and learned to negotiate with strangers from the age of 4, the girl was detached from the only environment to which she was accustomed without any cultural and social orientation. The boy, who was moved from his home facing many trials and experiences, knew at all times that this situation was temporary and that the familiar home was waiting for him at the end of the road. The girl grew up in a comfortable and warm environment with the knowledge that it was a temporary place and that she would have to leave it for a new place where she would be considered a stranger, at least until the end of her childhood.

THE ENVIRONMENTAL MODEL OF CHILDREN TODAY

Two approaches can be observed in the literature dealing with environmental influences on gender socialization in our time. The first ap-

[6]The stepmother appears only in girls' legends and only around the time of their puberty.

proach argues that, despite the increasing equality between boys and girls, there are still differences in the organization of their environment and in the way they are treated by their socializers. The second approach maintains that even when boys and girls grow up in the same environment, they are not influenced by it in the same way.

According to the first approach (represented by Eisenberg, 1983; Plomin, 1989; Liss, 1983; Pitcher & Schults, 1983; Hart, 1977; Whiting & Edwards, 1988, and others), the child is perceived as a passive member in his/her socialization process, directed almost entirely by his/her parents and educators. In this spirit, Plomin (1989) states that "Even small differences in relative parental affection within the family might have large effects on differences in siblings' outcomes" (p. 109).

Pitcher and Schults (1983) speak about the different toys parents buy for boys and girls and claim that parents play an important role in the creation of sex differences when they provide their children with different toys and therefore different play experiences. Hart (1977) points out that boys are permitted by their parents to enlarge their home range more than girls and speculates on the effect of the differences in the experience in open space on the differences in boys' and girls' abilities of orientation and performing spatial manipulations in geometry. The scholars who point out the dissimilarities in parents' behavior toward boys and girls believe that these explain why boys and girls prefer spending time with members of their own sex, play with sex-typed toys, prefer different activities, and develop different behavioral and cognitive styles.

Scholars who represent the second approach interpret the child as an active member in his/her own socialization process. These researchers (Carpenter, 1983; Weitzman, 1979; Pitcher & Schults, 1983; Lynn, 1969; Sutton-Smith & Rosenberg, 1971, and others) argue that the differences that have been observed between boys and girls do not result from dissimilarities in their environment itself but rather from the dissimilarity in the way both sexes relate to their environment and experience it.

Relating to the role played by the child in his/her socialization process, Whiting and Edwards (1988) state that:

> The growing awareness of gender makes the child more attentive to roles of same sex adults and older same sex children. It is evident that 4 and 5 year olds are acute observers; they probably learn more by observation than they do from statements of their teachers. They draw conclusions from observing regularities in the behavior of men and women, the clothes they wear, the content of the activities they perform, and their styles of interpersonal behavior, including speech habits, gestures, and other physical habits. (pp. 219–220)

Whiting and Edwards (1988) deal with societies in which the child grows up among adults of both sexes and can choose the appropriate model for imitation. In these societies the boy is attuned to male models and the girl to the female ones. In modern Western society, after the separation of the domain of work form the domain of home, with women predominating in the child's environment throughout the day (Kessen, 1979),[7] boys find themselves far from same-sex adult models for imitation. According to Pitcher and Schults (1983), when boys learn that they are "not female," they relinquish close identification with the mother and switch their gender identity to the less visible role of the father. Lynn (1969) has theorized that because boys have no direct exposure to male models they tend to develop stereotypical images of masculinity. In this respect, Sutton-Smith and Rosenberg (1971) claim that boys follow fantasy models in their imitative play (cowboys and Indians) and that girls follow realistic models in theirs (mothers, nurses). The researchers who represent the second approach agree that boys and girls who are brought up within a mainly female environment develop different behavior and cognitive styles when they become conscious of their sex.

Comparing these approaches, we see that both share the idea that differences in personality, social behavior, and cognitive style do exist between boys and girls; the first approach attributes these differences to parents' behavior, whereas the second one assigns them to the behavior of the children themselves. Both of them acknowledge the role played by the child's environment in generating the above-mentioned differences. By combining them we can deduce that children are aware of the environmental features around them but that they are selective in their responses to them. When children perceive the environmental occurrences as enhancing their development and as contributing to their enculturation process, they absorb even the messages that are implied.

If we ask how the child learns about his or her sexual identify, we learn from Kohlberg (1966) that children develop a conception of themselves as having an unchangeable sexual identity at the same age and through the same processes that they develop conceptions of invariable identity of physical objects. According to Kohlberg (1966), children *first* learn their sex identities and *then* attempt to acquire and master sex-appropriate activities (see also Inton-Peterson, 1988; Maccoby, 1988).

After recognizing his/her identity and the social anticipations that are attached to it, the child becomes a collaborator with his/her culture by relating particularly to the environmental stimuli that seem to enhance the traits of his/her gender identity. This kind of selective behavior is first expressed (according to Kohlberg, 1966; Pitcher & Schults, 1983; Edwards et al., 1986, and others) from the age of 2 to 3 among girls and 3 to 4 among boys.

---

[7]Kessen (1979) perceives the above-mentioned environmental change as one of the most important factors that affected children's lives and the child psychology of our times.

Perception of the child as an active participant in the process of gender socialization raises the question of what motivates him or her to do this? A possible answer is that every child wants to grow up and become an adult because the dimension of the future is an inherent part of the experience of childhood. Because adults are different from each other, children need to classify them and to find appropriate models for themselves. Gender, which the culture has marked with clear manifestations (clothes, hairdo, colors, repertoire of roles and behaviors, use of language, personal belongings including games, adornments, cosmetics, worktools, etc.), constitutes a useful key for such classification and supplies the child (whose cognition is still dominated by his/her sensory perception) with clear guidelines to orient his/her attention and direct his/her behavior.

CONCLUSION

A comparison of the developmental–environmental model of children in Western society today and the environmental models of boys and girls in the past shows that the fundamental differences between the girls' world and that of the boys (that were expressed in length of childhood and its division into stages, the scale and character of sociospatial experience at each stage, and the gradualness in the transition from one stage to another) no longer exist. On the whole, the girl and the boy in Western society today learn in the same classroom, play in the same yard, return to the same home, and complete their studies at the same age.

And yet, the books they read, the television programs they watch, and the clothes people around them wear broadcast messages that have prevailed in Western culture from the beginning of recorded history. From these messages they learn that they are not simply children but rather boys and girls who will mature as men and women, and who will have different status and different duties to fulfill in their society.

As individuals who demand to know themselves, grow, and achieve an equilibrium with their environment, boys and girls read and interpret their similar environments in different ways, conduct their activities in different places, organize themselves in groups of different sizes, move around in it at different speeds, and are involved with their surroundings in a different manner.

The design and organization of the children's environment are the infrastructure for their development, including their opportunities for social relations, physical activity, and sensory experiences. As such, the children's environment should correspond to the other factors that affect their education and should support the cultural mechanisms that direct the process of their enculturation (see Sebba, 1991).

For long periods, the various components that took part in the children's enculturation process corresponded and supported each oth er. However, during periods of change not all systems change at the same pace (Sebba, 1992), and as a result their mutual correspondence may no longer exist, and their messages may even contradict each other (Sebba, 1991). Children today are raised and educated in a society that has adapted itself to the demands of the present, without thoroughly changing its basic conceptions from the past. These values relate to the person's status in society, constitute the core of the culture (see Rapoport, 1983), and do not adapt themselves to the demands of time like the other cultural components. When we examine the relationships between the prevailing values and traditions and the environmental conditions of children in our society, we find that the actual environmental conditions shed light on the course that leads society to its future, whereas the traditional cultural customs preserve conceptions that were adapted to the demands of life in the past.

The environmental conditions of children today are reflected in their environmental model, which more than other educational means might give us a hint as to the direction society is advancing in. The traditional cultural mechanisms that still play an important role in children's education are, on the other hand, the center of gravity that ensures the stability of the culture and preserves its identity. Girls and boys, attuned to the contradicting cultural messages, create a bridge between yesterday's conceptions and today's environment and cause the culture to progress and change.

DIRECTIONS FOR FUTURE RESEARCH

> To understand the effect of culture, age and gender on the development of patterns of social interaction, one must study the characteristics of these settings. What is the nature of these environments where children learn patterns of interpersonal behavior? Who are the individuals who are available as role models? What are the most frequent opportunities for practicing various styles of social interaction?
>
> —*Whiting and Edwards, 1988, p. 35*

The concept of gender, according to which we interpret the behavioral outcomes uncovered by contemporary research, has very old origins. These origins still direct our behaviors and establish our conceptions by remote control, through our language, dress, social structures, and division of labor and by virtue of the spiritual inheritance of our religion, literature, and the arts. In order to better understand the cultural context to which the findings of today's research can be ascribed, we referred to the historical background of the socialization process in our society. Like the majority of the children that are studied in gender research in our society today, the children whose environments were reviewed in this chapter were educated according to theoretical educational guidelines and were never exploited as a source of labor.

However, because the aim of this chapter was to unveil the role of the environment in gender socialization, it is important to enlarge both the scope of the population and the environments and to investigate the implications of the organization of boys' and girls' environments in additional cultures and ethnic subgroups, in other socioeconomic classes, and in various places.

While preparing the research program and selecting the means of investigation, one must take into consideration the nature of the variables that are involved in such a culturally, environmentally, and developmentally oriented research. The main points regarding the characteristics of the variables that demand consideration in such research are:

1. Recognizing gender as a cultural concept, related to traditional conceptions and anchored in the principles of all religions, commits the researcher to presume that the explanations for a substantial part of the observed behaviors lie in the society's past, not in its immediate needs. The inertia of cultural values that is expressed in behavioral traditions (Geertz, 1975; Rapoport, 1983; Sebba, 1992), directs the researcher who is engaged in investigating gender socialization to be aware of the past of the society and to interpret the findings by using this knowledge.

2. Learning the child's environment, in order to uncover the different operative expressions of the education of boys and girls, necessitates the use of an environmental model similar to the one presented here, which includes all the environments with which the child is involved. The integration made by the child of the impacts of all the places he/she is involved with during the day and between the influences of past and present environments constitutes a crucial factor in his/her personality and compels us to analyze the child's environment as a complex of settings and not as a single place.

Examining the influence of the various environments with which the child is involved during his/her daily activities (along the horizontal axis of the model that represents the physical environment) is obligatory because children in many developed countries are brought up at least in two places (at home and at a public or private educational setting), often from the age of 2 years, and because the cultural correspondence between these places is gradually lessening (especially in countries of im migration and countries conducting state education for cultural minorities).

Examining the accumulated influence of the environments the child is involved with during his/her development (along the vertical axis of the model, which represents time) is necessary, because all the educational theories argue that each stage in the child's development is influenced by those preceding it. Such an examination appears necessary in particular with respect to physical environments, whose impact is gradual and not recognized consciously (Wagner, 1982).

3. The many studies dealing with gender socialization indicate concurrently that the environment plays an active role in influencing the child's development and that the child him/herself takes an active part in the same process, by choosing how to interpret and respond to the environmental stimuli. The child's selective behavior is attributed by Wachs (1987) to his/her individual organismic characteristics. Such interpretation does not explain why a whole group of children (boys) relates to the physical and social environment differently from another group (girls) (see Maccoby, 1990).

The fact that the difference between boys' and girls' behaviors emerges at the age of 3 to 4, parallel to the appearance of additional social skills and the fact that it develops with time (Maccoby, 1987) supports the hypothesis that the child behaves in a given situation according to values and knowledge that he/she internalized in preceding stages (Maccoby, 1988; Kohlberg, 1966), that is, under the influence of the past environment.

This brings us to Wagner's conclusion (1982) that the physical environment is interpreted diachronically and acts on the individual over time, as well as to the research implications derived from this conclusion. This clarifies why the environments in which we grew up affects not only the way we interpret our surroundings as adults but also how we perceive ourselves. As much as the dimension of the future is an inherent part of the experience of the child (who wants to grow up and become an adult), the dimension of the past (which is reflected in our childhood) is an inherent part of the experience of the adult.

REFERENCES

Ariès, Ph. (1962). *Centuries of childhood. A social history of family life* (Trans. R. Baldick). New York: Knopf.

Barry, H., III, Bacon, N. K., & Child, I. L. (1975). A cross cultural survey of some sex differences in socialization. In D. H. Spain (Ed.), *The human experience* (pp. 143–152). Homewood, IL: Dorsey Press.

Befu, H. (1986). The social and cultural background of child development in Japan and the United States. In H. Stevenson, H. Azuma, & K. Hakuta (Eds.), *Child development and education in Japan* (pp. 13–27). New York: Freeman.

Benedict, R. (1946). *The chrysanthemum and the sword: Patterns of Japanese culture.* Boston: Houghton Mifflin.

Bettelheim, B. (1976). *The uses of enchantment—The meaning and importance of fairy tales.* New York: Knopf.

Bower, T. G. (1977). *The perceptual world of the child.* Cambridge: Harvard University Press.

Bronfenbrenner, U., & Crouter, A. C. (1983). The evolution of environmental models in developmental research. In P. H. Mussen (Ed.), *Handbook of child psychology, Vol. 1: History, theory and methods* (pp. 357–414). New York: Wiley.

Carpenter, C. J. (1983). Activity structure and play: Implications for socialization. In M. B. Liss (Ed.), Social and cognitive skills, sex roles, and children's play (pp. 117–145). New York: Academic Press.

Cunningham, H. (1991). *The children of the poor.* Oxford: Blackwell.

Da Silva, A., Von Simcon, O., & Troutman, P. (Eds.) (1966). *Education—man through his art,* Vol. 4. Greenwich, CT: New York Graphic Society.

DeMause, L. (1974). The evolution of childhood. In L. DeMause (Ed.), *The history of childhood* (pp. 1–74). New York: The Psychohistory Press, Atcom.

Durantini, M. F. (1963). *The child in seventeenth-century Dutch painting.* Ann Arbor, MI: UMI Research Press.

Dyhouse, C. (1981). *Girls growing up in late Victorian and Edwardian England.* London: Routledge & Kegan Paul.

Eisenberg, N. (1983). Sex-typed toy choices: What do they signify? In M. B. Liss (Ed.), *Social and cognitive skills: Sex roles and children's play* (pp. 45–70). New York: Academic Press.

Edwards, C. P., Logue, M. E., Loehr, S., & Roth, S. (1986). The influence of model infant group care on parent/child interaction at home. *Early Childhood Research Quarterly, 1*(4), 317–332.

Feingold, A. (1988). Cognitive gender differences are disappearing. *American Psychologist, 43*(2), 95–103.

Geertz, C. (1975). The impact of the concept of culture on the concept of man. In D. H. Spain (Ed.), *The human experience* (pp. 21–38). Homewood, IL: Dorsey Press.

Gibran, K. G. (1980). *The prophet.* Tel Aviv: Tammuz Publishing House.

Gibson, E. J. (1969). *Principles of perceptual learning and development.* New York: Appleton-Century-Crofts.

Hall, G. H. (1904). *Adolescence: Its psychology and the relation to physiology, anthropology, sociology, sex, crime, religion and education.* New York: Appleton.

Halpern, D. F. (1986). *Sex differences in cognitive abilities.* Hillsdale, NJ: Lawrence Erlbaum.

Hart, R. A. (1977). *Children's place experience: A developmental study.* New York: Irvington.

Inton-Peterson, M. J. (1988). *Children's concept of gender.* Norwood, NJ: Ablex.

Jacklin, C. N. (1989). Female and male: Issues of gender. *American Psychologist, 44*(2), 127–133.

Kessen, W. (1979). The American child and other cultural inventions. *American Psychologist*, 34(10), 815–820.

Kohlberg, L. (1966). A cognitive-developmental analysis of children's sex-roles concepts and attitudes. In E. E. Maccoby (Ed.), *The development of sex differences* (pp. 82–172). Stanford: Stanford University Press.

Lever, J. (1976). Sex differences in the games children play. *Social Problems, 23*, 170–407.

Lever, J. (1978). Sex differences in the complexity of children's play and games. *American Sociological Review, 43*, 471–483.

Liss, M. B. (1983). Learning gender-related skills through play. In M. B. Liss (Ed.), *Social and cognitive skills—Sex roles and children's play* (pp. 147–167). New York: Academic Press.

Lynn, D. B. (1969). *Parental and sex role identification: A theoretical formulation*. Berkeley, CA: McCutchan.

Maccoby, E. E. (1987). The varied meaning of "masculine" and "feminine." In J. M. Reinisch, L. A. Rosenblum, & S. A. Sanders (Eds.), *Masculinity/femininity—Basic perspectives* (pp. 227–239). Oxford: Oxford University Press.

Maccoby, E. E. (1988). Gender as a social category. *Developmental Psychology, 24* (6), 755–765.

Maccoby, E. E. (1990). Gender and relationships: A developmental account. *American Psychologist, 45*(4), 513–520.

Maccoby, E. E., & Jacklin, C. N. (1974). *The psychology of sex differences*. Stanford, CA: Stanford University Press.

Maccoby, E. E., & Jacklin, C. N. (1987). Gender segregation in childhood. In E. H. Reese (Ed.), *Advances in child development and behavior*, Vol. 20 (pp. 239–287). New York: Academic Press.

Malinowski, B. (1927). *Sex and repression in savage society*. New York: Harcourt, Brace.

Marvick, E. W. (1974). Nature versus nurture: Patterns and trends in seventeenth century French child rearing. In L. DeMause (Ed.), *The history of childhood* (pp. 259–302). New York: Psychohistory Press, Atcom.

McLaughlin, M. M. (1974). Survivors and surrogates: Children and parents from the ninth to the thirteenth centuries. In L. DeMause (Ed.), *The history of childhood* (pp. 101–182). New York: Psychohistory Press, Atcom.

Mead, M. (1949). *Male and female*. New York: William Morrow.

Mead, M. (1952). *Sex and temperament in three primitive societies*. New York: Mentor Books.

Mead, M. (1953). *Growing up in New Guinea*. New York: Mentor Books.

Paoletti, J. B., & Kregloh, C. L. (1989). The children's department. In C. B. Kidwell & V. Steele (Eds.), *Men and women: Dressing the part* (pp. 22–41). Washington, DC: Smithsonian Institution.

Philip of Novara. (1988). *Les quatre ages de l'homme* (after 1265). Paris: Societe des anciens textes francais, Didot.

Piaget, J. (1968). *Six psychological studies*. New York: Random House.

Piaget, J., & Inhelder, B. (1969). *The psychology of the child*. New York: Basic Books.

Pitcher, E. G., & Schults, L. H. (1983). *Boys and girls at play: The development of sex roles*. New York: Praeger.

Plomin, R. (1989). Environment and genes: Determinants of behavior. *American Psychologist, 44*(2), 105–111.

Plumb, J. H. (1976). The great change in children. In A. Skolnick (Ed.), *Rethinking childhood: Perspectives on development and society* (pp. 205–213). Boston: Little, Brown.

Postman, N. (1982). *The disappearance of childhood*. New York: N. Postman.

Rapoport, A. (1983). Development, culture change and supportive design. *Habitat International, 7*(5/6), 249–263.

Read, M. (1968). *Children of their fathers: Growing up among the Ngoni of Malawi.* New York: Holt, Rinehart & Winston.

Robertson, P. (1974). The home as a nest. In L. DeMause (Ed.), *The history of childhood* (pp. 407–431). New York: Psychohistory Press, Atcom.

Rogoff, B., Sellers, M. J., Pirrotta, S., Fox, N., & White, S. H. (1976). Age of assignment of roles and responsibilities to children: A cross-cultural survey. In A. Skolnick (Ed.), *Rethinking childhood: Perspectives on development and society* (pp. 249–268). Boston: Little, Brown.

Rogoff, B. (1981). Adults and peers as agents of socialization: A Highland Guatemala profile. *Ethos, 9*(1), 18–36.

Rousseau, J. J. (1964). *His educational theories selected from Emile Julie and other writings.* R. L. Archer (Ed.). New York: Barron's Educational Series.

Sebba, R. (1991). The role of the home environment in cultural transmission. *Architecture and Behaviour, 7*(3), 223–242.

Sebba, R. (1992). The three faces of cultural change. *Presented at the IAPS 12 International Conference.* Porto Carras, Greece.

Shahar, S. (1992). *Childhood in the Middle Ages.* New York: Routledge.

Summerville, J. (1982). *The rise and fall of childhood.* Beverly Hills, CA: Sage.

Sutton-Smith, B., & Rosenberg, B. G. (1971). Sixty years of historical change in the game preferences of American children. In R. E. Herron & B. Sutton-Smith (Eds.), *Child's play* (pp. 18–50). New York: Wiley.

Van Gennep, A. (1960). *Rites of passage (1908).* London: Routledge & Kegan Paul.

Von Simonson, O. (1966). A donkey at school. In A. De Silva, O. Van Simson, & P. Troutman (Eds.), *Education—Man through his art,* Vol. 4 (pp. 46–47). Greenwich, CT: Graphic Society.

Wachs, T. D. (1987). Developmental perspectives on designing for development. In C. S. Weinstein & T. G. David (Eds.), *Spaces for children: The built environment and child development* (pp. 291–307). New York and London: Plenum Press.

Wagner, D. A. (1982). Ontogeny in the study of culture and cognition. In D. A. Wagner & H. W. Stevenson (Eds.), *Cultural perspectives on child development* (pp. 103–123). San Francisco: Freeman.

Weitzman, L. J. (1979). Sex role socialization: Behavioral studies of personal space during early adolescence. *Man–Environment Systems, 5*(5), 289–297.

Whiting, B. B., & Edwards, C. P. (1973). A cross-cultural analysis of sex differences in the behavior of children aged 3 through 11. *Journal of Social Psychology, 91,* 171–188.

Whiting, B. B., & Edwards, C. P. (1988). *Children of different worlds: The formation of social behavior.* Cambridge: Harvard University Press.

Whiting, J. W. M., Kluckhohn, R., & Anthony, A. (1958). The function of male initiation ceremonies at puberty. In E. E. Maccoby, T. M. Newcomb, & E. L. Hartley (Eds.), *Readings in social psycology* (pp. 359–370). New York: Holt, Rinehart & Winston.

Yamamura, Y. (1986). The child in the Japanese society. In H. Stevenson, H. Azuma, & K. Hakuta (Eds.), *Child development and education in Japan* (pp. 28–38). New York: Freeman.

4

Sociospatial Relations of Change

RURAL MEXICAN WOMEN IN URBAN CALIFORNIA

ELLEN-J. PADER

In our imaginations, we change what we cannot control.

—*Carlos Fuentes, 1991, p. 17*

When people relocate to a new environment, they invariably must re-conceptualize their daily activities; routes from home to schools, shops, work, friends, and family change. Neighbors are more likely to be strangers. The size and layout of rooms in the new home are not identical to those in the old. The greater the conceptual and physical distances between the old and new locales and the more traumatic the move, the greater the need to reconceptualize one's world becomes, simply to survive. And, perhaps, the harder this transformation is. The distance between a rural Mexican village and an urban Southern California city is immense. Yet, many villagers manage the transition, entwining strands of the familiar with strands of previously unimagined new ways, while letting go of anticipated, but unfulfilled, imaginings of how life would be in the United States.

ELLEN-J. PADER • Department of Landscape Architecture and Regional Planning, University of Massachusetts–Amherst, Amherst, Massachusetts 01003.

Women and the Environment, edited by Irwin Altman and Arza Churchman. Plenum Press, New York, 1994.

How does one draw on the imagination, image in the mind a realized past with an idealized future in order to create a new home world in the present? This question becomes more complex when the particular conditions leading to relocation are considered. Peter Marris (1974) argues that continuity is essential if a change of this magnitude is not to destroy an individual:

> Without confidence in the continuity of our purposes and sense of the regularity of *social* behaviour, we cannot begin to interpret the meaning of any event. But unless we are also ready to revise our purposes and understanding, we may be led to actions which are fatally misconceived. (p. 15, my emphasis)

How, then, does one achieve this flexibility of action? The sense of continuity is not just an individual endeavor devoid of sociocultural processes. Individuals, as products and producers of particular culturally based expectations and behaviors, look beyond themselves and into their surrounds for reassurance of their personal and social identity.

In middle- to upper-class U.S. society, the most familiar moves are job related. The individual tends to have a choice, and once having decided to accept the new position, moves to another middle- to upper-class community, often populated by other transplants like themselves. One buys an entire package of goods and services: Along with a house come schools, shops, transportation systems, and neighbors (Aaron, 1972), and, I would add, commonly understood and tacitly agreed upon landscape tastes, house styles, and general value systems. In these communities, a sense of connection with the past is further reinforced by, for instance, continuing to purchase the same brands of food, washing detergent, and clothing, perhaps in the same store chain, while maintaining a similar domestic routine and replacing one's familiar belongings in known and comfortable ways in the new home, which is probably designed according to similar underlying concepts as the one left behind (this will be discussed more later). Maintaining immediate voice contact with friends in the previous locale is simply a matter of a telephone call (as advertisements for long-distance telephone services continually remind us, and encourage us with their "reach out" and "friends and family" plans). Space and time become compressed, with the old remaining intact, as an anchor in one's memory, should you desire to return physically or emotionally. Thus, the home and community as integral facets of one's socially constructed reality are not continually tested.

At the other end of the continuum are situations in which one's understanding of reality are constantly tested. Among the most extreme situations are poor people who are dislocated in space and time by such disasters as an avalanche, war, or famine (Oliver-Smith, 1986). With no choice if they are to physically survive, these people become refugees, forced to leave behind a familiar community, taking with them few belongings, if any. Those who are left behind do not become an anchor —they cannot be telephoned and perhaps not contacted; their chances of still being alive might be minimal. Yet, as Oliver-Smith (1986) observes, refugees often find creative ways in which to recreate a sense of continuity even among strangers in relocation camps. For instance, in his study of Yungay, Peru, the survivors of an avalanche that razed an entire village quickly gave familiar street names to the paths between their tents. To have a home meant to create a sense of continuity between what was, what is, and what can be, regardless of how painful the memories of the massive loss of life and physical reminders of those lives. In this way they refined and redefined the sterile camps into familiar images. Following Marris, Oliver-Smith (1986) argues that by not denying the devastation, and hence the past, the people of Yungay managed to carry selected facets of the past with them into the future. "The past is a necessary element in the present, necessary for our efforts to impose a structure of logic on altered circumstances. It is crucial for creating and coping with change" (p. 17). Thus, the reconceptualization of sociospatial relations becomes a fundamental means by which change is accommodated in daily practice (see Bourdieu, 1979; Certeau, 1984; Giddens, 1979, 1985; and Soja, 1989, for theoretical perspectives on the role of daily practice for enabling and constraining social change).

Along the continuum between devastation and transnational moving vans are many discourses about moving; that is, many ways of talking about the move, reasons for relocating, responses and reactions to the move. The case of relocation I will discuss here is that of moving from a rural Mexican community to urban Southern California, and in particular the effect on, and role of, women in making this change. Mexicans go to the United States for a variety of reasons, the most common being economic, followed by adventure or personal reasons (Chavez, 1992). Often a man goes alone initially, sends money back home, and visits there regularly. Later his wife and children might follow and settle in the United States with him. It is the implications of this configuration that I will analyze here, drawing primarily from my fieldwork in La Chaneja, a mestizo village in rural Jalisco, Western Mexico,[1] and urban areas in Southern California, including Los Angeles and other smaller cities within 1 hour's drive from Los Angeles.

[1]The village name, La Chaneja, is a pseudonym. The fieldwork in Mexico and Southern California took place between 1986 and 1991. La Chaneja is a mestizo village of some 5,000 people (mestizo indicates that the villagers are of indigenous Indian and non-Indian background). The village has a primarily agricultural economy, although much of the money coming into the village is from family working in the United States.

The impact of the move from a small rural village to an urban locale is qualitatively different for women and men. In the village and in the city each lives by his/her own daily domestic routines and expectations. These must be differently accommodated in the new environment.

FROM MEXICO TO SOUTHERN CALIFORNIA

The sojourn from rural Mexico to urban California is replete with discontinuitities. In the United States, people not only look different and speak different languages, but houses are designed and sited in alien ways. Although most Mexican foods can be found now, where one gets them, the time of day when one eats them, and the social life surrounding walking to the local store are no longer commensurate. Many Mexicans say the food tastes strange, too. Expectations and laws are new. For instance, someone can be told that there are too many people sharing a rented apartment and therefore one or more householders has to leave. To limit the number of people per house according to a square-foot-per-person or number-of-people-per-bedroom ratio is an alien notion to the immigrants. However, in the United States such limitations are standard parts of rental agreements and are written into many local, state, and federal housing regulations, such as state sanitary codes, with the effect of potentially bringing into contestation many fundamental concepts about family and community (see Pader, 1994b).

As stated, whereas there are a variety of reasons why Mexicans come to the United States for work, the most common is economic. Many people cannot find work either in the vicinity of the village or in Mexican cities, and what work is available is often barely of subsistence level for a family. When work is available in factories, the pay tends to be extremely low. Even if a family has a small agricultural holding in the village, the crop cannot be guaranteed to feed the family and bring in sufficient cash for other needs. Women often participate in the informal sector, earning money through home-based work. One common way for them to earn money is by piecemeal work, such as knitting or embroidery (Figure 1). A day's work might bring in the equivalent of one dollar. Yet, the vest knitted in a day while chatting with friends, watching television or taking a break from other household chores, might earn the intermediary who commissions it $10 or $15 when sold in the United States. Women also have small businesses in their homes, such as turning the front room into a small shop where penny candies, soda, and other inexpensive but commonly used goods are sold. Others run larger shops from home or make and sell food outside their front door

Figure 1. *Hecho en México:* Young women knitting for the U.S. market.

(Figure 2). In this way, they not only earn some money but are engaged in the street and social life of the community. Such vending practices are common throughout the Third World (see, for example, Marris, 1962, and Moser, 1987).

The image of life in California from the distant view of La Chaneja is one of material riches and comfort. Relatives working in the United States send money home, they send clothing and photographs of themselves with their cars, and when they return for periodic visits, they tell of places and experiences previously unimagined in the village. Yet, over the generations since migration to the United States has become a common way of life, the stories create a palimpsest of images and expectations about how life might be. Often these stories are exaggerated and idealized, superimposed upon an experience of the world that is so far removed from life in the United States that the reality of the United States often is very difficult to conceive. This becomes part of the mythology of life in the United States. Chavez (1992) suggests that the very *idea* of working in the States is socially and culturally constructed. Thus, despite the reality of the sometimes extreme discontinuities of what life in the United States is, as opposed to one's imagined expectations of what it will be, the *concept* of living in the United States has been part of

Figure 2. This home has a small shop in the front room and women earn extra money by selling evening snacks to passersby.

many people's personal and community consciousness. How, then, is the breach between imagined expectations and the reality of life in the United States mediated by a family in order for them to be able to make the move?

THEORETICAL CONSIDERATIONS

I argue that women are central actors for enabling the transition between the Mexican homeland and the United States, and that it is through daily social and spatial practices within and around the home that much of the mediation between the past and the future takes place. The implication is that it is on the level of daily life in its most mundane domestic routines that many of the most important instigators of change and adaptation occur. It is important to note from the outset that this does not mean that the women adopt U.S. modes of thinking and acting wholesale, nor does it mean that they reject them outright. Rather, they combine facets of each society's tacitly accepted modes of action, arriving at a creative adaptation that is different from either of the others (see Rosaldo, 1975, on creative adaptations). Although, as many researchers have noted, women tend to be invisible and their voices "muted" (for example, Ardener, 1986, and Martin, 1990), in their quietly revised daily domestic practices, they are more influential than is often recognized.

In the new context, familiar objects and actions take on new meanings whereas unfamiliar objects and actions are defined in such a way that they make sense within the signification system of the immigrants. For example, in the village people do not think about the signification of the particular foods they eat; it is what they know and is taken for granted as appropriate. However, in the United States the same meal of beans, chili, and tortillas becomes a signifier of "Mexicanness," a subtle connector to home. Hamburgers, pizza, and take-out Chinese food become part of the connectedness to their new life, to being American. In fact, some women feel that once someone starts cooking with the aid of recipes, rather than making the known and familiar, they have, ruefully, symbolically passed the boundary into being more American. Material culture objects, such as food, dress, and architecture, are powerful conduits to social change in their seeming triviality.

An underlying premise of this study, then, is that the home is a particular form of material culture. In its design and use it becomes a culturally mediated phenomenon and a fundamental locale of enculturation (Pader, 1988, 1993). That is, one's daily movements through space, with the attendant activities and people associated with various spaces, are integral parts of the dynamic process by which one continually learns and revises the values of society (this will be discussed more later). The built environment is not a simple reflector of social relations, nor is it simply a mnemonic device that points people in certain predetermined directions. It is actively implicated in the entire enculturation process, enabling and constraining changing behaviors. Social and spatial practice in the home and community are intertwined with concepts of one's ethnic and self-identity. Social relations, in terms of socially constructed roles and hierarchical relations of power, of age and gender, are spatially created and reinterpreted by use within the home. A disjuncture between the physical environment and one's routinized actions can be very disorienting—literally and figuratively.

Explicating the relationship and meaning between the physical environment and routinized behaviors requires repositioning the emphasis of analysis from one of a chronological time frame of change to a more explicitly spatial frame. Soja (1989) contends that we should look at "simultaneous relations and meanings that are tied together by a spatial rather than a temporal logic" (p. 1). To accomplish this, one must place greater primacy on the impact of the spatial dimension for critical social analysis, on a dialectic of "space, time, and social being" (Soja, 1989, p. 3). The spatiality of social life, be it at the level of the nation or the home, the multinational corporation or the household, is ideologically and politically full, although these underlying structures are often barely visible. In this view, spatiality is simultaneously a product and a shaping force of social life. The imagination, too, it would seem, embraces this sense of simultaneity: Space and time become collapsed and reconfigured, while concurrently imagination affects how one sees and interprets their spatiotemporal environment.

The importance of this recognition is that while one might analytically differentiate space from time, or the imagination from the action, in reality each of these four elements is so deeply implicated in the other that a person's use and interpretation of space, time, social being (or social agency), and imagination in daily life profoundly affect one's social relations and ability to negotiate upheavals in one's sense of space and time. Yet, this negotiation is essential if one is to make the transition to a new space and time. An explicit, discursive awareness of the power of spatiality as actively engaged in the continuing process of enculturation, and hence social change, would empower the participant in a particular site of change while providing the researcher with greater insight into the transition process.

Thus, the "continuity of . . . purposes and sense of the regularity of social behavior" (Marris, 1974, p. 15) that is essential for successful adaptation to a new environment is fundamentally ensconced in the manipulation of domestic and community space. It is further recreated and reinterpreted via the temporal practices in the home, through routinized actions within the home space. Some of these practices inevitably must change in the new environment due to extradomestic contingencies (as will be discussed, for example, work schedules in the United States necessitate revising eating schedules), whereas others are responses to more subtle factors, such as home and community design and U.S. zoning regulations (see also Werner, Altman, & Oxley, 1985, and Harvey, 1989, for more developed studies of the temporal realm).

Understanding how variations in home and community design and use both enable and constrain change entails comparing the design of the homes left behind in La Chaneja with those moved into in California.[2] However, not only are the spatial arrangements of rooms with their

---

[2]There is a growing literature on domestic environments from a variety of perspectives, some substantiating others, some conflicting. Some of these include Altman and Werner, eds., 1985; Bourdieu, 1977; Browne, 1970; Churchman and Sebba, 1985; Low and Chambers, eds., 1989; Kent, ed., 1982, 1990; Lawrence, 1987; Pellow, 1988; Rapoport, 1982; Robben, 1989; Rodman, 1985. Lawrence and Low (1990) present an overview of the literature. Those that are concerned primarily with women and the domestic environment include Ardener, ed., 1981; Hayden, 1984; Matrix, 1984; Moore, 1986; and Roberts, 1991.

socially understood uses and meanings of diagnostic interest, but also how the inhabitants actually use those spaces in their negotiation and expectations of how life should be. Similarly, the organization and use of public village spaces also influence and are influenced by daily social practice.

People coming from different villages or living in different arrangements once in the United States will not respond identically to the people I describe here, nor will all people within a community respond with one voice. However, the encompassing *principles* of analysis and theoretical framework enable the sociospatial dynamics of change to be assessed for any community. Thus, whereas the specifics for each community are unique, including both the reasons people have for relocating and the locale from where they came, the larger implications and theoretical framework are more widely applicable.

The particular sectors of the Mexican-origin population in Southern California included in this study are settled long- and short-term immigrants and their families. That is, some are recent arrivals who plan to stay for a long time, if not forever, whereas others were born and raised in California. Some are undocumented immigrants, whereas others are documented. However, all live in apartments or houses; none are undocumented farm workers living in makeshift housing or specially built migrant-worker camps.

In order to put the deeper social implications of the Mexican spatial relations into relief, I will first discuss the Mexican context followed by the U.S. mainstream counterpart as it is this sector that largely determines the house type and regulations to which the immigrants are implicitly expected to adapt.[3]

LIFE IN LA CHANEJA, MEXICO

In many ways, life in La Chaneja is similar to that in many other Latin American peasant villages (see Lobo, 1982; Nash, 1985 [1970]), in which most people know one another, by sight if not by name. At any time, at least 60% of the households have at least one family member working in the United States. Often, a husband works 8 to 10 months a year in the United States and spends the rest of the year in the village with his family. During this time he is often not working, but living off

[3]By "mainstream" I refer to the dominant ideology in terms of middle- to upper-middle-class Euro-America. Although the United States clearly is an amalgamation of many ideas and values, it is this one that has largely been written into regulations and built into homes; it is this one that is, for the most part, taken as the marker of normalcy.

the money he has earned and spending time with friends. While away he has become a stranger to his children and has to try to reintegrate himself into his family. This sets up a particular dynamic in which he is, in essence, a known stranger. Wives of migrant workers often have ambivalent feelings about their spouses, who they expect will live mostly in the United States. Yet, even while he is away the husband tends to be the titular head of the household. When decisions have to be made the father will often be consulted by letter (which might take up to a month to reach him in the United States and another month for the response to reach the village). The decision might be about participating in a school outing, whether a girl is old enough to cut her hair or if she should accept a marriage proposal. However, for the most part, it is the wife who has responsibility for day-to-day decisions and discipline, although she will often make these decisions in the father's name. The reality of the relationship is clearly articulated by the comment of one woman to female relatives: "It's the same either way. He's here or he's there" (my translation).

Some women told me that it is the great responsibility of, in essence, being a single mother—raising the children properly, keeping them safe, clothed, fed, and out of trouble—that caused them to decide finally to leave their relatives and friends and join their husbands in the United States. Although in the village these temporarily single mothers have the support of relatives, they are still seen by their spouses and other villagers as primarily responsible for their own children's welfare. However, even when the father is living with the family, the children tend to be closer to her (see also Martin, 1990, and Mirandé & Enríquez, 1979). For many women, leaving their mother, sisters, sisters-in-law, aunts, and cousins is very difficult. Fortunately for many, however, people from the same village often move to neighborhoods where other villagers live. Thus, when they move to California some female relatives are likely to live nearby.

Economic differences within the village are apparent in both overt and subtle ways. Some women take in others' laundry to earn sufficient money to feed and clothe their own families, and some, obviously, can afford to pay to have their laundry done for them. The major disparity is based on whether or not someone is supporting you from outside the village—in some cases a husband or son works in Guadalajara, the second largest city in Mexico, about 3 hours away by bus—but most often, the money comes from *el otro lado*, the other side (of the border).[4]

[4]Some people earn relatively good incomes from owning local businesses in the village or the nearby town, or by having a large, productive piece of land.

People whose relatives in the United States help support them stand out by their possessions: They wear more American clothes, with U.S. clothes being considered intrinsically better and of higher status as part of the passed-down mythology of life in the United States; they have television, cassette players, better furniture, and other items not generally affordable. A side effect of these consumer items coming into the village is that they are fundamental factors in recreating a new sense of what is necessary, of what one's expectations of life are—and in a very visual manner, identifying and separating the *haves* and the *have-nots*.

WOMEN'S DAILY DOMESTIC ROUTINE

Women's daily routines are fairly standard throughout the village. In the early morning, at about 7 o'clock, women walk past blocks of attached houses to a shop off the plaza to collect their *nixtamal*, a dough made from corn and lime, needed to make tortillas. The evening before they will have left dried corn kernels in a bucket at the shop where they are then mechanically ground and mixed with the lime. Upon returning home with the *nixtamal*, breakfast is prepared: The tortillas are made, beans cooked, and chilis hand-ground to make a hot salsa. Sometimes parts of the meal are made the day before, and some women buy freshly made but mass-produced tortillas from a tortilla maker in the village. If a man or boy works in the fields or a local factory, he will leave the house before breakfast is made and return around 9 or 10 to eat with whomever else is at home. If the fields are far away, the wife might bring meals to him. With more children in school, however, breakfast routines have changed. Children eat before school—often a prepackaged cereal such as corn flakes—while workers eat later. Women serve the food, to men and boys first, and eat either after everyone leaves or after everyone is served. However, a woman is expected to be ready to stop eating to serve a second helping, anticipating the male's request.

After breakfast, general housekeeping begins. During the morning, buckets are filled with water that is stored in a large, covered barrel sitting on a flat roof, connected to a spigot in the courtyard. Water is carried to other parts of the home as needed. The women and girls wash the dishes, mop the floors (at least once a day), and sweep the courtyard. Many days laundry is hand-washed standing over a raised, stone *lavadora* situated in the courtyard. Washing and hanging clothes might take 3 hours, plus 1 or 2 hours more later for ironing. Sometimes, however, the town pump breaks down. When this happens the women wash their clothes at the river and the family bathes in the river, as was done before piped water came to the village (which arrived in the late

1960s). When the pump is down, women carry clay jugs and plastic buckets to the river where they dig small holes in the riverbank, draw water, and carry it up the hill to home for use with cooking and cleaning.

The main meal of the day is served at about 2 or 3 o'clock. In preparation, food is bought daily in one of the small village shops. This might be beans, vegetables, cheese, eggs, meat, fruit, milk, soda, or other foods the household members like and can afford. Occasionally a woman, accompanied by either a relative or children, will take the 15-minute bus ride into the nearby large town to shop at the fresh food market, the larger grocery stores with prepackaged products, or to make special purchases. The road out of town was built in the mid-1970s, making this a fairly new activity. After eating, wage earners return to work while the remains are cleaned away. The next meal of the day is a snack at about 8 o'clock. This might be leftovers, *quesedillas* (melted cheese on tortillas), or something as simple as store-bought white bread with jam.

These domestic routines are not as isolating as they might appear on the surface. During the day, a married daughter commonly visits her mother and joins in whatever task is being done, brings some work of her own to do, or just keeps her mother company while the mother continues with whatever she was doing. Other women, with children in tow, might stop by for a visit, which does not necessarily cause the householder to stop her tasks. However, she often stops work for a while and sits in the courtyard while chatting. Finally, and perhaps most importantly, children of the household are expected to participate in domestic tasks (Figure 3).

As is common in most peasant communities throughout Latin America and elsewhere in the world, children are actively involved with daily domestic tasks. As toddlers, boys and girls imitate their older siblings and mothers by play-sweeping or copying other chores. As soon as they are old enough, often at 5 or 6 years old, they are assigned tasks. Girls will care for younger siblings, fetch water, sweep, straighten bed coverings, or feed chickens, while boys will work in the fields or help with household tasks. Children might also be sent on an errand to a neighboring home (often a relative) or to one of the neighboring houses with a small store in the front room. Everyone knows their neighbors and is not fearful of a stranger mistreating their child. Although the number of cars in the village increases yearly, it is still safe for children to run across the street for an errand.

A woman is rarely alone on the street, even en route to a relative's home. Once married, many are not permitted by their husbands to go visiting without their knowledge and permission, even to her mother's

Figure 3. Visiting the courtyard.

home. Many women told me that men expect their wives to be home when they arrive, be it in the middle of the day, at mealtime, or late at night. When a woman is on the street, she tends to be accompanied by a child, another woman, or her husband. I once walked the two blocks from the house in which I live to the plaza, crossed the plaza, and went to a municipal building that housed what was then the only telephone in the village. Upon my return, my hostess and her two sisters-in-law looked at me and one asked with great surprise if I had gone by myself.

Most of a woman's socializing is with relatives, although with girls spending more time in school they are developing more nonfamily friends. Men have always interacted with both relatives and friends. Whereas the house is primarily the domain of women and children, the plaza is where men convene. Unemployed men, including migrant workers who are home temporarily, often spend a good bit of the day and evening sitting and chatting in the plaza. Employed men will often spend evenings at the plaza. Women walk through the plaza, buy from vendors situated at the plaza, but do not often sit there alone or with female friends.

As in many rural communities, one's home, in a broad sense, ex-

tends from the innermost walls of a particular physical dwelling, into
the encompassing community, and perhaps into the surrounding fields.
The central village plaza becomes a central focal point, a place that some
consider to be an outdoor, community living room (see Holston, 1989,
with reference to Brazil). Each of these locales has a different meaning.
The entire space of the house is associated primarily with women and
women's activities, which includes interacting with family and friends.
The streets are for all, but their uses, like different areas within the
house, are gendered. However, the distinction between house and
street is not physically impermeable. Although the house traditionally is
made of thick walls (adobe walls might be more than 1 foot wide, but
most new homes are built of brick), the front door is often left open
during the day, enabling passersby to see into the core of the house, the
courtyard (Figure 4). As with the central plaza at the community level,
the courtyard is the central focal point at the domestic level.

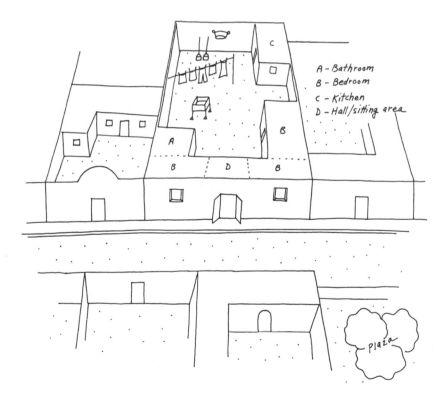

Figure 4. Domestic spatial arrangements in La Chaneja.

Here then, the tacitly understood, daily scheduled uses and meanings of domestic and community spaces for women, men, and children are intertwined in the dialectic of space, time, and social being. People's self-definition of others are inseparable from their spatiotemporal relations.

CHILD CARE

An essential facet of daily life is child care. In La Chaneja this is easily integrated into the daily movements through the spaces of home and community. The design of homes enables children and their care-takers to be almost continually within visual and auditory range of one another. This is not simply a fortuitous coincidence. A structural principle here, as in many peasant communities, is the importance of families with its emphasis on *inter*dependence and sharing (Griswold del Castillo, 1984; Mirandé & Enríquez, 1979). This value is built into the floorplan and reinforced by how the residents use the space: The Chanejan concept of the appropriate relationship among women, children, and sociospatial relations has led to a design that supports the social value of familism. As will be discussed, this value is in contrast to mainstream U.S. structural principles of independence and individualism. (For a detailed sociospatial comparison of La Chanejan and mainstream U.S. homes, see Pader, 1993; for a compendium of Mexican house styles, see López Morales, 1987.)

The courtyard is conceptually, and often physically, the center of the home. It is an outside room onto which other rooms usually connect. In some houses, the courtyard is at the back of the house, with the kitchen overlooking it and all rooms connected directly to one another, not separated by a hallway as would be expected in a U.S. home; yet sight and sound remain largely uninterrupted. Regardless of the particular house version, the courtyard is a safe place for children to play. It is swept daily and is where laundry and dishes are washed, and one commonly finds people washing themselves here, too.[5] Food preparation often takes place here, such as cleaning corn or beans and cutting vegetables. In the past, cooking tended to be done in the courtyard as well; kitchens with stoves run on bottled gas have made this less common. As stated, grown siblings, cousins, or other relatives and friends might stop by and chat while the work continues. Other children might be dropped off while their mother goes to the market.

[5]As new houses are being built more in the U.S. style, this is changing: Some kitchens and bathrooms now have piped-in water and considerably smaller courtyards. But most who move to the United States had lived in the traditional house.

Neither cleaning nor child care is an essentially isolating activity. Children play in the thick of the action, in full sight, not in a specialized children's play area. Even at bedtime, they fall asleep wherever everyone is sitting. Although more older children go to school than previously, and therefore are less available for child care and domestic tasks, women are not left alone with an infant or toddler all day. With visiting back and forth and walking the few blocks to a store several times a day during which time she visits with friends met along the way, there is substantial social interaction.

Thus, both in the design of the homes and the movements through the home and the village, there is much overlap between inside and outside, physically and conceptually. The most central, most used room inside the house is an unroofed, outside area—the courtyard. It is here that most social activity takes place, where family and friends are entertained when the weather permits.

The community outside the physical boundaries of the house is an extension of the inside. It is the sphere of the known, of friends and community. Once in the United States, these physical and conceptual spheres no longer mean the same. They are not only different visually, but their signification does not fit with previous experiences. They are sociospatially disruptive.

SOCIOSPATIAL DISCONTINUITY IN THE UNITED STATES

Domestic activities in the twentieth-century U.S. home tend to be much more compartmentalized into separate blocks of time and bounded spaces than in La Chanejan homes.[6] As Chant found in her study of women in Queretaro, Mexico, "Since the home was the area in which the majority of family interaction occurred, women tried to ensure that the homes were as pleasant and comfortable as possible" (1987, p. 41). This is more difficult when the most basic, taken-for-granted facets of the physical environment are transformed. Yet, it is the women who become the primary mediators between the old and new domestic worlds. Because the daily negotiation of domestic space is fundamental to the ongoing process of enculturation and social change, a woman's ability to creatively renegotiate these spaces in ways that make sense within her own continually changing conceptual framework is essential for her family to "make it" in their new environment. She is largely

[6]For historical perspectives on the change in U.S. and western European homes from more communal to more individuated, see Braudel, 1967; Rybcznski, 1986; and Wright, 1981.

responsible for drawing on familiar resources and reconceptualizing them in a meaningful manner.

A comparison of this new physical environment with the one left behind makes clear the radical, yet subtle, changes with which the family must deal. As has been described by a variety of researchers, the U.S. home typically is divided into backstage and frontstage areas (e.g., Altman & Chemers, 1980; Goffman, 1959; and Lawrence, 1987). That is, those areas in which activities that are deemed more private, for view by household members and, perhaps, close friends/relatives, are physically and conceptually located in the rear of the dwelling or on a separate floor. In general, these include bedrooms, laundry rooms, workshops, and, to a lesser extent, kitchens and bathrooms. Bathrooms are in a category of their own (Pader, 1993). Because the activities that take place in them, such as body washing and elimination, are considered the epitome of personal behavior, the room is conceptually backstage. However, it must be accessible to all who are invited into the home. As more bathrooms are included in a home (in large numbers since the 1950s), it becomes possible to differentiate between ones used by guests and ones closed to guests.

In contrast with these backstage rooms are those that are conceptually and physically open to nonintimates—living rooms, dining rooms, and front halls. Thus, the ethos around each room has a powerful effect on how one perceives people who do or do not/should or should not use each room (see Humphrey, 1974, on reification of people/place/position in the home). Sanctions are considered appropriate when these largely nonverbalized socially constructed rules are violated. Simultaneously, how one perceives of a room reinforces the role of the persons who may or may not use it and their relationship with others. Basically, there is a tautological relationship in effect.

The ethos of each type of room is further objectified by the circulation patterns, in the physical movements of people through the space of the home. In the United States, one moves through or past the more public, frontstage spaces to reach the backstage areas. To do otherwise "feels" wrong or uncomfortable. In La Chaneja the spatial arrangements are partially reversed, as is the signification of some spaces. With the bedrooms in front in the village houses, there is not the sense that these areas are to be visually and audibly removed from the circulation pattern of nonhouseholders. To reach the bathroom, kitchen, or central socializing area—the courtyard—one must walk past bedrooms, rooms that commonly have only an open curtain over the doorway opening. In the evenings, guests often join household members in the bedrooms to chat. Bedrooms are not part of the backstage.

Both the Mexican and U.S. patterns of movement become embedded in the minds of their respective users. They are part of each person's
socially constructed pattern of intra- and interhousehold social relationships, helping to create their sense of self and their place in society. For
most of the day in La Chaneja, it is women and children who repeat
these patterns of movement. They are akin to a well-choreographed and
well-practiced dance. I suggest that these movements help create that
daily sense of continuity that Marris (1974) argues is essential for the
creation of one's personal and social identity.

The choreography is not only through space and time but is encoded in the mind. It integrates with the nervous system through what
Gilfoyle, Grady, and Moore (1981) term the "spiraling *continuum* of
spatio-temporal adaptation" (p. 49, my emphasis). They state that infants, in the process of developing greater sensorimotor skills and
adapting to new environments and experiences "call forth past behavior
and activities to direct [their] effort at [a] higher level [of their brain]"
(p. 137). These researchers argue that motor activities, that is, physical
movements, interrelate with sensory information in a confluence of
past, present, and future. A fundamental factor in successful adaptation
to new situations, to space and time, is the degree to which sensorimotor skills are physiologically integrated through the adaptive facility of
the nervous system. Patterns of learning and one's system of organization, or categorization, are in part dependent upon the processing of
past and present movements in conjunction with other environmental
experiences. For these reasons "sensorimotor activity is important as an
integrating mechanism for linking together the developmental progress
of physical, intellectual, emotional and social components" (Gilfoyle et
al., 1981, p. 5).

They argue that the more often one repeats a physical movement
through space within a similar context, the more it becomes integrated
into the nervous system and "feels" right or natural; it becomes habit.
This routinization of action can be equated with what Lefebvre (1991)
calls one's "spatial code" and the process by which signification develops. This suggests that how one categorizes a particular environment
and one's relationship with that environment is a profound combining
of cultural and physiological experiences.

What then happens when a person is put into a new situation in
which the most seemingly trivial, everyday physical and social relations
are confounded, fragmented, and "feel" wrong, such as experienced in
the move from a La Chanejan home to a U.S. one? What prevents the
thread of continuity from getting stretched to its limit and breaking?
Perhaps, as some cognitive psychologists argue, memories are "recon-

stituted" in use rather than recalled precisely (Allman, 1989). Exactly how one recollects a past event is contextual; the memory is colored by the context in which it is recalled and is affected by such factors as verbal and environmental clues. To remember exactly how one imaged what the future in the United States would be like when living in the village is unlikely. It is far more likely that memories of past images will be reinterpreted in practice. In some sense, one reinvents the past and past expectations in the present, incorporating the changes into our memories. The thread of continuity, then, draws upon internal resources built up over years to reconceptualize the meaning of the present. We use the imagination to control facets of change that might otherwise feel too wrong, be too alien to established categories and spatial codes, and perhaps, therefore dangerously disruptive.

Thus, although the transition from rural Mexico to urban United States might be literally and figuratively disorienting, by the subtle processes of the mind, memory, and daily action, people who successfully make the transition presumably must manage to reconfigure the relationship among the individual, the group, and the environment. This is quite a remarkable feat. Within the new context, the old significations and fundamental categorizations of space and time, of action and spatiality, no longer interact according to expectation. Add to this the different ways in which space is used, the new work and school routines requiring new eating times and habits, and it becomes clear that the fundamental order that had always enabled and constrained social life is no longer dependable. Any existing conceptual framework exists in flux as it is continually altered in practice, albeit subtly. Changes in implicit spatial codes and their concomitant signification are integral to this process. However, because most of us tend to take domestic spatial arrangements so much for granted and do not think about the profound interrelationship among sensorimotor actions, socially constructed conceptual frameworks, and spatiality, some of the impact of the move from rural Mexico to urban California remains unrealized.

NEW HOMES, NEW ROUTINES, NEW CONCEPTUAL FRAMEWORKS

When a woman moves from her Mexican home to the United States, she has many levels of change with which to deal. Some are more easily incorporated into her conceptual framework than others. At a cognitive level, she has to reconceptualize her relationship with the immediate domestic environment: spatially, temporally, and technologically. Not only does the overall amount of space in the new U.S. home tend to be less, but visual and bodily access around the home is impaired. Tacitly understood spatial codes are no longer relevant. For instance, the courtyard, the physical and conceptual center of the home, no longer exists, nor is it easy to recreate in the U.S.-style home.

In addition, partially because rent is high and partially to ensure that no one is alone, it is not uncommon for a large family, or several smaller families to live together in the smaller, completely roofed home. A man whose family is in Mexico shares either with other men or a family of relatives. Yet, most would not consider denying a relative a place to sleep as long as there was a space on the floor available, a practice that leads to risks of eviction by the landlord. Sharing domestic space in this way is not considered a burden by most, nor do the inhabitants tend to complain of being overcrowded, as might be expected if judged by the mainstream U.S. perspective of appropriate spatial apportionment.

There is little material continuity between here and home. Having come with only a suitcase or two, a woman does not have many familiar mementos surrounding her. The neighborhood into which she moves is as alien as the apartment or house. Not only is the streetscape strange to her, but sometimes dangerous, both in terms of unknown people and the traffic-infested streets. In reminiscing about the differences between her expectations of what life would be like in the United States and her actual reactions once here, a woman who had moved to Los Angeles from La Chaneja 40 years before our meeting made these feelings of alienation and grief clear:

> I used to imagine that things were pretty in Los Angeles. It wasn't like that for me. From Tijuana I saw that the houses looked very clean, very white, and I thought they were pretty. But I wanted my adobe house [in La Chaneja] and I felt very sad because I didn't like being so far from my family. . . . For me, everything was strange. Although [the house in Los Angeles] had light . . . and running water, I didn't like it. I felt like when they keep a person just inside the house and they can't go out. It took me years to adapt to this life. Because I didn't feel free. . . . What I used to do is hide myself and not open the door to anyone I didn't know.

Women often comment that they cannot comfortably let their children out alone to run an errand or play for fear of their safety. Their feelings of alienation are exacerbated because daily routines are also disrupted. Everyone is out of the home early to go to school, which is compulsory for many more years than in Mexico, or to work, and no one returns until late afternoon or evening. The evening meal is now the only time when everyone is together. The woman often is minimally mobile and spends much of her time alone in the house. She does not know the ropes and must depend on her husband far more than before. After being the de facto head of house for years while he was away, this is a major change. When women are employed outside the home their world becomes even stranger, their schedules more alien, and often they remain primarily responsible for the daily domestic sphere as well.[7]

Within the home basic movements are reconceptualized due to fundamentally different daily routines of household members as well as different spatial arrangements and concepts about the use and meaning of each of these spaces. The new homes are designed with the U.S. values of individualism and independence as a conceptual base, as well as a strong, built-in separation of family and nonfamily. Back home, the appropriate structuring of domestic social and spatial relations discouraged individualism in preference for interdependence and did not have separate locales expressedly for nonfamily. These fundamentally different perspectives must be accommodated in the new environment.

For instance, as described, in the village the bedroom is in the front of the home; in the United States it is more secluded in the back. However, the front room, intended by the U.S. builders as a room for socializing, often becomes a sleeping *and* socializing room, just as it was in the village. This does not cause any problems as the "need" for physically bounded, private spaces for sleeping is not part of the La Chanejan conceptual framework. In one U.S. apartment an immigrant family made some physical changes to break down the frontstage–backstage divide. The apartment had been separated into discrete areas by a door between the living room and the hallway onto which the one bedroom and bathroom opened. They removed the door and in the process removed a physical barrier between themselves (parents and a daughter who shared the bedroom) and the two adult male relatives who slept in the living room. Other families live in larger homes, often single-family houses, with the same spatial arrangement, and have the same complaint about the impaired visibility created by the design.

Although the kitchen is spatially the back room in most U.S. houses, it is often turned into the conceptual center of the home by the immigrants. It is here that the family will gather to chat while women cook. One second-generation Mexican-American man from El Paso, Texas, told of his first encounter with the dominant U.S. domestic sociospatial relations and his Mexican-born grandmother's reaction to it. While at

---

[7]However, research indicates that the longer women are breadwinners, the more likely their spouses are to take over some domestic tasks. This is also a generational issue, in that people born in the United States are more likely to divide the household responsibilities (see Zavella, 1991).

university in the midwest, he visited the homes of friends. There, for the first time, he encountered an extra sitting room/parlor. He was amazed and reported this arrangement to his grandmother: "You know how we're in here [kitchen] all the time? There they have another room just for talking." She responded: "A room where you can sit and talk only? What do they use the kitchen for? Just to cook?"

Yet this, too, is often seen to change over time. For a Mexican-American woman from Texas, it was looking at middle-class, mainstream magazines such as *Good Housekeeping* and *Better Homes and Gardens* that gave her the idea to separate kitchen and sitting-room activities when she married and had her own home.

In the new U.S. home, the outside is no longer part of inside. The subtle implications of this reconfiguration were not part of the imagined life in the United States. There is no physically central point equivalent to the courtyard; no place where sight and sound is minimally impeded *and* where a great variety of activities are expected to take place simultaneously. In the new home, the kitchen might become the conceptual center, but it would be very difficult to have such a multiuse space. Several women mentioned that they do not like the new house style because they cannot see what everyone is doing or where they have gone.

Whereas child care and domestic tasks are more easily integrated into the La Chanejan woman's life, once in the United States she has to make adjustments. Child care is more problematic. Young children are kept inside while housework is being done; there is no outside room to take the place of the courtyard with its myriad of activities. These activities are now relegated to several physically bounded and differentiated spaces.

Visiting is more limited and with refrigerators, shopping trips might be less frequent. In some neighborhoods, there are small grocery stores specializing in Mexican foods, whereas in others women have to go a distance to a supermarket. Because of zoning regulations in most U.S. cities, small front-room shops are illegal, as is cooking and selling food in front of one's home. Thus, not only is a major source of income regulated out of the new life, but so is a major source of socializing with neighbors.

Ability to socialize or caretake children while completing domestic tasks is more difficult in the U.S. home. For instance, unlike in La Chaneja, movements surrounding washing are now differentiated by what is being washed: Washing the body, clothing, and dishes are conceived as discrete activities in the United States, each requiring its own appropriate locale.[8] The spatial arrangement of washing activities discourages casual conversation with friends or relatives, partially by the size of the rooms, partially by constantly moving for each task, and partially by attitudes surrounding what is being cleaned. Cleaning tasks, such as clothes washing, are considered personal; unlike in La Chaneja, it is not common to socialize while doing laundry. This belief is reinforced by the location of washing machines in the new home, which are generally in the basement or a back room; they are nearly always out of the general circulation pattern of nonhousehold members (women who use laundromats have an opportunity for socializing). Drying the laundry, when not in a machine, is relegated to the backyard, another backstage area. Dishwashing, too, is separated into a discrete, backstage locale, although one in which closer friends and relatives will go more readily than into a laundry room. The use of vacuums, which are loud cumbersome cleaning machines, is another means by which interaction is limited while cleaning tasks are performed.

In La Chaneja, carpets and the vacuums that clean them are idealized; they are part of the mythology underlying life *de otro lado,* as one of the benefits of living in the United States. The women and girls believe that these are labor-saving devices that will make life easier than the daily mopping of uncarpeted floors. They do not tend to realize that along with these commodities come greater isolation and a floor covering that is more susceptible to indelible staining. Although, perhaps softer for a child to fall on, carpeting also requires a new way of conceptualizing one's relation with one's home in some very subtle, but fundamental ways.

Carpeted floors require a reconsideration of what constitutes dirt. In La Chaneja adults and children might drop things onto floors (which are not carpeted) knowing the floors will be swept once or twice daily. Purposefully dropping things onto floors is a behavior that would be objectionable to many in the United States. However, not only do U.S. floors not tend to be cleaned as often, but they are covered by different materials. For instance, in U.S. kitchens, which tend not to be carpeted, food can be spilled and cleaned up. Not so for carpeted living rooms, dining rooms, or bedrooms, rooms that also have fewer uses than their Chanejan counterparts and in which activities that might stain the carpet are discouraged. To have a dining room, a room for eating in which

---

[8]Although clothes washing might be done in a bathroom or kitchen, they are not the most usual locations; however, this has not always been the case. For instance, in the old New York City tenements, bathtubs were often in the kitchen and served as sinks.

one has to eat more carefully than usual, is not within the Chanejan's experience. It breaks up activities that for them are appropriately combined. In Mexico, guests eat wherever family usually eats; generally in a kitchen or an uncarpeted dining area opening to the kitchen. The homes into which many Mexicans move in California do not have kitchens large enough to eat in and come with carpeting in the dining area. In this case, even daily eating becomes a more carefully controlled activity than it was at home; everyone must self-consciously avoid accidentally spilling anything onto the floor and creating a permanent mark. Much of the power of such seemingly trivial actions for engendering change lie in the subtlety of their reconceptualization in the move from new and unusual to taken-for-granted and habitual.

Another change that must be reinterpreted is the lack of plazas in the community. Public parks are neither centrally located nor physically arranged to encourage similar activities and interactions as in La Chaneja. However, as parks are outside the home like plazas, they are more likely to be the domain of men.

One disappointment to many women after living in the United States for a while is that previously imagined freedoms do not transpire. Women in the village often comment that it would be good to be independent and eat when you want; this is a bit of the freedom they imagine will transpire in the United States. While combing her child's hair, one woman stated: "Cook, get pregnant, wash and comb; women have much work" (my translation). When I asked whether women's work or men's work was better, she made the sign of money with her fingers: "We don't get paid." However, when I asked whose work was more satisfying, she was unable to answer. The gap between what is imagined to bring independence and the reality of the life known, and perhaps preferred, can be large.

Many women do work outside the home once in the United States, as opposed to earning money through the informal sector as was often the case in La Chaneja. The degree to which this affects internal social relations varies according to the household, although the longer both spouses work outside the home, the more the daily relations tend to change. For example, when the husbands were sharing living quarters with other men before their families arrived, they did their own cleaning and cooking, some cooking traditional Mexican meals. Once the family arrives, these skills are often "lost," and the division of labor common in the village is reinstated. However, if the wife does work full time outside the home, men's share of household tasks often increases. Nonetheless, it is still the women who tend to be seen as in charge of domestic life and daily child care, and hence who have much of the responsibility for figuring out how to incorporate the old with the new in the daily scheme of life. Some women clearly manage this better than others; some never stop missing La Chaneja and never adapt, whereas others come to prefer living in the United States.

Changing uses and meanings of space mutually reinforce and participate in the transformation of sociospatial relations. As women are most strongly identified with home and family, and hence with changes within the home, it is their actions that must be explored for understanding the larger implications of changes within the home—that is, the influence of these domestic changes in the extradomestic arena.

Two classic studies of the social effects of being forceably moved from a largely working-class Italian-American neighborhood in Boston clearly demonstrate the consequences of this dislocation on women (Fried, 1963; Fried & Gleicher, 1961). In the late 1950s this neighborhood fell to the urban renewal program; it was torn down to make way for luxury apartments and office buildings. The people who had lived there then scattered around the greater Boston area. Similar to the La Chanejan experience, men in the West End had always had a greater range in which to explore; their jobs took them out of the range of women's daily activities, and they hung out with friends at a distance from the house. Women tended to travel within a smaller radius from the home. The home and the immediate neighborhood were the focus of their lives, and central to their sense of identity. Shops and social networks were nearby. In the old neighborhood, women kept each other company and participated in an active street life.

Once relocated, these daily spatial and social expectations were no longer fulfilled for the women, and well-entrenched habits no longer made sense. For many, it was no longer possible to just walk outside and socialize, or walk down the block to the store. Continuity was severely strained, and imaginings of daily life had to be reconceptualized. The result was that many of the women suffered severe depression in their grief over losing their home and community. For some, the severity decreased after 6 months; for others it was still apparent at the time of the study, 2 years after the move. Men, Fried (1963) found, who had always been less dependent upon the home and its immediate environs, suffered less. With time, many came to feel more comfortable with their new homes—whereas some had been pleased to move from the outset.

The focus of Fried and Gleicher's studies was on documenting the incidence of grief as an effect of forceably fragmenting a stable community and understanding some of the fundamental social and spatial relations—at the neighborhood, not domestic, level—that were disrupted. Understanding the role of women, not only in grieving for the old, but in negotiating the new life must now also be explored.

WOMEN'S ROLE IN CHANGE

Although the impact of domestic sociospatial relations dynamically and interactively influence, and is influenced by, all householders, women and children tend to be most closely associated with the home on a day-to-day basis. For the most part, men's and women's activities, expectations, and needs are different (despite some evening out by more equal schooling). Their domains of real influence (as opposed to just socially sanctioned influence) are also different. As Moser (1987) has pointed out in her study of women, housing, and policymaking in the Third World, "Women, in their roles as wives and mothers, are the primary users of space both in their houses and in the local community. Yet their particular needs are often ignored or not recognized in both settlement planning and house design" (p. 17). Although she is referring specifically to professional planners as ignoring women's needs, I would extend her observation to include self-built, vernacular housing and the community patterns created by them. The role of the physical space of home in development and change is rarely considered.

Thus, when looking for the locus of "progress"—generally conceptualized in Western terms as greater purchasing power and more sophisticated forms of production—in Third World countries, researchers generally imply by omission that what goes on in the home is not a critical diagnostic (e.g., Massy, Alarcón, Durand, & Gonazález, 1987). It is seen as less important than, for instance, innovative means of utilizing land more efficiently. This assumes both that material culture, which includes house form as well as consumer products such as electric blenders that replace the mortar and pestle,[9] is not actively implicated in the creation, maintenance, and transformation of society, and that technological transformations at the largely female-oriented domestic level of interaction are less significant than those at the largely male-oriented extra-domestic level. Such positions do not take into account the generative and creative power of daily domestic and community life.

Studies that explicitly analyze Third World women's roles and contributions to home and community tend not to analyze the microlevel of guiding social change through domestic spatial relations and related

[9]Interestingly, many men complain that *chile* (salsa) made with a blender does not taste as good as *chile* ground by hand. Some say the seeds do not get well ground in the blender and change the flavor.

cognitive processes. More often they analyze the importance of women's role as producers, reproducers, and community and household organizers and appropriately analyze female and male discourse (see, for example, Benería & Roldán, 1987; Logan, 1984; Lomnitz, 1977; Martin, 1990; Moser & Peake, 1987, on Latin America). Women's voices, they find, are harder to hear than men's. Yet, as these authors and others have found (see Feldman and Stall, Chapter 7, this volume), when women organize and make people listen to their voices, it becomes clear that their contributions as mothers, wives, and community members have always insinuated themselves into the formation of their society.

DIRECTIONS FOR FUTURE RESEARCH AND POLICY

An individual or group of people might not be able to control the changes inherent in entering a new environment, changes such as home and community layout or patterns of behavior common there. However, with the aid of the imagination one can continually reconstitute and reinterpret past expectations of the present situation, and of the past itself. In this sense, the imagination is essential for controlling and enabling successful adaptation to an existing, external situation. It is largely during the renegotiation of the meanings and relations of one's spatial world that the past, present, and future are more or less successfully integrated. Even as new movements and daily routines insinuate themselves into one's memory and become part of taken-for-granted habit, as opposed to standing out in difference, they subtly continue to undergo revision in daily practice. It would seem, then, that via creative adaptations of the known with the unknown at the domestic level the thread of continuity is maintained, no matter how tenuously. And, as it is women who are primarily responsible for maintaining this domain, their role in creating a palimpsest of the new and old that makes sense within ever-changing conceptual frameworks is central to the success of the transition. They must make the discontinuity between here and there feel right in the process of reassessing daily domestic spatial, temporal, and social routines.

There is no one model or template that would fit all instances of individual or group relocation. Thus, whereas the details of the study presented here are not directly analogous to any other situation, the principles of analysis and the theoretical framework underlying the study *are* relevant to other situations. Some questions that were broached here need to be asked in all instances: How does one maintain, or regain, a sense of continuity with the past? How similar or different is the new home from the old, in terms of the sociospatial arrangement of both domestic space and extradomestic space? What role does disillusionment with expectations play in the ability or desire to make the new home work? How do different women, as central to the enculturation process in their roles as mother and wife, help mediate the changes, incorporating the unknown into existing and changing conceptual frameworks? How are social networks reconstituted in the new environment and what is the role of reconstructing some street life in this process? Is it possible to determine a range of creative accommodations to the new environment, in terms of spatiotemporal adaptations, necessary for relocatees to survive in their new home with minimum disruption? Would sensitivity to spatial habits and their transformations ease the sense of alienation many feel and foster a greater sense of continuity?

These questions informed this analysis and were formulated both by my particular theoretical perspective on the spatiality of daily life and other studies of relocation. Those studies tend not to concentrate on the microlevel of domestic spatial relations as was done here. Before we can participate in policymaking decisions that work for the people who need them, and not simply from our own culturally produced concepts of appropriate social and spatial relations, these issues must be more fully explored. This requires more comparative research at this level of analysis in other communities and under other conditions of relocation. An analysis of domestic and neighborhood spatial design and use in the home community will provide much insight to fundamental values and enable anyone assisting the relocatees to make their adaptations and thereby maintain some sense of continuity, and perhaps mitigate some grieving.

Whereas the data at the base of this study were gathered over a 4-year period that included extensive periods of participant observation, less-detailed sociospatial data can be very informative. Just asking people about their physical environment (and knowing the central questions to ask) and perhaps even having them draw pictures of the home left behind can be cathartic. Often this will lead into more extensive discussion of the past, the present, and hopes for the future. Although we cannot control mistaken imaginings or unrealized pictures of, in this case life in the United States, at the least we can help people to restructure the reality underlying the transition through a more profound understanding of the seemingly small, but highly significant, sociospatial relations of change.

It is especially important to consider the more subtle impact of women's lives in social formation and transformation. Women's invisibility and muteness make it easy to underestimate the ramification of women's work in the extradomestic realm. Yet, it is through the daily renegotiation of everyday experiences that conceptual frameworks and expectations slowly change. The emotional and physical survival of the family in the new environment is largely dependent on this ability and willingness to imagine the known in the face of the unknown, to gain some control over uncontrolled change.

Acknowledgments

I thank Peter Marris for having provided a critical framework in his own writings and for critiquing an earlier version of this chapter. Daniel Lizárraga and Sylvia Sanchez provided important insight into generational differences through their own experiences. The many families in La Chaneja and Southern California who welcomed me into their homes deserve special thanks. The illustration is by Jan Whitaker. Finally, I thank the funding agencies who made the research possible: The H. F. Guggenheim Foundation; UCLA's Institute of American Cultures through the Chicano Studies Research Center and the Program on Mexico; and a Faculty Travel Grant from the University of Massachusetts–Amherst.

REFERENCES

Aaron, H. J. (1972). *Shelter and subsidies: Who benefits from federal housing policies?* Washington, DC: The Brookings Institution.

Allman, W. F. (1989). *Apprentices of wonder: Inside the neural network revolution.* New York: Bantam Books.

Altman, I., & Werner, C. (Eds.). (1985). *Home environments: Human behavior and environment. Volume 8.* New York: Plenum Press.

Ardener, S. (1986). The representation of women in academic models. In L. Dube, E. Leacock, & S. Ardener (Eds.), *Visibility and power: Essays on women in society and development* (pp. 3–14). Oxford: Oxford University Press.

Ardener, S. (Ed.). (1981). *Women and space: Ground rules and social maps.* London: Croom Helm.

Benería, L., & Roldán, R. (1987). *The crossroads of class and gender.* Chicago: University of Chicago Press.

Bourdieu, P. (1977). *Outline of a theory of practice.* Cambridge: Cambridge University Press.

Altman, I., & Chemers, M. (1980). *Culture and environment.* Monterey, CA: Brooks/Cole.

Bourdieu, P. (1979). *Algeria 1960.* Cambridge: Cambridge University Press.

Browne, E. (1978). *El uso de las ciudades y de las viviendas.* Buenos Aires: Ediciones Siap.

Certeau de, M. (1984). *The practice of everyday life.* S. Rendell, trans. Berkeley: University of California Press.

Braudel, F. (1967). *Capitalism and material life 1400–1800.* New York: Harper & Row.

Chant, S. (1987). Domestic labour, decision-making, and dwelling construction: The experience of women in Queretaro, Mexico. In C. O. N. Moser & L. Peake (Eds.), *Women, human settlements and housing* (pp. 33–54). New York: Tavistock Publications.

Chavez, L. (1992). *Shadowed lives: Undocumented immigrants in American society.* New York: Holt, Rinehart & Winston.

Churchman, A., & Sebba, R. (1985). Women's territoriality in the home. In M. Safir, M. Mednick, D. Israeli, & J. Bernard (Eds.), *Women's worlds: From the new scholarship* (pp. 31–37). New York: Praeger.

Fried, M. (1963). Grieving for a lost home. In L. J. Duhl (Ed.), *The urban condition* (pp. 151–171). New York: Basic Books.

Fried, M., & Gleicher, P. (1961). Some sources of residential satisfaction in an urban slum. *Journal of the American Institute of Planners, 27,* 305–315.

Fuentes, C. (1991). Introduction. In A. Lundkvist. *Journeys in dream and imagination* (pp. 15–20). New York: Four Walls Eight Windows.

Giddens, A. (1979). *Central problems in social theory: Action, structure and contradiction in social analysis.* London: Macmillan.

Giddens, A. (1985). Time, space and regionalisation. In D. Gregory & J. Urry (Eds.), *Social relations and spatial structures* (pp. 265–295). New York: St. Martin's Press.

Gilfoyle, E., Grady, A., & Moore, J. (1981). *Children adapt.* Thorofare, NJ: Charles B. Slack, Inc.

Goffman, E. (1959). *The presentation of self in everyday life.* New York: Anchor Books.

Griswold del Castillo, R. (1984). *La familia.* Notre Dame, IN: Notre Dame Press.

Harvey, D. (1989). *The condition of postmodernity.* Oxford: Basil Blackwell.

Hayden, D. (1984). *Redesigning the American dream: The future of housing, work and family life.* New York: Norton.

Holston, J. (1989). *The modernist city: An anthropological critique of Brasilia.* Chicago: University of Chicago Press.

Humphrey, C. (1974). Inside a Mongolian tent. *New Society, 30,* 273–275.

Kent, S. (Ed.). (1990). *Domestic architecture and the use of space: An interdisciplinary cross-cultural study.* Cambridge: Cambridge University Press.

Kent, S. (1982). *Analyzing activity areas: An ethnoarchaeological study of the use of space.* Albuquerque: University of New Mexico Press.

Lawrence, D. L., & Low, S. M. (1990). The built environment and spatial form. *Annual Review of Anthropology, 19,* 453–505.

Lawrence, R. (1987). *Housing, dwelling and homes: Design theory, research and practice.* Chichester, U.K.: Wiley.

Lefebvre, H. (1991 [1974]). *The production of space.* Transl. Donald Nicholson-Smith. Oxford: Basil Blackwell.

Lobo, S. (1982). *A house of my own: Social organization in the squatter settlements of Lima, Peru.* Tucson: University of Arizona Press.

Logan, K. (1984). *Haciendo pueblo: The development of a Guadalajaran suburb.* Birmingham: University of Alabama Press.

Lomnitz, L. (1977). *Networks and marginality: Life in a Mexican shantytown.* New York: Academic Press.

López Morales, F. J. (1987). *Arquitectura vernácula en México.* Benito Juárez, México: Trillas.

Low, S. M., & Chambers, E. (Eds.). (1989). *Housing, culture and design: A comparative perspective.* Philadelphia: University of Pennsylvania Press.

Massey, D., Alarcón, R., Durand, J., & González, H. (1987). *Return to Aztlan: The social process of international migration from Western Mexico.* Berkeley: University of California Press.

Martin, J. (1990). Motherhood and power: The production of a women's culture of politics in a Mexican community. *American Ethnologist, 17*(3), 470–490.

Marris, P. (1974). *Loss and change.* New York: Pantheon Books.

Marris, P. (1982). *Family and social change in an African city: A study of rehousing in Lagos.* Chicago: Northwestern University Press.

Matrix (1984). *Making space: Women and the man made environment.* London: Pluto Press.

Mirandé, A., & Enríquez, E. (1979). *La Chicana: The Mexican American woman.* Chicago: The University of Chicago Press.

Moser, C. O. N. (1987). Women, human settlements and housing: A conceptual framework for analysis and policy-making. In C. O. N. Moser & L. Peake (Eds.), *Women, human settlement and housing* (pp. 12–32). New York: Tavistock Publications.

Moser, C. O. N. & Peake, L. (Eds.). (1987). *Women, human settlements and housing.* New York: Tavistock Publications.

Moore, H. (1986). *Space, text and gender: An anthropological study of the Marakwet of Kenya.* Cambridge: Cambridge University Press.

Nash, J. (1985 [1970]). *In the eyes of the ancestors: Belief and behavior in a Mayan community.* Prospect Heights, IL: Waveland Press.

Oliver-Smith, A. (1986). *The martyred city: Death and rebirth in the Andes.* Albuquerque: University of New Mexico Press.

Pader, E-J. (1988). Inside spatial relations. *Architecture and Behaviour, 4*(3), 251–287.

Pader, E-J. (1993). Spatiality and social change: Domestic space-use in Mexico and the United States. *American Ethnologist, 20*(1), 114–137.

Pader, E-J. (1994). *Spatial relations and housing policy: Regulations that discriminate against Mexican-origin households. Journal of Planning and Education and Research, 13*(2), 119–135.

Pellow, D. (1988). What housing does: Changes in an Accra community. *Architecture and Behaviour, 4*(3), 213–228.

Rapoport, A. (1982). *The meaning of the built environment: A nonverbal communication approach.* Beverly Hills, CA: Sage.

Roberts, M. (1991). *Living in a man-made world: Gender assumptions in modern housing design.* New York: Routledge.

Robben, A. (1989). Habits of the home: Spatial hegemony and the structuration of house and society in Brazil. *American Anthropologist, 91,* 570–588.

Rodman, M. C. (1985). Contemporary custom: Redefining domestic space in Longana, Vanuatu. *Ethnology, 24*(4), 269–279.

Rosaldo, R. (1985). *Assimilation revisited.* SCCR Working Paper No. 9, Stanford, CA: Stanford Center for Chicano Research.

Rybczynski, W. (1986). *Home: A short history of an idea.* New York: Penguin Books.

Soja, E. W. (1989). *Postmodern geographies: The reassertion of space in critical social theory.* New York: Verso.

Werner, C. M., Altman, I., & Oxley, D. (1985). Temporal aspects of homes: A transactional perspective. In I. Altman & C. M. Werner (Eds.), *Home environments: Human behavior and environment, Volume 8* (pp. 1–32). New York: Plenum Press.

Wright, G. (1981). *Building the dream: A social history of housing in America.* Cambridge, MA: MIT Press.

Zavella, P. (1991). *Mujeres* in factories: Race and class perspectives on women, work, and family. In M. di Leonardo (Ed.), *Gender at the crossroads of knowledge: Feminist anthropology in the postmodern era* (pp. 312–336). Los Angeles: University of California Press.

5

Environment and the Aging Woman

DOMAINS OF CHOICE

SANDRA C. HOWELL

SETTING THE STAGE

Entering the environments of older women affords us a unique opportunity to explore the potential of contemporary gender theories. One
aspect of feminist social science is a confrontation with the older sociological construct of "sex role," viewed as a determinant of behaviors and
self-definition across the life span, and attributed to gender socialization
in early life (Ferree & Hess, 1987; Riger, 1992). While gerontologists
continue to argue about continuity versus discontinuity of personality in
late life (Field & Millsap, 1991), an understanding of behaviors relative to
the social and physical environment may well expose both the mean-
inglessness of this supposed dichotomy and the intrusions of a gender-
based (male) structuralization of the issues. Social scientists have, for
decades, sought to describe sex differences in performance, affect, and
social behavior, while deemphasizing the variabilities within each gender (Riger, 1992). This presentation will attempt to illustrate, through

SANDRA C. HOWELL • Department of Architecture, Massachusetts Institute of Technol-
ogy, Cambridge, Massachusetts 02139.
Women and the Environment, edited by Irwin Altman and Arza Churchman. Plenum Press,
New York, 1994.

exemplars of class, race, cohort, marital and family status, competence, education, and environmental history, that gender-specific variability.

The subtitle "Domains of Choice" refers both to these mediating variables and to the belief in the agency of the individual woman to perceive and choose within the opportunities and constraints proferred by her society and the context within which she finds herself at particular points in her aging process. "Domains of Choice" also refers to perceived control, the extent to which an aging woman calculates the optimum context within which she can maintain a sense of continuity of self while both she and her environmental contexts are changing.

One construct that has gained popularity in attempts to understand the relationship between the inner person and environment is that of attachment to place. Rubinstein and Parmelee (1992) suggest a model of place attachment in late life that attempts an integration of both collective (social/cultural norms) and individual factors with physical, personal, and social factors. While not eschewing the importance of the collective factors, which cannot but influence the behaviors and beliefs of older women, this chapter focuses more on a refinement of what Rubinstein and Parmelee (1992) address as "personal definition" in attachment, namely the interactions of place, life experiences, and relationships. As these authors state "every person creates for herself a particularized version of the collective life course, a life story, depending upon her specific experiences and the meaning she attaches to them" (p. 144). One problem we have with a "collective definition," "roles," for example, is that they depend a great deal upon what the individual selects as her reference group to define norms at any given time. This will be most clearly seen as we more carefully dissect cohort and ethnicity influences on women.

Wapner and Craig-Bray (1992) and Altman (1992) develop the concept of "transitions" in life events as an operator through which we may better understand transactions of people and environment as both change over time. Mid- to late-life transitions for women (empty nest, widowhood) have been seen as particularly significant insofar as child-raising and homemaking roles were said to be the primary sources of self-definition and their loss is to be thought her loss. However, as we hear the stories of individual older women, as each reflects on her current and past relationships with environments, it becomes clear that domains of choice have not been so universal or narrowly and affectively defined by them.

For example, women who were widowed or divorced at younger ages showed tendencies to reach back toward work environments in the decade 1930–1940, and especially 1940–1950 when World War II opened new opportunities. Further, relationships with adult children do not universally enlarge environmental experiences for the older woman. This becomes evident when individual women described how infrequently they visited in the homes of children and grandchildren, particularly (but not only) when they lived farther than 30 miles away.

It is only recently that research on the behaviors and affects of that 5% of older women classified as single, never married has been demythologized relative to the "isolation and loneliness" previously laid on her (Rubinstein, 1987). Similarly, the woman who was widowed or divorced early and never remarried is beginning to be distinguished from her "on-time" sister in having had some experiences with autonomous environmental management, which seems to provide more choice (or perceptions of choice) in older age (Lopata, 1973; Troll, 1994).

In order to discuss the older woman's relationship with environment it is necessary to explore each woman's psychoenvironmental history. Although there may be some generalizations about aging and environment that will ultimately emerge from nomethetic research, the scholarly bias at this time is toward ideographics, within which the particular language of individual experience will become luminous. In taking this position, I side with the most recent thinking of Rubinstein and Parmelee (1992). These authors provide insight into the domains of "attachment of place" in old age by pointing to the individual as the interpreter of experience relative to collective definitions of person–place transactions, rather than as the automatic respondent to imposed norms.

Howard (1991) also argues for the fundamental insights to be gained by listening to stories individuals tell about themselves and their world. Working with story material however, is, itself, a subjective endeavor in which the scholar is required to specify the basis for the selection of particular narrative episodes as well as the interpretation and organization of verbal content.

It is because of the paucity of salient material about older women in the literature of both gerontology and environmental psychology that I have chosen to intermingle case or ethnographic examples with discussions of the domains of choice that middle-aged and aging women face and resolve with the environment. We will see that just as a woman plays out her own dynamics in the later decades of life, so the society is changing in the environmental affordances available to women. This is intended to be a positive thrust toward a feminist gerontology and environmental psychology, probably stimulated by a realization, in my review of the literature in both fields, that most of us have been constrained by the extant "definition of the situation" dominantly derived from a male-oriented social science in which women are rarely seen other than relative to their ascribed social roles.

It is rare, in the gerontological literature, for the discussion of gender or women to incorporate the environmental contexts within which the acting out of these roles occur, although the covert reference appears dominantly to be the home. Older women's extradomestic connections with environment have, to date, been poorly represented in studies, either by gerontologists or environmental psychologists. It is also because of the gap in descriptive data that this discussion will be based, predominantly, on case studies, as a potential basis for a grounded theory of female aging and environment.

An excellent example of the ways in which ideographic methods can provide a new definition of the situation is the study of the perception of leisure among older African-American women (Allen & Chin-Sang, 1990). The authors point to the striking difference in perceptions between their respondents, who tended in their narratives to wrap leisure into work activities, and studies of white men's perceptions that consistently show a clear separation of leisure from work activities and settings, a perception that had been assumed to hold for women in general, including any subgroups.

The women whose stories I have selected represent the variabilities that occur across and within aging cohorts. No two 70-year-old women will reflect the social and physical contexts of their same decades of development in the same ways. Where one continues to reside in the local house and neighborhood where she was born and lived during marriage, child rearing and widowhood, another has emigrated from a European country and has married, divorced, moved, and is without children.

Across cohorts, we see the coping strategies of a divorced mother in her 90s, still physically competent and actively engaged with both her daughters and community, contrasted to a still-married mother in her 80s who has been coping with increasingly restrictive physical disabilities and whose children are distanced geographically or emotionally. These instances may well argue for gerontologists to revisit the concept of cohort, insofar as it assumes some kind of normative impacts of generational events on later life behaviors and affects.

A key assumption underlying the cohort concept in gerontology is that people who have experienced common major societal events (i.e., the Great Depression, World War II, etc.) will exhibit similar psychological affects and, as well, respond differently to current situations from those who did not live through that period. Cohort effects are often called into play when selected variables cannot adequately account for the magnitude of a residual.

Although the cohort construct seems to be a very useful tool in explaining some psychosocial outcomes for particular subpopulations of aging (e.g., Holocaust victims, setting-specific union workers, ethnic-specific immigrants), for a general population there appear to be too many interactions between the original event and subsequent environmental transactions to which the individual responded to make "cohort" an informing construct.

The selection of cases and their narrative episodes was based upon a desire to illustrate the range of circumstances both within and across the cohorts of aging women. Thus, to be poor, frail, and locally oriented at age 71 can be contrasted with being a middle-income, active, 91-year-old cosmopolitan. Verbal content is inserted into behavioral and attitudinal descriptions as they were recorded, on tape or in notes, in the course of conversations or as they were written into open-ended questions of more formal interviews.

The presentation has been organized so that the reader can experience, first, what I have chosen to call "domains of choice." In this section the selected fragments of a life are brought into focus in order to suggest a theme that seems to govern the woman's transactions with the environment as she perceived it at the time of the interview.

Following this section, some broader issues, which are invited by prevailing social theories but which typically are outside of the consciousness of interviewees, are addressed.

Finally, future directions for research will be discussed as they are informed by this author's view of changes in environments and in women's self-perceptions.

DOMAINS OF CHOICE

The Reconstruction of Self-in-Place

The principle of perceived control is illustrated in the following two cases, separated by a continent, differing in socioeconomic class and marital status. Although the mediating variables in these cases are quite different, the determined choice to persevere in the home environment of middle age is the common theme.

When, at age 76, she was brought back to her Hollywood home from the rehabilitation center after a series of strokes, she was tearfully adamant to be in her (and her husband's) upstairs bedroom, surrounded by her most personal possessions, even though we had offered to prepare a space for her in the den downstairs, where she could be involved in daily activities and be among her valued furnishings and art objects.

Despite the fact that she had still to regain her speech, she was quite capable of making her needs and wants known. She would either call out or ring a bedside bell (with her unparalyzed hand) and when someone would come upstairs to her she would point and gesture until, by trial and error, she was brought what she required. For those first several months, although we did not initially understand, she requested all manner of objects unrelated to her physical care, but particularly photographs of family members, letters, and memorabilia from her desk or closets. When she became more mobile and had some return of speech, she asked to be assisted first to tour the entire second floor, particularly her adult children's former rooms and then to be taken downstairs where she was escorted, slowly, from room to room as she reacquainted herself with all of her favorite furnishings and the treasured objects, mostly in her inherited china cabinet, that she had collected throughout her married life. A valued family picture shows this cabinet in the background and reminds her of her childhood and celebrations in a midwestern state (see Figure 1).

During a subsequent taped interview, her motives became more apparent. Edith Cooper (my mother) had determined to recover her memory of herself in the systematic way she had achieved other goals

Figure 1. Edith Cooper, recovering from strokes, makes a first trip downstairs to review her china cabinet. Photograph by Daniel O. Howell, 1977.

she had sought throughout her life. In this difficult recovery, she had used the people around her, the places she had created, and the objects of meaning.

The lesson of this vignette is in line with a body of psychological research on aging: "As people age, they become more like themselves and less like everyone else their age" (Neugarten, 1964). More recent research on the continuity of personality indicates that stability may be somewhat uneven in later life and may be affected by environmental circumstances (Field & Millsap, 1991). What then must follow, although no strong research states this conclusion, is that the ways in which environments have been incorporated into a woman's life space will be revealed most clearly and individually during the late years of her life (Howell, 1983a).

If this conclusion is valid, it further contributes to the argument that ideographic data will offer more to our understanding of the environments of both older women and older men than will more traditional nomethetic explorations. In fact, in her most recent review of her own and others' research on older women and "attachment," Troll (1994) sees little to indicate gender differences in attachment and much to suggest that the people (and places) of old age reflect the cumulative history of those relationships for the individual woman or man.

That this runs counter to our stereotypes of older women may be explained best by past interpretations of gender and cohort role expectations. In the United States, from early in the twentieth century, the history of homemaking essentially has been a history of women's creation of the home environment (Wright, 1981). Women, currently 70 to 90 years old, were typically offered few options in the society to a primary focus on domestic activities and, therefore, psychologically, many validated their identity through investment in this environmental enterprise.

This investment became apparent in case studies of housing modifications among working-class families in East Boston, Massachusetts. Several older respondents commented on their attachment to house and neighborhood (Howell, 1983c). Recorded interviews reflected pride of place in the language of possession and active engagement over time with the physical aspects of their home environment.

In one case, a late middle-aged, Italian-American widow, with one employed adult son living at home, spoke of her environment.

"There are three floors, all one family, all mine. This house was nothing when we bought it—we modernized everything over 31 years. We did it all little by little, we're not rich. Put in oil heat [was all coal] there was nothing here. He [her deceased husband] did a lot of everything himself, plumbing, electrical connections. I had no closets, I had this put in. We had the ceiling lowered last year and I will continue repairs."

The woman remembers the original house—"like a dungeon, nobody took care of it, they closed doors off—we opened them. $3,600 bought the house 31 years ago." They added bathroom tiles, aluminum siding. "We're an average family, just working people. I live out of my kitchen—only go upstairs to do beds, kitchen is more important than living room with TV. For coffee, you have to sit at a table with people. Besides, I am a baker [used to run a bakery]. People say, 'You should get an apartment now your husband's gone.' No, this is all I want. Then I got the boy home."

She has three children, eight grandchildren, three great-grandchildren. "I have plenty of room for them. It's my own, that's all I care about. At my age, where would I go? My husband's gone, where would I be? In an apartment, no, after all these years. I couldn't live somewhere else and pay the high rent. At least I put everything in this, and it's mine. I put everything in this house. The house is paid for, $50 a month plus taxes. This is my home, I love it, I worked all these years, I wouldn't give it up for nothing. When I go down, the house goes with me. If you work hard for something, you want to hold on to it" (Howell, 1983c).

The Primacy of Nature

For other older women, in spite of the wider social mandates of their generation, attachments and relationships to specific environments are either weak or not home-based, as the following case will illustrate. The influences of early life geography and early marital dissolution, not factors of consequence in the prior cases, appear to dominate the psychoenvironmental history of this woman.

Eleanor lives in a subsidized elderly apartment on Martha's Vineyard, off the coast of Massachusetts. One of her two daughters, a recent widow age 70, lives within a mile, and they visit each other almost daily. Eleanor is a staunch environmentalist. From her concern about organically grown food to her involvement with recycling ("I remind my neighbors weekly about sorting their bottles and cans"), she lives out her principles. Eleanor is 91 years old but by no means is she frail. She represents one extreme of relationship with environment for her cohort of elderly. What is significant about Eleanor's sense of place is the consistency of her orientation over many adult years. When asked what environments have been important to her in the course of her life, Eleanor does not hesitate to report her early experiences in the mountains of Oregon and Washington. For Eleanor, it is the natural rather than the built environment that has meaning and reflects her identity.

This is not to say that her current private space is not meaningful. The walls of her apartment are filled with the seascapes painted by one of her sons-in-law (a former architect), and she maintains her setting as a functional place, both for her local activities (a typewriting table that represents her role as secretary to the on-site tenants' council) and her self-care life (a small free-standing freezer that allows her autonomy in food preparation) (see Figure 2).

Unlike the majority of American women of her cohort, Eleanor has been divorced since her mid-30s when her daughters were of school age. The long absence of a husband in the household may have modified the perceived need for her to focus her identity on her domestic environments; however, reports of her residential mobility suggest different saliencies.

For the divorced and widowed older woman, the choice of community and housing may be more related to the residential location of her adult children and grandchildren, than to her own earlier affiliated neighborhood (Longino & Serow, 1992). We know that most older Americans live within about 30 miles of at least one adult child (usually a

Figure 2. Eleanor's apartment, with functional supports of typing table and freezer. Photograph by Sandra C. Howell, 1990.

daughter); what is less understood is the trajectory that may have brought about this spatial proximity for the older woman. Eleanor's environmental history may suggest a future pattern, particularly with increasing numbers of divorced mothers.

Eleanor remained in the Northwest United States long after her two daughters married and moved East. She traveled to visit them and her grandchildren several times each year, until, on one visit when she was in her 60s, her youngest daughter begged her to move into a cottage on their farm in Tennessee. She lived there, happily near nature, about 3 years until they sold the farm and moved for job reasons. She then moved to White Plains, New York, into an apartment near her older daughter and husband, and, during that period of her late 60s, went to work as an assistant in a health-care agency.

When, about 5 years later, her son-in-law retired his architecture practice and they moved to the house he had designed on Martha's Vineyard, she moved there, too. It was already a familiar environment of recent summers past.

Eleanor is an active member of Elder Hostels, traveling to various workshops around the country. Last year she took advantage of a Hostel (whose topic was "Women and Environmentalism") to go to Atlanta, Georgia, where, not incidentally, she visited with her favorite granddaughter, who practices law in that city.

VOICES OF NEED AND LIMITED CHOICE

The following cases came from a 1981 federally funded study mounted to investigate the Determinants of Housing Choice among older people as they moved through the stages of "empty nest," retirement, illness of spouse, and widowhood (Howell, 1983b). The hypothesis that generated the research was that major life events are significant in aging people's decision about where and how they live. The research attempted to question stereotypes about people who move in retirement or after being widowed. In fact, with few exceptions, we found little to support this hypothesis for any event across all national samples, although women widowed young showed a small tendency to have moved within a year of the event.

One sample included women who moved into a 42-unit, gender-mixed, subsidized housing setting in Cambridge, Massachusetts, who had their own special stories about their environmental–social histories. These women tended to be frailer and with fewer social and economic resources than many of their age peers. A comparison group of women from the same working-class neighborhood were also included in this study.

Miss D. had been single for her 84 years and had previously lived with one or another of her three sisters. When each of them died and she, subsequently, broke her hip in a fall, she realized that she would be faced with an institutional environment if she could not find a community-based alternative. It was a nurse in the hospital that told her of the congregate option. She would rather, she commented, have more space, as she had with all her furniture when her last sister was alive. Although a Cambridge native, she disliked this particular neighborhood but repeated several times, "What choice do I have?" Before and after she retired from a textile mill, she lived in a house owned by her mother, who she took care of as the only unmarried daughter. She views her current two-room unit (without kitchen) as "just a place she happens to live" and the "place I'm going to die in."

Mrs. C., a neighbor in the same congregate setting and also a native of East Cambridge, at 71 years of age, has had a different history. As the widowed mother of three sons, she considers her current living arrangement to be the best solution to maintaining some independence in the face of her partial disability problems. When asked if she "thought of the place as her home or just as a place you happen to live?", she responded, "My son, the eldest, his place is *really* home. When he was [first] married they lived near us. I have a sofa I sleep on there." Despite her primary identification with her son's home in the same city, which she visits on weekends, she views the current rooms, building, and neighborhood more than just a place she happens to be. She likes the fact that she is "on her own" and close to stores. Her prior residence for 9 years was a "rest home" where she had to share a room and there were arguments all the time. Here she "can open the window whenever I wish" and her "bureau fits" into her second small room.

"Where are the stained glass windows that were in the chapel?", a woman resident of this Norfolk Street setting asked me during this study. She had been a lifelong member of St. Mary's Parish, and she knew the convent sister who had designed those windows ca. 1925, each of which represented a biblical quote. When I told her that my family had them, and they had been distributed and used in various contexts, she seemed relieved. When I asked her if she wished a segment of one of those windows for herself, she said, "Oh no, I am only glad that they were not destroyed in the conversion of the convent." In fact, she alone had chosen this setting just because it was familiar from her childhood, and the retention of many original architectural features provided her a sense of lifelong continuity-in-place.

"Wait for Spring. Everything will be fine in the Spring" was Mrs. E's late husband's response when she tried to discuss retirement housing.

Unfortunately, she was widowed young (her husband was only 49) and childless. She turned down a chance to buy a house in Walpole and decided to stay in Cambridge "because friends and family [mostly nieces and nephews] are here." "They all own houses." She also remarked that "your own furniture [and my knick-knacks] make your own home."

Mrs. E., age 87, retired from Bell Telephone in 1958 (at age 65), but reports that when she married she was demoted from a management position "because you can't be a married supervisor." This example of a "cohort effect" specific to women now older may have implications for environmental attitudes toward past work environments. Illustrative of such attitudes was the initial community resistance, particularly among potential elderly women tenants, to the conversion of an old textile mill in Lowell, Massachusetts, to subsidized apartments for elderly. Many thought it "weird" to think they would want to live in that "sweat shop."

Mrs. E. is legally blind, and this has influenced her decision to remain in her four-room apartment of 39 years because "I know the place inside so well [and] I can walk to the Square and back." She is one of several respondents in our study that commented on the poor sidewalk maintenance in her neighborhood that makes her outside activities more hazardous.

Several older women living, as does Mrs. E., in the neighborhood of Norfolk Street Congregate housing remarked on their complete unwillingness to share a kitchen, required by the design of that setting. Looking in from the outside, they perceived the environment to lack the privacy they so cherished in their own, more traditionally complete, residences.

We often ask respondents to give us their preference of living arrangements without probing into the basis for their judgment—(i.e., "compared to what?"). For women living in their rooms of the Congregate housing, the comparison is the alternative they have already experienced or anticipate—a nursing home, where privacy and freedom to choose activities and use of time are at their most minimal.

Mrs. S., a 71-year-old widow born in Lithuania, still lived in the (four-unit) apartment building she inherited from her father and to which she brought her husband on marriage in 1934. Like this mother, her own daughter has lived downstairs with her family since her marriage.

Though, clearly, time and family events have attached her to the place, she worries about what might happen if her daughter and son-in-law should decide to move to a small house they own (and rent out) in Quincy. It would be too small for her, and she does not feel she would be comfortable with their "lifestyle" and social life—she imagines she might feel she would "have to lock herself in her room so as not to intrude on them." She volunteered that her grandson used one of the spare bedrooms in her upstairs unit for his train collection for several years. He has now "moved out of the train room to become a real railroad man with the B&M in Maine." she has thought about moving to Elderly Housing because her house now seems too big to manage, but her daughter urged her to stay with her in the "family building." Her attachment to the neighborhood has been weakened by the demise of all her neighbors and the independence of her three grandchildren. Mrs. S. and her husband thought "we'd find a smaller place maybe on the Cape" after he retired, "but he didn't live to retire."

This sampling from a local population suggests a possible personal dimension to be referred to as low-risk takers. The cases sited, whether residing in their own homes or in the congregate setting, seem to be "making do," not pushing the boundaries of their situations. That this propensity is not primarily a reflection of either the lower socioeconomic status of these women or of their frailer conditions will be seen in the later discussions of cohort and migratory patterns.

Organizing the Environment: The Frail, Oldest Women

Soldo, Wolf, and Agree (1990), using data from the 1982 Long Term Care Study, developed a model of care arrangements of frail older women based on living arrangement and availability of kin. They found that being a no-longer-married, older woman having adult older children (whatever number or gender), increases the probability of coresidence or informal (nonprofessional) care giving. If an adult child is geographically available to provide needed services it appears to be more likely that the frail older mother will continue to live alone. "Daughters are considerably more likely than sons to live with [or house] their frailer mothers." The availability of sons appears to promote the use of formal (professional agency) caregivers, when the mother is independently housed.

As the number of children increases, older frail mothers have a greater likelihood of living alone because of more people able to meet the varied lifestyle needs of the aged parent. "Frail older women who persist within the community," the authors suggest, "appear to organize some type of supportive living or care arrangement" (within the constraints imposed by familial and financial resources). Krivo and Mutchler (1989) also address these issues. That the frail older woman's personality and social–environmental history can also overcome the limitations on availability of adult children is illustrated by Clara's late life history.

A retired New York City schoolteacher, her environments for 50 years of adult life were divided between Brooklyn, New York, and Martha's Vineyard, Massachusetts, where she and her teacher-husband had bought land and a house in 1935. One of the understudied middle-income, long-term renters, this aging couple finally decided to give up their apartment in Brooklyn and move, permanently, to their summer location in 1982. The husband and wife were then in their mid-70s and in relatively good health. They arranged to spend the months of October to April in a rented apartment because their summer house on the water could not be easily insulated. About 4 years after this permanent move, Clara's husband's health began to fail and his increasing disability required her care night and day, as he ultimately became bedridden. Clara maintained, through this period of caretaking, an active role in a wide variety of community services, and she solidified a network of people that would deliver groceries, transport her to events, invite her to social occasions. She had one living son (and daughter-in-law) who had moved from the midwest to a nearby Cape Cod town to work. They monitored the welfare of the couple but maintained their own autonomy and distance (i.e., they were not available for daily needs) and visited on their own schedule about every other month. As her husband became totally bedridden, he was moved downstairs to his small study off the living room of their summer house. She continued to sleep in their upstairs bedroom until she realized how much she was going up and down stairs for his care. She then took over a spare bedroom off the kitchen. Her confidence that she "knew this house in the dark" resulted in a fall that broke an arm. An accident "post mortem" that I conducted led to her upgrading the night lighting between her bedroom and her husband's. Her husband subsequently died and for 2 years she maintained the pattern of living in her summer home and wintering in the rented apartment.

Several months before she died, Clara, perhaps unconsciously aware that she was terminally ill, decided to apply for an apartment in nonprofit-sponsored elderly housing within the town, rather than face the move from summer house to winter apartment. Because of her network, which included some local political connections, she obtained an apartment 1 week before she entered the hospital for treatment of incurable cancer. She insisted that no one know her condition lest the apartment (for "well-elderly") be denied her. I and several long-time friends moved her possessions into her new apartment, overlooking the Sound she knew so well. She lay in bed, carefully instructing us on every detail, what she did and did not want moved and where she wanted each item placed. A particular issue of "control" occurred over where the telephone, clock, and room-light controls would be placed—within arm's reach of her bed. Lawton (1990) refers to this consolidating behavior as it can often be demonstrated among frailest elderly.

Recently an architect colleague reported on the reorganization of her home supervised by his 94-year-old mother still dwelling in the house he had designed over 30 years ago. Her objective was not only to consolidate necessary activities in space but also to move to the front of the house where she had control of the entry and, as well, could more actively "participate" in the life of her neighborhood, waving to neighbors and familiar tradesmen.

Older women who have, for many years, cared for frail husbands also participate in organizing the environment often in order to facilitate their own autonomy. For such older women, the stresses involved in caring for a disabled husband may not be too apparent if the disability is of many years duration and the couple has, during that time, actively engaged in these environmental modifications.

A recent communication from a friend in her early 70s, whose husband is a retired academician with progressive blindness and a childhood physical disability that disallowed driving is illustrative:

"We are now equipped with an electric wheelchair and van which not only make J.'s 'expert witness' work much easier but make it possible for us to go to basketball games and to take [our granddaughter] to shows. We're enjoying the new freedom" (Henderson, personal communication, 1992).

In another case, the husband, a retired researcher in his mid-70s, has had a lifelong battle to control the effects of muscular dystrophy. While the wife, also a retired professional, historically has provided assistance to him in personal care, he has learned to find and deploy compensatory environmental supports in order to retain a high degree of autonomy. For example, some years ago he procured from the Dystrophy Association a large automatic upholstered chair to allow himself to sit and stand without assistance. He has placed it in a corner of their living room, surrounded by his computer, printer, and modem-telephone, and in this way can spend many satisfying hours still actively engaged in explorations (such "control centers" are described by Lawton, 1985). This couple, as well, has a van equipped for a disabled driver/passenger, and they now take several long trips each year, usually visiting places of scenic beauty from Canada and the West Coast to Utah and, most recently, revisiting the Carolina coast.

Because of these environmental supports, the wife has maintained a very active role outside the home with the Gray Panthers and social contact with her women friends. Indicative of the joint micromanagement of environment by this couple was a recently overheard request by the husband for the wife to purchase brass handles and mount them on the door frames of the kitchen and bathroom so that he could more safely cross the hall without losing balance.

These two cases are included to point out that for the older woman, the quality of the relationship with a long-term partner can inhibit or enhance her perception of environmental control. How, as a couple, they have approached and coped with environmental opportunities and experiences over many years is an unmined body of knowledge in the heads of these older women respondents. We cannot talk about older women and environment without entering the effects of key, long-term relationships.

COHORT EFFECTS AND MIGRATORY HISTORY

Certain cohort effects may have unique relevance in understanding some of the weaker relationships between older women and their physical environments. While the impact on older men of work environments, the Great Depression, and military service has often been discussed, the experiences of older women during their formative and earlier adult years have been poorly specified.

One type of historical event and cohort effect that may prove to provide richer insight into environmental meaning for older women are the waves of emigration to the United States and migration to western states during the 1930–1950 decades and later. In addition, for women, cohort experiences may interact with marital status to create special relationships with children that induce migration and loosen environmental attachment.

Of the 32 women in our 1981 Glendale, California Determinants of Choice sample, 89% (28) were born *outside* of California, and none counted the Glendale area as the place of family origin. By contrast, among the earlier reported Cambridge, Massachusetts, sample, 33% were native to Cambridge or the Greater Boston area, and only 51% were born out of the state, but mostly in New England (Howell, 1983b).

One migratory wave brought Europeans to America after World War II. For a 76-year-old German war bride (Johanna B.), emigration, she claimed, was pushed by her divorce and her children's wish to move to Canada and then to the United States. She first lived in a rural area of California with a daughter and her family for a year. Her main reason for moving to Glendale, California, was a sense of "isolation in a country environment," having grown up in a city. Her expressions of attachment to place were very weak; she had moved nine times between 1950–1981, often in close consultation with her three children, who are her primary attachments. A 50-year-old son was reported to visit her daily and another weekly.

The combination of economic depression and early widowhood is reflected in the environmental history of Enid P. (age 85) who was born in Severence, Kansas. Widowed in 1936 with four children, she moved in with her mother because of "lack of money for food for her children." She had moved five times between 1950–1981. One of these residences was in the home of her son and his family in Wichita, Kansas, moving out when her son moved to Southern California for work in 1973. Shortly thereafter, having retired from a secretarial job, she followed and has rented apartments in Glendale, California, ever since.

O'Bryant (1987) sees her Columbus, Ohio, sample as more broadly "typical" of American elderly widows, the majority born in the state they own their home in and most of whom have at least one middle-aged child in the same city.

Late-life migration studies refer to subpopulations who return to their birth-home (Rowles, 1983) but more typical of those who live out their older years far from their place of origin are those who remain nearer where their adult lives transpired. The complex psychology involved in decisions to age in place is notable in the responses of the vast majority of our samples, from varied sites around the country.

KEEPING UP WITH AGING FRIENDS AND RELATIVES

In the past year, I have been confronted with the voluntary moves of several dear relatives and friends, announced through change-of-address cards (otherwise unexplained) or through Christmas greetings (often with a partial explanation of their decision).

Given our concern in gerontology with the maintenance of networks, it seems to me that we now ought to spend some research energy on the continuities and discontinuities in female-to-female relationships in older age in relation to geographic mobility.

My friends and relations seem positively excited about the moving decisions they have made. They ask me to "keep in touch" and "to visit." In one case, the new residence is 50 miles north of Seattle, Washington: in another it is 50 miles from Brownsville, Texas. Neither location is easy to access.

The "vagabonds" (as one cousin called herself) seem mostly to be couples and I worry about what happens to the wife in this very new scene, if, as so often happens, the husband dies. On a more positive note, it also seems worth exploring the gratification of new identification in place and of perceptions of continued control. Such a subgroup of late-life women movers to environments radically different from their past might be defined as high-risk takers.

Studies of determinants of housing choice among elderly now most often show either a preference for remaining in place in a long established home and neighborhood or a push toward a health-related environment due to actual or perceived deterioration in capacity to handle activities of daily living. Although networks are considered secondary, but important, in both of these sets of respondents, they seem decidedly and surprisingly distant in the minds of this mobile subgroup of friends I am now encountering—rather more like a geographically (but not socially) "disengaging" population. My correspondents describe new affiliations with folk dance and church groups, fresh encounters with nature and, perhaps, an extension of identity in affirmation of continued vigor.

CULTURES AND AGING WOMEN: GRANDMOTHER AS HOUSEHOLD HEAD

Older women in extended families have been traditional in Japan. In recent years, there has been a movement among older, middle-class, urban widows to remain independently housed or, at least, to attach a separate complete unit on their site for an adult child/grandchildren. An interesting mixture of traditional and modern female lifestyle was studied in 1987 in a village outside Nagoya, Japan.

Sited on an 11-generation family compound, a traditional core house has been expanded in relation to additions to and changes in the family.

Over the 2-day visit, there was no doubt who ran the Ohta household. Grandmother (*Obason*) directed where I was to sleep and prepared the futon, supervised the activities of the grandchildren, and directed her daughter-in-law (an elementary-school teacher) and granddaughters in the preparation of meals and serving-cleaning activities. In one interaction, the battle for control so universally typical of the teenage girl with her mother occurred, in this case, with her grandmother. A miniature hat had been placed by the granddaughter over the light switch in her room. The grandmother attempted to remove it, to the great exasperation of the granddaughter who, at least in my presence, maintained control of her space. It is *Obason's* morning task, as it has been that of the oldest woman in this household for 11 generations, to retrieve yesterday's rice ball from the family shrine and to add this blessed morsel to today's newly made rice. The 35-year-old wife of the eldest son will very likely continue this ritual inside that historic house, however, because it is the grandson who will inherit, there is some question, given emerging female perceptions of emancipation in Japan, that the two granddaughters will even be dwelling in three-generation households, much less perform similar obligatory rituals for their husband's family (Bernstein, 1976). This straying from ritual was, in fact, seen in most of the independent households of Japanese middle-class families I studied during the period 1978–1990, where, in virtually all instances the young middle-aged wife worked outside the home. It has also been documented in sociological research on attitudes toward the three-generation family household by younger and older Japanese women who live together with or separate from children (Brody & Campbell, 1986).

"Affiliative" is a word applied to people who relate closely and frequently with members of their own kin group. In the sense of intergenerational living arrangements and living with other relatives, African-American households headed by older women are significantly more frequent than among other U.S. households of aged (Taylor, 1985). Several studies indicate that the presence of other relatives (aunts, uncles, cousins) are often also included, if not continuously, for varying periods of time. In contrast to white households where an occasional older woman is living with adult children in their home, older African-American women tend to take their adult children into their owned or rented home. Given that the combination of economic imperatives and a shortage of adequate housing have been oppressive problems for these Americans (both urban and rural), it would be difficult to argue that these living arrangements are all by "preference" and are inevitably psychosocially satisfactory. A documentary film made in the late 1970s, *Mrs. Graham's House*, by Topper Carew (writer/producer) and Tunney Lee (urban planner) reflects both the pleasant social chaos and the stressful overcrowding that may occur in the course of daily living in such settings. Establishing family rituals appears to be particularly difficult, in that interior space often does not allow regularized family meals at a common table and sleeping arrangements for children and adults are distributed throughout the house so that sleep, homework, and social activity is unpredictably interrupted. The older women on these domestic scenes (grandmothers and aunts) carry the brunt of the household tasks along with the emotional baggage the other family members bring (Taylor, 1985).

The pain of change within a culture is beautifully visualized in *Farewell*, a 1983 Soviet film, which presents the ultimate statement about the "old woman," wrapped in traditional identity with place and in conflict with modernization and technology. All but a few of the other villagers, on an island to be flooded by a new hydroelectric dam, leave for new and modern apartments on the mainland, including her son and grandson. With a handful of remaining villagers, mostly women, watching, she scours the walls and floors of her rural cabin, brings flowers from the fields, and hangs freshly washed curtains. She visits her father's grave. "Which is back, which is forward," her son asks (symbolically) as he tries to reach the island to rescue her by boat, in an intense fog, before the flooding of the island.

WOMEN AND ENVIRONMENTAL IMAGING

What might the most current discussions of interpersonal attachments in old age suggest about the relationships between older women and past and present environments? While Troll (1994) particularly addresses the bonding among three generations of women, she incidentally raises a number of questions about the ways in which objects and places experienced in the past can reinforce these attachments.

To the extent that the mother–daughter relationship in the United States often culminates in the daughter(s) inheriting the bulk of the parents' valued objects and even frequently selects those that hold most meaning to her, we may postulate that, at least for some aging women, being surrounded by these memories of place does regularly recreate the selves of the past and reaffirm identity. That the identity reaffirmed need not necessarily be a positive experience might be tested by addressing reports of inherited "white elephants" or negative memories of place and event associated with certain inherited objects. No focus on this has appeared in the social science literature, in fact there appears to be a tendency to view both attachment and identity as always positive affects.

A methodological note needs to be made in the case of inherited and valued objects and the environmental memories they may elicit. When Rubenstein (1987) asked older people to name and describe the significance of objects in the home that had "personal meaning," he found, in content analysis, that people, self, and events rather than place were primary responses. It may well be that a rephrasing of the initial question and the probes, so that place becomes primary to the recall of the respondent, would result in a much richer collection of past environmental images. As a niece of mine commented on my gifting her one of my mother's seascapes: "Whenever I look at this I will remember walking down grandma's staircase and viewing the whole set of these paintings." She could not have been a more frequent visitor than six times per year to her grandparent's home, but the revisualization was clear to both of us, as I am sure it would be to older inheritors.

Frequency of experiencing a place is often used as a measure of the importance of the place to an older person. I find this measure rather shallow and distant. The issue of salience of environments (positive or negative) to an older woman does not likely correlate with frequency as an independent variable, though possibly it is a mediating variable where other, more intrapsychic issues, are strong. Further, frequency is likely to be only one factor in relation to memories elicited. The power of the event or the interpersonal transaction, relative to the intrapsychic dynamics of the individual, is what gives "place" salience.

FUTURE DIRECTIONS FOR RESEARCH

FUTURE ENVIRONMENTS AND FUTURE WOMEN

Environmental gerontologists have been addressing the current cohorts of over-65 people. These women were born in decades beginning around 1900 and extending to about 1925. Those age cohorts, according to O'Bryant's study of older Ohio widows (O'Bryant, 1987) reflect quite unique and intermittent relationships with work, transportation, and educational environments. Since the cohort beginning 1930, where women came of age near 1950, American women have been exposed to an ever-widening experience of environments, particularly environments of work and education.

Gerry is an interesting example of this cohort. Now 70, she considers her work as an airplane mechanic during World War II only an interlude worthy of a life-sized photo poster permanently installed on a den wall. At age 50+ she had no compunctions about gaining her degree in social work and became, for 20 years of her life, a significant leader in social service planning for the Washington, DC low-income elderly. Her weekly home range, still at this age, is the entire Washington, DC metropolitan area.

Irene, now just 60, who had been an artist, but mostly home-bound in motherhood, took a similar course as a late-life student of social work to accomplish, in her 50s, a leadership role in state mental health planning. Both of these women had few economic pressures to enter the work environment, having intact marriages, professional husbands, and adult children. They are an interface cohort. Most of us in our sixth decade drove cars from adolescence, among the current 75-to-90-year-olds many did not (Lopata, 1980). We traveled beyond our local community and state, many 80-to-90-year-old women did not. The 60 to 75 cohort had television, which showed us, early in adulthood, the places of the world. The 80-to-90-year-olds did not but now do. The domains of choice have clearly expanded for younger women growing older.

If environments and aging women are to be of consequence to the development of feminist knowledge, then cross-sectional research on environmental experiences must be combined with retroactive longitudinal explorations of now older cohorts of women. Many of us in our fifth and sixth decades have never spoken to researchers about our environmental experiences, particularly with regard to work-setting attachments. Women in their third and fourth decades are now, in the United States, increasingly involved in work settings. How will these future elderly view the significance of their varied environments in relation to the aging process? Will they reminisce on the work settings and the relationships attached to them, as men often do? Will the domestic scene be less cardinal to their continuing identities and, thus, less invested relative to their propensity to move in late life?

Environments Outside the Home

If you want to know about the environments inhabited by older women, in any society, reflect on the local activities of daily life and follow these social patterns.

For example, a "behavior setting" in the United States to which a very large proportion of women over the age of 50 are loyally affiliated is the beauty shop. The psychosocial significance of this setting in maintaining self-image and social contact, while not formally validated, is evidenced by the increasing inclusion of such settings as critical services in elderly housing and retirement communities. But the ubiquity of such settings in most normative urban, suburban, and small-town neighborhoods also attests to their active use (see Figure 3).

As well, the shopping mall has become a major, weekly setting to be occupied by women of late middle to older age. Although purchases by this population are relatively small, these locales provide stimulation and active exposure to a broad range of other age groups and to changes in the variety of consumer goods that would otherwise only be incidentally exposed in the media (see Figure 4).

CONCLUSION

Wapner and Craig-Bray (1992) classify the domains of environmental transactions as biological, cognitive, sociocultural, and "personality" or intrapsychic. In the development of understanding of the relationships between the aging woman and her environments, I have chosen the phrase "domains of choice" because it seems, in reviewing individu-

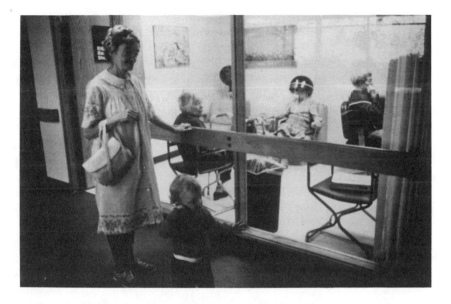

Figure 3. A beauty parlor incorporated into a congregate setting for the elderly in Newton, Massachusetts. Photograph by Sandra C. Howell, 1988.

Figure 4. Older women converge daily in front of the mall/grocery store at Wah Fu housing project in Hong Kong. Photograph by Sandra C. Howell, 1978.

al case material, that different and changing contexts and histories call upon a woman to differently employ one or more, likely several, domains in constructing the environmental surrounding and environmental memories that appear best to meet her perceived needs at different points in her own aging continuum. This conceptualization, although operationally difficult to handle, does more explicitly entertain the temporal processes, so aptly introduced by Altman and perhaps most clearly seen in human transitional states (Altman, 1992).

The special contribution that studies of aging women may make to environment–behavior transactional theory is in the quite striking within-cohort differences we see in transactional modes. Cross-cohort studies of middle age and older women also evidence quite variable environmental experiences, despite the dominance of the local domestic in the oldest cohorts.

In this chapter, I have adopted biographical narratives as the method for uncovering the possible variable that may affect the relationship between older women and the environment. This is an alternative to the search for invariant and universal rules for behaviors in environments, which I see as a premature effort. In a critique of age-based generalizations that neglect within- and between-cohort variability in gerontology research, Nelson and Dannefer (1992) report that a majority (65%) of studies that do report on dispersions show increases in variability with increasing age. Ceci and Bronfenbrenner (1991) ask, "What if the very essence of what is being studied is variable and systematically differentiated by the ecology in which it unfolds?" (p. 30). I agree that this admonition is particularly relevant to begin to understand the multiple processes of building a self-in-environment "story" unique to women. The growing legitimacy of this method has been reviewed by Howard (1991). It is here asserted that no amount of accumulated gender difference data will likely uncover the mechanisms by which individual women process their own environmental history.

Is it likely that recall (however flawed) of past environments and one's evaluations of events related to and decisions made about them reflect the individual's relationship to current environment? We would argue that it is very likely and, indeed, would further put the case that it is the very selectivity of this environmental recall that is fashioning the older individual's model of herself-in-place (see Rowles, 1978; Conway, 1991, on "Everyday Memory"). It is not the response to interview questions from an older woman about her relationship with environment that counts the most in theory building, it is the manifest behavior of the older woman in her acting-out her identity that is most telling. When Edith Cooper moves her way back, in memory, from most personal to broader social spaces and Eleanor persists in her environmental activism, they are making their statement. Consistent manifest behavior in the older woman reflects latent or intrapsychic intentions, I would argue. The reduction of inhibition consequent to personality transformation, which has been commented upon relative to the older woman, allows this conclusion (Gutmann, 1987).

To focus on the woman as self in place and time is a peculiarly Western, even North American, perspective. That is not to say that I am not convinced that this construct has a universal quality but rather that the individual has gender and, thus, literally incorporates a gender identity that places her in a collective. Across the world we learn to be female from our mothers, grandmothers, aunts, and sisters.

Future research should build a redefinition of the experiences of being a woman in changing environments across cultures and across stages in the adult life cycle. The adoption of universal policies that attempt to create gender and age—separating environments for older women, a tendency in the United States, appears to contradict the more integrative direction in environmental experience of younger and middle-aged women in many societies.

The older woman has, at last, nothing to lose by asserting her hegemony over her environment (as our East Boston women demonstrate). In this regard, future cohorts of older women may be psychoenvironmentally closer to their younger, now more assertive, sisters than has, perhaps, been true in the past. To the extent that more women will have experienced educational, work, leisure, travel, and even active political environments in their middle years, we can expect much wider variance and less stereotypic expression in behaviors, cognitions, and affects relative to environments among older women.

Acknowledgments

The author would like to express appreciation to the following people for their contributions to and criticisms of this chapter: Marcella Bothwell, Margaret Huyck, Patricia Parmelee, Shirley O'Bryant, Lillian Troll, and Barbara Turner. The author alone takes responsibility for interpretations of referenced texts.

REFERENCES

Allen, K. R., & Chin-Sang, V. (1990). A lifetime of work: The context and meanings of leisure for aging Black women. *The Gerontologist, 30,* 734–740.
Altman, I. (1992). A transactional perspective on transitions to new environments. *Environment and Behavior, 24,* 268–280.

Bernstein, G. L. (1976). Women in rural Japan. In J. Lebra, J. Paulson, & E. Powers (Eds.), *Women in changing Japan* (pp. 25–49). Stanford: Stanford University Press.

Brody, E. & Campbell, R. (1985). Attitudes toward three generation living among Japanese and American women. *The Gerontologist, 25,* 584–592.

Ceci, S. J., & Bronfenbrenner, U. (1991). On the demise of everyday memory. *American Psychologist, 46,* 27–31.

Conway, M. A. (1991). In defense of everyday memory. *American Psychologist, 46,* 19–26.

Ferree, M. M., & Hess, B. B., (1987). Introduction. In B. B. Hess & M. M. Ferree (Eds.), *Analyzing gender: A handbook of social science research* (pp. 9–30). Newbury Park, CA: Sage.

Field, D., & Millsap, R. E. (1991). Personality in advanced old age: Continuity of change. *Journal of Gerontology, 46,* 299–308.

Gutmann, D. L. (1987). *Reclaimed powers: Toward a new psychology of men and women in later life.* New York: Basic Books.

Howard, G. S. (1991). Culturetales: A narrative approach to thinking, cross cultural psychology and psychotherapy. *American Psychologist, 46,* 187–197.

Howell, S. C. (1983a). The meaning of place in old age. In G. Rowles & R. Ohta (Eds.), *Aging and milieu* (pp. 97–107). New York: Academic Press.

Howell, S. C. (1983b). *Determinants of housing choice.* Final Report. Cambridge, MA: MIT Department of Architecture.

Howell, S. C. (1983c). *Women, housing and habitability.* Unpublished paper. Symposium on gender-related issues: Women in housing. Seattle, WA: University of Washington.

Krivo, L. J., & Mutchler, J. E. (1989). Elderly persons living alone: The effect of community context on living arrangement. *Journal of Gerontology, 44,* S54–62.

Lawton, M. P. (1990). Residential environment and self-directedness among older people. *American Psychologist, 45,* 638–640.

Lawton, M. P. (1985). The elderly in context: Perspectives from environmental psychology and gerontology. *Environment and Behavior, 17,* 501–519.

Longino, C., & Serow, W. (1992). Regional differences in the characteristics of elderly return migrants. *Journal of Gerontology, 47,* S38–43.

Lopata, H. Z. (1980). The Chicago woman: A study of patterns of mobility and transportation. *Signs: Journal of Women in Culture and Society, 5,* 161–169.

Lopata, H. Z. (1973). *Widowhood in the American city.* Cambridge, MA: Schenkman.

Nelson, E. A., & Dannefer, D. (1992). Aged heterogeneity: Fact or fiction? The fate of diversity in gerontological research. *The Gerontologist, 32,* 17–23.

Neugarten, B. L. (1964). *Personality in middle and late life.* New York: Atherton Press.

O'Bryant, S. (1987). Attachment to home and support systems of older widows in Columbus, Ohio. In H. Z. Lopata (Ed.), *Widows: V2: North America* (pp. 48–70). Durham, NC: Duke University Press.

Riger, S. (1992). Epistemological debates, feminist voices. *American Psychologist, 47,* 730–740.

Rowles, G. (1978). *Prisoners of space?* Boulder, CO: Westview.

Rowles, G. (1983). Between worlds: A relocation dilemma for the Appalachian elderly. *International Journal of Aging and Human Development, 17,* 301–314.

Rubinstein, R. L. (1987). Never married elderly as a social type: Re-evaluating some images. *The Gerontologist, 27,* 108–113.

Rubinstein, R. L., & Parmelee, P. A. (1992). Attachment to place and the representation of the life course by the elderly. In I. Altman & S. Low (Eds.), *Place attachment* (pp. 139–163). New York: Plenum.

Soldo, B. J., Wolf, D. A., & Agree, E. M. (1990). Family, households and care arrangements of frail older women. *Journal of Gerontology, 45,* S238–249.

Taylor, R. J. (1985). Extended family as a source of support to elderly Blacks. *The Gerontologist, 25,* 488–495.

Troll, L. E. (1994). Family connectedness of old women: Attachments in later life. In Barbara F. Turner & Lillian E. Troll (Eds.), *Women growing older: Psychological perspectives* (pp. 169–201). Thousand Oaks, CA: Sage.

Wapner, S., & Craig-Bray, L. (1992). Person-in-environment transitions: Theoretical and methodological approaches. *Environment and Behavior, 24,* 161–188.

Wright, G. (1981). *Building the dream: A social history of housing in America.* Cambridge, MA: MIT Press.

—— 6 ——

Working at Home

FRAMEWORKS OF MEANING

KATHLEEN CHRISTENSEN

INTRODUCTION

More women are gainfully employed than at any other period of U.S. history. There has been a particularly rapid growth in the labor force participation rate of women with children. In fact, the labor participation rate for women with children under the age of 6 has doubled since 1970. By 1991, 60% of these mothers were gainfully employed, compared to 30% in 1970 (Institute for Women's Policy Research, 1992, p. 3).

The task of combining work and family for most working mothers remains difficult. The division of domestic labor continues to fall disproportionately on women in the family, prompting most to work what has been referred to as a double shift (Hochschild, 1990). Many working mothers pursue a variety of strategies to offset this burden of two full-time jobs, including ceding a bulk of the domestic responsibility to nannies, child-care centers, or housekeepers; reducing their work schedules to part-time or job-sharing arrangements; or bringing their paid labor into the home. It is those in the last category who are the focus of this chapter. If these home-based working women are company employees, they are typically referred to as telecommuters; if they are self-employed, they are characterized as home-based business owners or independent

KATHLEEN CHRISTENSEN • Environmental Psychology Program, Graduate School and University Center, City University of New York, New York, New York 10036.
Women and the Environment, edited by Irwin Altman and Arza Churchman. Plenum Press, New York, 1994.

contractors. The objective of this chapter is to examine how and why some women with young children are more effective than others at working at home.

Given the fact that both public policy and private initiatives in the United States and abroad promote work at home as a strategy for solving work–family demands, it is critical to examine the conditions under which working at home becomes a viable work–family strategy.

WOMEN WORKING AT HOME

According to the most recent national figures released by the U.S. Bureau of Labor Statistics (BLS), approximately 4 million women work 8 or more hours per week at home as part of their primary (nonfarm) jobs (Horvath, 1986). The majority appears to be women who bring work home as overtime from their primary jobs. But 1.3 million of them work exclusively at home; they are predominantly white, married, self-employed women who work an average of 27 hours a week and live in two-parent households. Approximately 600,000 of these 1.3 million women have children under the age of 6. Proprietary market research indicates that these numbers of home-based working mothers have increased steadily since the BLS figures were collected in 1985 (Miller, 1992).

Although an interdisciplinary body of literature on women who work at home is developing, it remains relatively nascent. As recently as 1983, when I began my research, the indexes of major U.S. periodicals did not include such key words as "home-based work" or "telecommuting," that is, the substitution of the computer for the commute for company employees. Yet, in less than a decade, a body of not only interdisciplinary but also international research has emerged that examines the phenomenon of women and home-based work from a multitude of critical perspectives, including historical trends in the United States (e.g., Boris, 1989a,b); persistence of industrial homework in the United States (e.g., Beach, 1989; Fernandez-Kelly & Garcia, 1989a; Dangler, 1989); the relationship between occupational status, particularly professional and clerical, and the experiences of working at home (e.g., Ahrentzen, 1990; Christensen, 1985b, 1988a, 1989b; Costello, 1988, 1991; Gerson & Kraut, 1988; Horowitz, 1986); the role of home-based work in the informal and contingent economy (e.g., Christensen, 1988c; Christensen & Murphee, 1988; Fernandez-Kelly & Garcia, 1989a,b; Lozano, 1989); the relationship between the state and homework (e.g., Daniels, 1989; Iverson, 1988; Simonson, 1988); organized labor's positions on professional and clerical work at home (e.g., Chamot, 1988; Christensen, 1993a; Costello, 1991; du Rivage & Jacobs, 1989; Gerson, 1993); the

manifestation of work at home across the life course of women (Christensen, 1993b); corporate policies and programs regarding work at home
(e.g., Christensen, 1989c; International Labour Office, 1990; Olson,
1988, 1989); and roles and role expectations, both implicit and explicit,
women bring to the experience of working in their homes (e.g., Ahrentzen, 1990, 1992; Christensen, 1985b, 1988a; Costello, 1990, 1991, Gerson
& Kraut, 1988).

Although the majority of empirical research done on home-based
work in the United States has focused on white middle- and working-
class women, recent efforts have broadened this focus to include the
experiences of African-American women (Ahrentzen, 1992; Boris, 1989b)
and Hispanic women in the United States (Fernandez-Kelly & Garcia,
1989a,b). There has also been a growing body of work on home-based
working women of different classes in Canada, as well as in Great Brit-
ain and Mexico (e.g., Allen & Wolkowitz, 1987; Huws, 1984; Johnson &
Johnson, 1982; Beneria & Roldan, 1987). In addition, two recent issues of
the *Conditions of Work Digest* published by the International Labour Organization (ILO) have examined contemporary international experiences
with industrial homework and professional and clerical telework (International Labour Organization, 1989, 1990).

Despite this growing body of research on home-based work, little
systematic research has examined the conditions of work and their relationship to the physical environment of the home. When the environment has been addressed, the research has primarily focused on how
the women establish spatial, social, and temporal boundaries between
their wage and nonwage work in the home (e.g., Ahrentzen, 1990;
Christensen, 1988a; Costello, 1991; McLaughlin, 1981). Both Ahrentzen's
and McLaughlin's research, however, have extended beyond the boundary-
setting question. Based on her study of 104 male and female home-based
workers' experiences in working at home, Ahrentzen (1989) provided a
detailed assessment of the physical features that these workers, typically
self-employed, wanted in their actual work spaces and in situating those
work spaces vis-à-vis other rooms in the house. This research also examined the access of the workers' home to other services in their immediate
neighborhoods. McLaughlin's work (1981) found that the nature of the
physical work space was a major determinant of the women's satisfaction in working home.

With the exception of McLaughlin's work, however, there has been
limited theoretical and empirical attention paid as to why or how some
women are satisfied and successful in working at home and others not.
Addressing that question in the context of my long-term research is the
aim of this chapter.

Since 1983, I have conducted research on the experiences of people, particularly women, who work in their homes. In January 1985, I directed a survey of 13,521 women who either already worked at home or who wanted to work there[1] (Christensen, 1985a, 1988a, 1989b). Of that total, 53% (n = 6,200) were engaged in wage-earning work at home; and 55% of those actually working at home (n = 3,379) had children 17 years or younger (Christensen, 1988a, 1989b). As was the case with the BLS statistics on female home-based workers, the women in my sample were predominantly white, married, self-employed, and working on part-time bases.

Subsequent to this survey, I conducted in-depth, in-person interviews with 100 of the survey's respondents in their homes in the three metropolitan areas of New York City, Chicago, and San Francisco. Although the purposes of the research were multiple and have been described elsewhere in more detail (Christensen, 1985b, 1988a,b, 1989a,b, 1993a,b), a question continued to recur: Why is it that some mothers were better able than others to do wage-earning work at home?

Each of these female homeworkers was faced with having to work in an environment that had a number of competing family demands on it and that had traditionally been defined as a private, domestic sphere and not a public wage-earning one. Although, as noted, earlier research focused on the nature and exclusivity of the worksite as a factor in successfully working at home (McLaughlin, 1981) that did not appear to be a sufficient explanation for success in light of my research. In analyzing the transcripts and the survey results, it appeared that the ability to work at home was not a simple function of the availability or size of the work space or of its exclusivity for work.

I observed women with their offices in small closets who could work effectively there, whereas others with large rooms on separate levels of their homes who could not. I saw women who worked at small work stations in the corners of kitchens or dining rooms, shared with other family activities, who functioned as adequately as those who had taken over extra bedrooms.

FRAMEWORKS OF MEANING

It became clear to me, through the analysis of my interview data, that the ability to work successfully at home requires a mutually enhanc-

---

[1]The survey, entitled National Survey on Women and Home-Based Work, was published in *Family Circle Magazine*, January 15, 1985. This survey was a part of a 3-year research project funded by the U.S. Department of Health and Human Services. The full results of the survey data are reported in Christensen (1989a). Selected data on clerical homeworkers are included in Christensen (1989b). Case studies that were conducted as a follow-up to the survey are reported in Christensen (1988a).

ing configuration of space, time, social relations, and self-identity.[2]
These four frameworks of meaning coexist and jointly define one another, with the self serving an integrative function in both shaping and
being shaped by the frameworks of time, space, and social relationships.

Rather than conceiving of space, time, social relationships, and self
as mutually interdependent parts, I think it more productive to conceive
of them as *frameworks*, in essence, as organized and organizing structures of meaning. For example, the framework of space, whether it
involves the physical patterning of a home, workplace, neighborhood,
or other place has its own internal organization of meaning that helps to
organize the self's actions and relationships with others. In effect, a
space carries meaning that does not nor cannot exist independently of
the self and that can change dynamically over the course of time in
evolution with changes in the frameworks of self and social relations.

It follows from this line of reasoning that the spatial framework,
that is, the physical environment, cannot be treated as if it exists independent of the self, nor can the self be treated as if it exists independent
of the physical environment. In effect, the self is constitutive of the
world, and the world is constitutive of the self.

Self and environment are primordially bound together and can be
conceptually separated for purposes of analysis, but in that separation
also lies a violation of their underlying being. One cannot have self
without environment, and one cannot have environment without self.
Therefore, to understand the complex, symbiotic relationship between
self and environment, we need to make transparent how the self is not
separate from space; but space, like time and social relations, is an a
priori framework by which and through which the self gives meaning to
his or her actions and that, in turn, can evolve and change over time.[3]
Although the emphasis has thus far been on the self as the integrative
force in mediating the other frameworks of meaning, social relations and
culture can also play such roles.

Working at home, as an event, does not occur in a space, time, or set
of social relations that have no organized meaning. Rather, when a
woman conceives of or begins to execute work at home, the three frameworks of meaning, space, time, and social relations, in which she oper-

[2]The theoretical basis for this point of view is embedded in the transactionalist approach.
See Altman and Rogoff (1987) for a more thorough discussion of the transactional approach to psychology. Also, see Werner, Altman, and Oxley (1985) for a transactionalist
analysis of home environments.

[3]For a detailed philosophic exposition of the relationships among culture, space, and time,
see Ernest Cassirer (1977). Standing in a Kantian tradition, Cassirer argues that space and
time are a priori categories of the mind that take on different forms in different cultures
and at different points in time.

ates, already possess certain organized meanings that must be adapted to accommodate her work. The home has its own internal design and organization; the timing for family events have their own rhythm; and the social relations with her spouse and children reflect negotiated roles and role expectations. Each woman has varying degrees of freedom within which she can negotiate the reconstruction of her own self and the frameworks of space, time, and social relations in her efforts to work at home.

My research thus far indicates that the most viable configuration of self, space, time, and social relations for a woman working at home is one in which she has strong, clear, multiple role identities, a well-defined workspace, clear, mutually agreed upon social roles and relations within the family, and predictability and control over events in time. Before presenting the three case studies, it is important to explicate in more detail what I mean by these four frameworks of self, space, time, and social relations.

The concept of *self* has a long and complicated tradition in philosophy and psychology. For purposes of my analysis, I focus on one dimension of the framework of self, the dimension of role identity—how one self-consciously defines oneself as a function of the social role(s) one plays. It has formally been defined in psychology as the "character and the role that an individual devises for himself as an occupant of a particular social position" (McCall & Simmons, 1978, p. 65).

It would be a mistake to think of role identity in a socially isolated fashion. One's role identity is constructed by an individual in a social context; each role, in effect, is imbued with both the idiosyncratic expectations of the individual, as well as being informed by prevailing social and cultural norms (Deaux, 1993). For each role, there are certain implicit and explicit expectations about appropriate behaviors that can lead to specific social rules. Each self typically has multiple role identities, although one may be more salient to that person's overall self-definition than would be others (Stryker & Statham, 1985).

In the three case studies presented in this chapter, each woman has at least four role identities, that of wife, mother, homemaker, and wage earner. The saliency of role identities and the degree of confusion or conflict with her roles will vary across women, however.

At the most primordial level, the self never stands alone. Self always stands in a tradition of *social relations* that include the relationship between self and spouse and with members of the nuclear family, extended family, workplace, ethnic, or religious community. These social relations, in turn, stand in a culture shaped in part, by generational norms. The individual self can never be separated from the social or cultural traditions in which she stands. How one thinks of oneself and sets one's course of action is tied to who one is vis-à-vis these multiple and overlapping social and cultural traditions in which one is embedded. For purposes of this chapter, the social relation's framework by which and through which the self defines herself and configures space and time include the self's multiple relations with spouse, children, parents, and work and religious communities.

For purposes of this chapter, *space* is not defined, in a Newtonian sense, as a container separate from the self in which activities occur. Rather, the macrogeography of the home, including the spatial configuration of the rooms and the microgeography of the individual work space constitute the physical frameworks in which, through which, and by which women give physical definition to their work and communicate that meaning to their family or colleagues. As has been noted, the home is an inherently ambiguous place in which to locate wage-earning work. Although exceptions exist (e.g., Ahrentzen, 1992; Hewes, 1981), most extant homes in the United States have not been designed to accommodate wage-earning work. In most cases, traditional domestic spaces are used for wage-earning activities. This traditional spatial framework of meaning renders many home-based working women vulnerable to the domestic messages of the home (Ahrentzen, 1992; Christensen, 1988a).

As one woman I interviewed claimed regarding working at home:

> You're juggling so many things, and it's constantly there. When you're in an office, the only thing you really do is work. You might think of the house, and say, "Oh God, I've got to cook something for dinner," or "Did I defrost the roast?" But when you get up to go get a soda from the soda machine, that's all you're doing. At home I get up to get a soda, and the refrigerator says, "Better clean me." Or I go to the bathroom and I think, "I better clean that." It's always there, hitting me in the face. (Christensen, 1988a, 2b)

As a result, many women must rethink and literally reconfigure their physical homes and their traditional meanings of it so that the home supports rather than impedes their activities of work and their identities as wage earners. To do so may require a concomitant reconfiguration of their role identities and responsibilities vis-à-vis their domestic spaces. The more the self and the members of her family agree about her roles and her work, the easier it will be to reconfigure the physical and social meanings of the home.

In itself, *time* possesses a very complicated structure and even more so when applied to the home (Werner, Altman, & Oxley, 1985). For purposes of this chapter, I look primarily at time in the sense of cycles in which and by which events and experiences occur and recur. These cycles have their own rhythm, predictability, and pace. Pace refers to the relative rapidity or density of experience (Werner, Altman, & Oxley, 1984). A viable arrangement is one in which the events of work and their relationship to the events of family have their own rhythmic cycle, such as working Monday through Fridays, 9 A.M. to 12 P.M. This rhythm, in turn, usually reflects a certain even volume and pace of work and affords the women working at home a high degree of predictability and control.

An arrhythmic pattern often reflects an uneven volume or pacing of work, which can, in turn, lead to a lower level of predictability and control. Not surprisingly, higher levels of predictability and control lead to greater satisfaction in working at home than do lower levels. In effect, certain temporal qualities such as rhythm and pacing constitute a framework by which events in the family and work can be organized, controlled, and predicted.

About This Chapter

This chapter will be structured around three case studies that I have conducted as part of my longer-term research project. As reflects the BLS figures on mothers working at home, each of the women profiled is white, married, and living with her husband. Each is also the mother of a child under the age of 6. All live in single-family detached homes in suburban U.S. communities. I have changed their names and hometowns to ensure that their anonymity is protected, although the facts are true and their quotations are direct.

CASE STUDIES

I will present and organize each case study around the four frameworks of meaning: self, social relations, time, and space. It will be apparent by the organization of each case how the frameworks coexist and jointly define the situation in which the woman lives. In some cases, individual frameworks are so profoundly interdependent with others that individual sections cannot be written for each but rather must be presented together.

Jennifer Young

A strong, confident woman, Jennifer feels that she has been capable of exercising her choices all of her life. The eldest of four children, she was brought up to believe that no difference existed between boys' chores and girls' chores. She did them all—from chopping wood to mowing the lawn to sewing, cleaning, and cooking. "It made me feel like I could do anything I wanted, that I was not limited." And what she wanted more than anything was to have a family and be the kind of wife and mother she was brought up in her Mormon faith to revere.

As will be clear in the subsequent case study, Jennifer's case reflects a successful configuration of role identities, social relations, space, and time. As an active member of the Church of Jesus Christ of the Latter Day Saints, she receives strong social support for her domestic roles as wife, mother, and homemaker. Perhaps because of this support from fellow Mormons, she feels empowered in her domestic roles, enabling her to justify her pursuit of a wage-earning identity. Perhaps more than any other woman I interviewed, Jennifer possesses the strongest and least conflicted role identities, allowing her to structure her work in space and time in a clear and effective manner.

Role Identities and Social Relations over Time

From a young age, Jennifer knew who she was and what she wanted. After high-school graduation, she attended a local college for 2 years but quit when she married her high-school boyfriend, Jim, also a Mormon. Because her primary goal was to be a good wife, mother, and homemaker, Jennifer saw no need to finish college or make specific plans for a wage-earning career.

By the time they married, Jim had already started a construction company, capitalized through family loans. He and Jennifer had a clear understanding about their priorities: They were determined that after the birth of their first child that they would never put themselves in a financial situation that required Jennifer to take a paying job. To do otherwise would undercut Jennifer's beliefs about her role and responsibilities as a mother:

> I decided that I couldn't have kids and delegate that responsibility to some one else. If I made the decision to have children, then it was my responsibility to raise them. You make a compromise when you delegate that authority to someone else.

It was a compromise she was unwilling to make. According to Jennifer, a good mother is not just a child's physical caretaker but more importantly is his or her moral teacher.

> If I let someone else raise my child, they would teach my child what is acceptable and not. They would teach them what is right and wrong. What

they teach might be different from what we believed. Then I would have to
live with my children as they were raised by someone else.

Raising her children has also meant being completely involved in
their lives and being there even when they are not aware and do not care
if she is around. Jennifer wants to ensure that her children have the
security and knowledge that she is always available to them. These
terms for being a full-time mother are deeply ingrained. "Of course, this
is what a good mother is. I just couldn't be any other way. I never
thought to question it. This is what I was brought up to do."

As an active member of her church, Jennifer is surrounded by
friends and family who share her values. She can depend on them for
moral, social, and practical support as needed. Furthermore, these
religious-based values have enabled her to resist what often is a strong
message from the larger secular society that the role of homemaker is a
devalued one. As a result, Jennifer maintains very positive and unconflicted notions about herself in her domestic roles. "I love to clean. I love
to cook. I love to sew, and I love to decorate things. I even love to do
the grocery shopping—weird house-wifely kinds of things. It is really
an art."

She takes great pride in doing all of these things well. "You can be
either a frump or you can really be an all-out, knock-out, drag-out, walk-
right-out-of-Vogue housewife. That's what I want to be."

And she is. At 5'10", she walks with the pronounced confidence of
someone at peace with herself. Because of this confidence, Jennifer experiences little difficulty in asserting her needs as they develop and
change over time. This became apparent in her need for wage-earning
work. Although she and Jim structured their lives so they could live on
his annual income, she decided shortly after the birth of their first
daughter, in 1980, that she wanted to earn money:

> I am a very independent person and the thought of Jim making all the money
> and me spending all the money kind of grated against my nerves. Also, I
> didn't want to be just a mom, because I am a person before anything else,
> and I thought it was important that my children see me in a many-faceted
> way.

She recognized that her job at home as wife and mother was full-time
and fulfilling, but she wanted to keep some of her individual identity
through a paying job.

She had been sewing since she was a teenager and decided to start
sewing for pay. "I was basically lucky. I had a talent that was marketable
and that I could do from home." Jim understood her desire to work for
pay but also felt that she should do it at home so she would continue to

fulfill her role as a stay-at-home mother. "He and I came up with the idea of me working at home. It wasn't like I had to sell him on it. He was open to it. His only concern was whether I could handle it."

Her priorities were clear from the start. "Work is real important to me as an outlet, but it will never be the number one thing in my life. My family will always come first and I will never put work before it."

The couple had their second child in 1982 and their third in late 1983. By the time Jennifer was 26, she had three children under the age of 5 and was working 25 to 30 hours a week sewing for clients. Because she works more out of psychological need than for financial survival, she has a traditional attitude toward her earnings: "My money is my money—it's the fun money. His money is boring—it pays the bills. My money pays for us to go out on Friday nights or to take the kids to the zoo or to McDonald's."

This attitude toward money is deeply buried in the traditional terms of marriage in which the woman does not have to work for pay, because she has the full responsibility for being wife, mother, and homemaker. Any work she does for pay is done out of choice and pursued only so long as it does not in any way hinder her abilities to fulfill her obligations at home. It is within this kind of value structure that the notion of "pin money" arises, as well as the notion of women's work out of interest, whereas men work out of necessity.

Although their paying work may not be taken as seriously as their husband's, their unpaid work in the family is. In traditional marriages, such as Jennifer and Jim's, the roles of wife and mother are so powerful that a woman does not need a paycheck to exert power and influence in the home. Her ability to exercise influence—particularly over the private spaces and matters of the family—derives from her domestic role identities.

Space

One of the marks of influence for a woman who works for pay at home is her ability to claim work space. Two things are interesting in Jennifer's case. One is that it appears to be the power of her domestic roles that have enabled her to claim space for wage-earning work. And, two, sewing historically has been the only work a woman could do that allowed her to claim private space in the home. Except for sewing rooms, the American home has never been designed to give women separate workrooms of their own. Men have had their studies, libraries, dens, workrooms, and even garages. Children have had bedrooms, which often in the middle class are not shared, playrooms, and tree houses. But most women have never had a room they could completely call their own. They share their bedrooms with their husbands and manage the remaining home and its operations.

As a result, most women who work for pay at home have to carve out a space for themselves that was initially devoted to some other purpose. Typically they take leftover space such as a spare bedroom or a corner of the basement, or they share space with other activities such as in the living or dining rooms, the master bedroom, the family room, or the recreation room. In the course of my in-depth research, Jennifer emerged as the only woman who physically displaced family activities in order to provide herself with a separate room for her work.

She was convinced that as long as she was going to work on delicate and valuable fabrics, she deserved and needed a separate place in which to safeguard them. Yet, their small three-bedroom ranch house provided no extra room. If she was going to have separate work space with a door, she would have to use one of the bedrooms, which entailed putting all three children into another bedroom—which she did.

She took the smallest of the three bedrooms and converted it into her sewing room. Facing the front yard, it's filled with morning sunlight, filtered through plants that hang in front of the window. A large table holding her sewing machine, telephone, and daily working sits at right angles to the window. Next to the table stands a tall wardrobe in which hang her clients' projects, and across the room is a hopechest she has covered with cushions to serve as a couch on which the children, clients, or visitors can sit. In addition, a large, comfortable recliner is in the corner.

> I have made this room just like I like it. It is sacred territory. I revere this room
> to the point where I have two locks on the door. If we go out at night, we
> make it very clear to the baby-sitter that the kids are not allowed in this room.
> I have it as a real sanctuary.

Every evening after she puts her children to bed, she goes to her sanctuary to study and prepare her next morning's seminary class that she teachers Monday through Friday.

By creating this room to suit her work and personal needs, Jennifer reinforces her identities as a wage earner, Mormon, and her own person. The room becomes a powerful means by which she expresses herself and supports who she is. But space in and of itself is not capable of completely framing a person and the activities of her roles. Time also serves as an important framework by which and through which she can assert who she is. The more control she exercises over the volume and pacing of work within the rhythm of family rituals the more effective she can be in predicting her schedule for executing her domestic and wage-earning responsibilities.

Time

Jennifer tries to keep to a regular work schedule, sewing in the mornings from 10:00 to 12:00, in the afternoons from 1:00 to 3:00, and some evenings from 8:00 to 10:00, but she changes her times if her children need attention. Otherwise, the children are welcome in her room while she works because she normally can talk to them while she sews. They never feel entirely left out. This arrangement allows Jennifer to work while the children are awake, rather than having to work only when they are asleep or out of the house. Because there are three of them, they occupy themselves playing—and fighting—with each other. She keeps the door open to monitor them and can quickly tell if they need her attention.

Because Jennifer does not "need" the money and does not want to work into the night, she sets limits on what she can accomplish.

> You just have to have a basic sense of priority. I can just look at what I have to do that day and set my priorities—I can do this and I can't do that. I can only spend so much time on this and I need to leave that open. If clients call and ask for more, I just say no.

Although she is very professional and will not disappoint a client to whom she has made a commitment, she has the luxury of turning down additional work.

Jennifer has been successful in controlling and predicting her flow of work in her home, but less successful in integrating her work schedule into her daughter's school schedule, largely because people often do not take working at home as seriously as they do work that is done outside of the home.

> Most people can't get it through their thick heads that I work since I work at home. Like at my daughter's kindergarten. They asked whether I wanted her in the morning or afternoon sessions and I said morning. They asked me if I worked and I said yes. Then they asked where and I said at home. They acted like I didn't really work.

As a result, Jennifer has become an outspoken advocate of women who work in their homes. "I really push the point. I say 'I work.' I don't care where I work, I work."

In many respects, Jennifer's case represents the most viable configuration of self, space, time, and social relations for working at home. Her multiple role identities are clear, strong, and confident; she knows who she is and what her priorities are regarding her identities. She exercises control over the temporal pacing of her work and over the spatial allocation of work activities and family activities. As a result of this control, her work possesses a predictability in time and space. She knows when and where she is going to work on daily, weekly, and monthly cycles. Her role responsibilities regarding her family and work are well-defined and complimentary to the role responsibilities of her husband. Because the nature of her work allows her children constant access to her, the work has not undercut her ability to meet the terms of the good mother that she set for herself.

SUSAN CARLTON

On a continuum of viability for work at home, Jennifer's case clearly represents the high end of viability. Susan Carlton's case, on the other hand, represents the low end of that continuum. Her particular configuration of self, space, time and social relations make working at home difficult. It is not surprising, therefore, that in contrast to Jennifer's satisfaction with her arrangement, Susan is profoundly dissatisfied.

Role Identities over Time

Susan's self-definition has historically been vague and unfocused. As a sophomore in high school, she began working as a salesclerk at the local JC Penney store. After graduation she stayed on not so much because she liked the work, but because she had little interest in pursuing other options. After 4 years at Penney's, Susan married Michael, got pregnant the next year, and quit her sales job. "Deciding to quit never fazed me, I guess. I really didn't think too much one way or another about whether I would ever work again."

When asked how she initially thought of herself and her relationship with her husband, Susan spoke of her roles as wife and mother in traditional terms. She assumed that her husband would financially support the family and that she would run the household and raise the children. If she was ever to decide to work for pay again it would be because she wanted to, not because she needed to. Circumstances proved her wrong. When she was 27 with a 4-year-old son and a 1-year-old daughter, her husband was laid off, leaving them with a considerable monthly mortgage payment on their three-bedroom split-level house in the Milwaukee suburbs. Their minimal savings were quickly depleted, and Susan was forced to take a job. Fortunately, her cousin, who owned a local printing business, needed a technical assistant and was willing to train her and let her do the work in her home. She took it. Given that she had no time to prepare emotionally or practically for this change in her role identities and responsibilities, Susan never developed a well-articulated plan for incorporating paid labor into her home and into her family's routine.

After a brief initial training period, Susan started work. Her basic responsibility involves taking the raw text and turning out a final mechanical layout for printing. The work requires concentration, precision, and attention to detail.

Susan took the job intending it to be a transitional arrangement until her husband could find work, but again circumstances intervened. When Michael found his new position, it involved a substantial cut in pay that left him unable to cover their fixed monthly expenses. Susan was forced to keep her home-based work.

Conflicts in Time and Role Identities

Susan's work situation is made particularly difficult because she exercises no control over the volume of work she gets, when she gets it, and when she must complete it. She never knows if she'll get a project that day or the next. And work could come in on a Friday or Saturday as well as on a Monday or Tuesday. The typical cycle of a 5-day work week from Monday through Friday does not hold for Susan. When she does get a project, she has less than 24 hours to turn it around.

On a typical work day, Susan gets a call from her cousin in the morning informing her a job is coming in for her; she picks up the work in midafternoon at his business; and then she drops off the completed job by the next morning.

In addition to the lack of control over the work flow, Susan also experiences difficulty in scheduling work at home. Because her work requires concentration and precision, she cannot do it when her children are around needing her attention and making demands of her. An obvious solution would be for her to hire someone to help care for the children, but she doesn't feel justified in paying for help. Although her work enables the family to pay their mortgage, she feels that because she is home during the day she should watch the children and not spend money for child care.

As a result of not having help, Susan ends up doing most of her work after the children go to sleep at night, resulting in long, exhausting days.

> I get up with my husband about 7 A.M., go downstairs about 7:30, get in 2 hours of work in the morning before my daughter gets up, while my son

> plays in my office with me. He is pretty good. I start work again after they are
> in bed, and work from about 8:30 or 9:00 P.M. and go until 1 or 2 A.M. Then
> my husband still expects me to get up at 7 A.M. and carry on.

This combination of full responsibility for housework and child care
and the lack of control over the amount and pacing of her work have left
her ambivalent about her work and her self-definition as a wage earner.

> My work gives me some self-satisfaction and pride. Before I started working,
> I didn't think I was doing anything particularly worthwhile in my life. So the
> work feels good. But on this particular day and this particular week, I'd like
> to just chuck the whole thing.

Conflicts in Social Relations, Space, and Time

Susan would like to work during the early evening when her husband could watch the children but has found she cannot rely on him for
help. Susan set up her office in a separate room on the lower level of her
home next to the family's recreation room, in which the television set
and children's toys are located. In the evening, she asks her husband to
act as a gatekeeper to keep the children from bothering her while she is
working. She experiences little success.

> I try to go downstairs to my office to work while they are up, but I get a
> million interruptions. It is always, "Mommy this" and "Mommy that." If I try
> to close and lock my door, they just scream. The fact that I am here means
> that I am always interrupted.

A spatial boundary, such as a door, between a woman and her
children proves effective, only insofar as there are social rules of enforc-
ing the separation. In the case of Susan and her husband, the social rules
are nearly nonexistent because their roles are incompletely defined,
leading to conflicts in their social relations.

Rather than seeing his wife as a wage earner who needs support
from him, Michael holds out his assistance in the evening as a bargain-
ing chip to get her to stop work in time to go to bed with him. Many of
their arguments result from a failure in this barter system. "If I ask my
husband to watch the kids, he gets ticked off if I *don't* finish by 11." But
she thinks his help is really no help, anyway.

> Asking him to watch the kids is a joke. I get paid by the hour so every time I
> get interrupted I have to write it down on my log. Some nights there are 20
> entries in a matter of 2 hours. There are times when I feel bitter.

Because she cannot rely on his assistance in the early evening when
the children are awake, she works late at night as her only recourse. "I

can get 5 or 6 hours of straight time in. So I have no choice. I need 5 hours to sit and concentrate and get the job done."

This schedule exhausts her and angers her husband. He can't understand why she can't get her work done during the day, thereby enabling her to spend the evening with him. He fails to recognize or appreciate that during the day she already has a full-time job as mother and homemaker. In fact, Michael feels that Susan works at night for other reasons.

> He told me that he thinks that I use my work as an excuse to avoid being with him. I said that wasn't true, but who knows? Maybe I don't spend as much time with him as he thinks I should. That was one of the things he said last night which made me realize that I never thought about it. He told me that there are some nights when he wants me to go to bed with him, and he thinks that I use work as an excuse not to go to bed together. I never realized that, but maybe subconsciously I have done that in the past. There was never a night where I pretended that I was working. There might be something that would take me 2 hours to do that I could do the next morning, but I will do it at night. Maybe he is right.

His overall attitude perplexes her. "He may not like the time I spend working, but he sure likes the money I bring in. I don't understand his reasoning."

His reasoning seems transparent—he wants a traditional wife, mother, and homemaker who assumes overall responsibility for the home and family, but at the same time his financial circumstances require that he have a wage-earning partner. In his competing expectations for her, he assumes implicitly that it takes little effort to fulfill her domestic roles. He doesn't appreciate the demands of caring for a family and the difficulties Susan encounters in trying to do paid work at home without any effective separation between work and family. He thinks that because she's "just staying home," she should be able to do it all.

There has been a clear breakdown in their understanding of their roles in the family. As a result, Susan has grown increasingly resentful of her husband's critical attitude and feels he has a much easier life, working a 5-day workweek out of the home.

> He can leave his job at the end of the day and say goodbye until the next morning. He knows he never has to work on weekends. There are a lot of weekends that I have to spend at home working, instead of going out and doing something. I never know exactly when I am going to get a job to do.

An essential difficulty in Susan's situation is that Susan has not come to terms with the demand of being a wage earner. Therefore, she has not used her wage-earning role a platform from which to renegotiate the domestic division of labor in the home. Instead, she continues to feel it is her responsibility to care, cook, and clean. She has so internalized these domestic responsibilities that she cannot conceive of other alternatives. As she herself recognizes:

> I don't have the time to do everything I have to do. There are times when my husband comes home from work and I haven't even been able to start dinner. If I am not here to do it, then who is going to?

She justifies continuing as a full-time homemaker by saying, "I am not working full-time, so I guess that the housework is part of my job."

But she's not happy with the arrangement. She would like her husband to offer to help out:

> If he would just offer, just once, to push the vacuum around, to run to the store, to clean a toilet, it would make all the difference in the world. I don't want to have to be a nagging witch, but if he would just take the time to offer once in a while, that would be the most wonderful thing in the world.

Although she wants things to change, it is more of a wish than a demand:

> I wish there was some way that society had brought us all up so that men could take turns with women. A lot of women carry on in the same job a man has, but I don't think men really conceive of what women do all day at home. Whether it is cleaning the toilet, scouring the sink, doing laundry every single day, washing the same dishes every single day—all those sorts of things. I think everybody should go through that.

Susan has forfeited her traditional position of "not working." She feels stressed, overextended, and confused.

The entire domestic scene, involving the question of who is responsible for housework and child care, has never been renegotiated or discussed in any definitive fashion in Susan and Michael's household. Domestic roles have stayed traditionally divided, despite the fact that Susan has taken on a wage-earning role over which she has little temporal control. Despite these difficulties Susan still finds the work intrinsically gratifying, particularly compared to how she thought of herself before she started working for pay. As she noted earlier, "Before I started working I didn't think I was doing anything particularly worthwhile."

Susan's case reveals a configuration of self, space, and time and social relations that is not mutually enhancing and does not create viable conditions for working at home. Ironically, the only framework that works somewhat well in her case is her work space that, in principle, could be sufficiently separate from the family. But in lieu of well-defined social rules and relationships it's not effectively separate. As her case clearly illustrates, the spatial framework, although a necessary condition for work at home, is by no means a sufficient one.

Although Jennifer's and Susan's cases represent opposite ends of the spectrum regarding viability of work at home, the next case represents a middle-ground position. Although Lisa Jacobi's case reflects various role confusions and conflicts, she has been able to configure reasonably well the space of her home, the timing of her work, and her relationship with her husband in such ways that working at home works, but within bounds and not without costs.

LISA JACOBI

Throughout the 1970s and later, many women eschewed the traditional roles of wife and homemaker, adopting a framework of identity that focuses more on pursuing college educations, careers, and equitable division of labor in the home. As a result, the salient identity for many of these women is that of the working woman—at least, until they have children. Lisa Jacobi is a case in point.

Role Identities and Social Relations over Time

At 22, Lisa Jacobi would have been shocked to hear that one day she would quit her job to stay home and raise her daughters. She had graduated from college, and was hired as a management trainee with the East Coast offices of AT&T, with every intention of working her way up the corporate ladder. Over the next 10 years, she did exactly that, eventually being promoted to regional manager, a job she loved:

> I had to meet regularly with managers and employees in our stores. It required me to be on the road a lot. I loved my job. I loved working with people. I always felt like I was on stage.

During that time, she met and married Stewart, an economist for the federal government. From the outset they had an explicit understanding that in their marriage they were full partners—both in the workplace and home. Neither's career was to be subordinated to the other's. As their incomes were virtually identical, it was easy to avoid the trap of assuming that the person with the higher income would exercise greater power in the family's decision making.

Although Lisa assumed overall responsibility for the house, Stewart took on many of the tasks so that the burdens were more evenly divided than in traditional marriages, such as those of Jennifer's and Susan's.

Given the significance of both Lisa's and Stewart's careers to their identities and the parity of their relationship, it was assumed that both would continue to work after they had children. "I always thought it wouldn't be a big deal, that somehow I'd juggle everything," said Lisa.

At 32, Lisa gave birth to their first child, Ellen. To Lisa's surprise and bewilderment, becoming a parent caused her to reevaluate her situation. While on maternity leave she began to take a hard look at her job, its travel demands, the realities of motherhood, and her conception of herself as a mother. She no longer wanted to be on the road several days a week. Furthermore, she quickly learned that although she previously could exercise a fair degree of control over her work schedule, she could not do so over her home schedule—"a baby just doesn't adhere to any type of schedule." She also found it difficult to find appropriate infant care. She spent the first months of her maternity leave scouting out child care. She was horrified at much of what she saw, finding some unfit "even for a dog." But even when she did find quality care, she remained reluctant to leave her baby in the care of someone else. She began to remember the emotional texture of her own childhood. As a child in the 1950s, she recalled that

> my mom was always there when we got home. We were always able to burst in the door and tell her what we did. I remember how annoyed I was the few times she wasn't home. How dare she not be home? I wanted my mother to be there.

She began to translate these memories into standards for her own life as a mother and became convinced that staying at home was the only way that she could provide the moral guidance she wanted to give her children.

> If you have a set of values that are real important, you want to be able to transfer them to your children. If you are away from the home 40 to 50 hours a week, then someone else is influencing your children a lot more than you are.

Confusions in Role Identities

She and Stewart concluded that one of them had to stay home. Stewart was interested in and willing to be the prime nurturer and would have been able to because he had accrued extensive leave time at his job. But to add to Lisa's confusion, she found that she couldn't accept that possibility or its implications.

> I know that this feeling of mine isn't innate, that it comes from all the conditioning I had as a kid. Mothers were always the ones who stayed home and took care of the kids. When Stewart offered to do that, I could not accept

the idea that he'd be the mom and I'd be the breadwinner. I just couldn't reconcile that switch within myself.

Although she was not emotionally prepared to switch roles, she also was not sure she could be a full-time, stay-at-home mother either. Therefore, she approached her employer to see if they'd let her work at home rather than the office. The novelty of her proposed telecommuting situation, coupled with what they perceived as difficulties in creating and supervising a home-based job, led them to say "no." It became clear that if she wanted to stay home, she would have to leave her corporate career. The prospect did not please her. In fact, it terrified her.

Her career meant so much to her—it provided her with a sense of power and status and it gave her the income that she felt was an important factor in the equality she shared with her husband. The regularity of a paycheck contributed to her strong self-identity and independence.

> I had a paycheck since I was 16. Now, all of a sudden, I had to decide for the first time in my life not to have a job and to depend on someone else for support. I know there's no logic to it. I know that when you're at home you work, but I think that having that paycheck in my name was real important. I just knew that I needed to feel like I was contributing to the support of our household. I've always felt like that—even as a kid. I just can't get the words out to ask for money.

It was a difficult and confusing time for Lisa. She was unsure about giving up her job and career identity but could not see how she could maintain her dual and, what felt like, competing allegiances to her employer and her child.

> I didn't think it was fair to go back to the company. I had such loyalty to them. Before I had my children, I was able to commit to long hours. After Ellen was born, I couldn't commit the same types of hours. I had to be with her. I knew that I just couldn't give the company 100% like I had before.

Although her employer offered Lisa several other assignments during her maternity leave, each required extensive travel or long hours. None fit her needs as a parent. Although pleased that the company didn't want to lose her—she loved working for them and wanted to continue—she saw no alternative but to quit.

Lisa faced what she saw as a choice between herself and her child. She chose her child. "I went through what I guess a lot of women go through—wondering if you're doing the right thing. Are you being selfish if you work? Are you giving enough time to your kids?"

Lisa left her job but was not ready or able to leave the work world. Lisa knew she had to continue to earn money both to support her family and to maintain her identity as a wage earner.

Working at home seemed to offer what she needed. She could earn money and yet avoid being typecast as a homemaker, an identity she had assiduously avoided her entire life.

One of the most striking aspects of Lisa's search for suitable home-based work was her loss of confidence and confusion in setting a direction. Although she had over 10 years of corporate experience, she initially saw no way to translate that experience into starting a home-based business. Instead, she began a frantic search of newspaper ads to find any kind of work she could do at home.

> I wasn't proud. I'd do anything. I just needed to prove to myself that I could do something at home and use the skills that I had spent all those years acquiring. I found a secondhand store through the newspaper that wanted someone who could call up people and ask for donations. They hired me, and I did it 2 hours in the morning and 2 hours at night. On Sunday nights, Stewart would help me. I only made a little money, but that was all I needed to know—that I could do something at home.

Lisa used her telephone solicitation job to gain enough confidence to figure out her next step. She became convinced she wanted to start a business. Her husband's personal computer seemed the natural starting point for one, and she knew Stewart would show her how to use it.

Stewart was enthusiastic about Lisa's desire to work at home but skeptical about her idea that the computer would be the best cornerstone for a business. He was not impressed when, in the middle of the night, a very excited Lisa shook him awake, blurting out, "Mailing lists!" Direct mail was not yet the business it has now become, and he could not believe someone would pay her to put together lists of names. He remained unconvinced until Lisa secured her old employer as her first client. From that moment on, he was her biggest supporter.

In addition to direct-mail services, Lisa decided to provide word-processing and data-entry services to local companies that were too small to have their own secretarial assistance. She began her business with one personal computer and within 6 months added two more personal computers and two printers, locating everything in an extra upstairs bedroom that she converted into her office.

Disruptions in Social Relations

For Lisa, the home-based situation has not been without costs. She went from a high profile, socially complex identity as a corporate middle manager to working alone on a personal computer in an upstairs bedroom. With the exception of her parents who became her children's caregivers, she lost adult companionship during the day. "There is no one in this neighborhood under 50. All the younger people are out working." This has been particularly difficult because she used to depend on her workplace for friendships.

> All my friends were the people at work. When I started working at home, I really missed the adult companionship. It was funny, but all I did was talk about my old company for the first 9 months after I left. If someone came over, it was just so natural to get into that conversational pattern of checking out who was doing what and who was responsible for what. It's like an addiction.

Despite these difficulties in defining her roles and her community of support, Lisa has been able to configure a viable and satisfying work at home situation, partially because of her ability to control the temporal pace of her work.

Time and Social Relations

Lisa developed a strict work schedule. She works from 9 A.M. to 5 P.M., 5 days a week, at minimum. At first she took care of her daughter herself, but as her business grew she realized she needed help. Fortunately, her parents were available. Her father had recently retired, so each morning at 9, both her parents arrive and assume full responsibility for Ellen. Lisa heads upstairs to her office and works until noon, when she breaks for lunch, usually coming downstairs with a bag of laundry in tow. "I'll put it in while we have lunch, and then I'll take another load back upstairs after lunch." She works in her office until 5.

> I quit at 5 sharp; then the evening routine starts. My parents leave, I start dinner, run around and put in more laundry, and Stewart arrives at home at 6. We eat and put the kids to bed. Then we both go back in the office at 8:30. I usually poop out at 10:30 or 11:00, and he works a lot later.

The demands of the business have created some unanticipated strains in her marriage. For one thing, Stewart and Lisa have very little time together in the evening just to relax.

For the most part their personal time together consists of working side by side at their computers. Stewart takes the information Lisa has gotten from a customer and designs the appropriate software programs.

Lisa's family has grown as quickly as her business. Within the first full year of business she gave birth to their second child, Jeremy. Although Lisa's home-based business provides immediate and sustained access to her children, it has not resulted in any significant increase in the amount of time she spends with them on a daily basis. In fact, she has had to struggle to maintain not only temporal, but also spatial boundaries between her work and family.

Breakdowns in Space and Social Relations

Having a separate office upstairs has helped Lisa in her efforts to keep her work activities separate from her family life. Nonetheless the two often blur. Her daughter often can't understand why Mommy wants to be left alone.

> Sometimes Ellen stands at the door and pounds. There are times I am in the middle of a telephone conversation, and it's just not appropriate to put the receiver down and growl at a 3-year-old. At that time I try to block out what is going on outside and hope the customer doesn't think I am beating someone. Other times I have to go discipline Ellen because she can get out of control. She can work herself up to a fever pitch, and then we've lost the rest of the afternoon. As long as she knows she isn't locked out of my office and she knows she can come and go, she loses interest. The problem comes when she knows the door is locked and she can't come in.

Lisa has tried to make room for her daughter as much as possible in the office, including setting up a miniature work area for her.

> My little girl has her own little desk and yellow phone over in the corner of our office. She says she has her own company and she named it after me, "Lisa's company." Sometimes I will get on the telephone and she gets on her yellow phone, and she pretends she is talking to her customers. I have one client, Mr. Matthews, who is a real pain. So she gets on the phone with Mr. Matthews and talks to him all the time. Ellen is very professional and really self-assured. I don't know if that is just her personality, or the fact that she knows I'm here.

As Lisa's business develops, new pressures and problems develop. Periodically she finds it necessary to hire temporary help, which proves difficult. For one thing, she now knows that most temporary agencies don't want for security reasons to send their workers, mostly females, out to private homes. Secondly, temporary help places more demands on the physical setup of the house.

Because her upstairs office is too small for the additional workers, they end up spreading out through the house. For example, one time Lisa was under a tight deadline to send out a mailing. She had three temporary workers, plus her mother, hand-labeling envelopes at the dining room table. Rubber bands and red dots were all over the floor, and the baby had to be kept in the living room with the gate up.

> Jeremy started screaming—babies know when you are desperate, that's when they start acting up. Then the phone rang in our upstairs office, I went to get it, and Ellen came with me. While I was talking to this customer, she knew my defenses were down so she just started slapping labels on the walls and windows. There was enough sun that day to attach them permanently. I still haven't gotten the razor out to take them down.

By locating her work in the home, Lisa has also lost the luxury of "going home" and leaving her job behind.

> Sometimes when you work in the same place you live, you get the feeling that you never get away. There is a need to get out and get away, to break the monotony of being in one place for such long periods of time.

In her worst moments, Lisa even longs for the crowded, dirty commuter bus she used to take to and from work. Those 30 minutes each way at least gave her some time alone and a temporal and emotional transition between her roles as career woman and mother/homemaker. Now, as soon as she walks out of the office and down the stairs she's "home."

Space and Role Identities

Even though she owns a business, being home has made Lisa feel vulnerable to being stereotyped as "just a homemaker."

> Because I am a woman, people imagine me wearing an apron. I've heard it in people's voices over the telephone, when I tell them my office is at home. They can't understand that I can have a business and not be making cookies or fudge. They see it as the same kind of thing. They don't see professionalism in it. They might see it when the product is generated, but they don't quite understand. I resent it. I don't get this kind of reaction from women who have had children and may have been torn leaving their children with a baby-sitter. But I do get it from men, even my own brother.

Despite the role confusions and the conflicts in space that her situation entails, Lisa feels that owning a home-based business offers her the control over her life and work that she wants. She likes being geographically available to her children and having the autonomy and flexibility that come from being self-employed. In addition, Lisa also enjoys strong social support for her efforts from both her husband and her parents.

Working at home has become a way of life that allows Lisa to live and work as part of an extended family. She often likens her situation to that of the traditional family farm in which grandparents, children, and children's children live and work in the same environment. It is not surprising that, given her autonomy, flexibility, and lifestyle, Lisa claims she will never return to the corporate world as a company employee.

DIRECTIONS FOR FUTURE RESEARCH, ENVIRONMENTAL DESIGN, AND POLICY

As the case studies in this chapter illustrate, women with young children experience varying levels of success in their efforts to work at home as a strategy for balancing their work–family obligations. The most successful configuration for work at home exists when the women have clear multiple role identities, strong social support from their spouses and members of other relevant communities, and clear control and predictability over their space and the timing of their work. Yet, having said this, it is also important to note that more research is needed on women who work at home.

IGNORED GROUPS

The case studies in this chapter reflect the experiences of white, married, middle-class women with young children who work at home on self-employed bases. This bias is warranted, in part, because the most recent federal statistics indicate that the majority of women who work at home are white, married, and self-employed. Yet, research should be expanded to include the home-based work experiences of a wide range of other racial, cultural, religious, and economic groups.

In the barrios of Spanish Harlem, on the stoves in Silicon Valley homes, and at worktables in the lofts of New York City's Chinatown, women enter data, assemble computer chip casings, and construct garments. In Chicago, a project was undertaken in the 1980s to provide assistance to women on public welfare to start their own home-based businesses. In central New Jersey, efforts have been made to establish home-based work opportunities for orthodox Jewish women married to Talmudic scholars who study rather than engage in income-producing work.

Although recent research has been conducted on the historical, as well as contemporary, experiences of African-American and Hispanic women who work at home in the United States, the efforts have been limited and need expansion (e.g., Ahrentzen, 1992; Boris, 1989b; Fernandez-Kelly & Garcia, 1989a,b). Research should also be conducted on the relationship between welfare policies and the cultivation of home-based businesses, as well as on the viability of home-based work as a rural economic development strategy.

As the political rhetoric around family values increases, it is important to understand not only how families of diverse racial, religious, and socioeconomic status cope with the experiences of bringing paid labor into the home, but also how families with different structures cope. Increasing numbers of American families deviate from the traditional Ozzie and Harriet two-parent household.

Although in the statistical minority, some single mothers do work at home, typically with full responsibility for supporting themselves and their children. Research is needed on how they define and find appropriate social support systems. In addition, statistical figures also indicate that roughly half of the women who work at home have no children. Some are young, some older; some are single, others married, but with no children or with children who have grown and left home. These older women without children fall into three groups: reentrants to the labor force; preretirees who are trying to save for retirement; or retirees who must continue to work because they are inadequately covered by social security, pensions, or health-care benefits. Although I have profiled the experiences of many of these women in my research (Christensen, 1988a, 1993b), they have yet to be studied systematically as groups.

Research is also needed on the conditions of work at home when both parents own and operate a family business and on how that affects role identities, social relations, including the division of domestic labor, and the delineation of public versus private space in the family. In my earlier research, I found two models for home-based family businesses, one in which women played behind-the-scenes roles in running the business and the other in which the women were full-functioning partners (Christensen, 1988). These models could be further tested and expanded upon.

Given the focus of this volume, my comments have been primarily directed toward the experiences of women in these ignored groups. Needless to say, the experiences of men working at home and their differences with women would form another entire set of directions for home-based work.[4]

DIFFERENT EMPLOYMENT CONDITIONS

As noted earlier, most of the contemporary research has focused primarily on the experiences of the self-employed at home. In my early work, I showed that there are major differences among the self-employed, particularly those who are genuinely self-employed versus those who are hired fraudulently as independent contractors (Christensen, 1989b). However, there has been no systematic research comparing the experiences of the self-employed home-based worker with those of the telecommuter, that is, the company employee who works at home. It is likely that the self-employed differ from the employed on a number of

[4]The author has worked with Margrethe Olson on a gender analysis of home-based work. Olson conducted a survey of *Datamation* readers, in 1985, using the survey instrument that the author developed for the *Family Circle Magazine*. Her respondents were primarily male; the *Family Circle* respondents predominantly female. The preliminary analysis of the two samples indicated dramatic differences. Also see N. Gottlieb (1987).

dimensions, including the nature and strength of their work role identity; the nature and complexity of their social relations; and the control over their time. For example, a telecommuter will have a work identity that is shaped in large part by her corporate culture; she will be nested in a complex social network that intersects both the family and her office; and she will likely spend proportionately less time working at home than would the self-employed. Currently, most telecommuters only work a fraction of their work week at home, spending the rest in the office. On the other hand, the self-employed may make different demands on the home and family if she has to bring clients into her home.

These differences in conditions raise not only questions about the social and psychological experiences of the telecommuter versus the self-employed, they also raise an important design question. Does a home-based work setting need to be differently designed for different employment conditions? This question is only a piece of a broader effort to understand the design implications of home-based work.

DESIGN

Most of contemporary thinking about the design aspects of work at home focuses on the physical features of the work space and its relationship to the remainder of the home, which typically is a single-family detached or semiattached house (Ahrentzen, 1989, 1992). More research is needed on three related design issues: the relationship between the home-based office and the type of housing in which the office is situated; the way that design, role identity, and social relations work together to create an effective work space and work dynamic; and the way in which home offices are part of a broader effort to decentralize the workplace.

It is important to evaluate home offices as they occur in different types of housing and different types of social relations supported by that housing. For example, in my earliest work, I was impressed by how socially well-connected people were whose home offices were located in apartment complexes rather than in single-family detached houses. Following this line of thought, it would be interesting to study how home-based work has been or could be integrated into housing developments that have very distinct social philosophies, such as the cohousing efforts in Davis, California or Boulder, Colorado.

One clear message from the case studies presented in this chapter is that no home-based office, no matter how well-designed and situated it is, will be effective unless it is well integrated into the social dynamics of the household. Research must be conducted that examines how different designs of home-based offices enhance, rather than inhibit, the social organization of work and family in the home.

It is also important to think of the home office as symptomatic of a broader effort to decentralize work from the conventional office. In this context, it would be of value to examine the differential effects on work and family of a woman working in her home office versus working in a satellite office, located midway between home and the conventional workplace. An effort is currently underway in the state of California to develop 15 satellite offices; this could provide an important laboratory in which to study the broader issues related to the decentralization of work.

THEORETICAL ISSUES

There are a number of theoretical models one could adopt in examining women and home-based work, including role theory, stress, place attachment, privacy, and territoriality. Rather than focus on any one theory, I found it appropriate to introduce a transactional metatheory, that of frameworks of meaning, which maintains that a woman who works at home is simultaneously situated in multiple frameworks of meaning, including space, time, and social relations. As the case studies suggest, the role identities of a woman are shaped by and in turn reshape these frameworks of meaning as she attempts to bring paid labor into the home. Yet, the case studies also illustrate the need for additional research on how the frameworks of meaning are conjointly formed and reformed over time.

One direction of research that could show this dynamic process would be to extend current place identity theory, which postulates that significant places affect how one thinks and feels about oneself (Proshansky, Fabian, & Kaminoff, 1983). This theory is one directional in its emphasis on how places affect identity, failing to show its corollary, that identity affects environment: How one thinks and feels about oneself affects one's ability to shape her social and physical environment to suit the needs of her role identities. For example, if a person has a strong work-role identity, as does Jennifer, one would expect that she would be better able to create a social and physical work environment than would a person, such as Susan, who has a weak and conflicted work-role identity. In other words, how one thinks about oneself affects one's ability to structure the physical and social environment in ways necessary to support the demands of that identity. In turn, a well-structured environment, one that is well-designed and socially regulated, will further strengthen one's identity; a poorly structured environment will further undercut how one thinks of oneself.

A discussion about public versus private space could also be integrated into the metatheory of frameworks of meaning. Whereas conventional sociological research posits work as the public sphere and family as the private one, work at home renders such a distinction virtually meaningless. What has been private, that is the home, now becomes public and what has been public, that is the workplace, now becomes private. This raises the question of how home-based workers and their families conceive of a public–private boundary and how they renegotiate space and social relations to maintain it. In other words, does the public–private boundary exist for them and, if so, in what form or forms? For example, in one family I studied, the husband adjusted relatively well to the demands that his wife's home-based business placed on the privacy of his home and family. He could live with the fact that her four employees plus their children worked in his home daily. Yet, he would throw a fit if he went to the refrigerator and found that someone had drunk his apple cider. The idea that his refrigerator and his valued foods were not private was unacceptable to him. In effect, the boundary between public and private for him started and stopped, not at the front door as it does for most people who work outside the home, but at the refrigerator door.

The case studies in this chapter also argue for research that could identify the factors that contribute to strengthening one's role identities. For example, why or how did Jennifer develop such strong, clear, unconflicted role identities, whereas Susan did not?

POLICY

Several political forces are converging to create a very favorable political climate for work at home. Telecommuting is being promoted as a solution for work–family problems, traffic congestion, poor air quality, and improved land use. For example, the notion of working at home fits fine within a political climate that, in part, argues for women to return home. Telecommuting is being actively promoted under new federal and state clean-air regulations as a solution companies can employ to cut car trips, decrease traffic congestion, and improve air quality. Cutting the number of car trips is also viewed as a way to reduce demand, and ultimately cost, for expanded highway infrastructure. Telecommuting is also viewed as a way to effectively handle undesired urban sprawl because people could move further from major metropolitan areas and live in small, economically self-contained and self-sustaining small towns. A hot topic at a recent meeting I attended at the U.S. Department of Transportation, in fact, was whether increased telecommuting would lead to the abandonment of downtown metropolitan areas. It is clear that the agendas of both the federal government and many state governments, including those of California and Washington, are raising issues that researchers would be well served to study.

Behind many of the policy claims regarding work at home and family values is the notion that people make tradeoffs in their efforts to balance work and home. A thorough systematic study of the tradeoffs between space and time is needed. For example, a particular study is needed that evaluates the relative effectiveness of changing work locations, such as in working at home, versus changing work schedules, such as in reduced time schedules that include part-time work or job sharing. Working women with family responsibilities are constantly making decisions that involve tradeoffs among space, time, and money, and it would be good to better understand how those are made and which are most effective for meeting their needs.

It is also important to evaluate, from a policy perspective, the effectiveness of working at home for women caring for elderly family members versus young children. We know from current research that work at home has limited utility as a form of child care for pre-school-aged children. But we do not know how well it works as a form of elder care. As the baby boom continues to age, increasing numbers of women will assume elder care responsibilities and strategies must be developed for them and their spouses in shouldering these responsibilities.

In conclusion, working at home serves as a powerful lens through which we can examine how work and family are being reconfigured in the political, social, and economic climate of the 1990s.

REFERENCES

Ahrentzen, S. (1989). A place of peace, prospect, and of P.C.: The home as office. *Journal of Architectural and Planning Research, 6,* 271–289.

Ahrentzen, S. (1990). Managing conflict by managing boundaries: How professional homeworkers cope with multiple roles at home. *Environment and Behavior, 22,* 723–752.

Ahrentzen, S. (1992). *Hybrid housing: A contemporary building type for multiple residential and business use* (Report R 92-1). Milwaukee, WI: Center for Architecture and Urban Planning, Publications in Architecture and Urban Planning.

Ahrentzen, S. (1992). Home as a workplace in the lives of Women. In I. Altman & S. Low (Eds.), *Human behavior and environment: Vol. 12. Place attachment* (pp. 113–138). New York: Plenum Press.

Allen, S., & Wolkowitz, C. (1987). *Homeworking: Myths and realities.* London: Macmillan.

Altman, I., & Rogoff, B. (1987). World views in psychology: Trait, interactional, organismic and transactional perspectives. In D. Stokols & I. Altman (Eds.), *Handbook of environmental psychology* (Vol. 1, pp. 1–40). New York: Wiley.

Beach, B. (1989). The family context of home shoe work. In E. Boris & C. Daniels (Eds.), *Homework: Historical and contemporary perspectives on paid labor at home* (pp. 130–146). Urbana: University of Illinois Press.

Beneria, L., & Roldan, M. (1987). *The crossroads of class and gender: Industrial homework, subcontracting and household dynamics in Mexico City.* Chicago: University of Chicago Press.

Boris, E. (1989a). Homework and women's rights: The case of the Vermont Knitters 1980–85. In E. Boris & C. R. Daniels (Eds.), *Homework: Historical and contemporary perspectives on paid labor at home* (pp. 223–257). Urbana: University of Illinois Press.

Boris, E. (1989b). Black women and paid labor in their home: Industrial homework in Chicago in the 1920s. In E. Boris & C. R. Daniels (Eds.), *Homework: Historical and contemporary perspectives on paid labor at home* (pp. 33–52). Urbana: University of Illinois Press.

Cassirer, E. (1977). *The philosophy of symbolic forms* (Vols. 1–3). New Haven: Yale University.

Chamot, D. (1988). Blue collar, white collar: Homeworker problems. In K. Christensen (Ed.), *The new era of home-based work: Directions and policies.* Boulder, CO: Westview Press.

Christensen, K. (1985a, January 15). National survey of women and home-based work. *Family Circle*, p. 58.

Christensen, K. (1985b). *Impacts of computer mediated home-based work on women and their families.* Final report submitted to the Office of Technology Assessment, U.S. Congress, for their study *Automation of America's offices, 1985–2000* (OTA-CIT-287). New York: Center for Human Environments, Graduate Center, City University of New York.

Christensen, K. (1988a). *Women and home-based work: The unspoken contract.* New York: Henry Holt.

Christensen, K. (Ed.). (1988b). *The new era of home-based work: Directions and policies.* Boulder, CO: Westview Press.

Christensen, K. (1988c). Introduction: White-collar home-based work: The changing U.S. economy and family. In K. Christensen (Ed.), *The new era of home-based work: Directions and policies* (pp. 1–11). Boulder, CO: Westview Press.

Christensen, K. (1989a). *Impacts of home-based work on women and their families.* Final Report to the U.S. Department of Health and Human Services on Grant #90-DD-86562. New York: Center for Human Environments, Graduate Center, City University of New York.

Christensen, K. (1989b). Home-based clerical work: No simple truth; No single reality. In E. Boris & C. Daniels (Eds.), *Homework: Historical and contemporary perspectives on paid labor at home* (pp. 183–197). Urbana: University of Illinois Press.

Christensen, K. (1989c). *Flexible staffing and scheduling in U.S. Corporations* (Bulletin No. 240). New York: The Conference Board.

Christensen, K. (1993a). Re-evaluating union policy toward home-based work. In S. Cobble (Ed.), *Women and unions: Forging a new partnership.* Ithaca: NY: ILP Press.

Christensen, K. (1993b). Eliminating the journey to work: Home-based work across the life course of women. In C. Katz & J. Monk (Eds.), *Full circle: Geographies of women over the life course.* London: Routledge.

Costello, C. (1988). Clerical home-based work: A case study of work and families. In K.

Christensen (Ed.), *The new era of home-based work: Directions and policies* (pp. 135–145). Boulder, CO: Westview Press.

Costello, C. (1991). *We're worth it! Women and collective action in the insurance industry*. Urbana: University of Illinois Press.

Daniels, C. (1989). Between home and factory: Homeworkers and the state. In E. Boris & C. Daniels (Eds.), *Homework: Historical and contemporary perspectives on paid labor at home* (pp. 13–32). Urbana: University of Illinois Press.

Dangler, J. (1989). Electronic subassemblers in central New York: Nontraditional homeworkers in a nontraditional industry. In E. Boris & C. Daniels (Eds.), *Homework: Historical and contemporary perspectives on paid labor at home* (pp. 147–164). Urbana: University of Illinois Press.

Deaux, K. (1993). Reconstructing social identity. *Personality and Social Psychology Bulletin, 19*(1), 4–12.

du Rivage, V., & Jacobs, D. (1989). Home-based work: Labor's choices. In E. Boris & C. Daniels (Eds.), *Homework: Historical and contemporary perspectives on paid labor at home* (pp. 258–271). Urbana: University of Illinois Press.

Fernandez-Kelly, M. P., & Garcia, A. (1989a). Hispanic women and homework: Women in the informal economy of Miami and Los Angeles. In E. Boris & C. Daniels (Eds.), *Homework: Historical and contemporary perspectives on paid labor at home* (pp. 165–179). Urbana: University of Illinois Press.

Fernandez-Kelly, M. P., & Garcia, A. (1989b). Informalization at the core: Hispanic women, homework and the advanced capitalist state. In A. Portes, M. Castells, & L. Benton (Eds.), *The informal economy: Studies in advanced and less developed countries*. Baltimore: The Johns Hopkins University Press.

Gerson, J. (1993). Home-based clericals: Are they organizable? In S. Cobble (Ed.), *Women and unions: Forging a partnership*. Ithaca: ILR Press.

Gerson, J., & Kraut, R. (1988). Clerical work at home or in the office: The difference it makes. In K. Christensen (Ed.), *The new era of home-based work: Directions and policies* (pp. 49–64). Boulder, CO: Westview Press.

Gottlieb, N. (1987). *Gender differences in the experiences of working at home*. Unpublished master's thesis, Graduate Center, City University of New York.

Hewes, J. (1981). *Worksteads: Living and working in the same place*. Garden City, NY: Dolphin Books, Doubleday.

Hochschild, A., with A. Machung. (1990). *The second shift*. New York: Avon Books.

Horowitz, J. (1986). *Working at home and being at home: The interaction of microcomputers and the social life of households*. Unpublished doctoral dissertation, Graduate School and University Center, City University of New York.

Horvath, F. (1986). Work at home: New findings from the current population survey. *Monthly Labor Review, 109*, 31–35.

Huws, U. (1984). *The new homeworkers: New technology and the changing location of white collar work* (Pamphlet No. 28). London: Low Pay Unit.

Institute for Women's Policy Research (IWPR). (1992). *Are mommies dropping out of the labor force? No! Research-in-brief*. Washington, DC: IWPR.

International Labour Organization (ILO). (1989). Home work. *Conditions of Work Digest, 8*. Geneva, Switzerland: ILO.

International Labour Office (ILO). (1990). Telework. *Conditions of Work Digest, 9*. Geneva, Switzerland: ILO.

Iverson, K. (1988). The government's role in regulating home employment. In K. Christensen (Ed), *The new era of home-based work: Directions and policies* (pp. 149–156). Boulder, CO: Westview Press.

Johnson, L., with R. Johnson. (1982). *The seam allowance: Industrial home sewing in Canada.* Toronto: Women's Press.

Lozano, B. (1989). *The invisible work force: Transforming American business with outside and home-based workers.* New York: Free Press.

McCall, G., & Simmons, J. (1978). *Identities and interactions* (rev. ed.). New York: Free Press.

McLaughlin, M. (1981). *Physical and social support systems used by women engaged in home-based work.* Unpublished Master's Thesis, Cornell University, Ithaca, NY.

Miller, T. (1992, May). *Presentation of research findings of Link's annual surveys on work-at-home.* Paper presented at the U.S. Department of Transportation Workshop on Telecommuting, Washington, DC.

Olson, M. (1988). Corporate culture and the homeworker. In K. Christensen (Ed.), *The new era of home-based work: Directions and policies* (pp. 126–134). Boulder, CO: Westview Press.

Olson, M. (1989). Organization barriers to professional telework. In E. Boris & C. Daniels (Eds.), *Homework: Historical and contemporary perspectives on paid labor at home* (pp. 215–230). Urbana: University of Illinois Press.

Pfeffer, J. (1985). Organizations and organization theory. In G. Lindsey & E. Aronson (Eds.), *Handbook of social psychology* (3rd ed., Vol. 1, pp. 379–431). New York: Knopf.

Pratt, J. (1984). Home teleworking: A study of its pioneers. *Technology Forecasting and Social Change, 25,* 1–14.

Proshansky, H., Fabian, A., & Kaminoff, R. (1983). Place identity: Physical world socialization of the self. *Journal of Environmental Psychology, 3,* 57–83.

Simonson, J. R. (1988). The protection of clerical homeworkers: From what, by whom? In K. Christensen (Ed.), *The new era of home-based work: Directions and policies* (pp. 157–167). Boulder, CO: Westview Press.

The Politics of Space Appropriation

A CASE STUDY OF WOMEN'S STRUGGLES FOR HOMEPLACE IN CHICAGO PUBLIC HOUSING

ROBERTA M. FELDMAN AND SUSAN STALL

INTRODUCTION

> So I'm just saying this to tell you, there just comes a
> point and a time when there's a need for something,
> and a group of people gather and decide that they are
> going to do this for the benefit of their community—
> they can do it.
> —*Mrs. Hallie Amey, Wentworth Gardens resident, 1988*

The point and time was the 1960s when public housing in the United States was beleaguered by disinvestment—a reduction in maintenance, services, and programs. Daily life in Chicago Housing Authority (CHA) housing was beset with deteriorating physical facilities and inadequate services to meet the residents' needs (see Kotlowitz, 1991; Slayton, 1988).

ROBERTA M. FELDMAN • School of Architecture, University of Illinois at Chicago, Chicago, Illinois 60607-7024.   SUSAN STALL • Department of Sociology, Northeastern Illinois University, Chicago, Illinois 60625.
Women and the Environment, edited by Irwin Altman and Arza Churchman. Plenum Press, New York, 1994.

For Mrs. Hallie Amey,[1] a resident of Wentworth Gardens and key figure in local organizing efforts, the point and time she was describing was when she and other women residents decided to challenge the closing of Wentworth Garden's field house and the dismantling of the youth recreation programs.[2] According to Mrs. Amey, this was the precipitating incident that compelled Wentworth women residents "to venture out into the community." It marked the beginning of three decades of these women's grassroots activism to act on their own behalf and on behalf of other Wentworth residents to maintain and improve their housing development, their "home."

For policymakers and the public alike, the role that women in public housing have played in their struggles to save their homeplaces, as well as the struggles of other low-income women of color, all too often remain invisible. Rather, the media portrayal of this societal crisis is one of hopelessness and despair. For instance, the Public Broadcasting System aired (January 6, 1989, in Chicago) a documentary about life in Robert Taylor Homes, the largest CHA development, titled, "A Crisis on Federal Street." Public housing residents were depicted as both helpless and predatory, and their housing environment as irreparable. In a 12-part series, the *Chicago Tribune* (December, 1986, p. 1) called its city's public housing "The Chicago Wall"—"a physical barrier of brick and steel and concrete that separates black from white, rich from poor, hope from despair." With increasing frequency, the proposed solution is the call for the dismantling of existing public housing. The traditional social-science characterization is hardly more favorable. Low-income people are typically depicted as helpless and apathetic victims of despair (reviewed in Kieffer, 1984; Naples, 1988; also see Rappaport, 1981). Although scholars refrain from "blaming the victim," they portray an oppressed, alienated, passive, and powerless resident population victimized by stigmatization, poverty, and racism. For instance, in characterizing the purported ineffectiveness of the "War on Poverty" of the 1960s, social-science explanations focused on the " 'failure' of 'deprived' cultures, the 'pathology' of the 'underprivileged,' and 'obstructions' to the empowerment of the 'culturally disadvantaged' " (Kieffer, 1984, pp. 10–11). In discussing the "paternalistic philosophy" of both social reformers and public officials specifically toward public housing residents, Bowley noted:

[1]We use the prefix "Mrs." when referring to the residents because this is the manner in which they address and refer to each other in daily interactions.
[2]Mrs. Hallie Amey exemplifies Karen Sacks's (1988) concept of "centerwoman," a leader who engages with people one-on-one, enlisting their skills and ensuring that obligations are fulfilled. Through her enthusiasm, Mrs. Amey ignited other residents to join her in community efforts.

> The residents were treated like children, and the tragedy is that for some it
> was the self-fulfilling prophecy—they acted like children and were satisfied
> to have public housing and welfare policies control their lives. Public housing
> thus tended to perpetuate a permanent class of dependent people, unable to
> fend for themselves. (1978, p. 224)

Often cited studies of the experiences of public housing residents view
them as on the defensive, attempting to protect themselves from surrounding human and physical threats (cf. Newman, 1972; Rainwater,
1966). Furthermore, it is presumed that low-income people are incapable
of forming and participating in an active, productive community. It has
been an "assumption in social reform efforts that low-income people
lack social organization" (Naples, 1988, p. 30).

In this chapter we offer an alternative portrayal. We show that for
residents, public housing is their home and their community, one they
would like to see improved. Rather than "conditioned acceptance," Chicago's Metropolitan Planning Council (1986, p. 3) found in resident-
conducted surveys in three high-rise CHA developments that CHA residents suggested innovative ways to improve their housing environment
and services; furthermore, residents reported a willingness to devote
some of their own time to assure these improvements. This is the other
side of CHA and of public housing residents, a side we seldom hear
about.

In our ongoing case study of Wentworth Gardens residents' grassroots activism, we have found that residents are working toward alter-
ing living conditions that threaten public housing viability. We describe
this ongoing history of resident-initiated collective actions to improve
their everyday lives and explain how these actions provide a rich environment for nurturing individual and collective empowerment despite
limited economic and political resources. We conclude with a discussion
of a comprehensive interpretive framework to understand social change
in everyday life. This framework will include elaborating upon the feminist and social-science empowerment literature to further explicate the
politics of community activism among poor and working-class women.
In particular, we will extend this literature to disclose the ways in which
struggles to appropriate the physical settings of their housing developments contribute to public housing residents' empowerment.

A BRIEF HISTORY OF CHICAGO PUBLIC HOUSING

Despite its numerous problems—bad design, poor management,
inefficiency, and inadequate maintenance—public housing in the United

States remains the federal government's primary housing program for low-income Americans. More than 3 million people live in public housing units, and most large cities have long waiting lists with names of applicants eager for apartments (Pynoos, 1986). In Chicago, public housing provides 29,000 family units, or nearly 30% of the housing needs of low-income families (Metropolitan Planning Council, 1988).

In the United States, public housing was launched in 1933 as part of President Franklin Delano Roosevelt's New Deal program in response to severe economic problems during the Depression era. The Housing Division of the Federal Public Works Administration (PWA) was charted to build and manage housing projects in order to increase both employment and provide low income housing. According to Devereux Bowley, Jr. (1978, p. 18), in his historical study of subsidized housing in Chicago, *The Poorhouse*, "The movement of government into this area of activity was controversial to many people, but was made more palatable by the designation of the initial developments as 'demonstration' projects, built during a time of national economic emergency." As documented by Bowley, Jr. (1978), the PWA built three public housing projects in Chicago in the pre-World War II period and selected a site for a fourth project. These four projects are important because they set the precedent for the quality of the public housing that followed. To insure that these projects would not compete with the private residential market, the investment cost per unit averaged about 20% below the cost of for-profit construction in the area. The units were designed to be "stark, each building like the one next door, except for some variations in height, and each project clearly isolated from the surrounding community" (Bowley, 1978, p. 33).

In 1937, through the U.S. Housing Act, the responsibility for the construction of public housing was transferred to local agencies. The CHA, which had managed PWA housing from the onset, now was in the construction business (Bowley, 1978).[3] Although the majority of the existing 19 CHA family developments were built prior to 1955, the greatest number of units in large-scale high-rise projects were constructed in the later 1950s and early 1960s (Bowley, 1978).

The years 1937 through the early 1950s have been called the "happy years" of public housing across the United States (Scobie, 1975, p. 2). In the words of Elizabeth Wood, a prominent national housing figure and

---

[3]The CHA was charted in 1937. Although CHA legally exists as an independent agency, it functions as an arm of city government. The CHA commissioners are appointed by the mayor, and they must submit an annual report to the mayor. Much of CHA planning is provided by city agencies, and CHA sites must be approved by the City Council (Bowley, 1978).

the first executive director of the CHA, "The original tenants included many families, middle class as to living standards but caught in the depression and with low incomes. They used the projects well and happily" (Fischer, 1959, p. 164). But, by the mid-1950s, family public housing experienced a shift "from poor, white tenants, either temporarily unemployed or working, to primarily welfare-dependent minority tenants" (Pynoos, 1986, p. 190). The underlying racial discrimination that propelled political forces in Chicago to orchestrate this shift in public housing's population are well documented in Hirsch's *Making of the Second Ghetto* (1985). There is ample evidence to demonstrate, as Bowley (1978, p. 225) contends, that "a de facto purpose of public housing, at least after the firing of Elizabeth Wood in 1954, was to isolate the poor and especially, the black population away from the white-middle class areas of the city" by constructing its major projects in existing ghettos. The demographic statistics of residents in family-occupied public housing show that in 1951, 60% were nonwhite (*Chicago Tribune*, 1986), whereas in 1991 91% were nonwhite (*Chicago Tribune*, 1986).

Another major cause of the shift in the population composition of family public housing units has been the increase in the numbers of public-welfare recipients needing affordable housing among the general population (Pynoos, 1986). Indeed, Wacquant and Wilson (1989, p. 9) argue that "joblessness and economic exclusion, having reached dramatic proportions, have triggered a process of hyperghettoization" in Chicago's inner city. In 1960, approximately 50% of CHA families received some type of public aid (*Chicago Tribune*, 1986), whereas in 1991, about 83% were public assistance recipients (Chicago Housing Authority, 1991).

Finally, the shift has gender implications. With the feminization of poverty (see Pearce, 1978, 1983), more women and female-headed households are found in the lowest income categories. Therefore, they are likely to require subsidized housing (e.g., Leavitt & Saegert, 1984; McClain, 1979–1980; National Council of Negro Women, 1975). As noted by Leslie Kanes Weisman:

> The extent to which American women of diverse racial backgrounds are unable to find adequate shelter, and therefore depend on public housing, is a bitter comment on the prevalence of women's poverty. With the exception of the Federal Housing Administration (FHA) and the Veteran's Administration (VA) programs, federal housing programs are essentially women's programs. (1992, p. 106)

In Chicago's public housing in 1991, 85% of the families listed a woman as the primary lease holder (Chicago Housing Authority, 1991).

"Today, Chicago Public Housing is for people who are black, poor and unemployed and living in families headed by single women" (*Chicago Tribune*, 1986, p. 1). In spite of the unresolved issues of racism, classism, and sexism that intersect within subsidized housing developments, women residents have historically fought and continue to fight for their right for safe and decent shelter (see, e.g., Birch, 1978; Feldman & Stall, 1990; Keys, 1991; Lawson & Barton, 1980; Leavitt & Saegert, 1990; Weisman, 1992; Wekerle, 1980). Patricia Hill Collins in her book *Black Feminist Thought* (1991) cautions against portraying Black women "solely as passive, unfortunate recipients of racial and sexual abuse" or "solely as heroic figures who easily engage in resisting oppression on all fronts" (p. 237). Rather, Collins points to the need to uncover "the ongoing interplay between Black women's oppression and Black women's activism [because it] presents the matrix of domination [gender, race, and class] as responsive to human agency" (p. 237).

THE POLITICS OF SPACE APPROPRIATION

In our research we have found that residents' struggles over the physical settings of their public housing development and the consequences of these struggles are a necessary, albeit a single factor in conceptualizing resident activists' efforts toward social change. We have observed that low-income African-American women's power to influence change lies in part in the empowering experiences of the everyday, ongoing struggles to appropriate their homeplace.

Appropriation of space is a term that has been used in environment and behavior research to describe individuals' and groups' creation, choice, possession, modification, enhancement of, care for, and/or simply intentional use of a space to make it one's own (see Korosec-Serfaty's edited volume, 1976). Space appropriation is conceptualized as an interactive process through which individuals purposefully transform the physical environment into a meaningful place while in turn transforming themselves.

The concept was originally adapted from Marx who proposed that the individual constructively acts upon and uses "nature" and in the process realizes her or his powers and potentialities, her or his own nature (Graumann, 1976; also see Ollman, 1971); that is, in the process of appropriating a physical setting, the self is actualized and expressed in the material form. Theorists have further argued that appropriation of space is not a solitary process; the individual actions and meanings of space appropriation always are realized within the broader society (Chombart de Lauwe, 1976; Graumann, 1976). Inquiries into space appropriation have sought to uncover the societal conditions that structure opportunities for and obstacles to space-appropriation processes. They are framed around the question: "Is the appropriation of space by all possible?" (Chombart de Lauwe, 1976). Some researchers have examined people's economic and political power, and the technological and social transformations of industrial society that enable or hinder people's relative power or ability to appropriate space (see Korosec-Serfaty's edited volume, 1976). Others have examined the societal modes of relating to places that are appropriated through the codification, institutionalization, and organization of space according to sociocultural and professional models (see Korosec-Serfaty, 1976; also see Werner's edited issue of *Architecture & Behavior*, 1992).

In our conceptualization, we have attempted to integrate the various definitions of space appropriation in the literature (reviewed in Proshansky, 1976), and to reflect the origins of this concept. Although some researchers make direct reference only to the actions necessary to control spatial resources and others focus on the purposes and/or experiential outcomes, we include both the means and ends of the process. Furthermore, we define homeplaces broadly to include nested scales of the residential environment from the dwelling up to the larger neighborhood environment.

In the United States, however, conventional wisdom presumes that appropriation of space refers specifically to the dwelling (reviewed in Despres, 1989; Duncan, 1981; Hayden, 1984; Wright, 1981), and that the dwelling is the best place to satisfy and express appropriation "needs" (reviewed in Despres, 1989; also see Cooper, 1974). Yet, researchers studying working-class and lower-income communities have challenged this view (Fried, 1963; Fried & Gleicher, 1970; Gans, 1962; Haywoode, 1991; Leavitt & Saegert, 1990; Suttles, 1968). Their studies provide a broader understanding of the ways class and race and ethnicity mediate acts and experiences of space appropriation. In particular, they have shown that actions and experiences indicative of the appropriation of homeplace extend well beyond the confines of the dwelling into the neighborhood environs. In fact, Chombart de Lauwe (1976, p. 27) argues that appropriation of homeplace cannot be understood "without reference to the lodging's surroundings, and more broadly, to the neighborhood and the city" (p. 27).

THE APPROPRIATION OF HOMEPLACE

Of all the physical settings that comprise everyday environmental experience, the appropriation of homeplace is deemed most important, if not universal: "Hearth, shelter, home or home base are intimate places to human beings everywhere" (Tuan, 1977, p. 147; also see Buttimer, 1980; Cooper, 1974; Csikszentmihalyi & Rochberg-Halton, 1981; Relph, 1976; Seamon, 1979). Considerable effort has been spent attempting to demonstrate that appropriation of the meanings of home is a universal and vital process of "at-homeness" or of "dwelling in the world," one that is essential to psychological well-being and the experiences of harmony with the world.

Bell Hooks, while not directly utilizing the space-appropriation concept, reminds us of the historical importance of the political dimensions of the appropriation of homeplace in African-American women's lives:

> Historically, African-American people believed that the construction of a homeplace, however fragile and tenuous (the slave hut, the wooden shack), had a radical political dimension . . . it was about the construction of a safe place where black people could affirm one another and by so doing heal many of the wounds inflicted by racist domination. (1990, p. 42)

Hooks's thesis amply speaks to the importance of both the societal and experiential dimensions of the politics of space appropriation. She addresses the obstacles imposed by racism, classism, and sexism on African-American women's freedom and power to appropriate space to make it one's own place. Their dwelling, no matter how simple, was typically the only physical setting that they could, with some reliability, call their own (also see Rainwater, 1966). Yet, Hooks also recognizes the central importance of the experiences of at-homeness. Her descriptions of the "feeling of safety, of arrival, of homecoming" (p. 41) upon arrival at one's home, and of black women's central responsibility in constructing "domestic households as spaces of care and nurturance" (p. 42) are indicators of experiences that are central to conceptualizations of at-homeness. Hooks, however, views these experiences as not ends in and of themselves, but rather as central to conceptualizing homeplace as political—the construction of a safe, nurturing place "where people can return to themselves more easily, where the conditions are such that they can heal themselves and recover their wholeness" (Hooks, citing Thich Nhat Hahn, p. 43) in "the face of the brutal harsh reality of racist oppression, of sexist domination" (Hooks, p. 42).

In the following case study of the history of Wentworth women residents' grassroots community activism, we will elaborate on the political dimension of both the means and ends of the appropriation of homeplace. We will examine the power relations that constrain and enable these ongoing, everyday material acts. And we will illustrate the transformative powers of the process of space appropriation in the service of resident empowerment and social change.

A CASE STUDY OF THE INVISIBLE STRUGGLES FOR HOMEPLACE

Wentworth Gardens is a low-rise public housing development located on a four-square-block area on Chicago's southside (see Figure 1). One of the 19 family public housing developments in Chicago, Wentworth Gardens was originally planned for Black war workers. Project construction was started in 1945 and completed in 1947. The development has 422 units within 37 buildings. Twenty-eight of the buildings are two-story row houses with a cluster of nine three-story apartment buildings in the center of the development (Bowley, 1978). Built in a largely industrial area, it is currently bounded by a major highway, the Dan Ryan Expressway, on the east; the White Sox Stadium, Comiskey Park, on the north; an industrial park on the west; and a small deteriorating commercial strip on its southern boundaries.

The first Wentworth residents were, and continue to be, low-income African-American families. Home to 1,264 people, Wentworth Gardens' buildings are in great disrepair. Its physical deterioration is common to all CHA properties: As of 1988, CHA claimed that it needed approximately $750,000 in order to repair and bring its physical plant up to standard (Slayton, 1988). In 1989, when our fieldwork began, signs of the poor physical condition of Wentworth Gardens were highly visible and posed a safety hazard. A woman resident activist described the situation this way:

> You really just haven't seen how some people are living over here. We have potholes over here large enough for a small child to fall in, and we have roof leaks. It doesn't make sense for somebody to be living like that, all from roofing and tuckpointing.[4]

In our ongoing participatory research study (see Petras & Porpora, 1992), we are using techniques of direct observation and structured and open-ended interviews with selected female residents at Wentworth Gardens. As participatory researchers, we seek to develop an understanding of grassroots organizing in the everyday lives of women activists through their words and actions; and furthermore to use this knowledge to contribute to social change that addresses socioeconomic and

[4]Tuckpointing is a process to replace and repair the mortar between the bricks of the exterior walls in order to prevent water from seeping into the interior of a building.

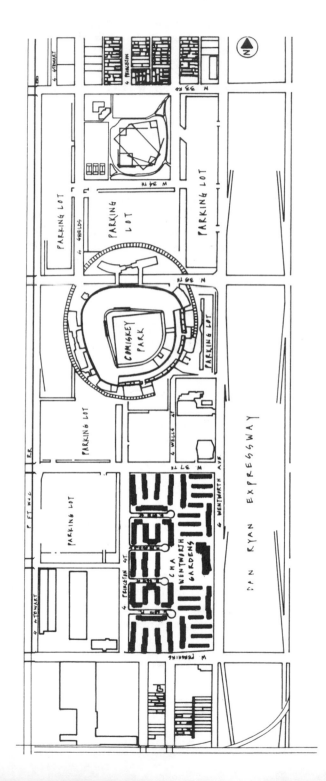

Figure 1. Site plan of Wentworth Gardens and the surrounding neighborhood (drawn by Loree Sandler).

political injustices.[5] We are utilizing a sociological case-study method because it has proven to be the most effective means to investigate process (Becker, 1966, as reported in Stoecker, 1991). It facilitates the explication of the historical causal process behind a particular event or variable (Platt, 1984).

Our initial observations and interviews led us to conclude that Wentworth women's grassroots activism is rooted in the social fabric of community (Feldman & Stall, 1990). Through our continuing fieldwork, we have come to recognize that the social networks so vital to Wentworth resident activism not only were substantially locally based, but moreover, were connected to homeplace appropriation. It is to these observations that we now turn. Of all the struggles to appropriate homeplace, there are two sustained efforts that continue to be of particular significance to the Wentworth resident activists: the field house and the laundromat.

APPROPRIATING THE FIELD HOUSE: MODEST STRUGGLES

According to Wentworth Garden activists, all of the housing development and the surrounding neighborhood is their "home," a place they care deeply about and one in which they find nurturance. Furthermore, their actions to improve and maintain the physical setting of their

[5]This chapter is primarily based on interviews and observations we conducted in the fall and winter of 1988 and in the winter of 1991. Before formally interviewing Wentworth residents and other organized participants in the Wentworth struggles, we had met and worked with the residents in other settings. In 1986–1987, one of us, Susan Stall, as coordinator of the conference project "Women and Public Housing: Hidden Strength, Unclaimed Power" became acquainted with the activism of the Wentworth Garden Residents and with individual resident organizers. Roberta Feldman prepared the photodocumentary for this conference's plenary session, "Sharing Our Homes, Sharing Our Communities." Immediately following this conference, Susan Stall, as a community consultant, worked with public housing residents, including representatives from Wentworth Gardens, to form the citywide advocacy organization, Chicago Housing Authority Residents Taking Action. And, both authors have been members of the Wentworth Gardens Resident Management Community Advisory Board, which supports the broadbased efforts of resident activists since its inception in 1989.

We have shared our research articles and scholarly papers with residents. Their comments were invited and incorporated into our revisions. As participatory researchers we are cognizant of our responsibility to reciprocate the Wentworth residents' contributions. We have assisted activist residents by documenting and giving recognition to their past achievements. Our writings provide formal documents for grant proposals. They also serve to share the successes of Wentworth women activists with nonactivist residents and potential community supporters. For example, we have written an article for publication for community activists and reformers (Feldman & Stall, 1989) and have prepared a museum exhibit.

housing development serve as visible expressions of their ongoing struggles to appropriate their neighborhood as their homeplace. Their struggles to reopen and maintain the field house for youth-related activities are a telling, visible example.

In the early 1960s, when the CHA closed the on-site field house, and thereby eliminated a youth recreational facility, some residents did not passively acquiesce. During this same period of time, with the help of a tenant relations representative from CHA, the residents had managed to organize four of the seven blocks in Wentworth and had formed a development-wide elected Resident Council. A small core of volunteers expanded to 15 committed activists. (Over the last three decades, the core group has fluctuated between 10 to 20 women.)

According to Mrs. Hallie Amey (at that time the Resident Council President) it was a local youth protest against the lack of community recreational programs that mobilized her and several other Resident Council members into action to attempt to take control of the field house and assure that the physical facility and youth programs would begin to function. Mrs. Amey describes this precipitating event:

> One day I looked out the window, I think we [the Resident Council] were giving a small fish fry or something, and there was a group of boys marching through the area with picket signs on them, picketing CHA. And I told the ladies, "They're picketing the wrong group. They [the boys] should be picketing us." I said, "If anything comes up in here for us, it's going to come through us."

In the mid-1960s, women resident activists through the Resident Council pressured the CHA to authorize them to operate a youth program in the field house. When continued appeals to CHA and on-site management failed to make CHA accountable, Mrs. Amey and several other residents attempted to press management to allow them to run a program in the field house. But management declined. They deemed the residents unreliable and incapable. These women's frustrations were palpable. According to Mrs. Amey:

> This space [the field house] was used for recreation and it had refrigerators and stoves in it! What little recreation material was there was locked in a closet, and they wouldn't even give us that.

With no options left, these Wentworth women decided to act on their own with the material resources that they could count on as their own. They created a preschool program in one of the field house rooms. Mrs. Amey explained that "the only thing we had was a desire to start":

> We didn't have anything. So what we did, we sat down and decided, what could we start with nothing. . . . [W]e decided we'd start a small preschool program because one would bring a ball and different little things that we

had at home, and that's how we began. And we carried that program on for about two years.

This successful preschool program, which accommodated 25 to 30 children, operated 5 days per week through the work of resident volunteers. When the program was well established, the CHA did officially grant the residents control of the field house facility. Ultimately, with technical assistance the Resident Council sought from The Illinois Institute of Technology and other outside institutions, the Chicago Park District was pressured to assume responsibility for youth recreation programs. The Park District is still there today.

In organizing the preschool program and securing the reopening of the field house for youth activities, the residents achieved "modest victories, small fragmented but positive changes in their lives" (Feldman & Stall, 1990, p. 114). The notion of modest victories was adopted from Celene Krauss's (1983, p. 54) concept of "modest struggles," "small, fragmented, and sometimes contradictory efforts by people to change their lives." In conceptualizing the influence of modest struggles on empowerment, we have found that these struggles are not enough; rather, some modest victories are necessary to engender self-esteem and confidence for further action. Although they are small, modest victories are not insignificant. These short-lived successful protests of everyday life illustrate the possibilities for social change from the bottom up.

The residents' struggles to control the spatial resources necessary to operate the youth program were integral to these modest victories. Initially, when unsuccessful in their attempts to pressure CHA to reopen the field house for needed youth recreational activities, Wentworth women relied on their own initiative and resources. With this modest victory they gained the self-confidence and skills to challenge CHA successfully to give them control over the field house facility. Through these actions, Wentworth women were "confronting institutions" and came "to a better understanding of the power relations that affect their lives and of their own abilities—together with others—to have some influence on them" (Ackelsberg, 1988, p. 304).

Wentworth Gardens Laundromat: Building Community

The Wentworth residents' ongoing struggles to maintain and improve the field house facility and its programs illustrates the synergistic relationship among individual and collective space appropriation processes and community building. In a review of the literature on women and community, Shulamit Reinharz (1984) defined community-building activities as "those actions engaged in by a group of people on their own initiative in order to increase social cohesiveness of unrelated persons or to enhance the opportunities or redress the injustices of persons with whom the group identifies beyond their own family" (p. 20). To accomplish their objectives, residents did not, nor could they effectively act alone. In fact, their efforts to control the field house were motivated by a strong sense of rootedness in a community, a sense of pride and determination, and a sense of attachment and support within a caring community of neighbors. Informal and organized means to further develop community were necessary for residents to take and sustain control of the field house that, in turn, provided critical resources to appropriate other physical settings in their housing development. One such setting is the laundromat.

Founded in 1968 by the Resident Council, the laundromat is a place for neighboring and a primary recruitment ground for community activists. Prior to 1968, Wentworth Gardens had no laundry facilities.[6] The nearest retail laundromat was 10 blocks away through the "unsafe turf" of other low-income neighborhoods.

It was Mrs. Taylor who "instigated" the idea for the laundromat and organized volunteers to supervise the original five machines. It was Mrs. Amey, with the help of other residents who pressed the CHA for the space—a centrally located, unused basement of a garden apartment building—and funds for the initial leasing costs. And, it has been the ongoing volunteer work of women residents spanning two decades that has assured the laundromat's continued operation. Most volunteers work several 3-hour shifts per week in order to keep the facility open from 7:00 A.M. to 7:00 P.M., 6 days per week—women like Mrs. Mae Frances Jones, one of the original laundromat volunteers, who, for 17 years, has worked for up to 3 hours per day, 4 days per week; and Mrs. Henrietta Shah, described as the "Rock of Gibraltar" because in addition to her own shift (working up to 4 days per week), she often relieves other operators as the need arises and does simple washer repairs learned through years of volunteering.

The visible signs of space appropriation are numerous. The darkness of the basement is lightened by fresh paint, a full announcement board, birthday cards adorning the walls, and the activity of residents doing the ordinary domestic work of clothes washing. Visibly impressive are the 12 new washers purchased with monies earned through years of an efficiently organized operation.

[6]Originally the Wentworth Gardens development had a laundry room located in each of the seven blocks. Residents purchased a key to their facility. When the overhead to maintain these laundry rooms became too high, the CHA discontinued this on-site service.

For the women who care for and operate the facility, the laundromat is "their" facility, one they speak about with great pride. Furthermore, when interviewed, the laundromat operators expressed intense attachment to this place. One woman who had volunteered for nearly 20 years described the laundromat as "our community." Others mentioned the friends they've made through their work—Mrs. Mary Rias explained that she loved her laundromat work because, in her words, "I like meeting people, and you know everybody in the community." And there are the rituals that reinforce solidarity such as birthdays celebrated "right down here." Perhaps the high degree of social cohesion and interdependence generated through appropriation of this physical facility can best be demonstrated by Mrs. Lucille Burns, who although she and her husband moved out of Wentworth several year ago, still returns three times a week to work in the laundromat.

In the process of providing a service to their communities, the laundromat operators are deriving a sense of significance by being a part of this core group of volunteers. They share a sense of achievement in the laundromat's success. Wentworth residents rely on this facility; it is cost-efficient and convenient. One volunteer explained that the residents "had a fit" when the laundromat had to close for a month for painting. Volunteers take great pride in the new washers purchased in 1988 with $20,850 saved from laundromat proceeds. All profits above maintenance, repair, and replacement costs are returned to the community. A Resident Service Committee, made up of laundromat volunteers, meets monthly to resolve problems and to prioritize requests for laundromat profits. Regular recipients have included yearly community festivals and scholarship funds.

Through their actions and experiences to appropriate the laundromat and field house, women volunteers have provided a necessary service as well as created a sense of solidarity and of significance that are fundamental to the experience of community (Clark, 1973). Moreover, they have developed skills and self-confidence to sustain the development of community. In their struggles to create, maintain, and enhance both the field house and the laundromat facility, their conventionally defined domestic role was expanded to community organizing. Similarly, the traditionally defined private, domestic domain of doing household laundry and caring for children has met the public world of business. In providing a domestic service for the community's residents, these women have run the laundromat, an enterprise that makes a profit and selectively distributes the profits to further community development.

In their attention to community activism, Sara Evans and Harry Boyte (1981) have offered historical evidence that rootedness in communal settings and participation in communal structures "can serve as the arenas where people can distinguish themselves from elite [societal] definitions of who they are, [and] gain the skills and mutual regard necessary to act as a force for change" (1981, p. 56). Particularly for women, communal structures can serve as "free spaces" offering arenas outside of the family where women can develop "a growing sense that they had [have] the right to work—first in behalf of others, then in behalf of themselves" (Evans & Boyte, 1981, p. 61; Evans & Boyte, 1986). Implicit in the Evans and Boyte work is that free spaces are place-bound settings. Our observations illustrate that the laundromat and field house are "sited" free spaces.

THE STRUGGLES TO SAVE HOMEPLACE

The history of invisible struggles that Wentworth women resident activists engaged in to create and sustain their homeplace and to alter conditions that threatened their community viability prepared them and their neighbors for visible action in the high-stakes political arena. It was the threat to the physical survival of Wentworth Gardens and its surrounding neighborhood posed by the proposed construction of the new Chicago White Sox Stadium that brought Wentworth residents into the political arena to do "battle" to protect "their homes." A resident initiated on-site action committee had been meeting regularly for more than a year to assist the Local Advisory Council (LAC), the CHA designated site representative, in their ongoing frustration with the nonresponsiveness of CHA to attend to years of deferred building and site maintenance and inadequate services to meet basic daily needs of the residents.[7] The action committee became the focal group moved to collective action by what they believed to be the "crisis" posed by the new stadium, a crisis with an immediate, tangible impact on their community. To assist them, the committee sought help from a local community organizers, Sheila Radford-Hill, lent by a Chicago citywide not-for-profit organization. Sheila Radford-Hill had worked previously in the community with Mrs. Amey on local educational issues (setting up a School Watch Program). After meeting for several weeks, the committee selected a name for itself. Mrs. Amey stated:

[7]Officially, residents at each of the 19 CHA developments are represented by a CHA-designated structure called the Local Advisory Council (LAC). LAC officers are elected locally, but LACs vary widely across developments both in terms of their respresentativeness and effectiveness in dealing with on-site issues.

[I]t was decided and approved that we would choose the name—Wentworth Garden Residents United for Survival—because we felt at that point that's what we really would be. Because here were the White Sox right up on us threatening to take our home, and here's CHA doing nothing for us in here—it was the only name that really fit what we were about to be about!

In 1987, through strong leadership and persistent organizing efforts, the committee was officially incorporated as the Wentworth Gardens Residents United for Survival (Wentworth United) (see Figure 2). Although the White Sox Stadium struggle served as the central focus for this group, a more immediate need was the physical deterioration of the field house. Once again this necessary facility required local organizing efforts. The field house roof was in such poor repair that the scheduled children's summer food program was at risk of being canceled.

The women of Wentworth United began to attend the weekly public CHA Board of Commissioners' meetings to pressure for the roof repair. Time and persistence resulted in CHA's approval of the roof repair, but no available funds. Undaunted, Wentworth United women persevered and continued to press the CHA Regional Supervisor until repair monies were located and allocated, and the field house roof was not only repaired, but replaced.

For the Wentworth United women, the repair of the field house roof served their goal to provide a visible, tangible sign of their growing political effectiveness not only for themselves, but for all residents of the Wentworth Gardens development, and for CHA and municipal officials. This was a proud time for Wentworth United activists.

With the summer food program in place, Wentworth United focused its attention on the impending stadium construction. It is to the credit of the organizational reputation and expertise of women activist members of Wentworth United that they provided local leadership among impacted home owners, renters, and CHA residents in the political and legal actions against the Illinois Sports Facility Authority,[8] the White Sox Corporation, and the City of Chicago. Mrs. Amey explained how their home-owning neighbors learned about their organizing efforts:

Some of the folk who live down there have relatives in here. And they were telling them about the flyer. We sent out a very, very colorful flyer. We had a little man on it. Had a map drawn on the paper and [the flyer] said, "Have you seen this?" And the man was pointing to the map about the White Sox

[8]"In January 1987, Governor Thompson of Illinois and Mayor Washington of Chicago signed a law that formed the Illinois Sports Facility Authority (ISFA). This Authority was specifically set up to build a new stadium for the Chicago White Sox team. By 1988, ISFA had decided that the new stadium would be south of 35th Street, directly south of Comiskey Park" (Wright, 1988, p. 2).

Figure 2. A Wentworth Gardens Residents United for Survival Meeting, December, 1989 (photographer, Diana Solis).

Park and how far it was coming, and how much of Wentworth was going to be taken away.

Members of Wentworth United were approached by their home-owning neighbors for organizing assistance. Mrs. Marcella Carter, a Wentworth United activist, shared:

> A group of residents [from the surrounding neighborhood] had come to us and asked us, would we help them, because the White Sox were going to tear their homes down. They didn't have any idea about a council or anything so we helped them. We got Sheila [Radford-Hill] to come out and we helped them to form the South Armour Square Neighborhood Coalition.

Aided in their organizing efforts, once again by Sheila Radford-Hill, the South Armour Square Neighborhood Coalition (SASNC) was formed in response to a direct threat to their neighborhood. SASNC included not only Wentworth residents, but homeowners from 178 homes within the site of the proposed stadium, residents in a neighboring senior housing development, T. E. Brown Apartments, and renters from Bridgeport and Fuller Park. The coalition voted to oppose the stadium construction because of the devastating effect it would have on South Armour Square, a stable community since 1945 (Wright, 1988).

The Wentworth United activists, now as part of SASNC, began the battle by lobbying appropriate public officials. Coalition members first attended Sports Authority meetings at the old ballpark, Comiskey Park. Mrs. Carter, now the South Armour Square Coalition's secretary, explained the strategy they used to make their presence known:

> There was one time when we went to the stadium, to the Sports Authority meeting, and we had little crickets [noise makers]. And everytime they said something we didn't like, we'd crick them. They were going off at the meeting and naturally they threw us out.

As coalition members, the residents also made four trips to lobby the state legislators, including the Black Caucus in Springfield, Illinois, to block a bill that supported the stadium construction at the proposed site. Promises were made by legislators and later broken; the bill to build the new stadium was passed. The Illinois Sports Facility Authority, in an agreement with the homeowners within the proposed site began purchasing the property in August, 1988; this resulted in the homeowners leaving the coalition, although the remaining residents continued to oppose the stadium development (Wright, 1988). According to the dissenting coalition board members, this agreement was never ratified because it was not properly approved by the board.

The coalition continued for 2 years to organize and attempt to negotiate with the Sports Authority to modify the site plan to locate the stadium south of 35th Street. On February 8, 1989, the coalition filed a lawsuit against the City of Chicago, the Sports Facility Authority, and the White Sox Corporation. Initially, the lawsuit aimed to halt the stadium development on the grounds that planning and decision making for the stadium site were done in violation of the civil rights of community members. Unsuccessful in their attempts to halt the construction of the new stadium, which opened in the spring of 1991 (see Figure 3), the coalition altered the demands of their suit. Mrs Carter, who remains an active Wentworth representative in the coalition, explained the purpose of this pending lawsuit (also see Zhang & Wright, 1992):

> We want them to rebuild the neighborhood. We want them to build some houses over there by the park on 37th [Street], and put a commercial strip up and down 39th [Street]—stores, cleaners, a medical center. We had stores; we didn't have any medical center, but we had stores . . . and we want them back.

This lawsuit is expected to be settled in the near future.

In doing battle to reappropriate their homes, Wentworth resident activists extended their range of actions and experiences into the sur-

Figure 3. The west side of Wentworth Gardens in the shadow of Comiskey Park, 1991 (photographer, Susan Stall).

rounding neighborhood. They acted independently of the CHA in the public domain. In the process, they formalized their organizational structure. In publicly confronting formidable opponents, Wentworth resident activists increased their knowledge of how the city and state political system functions while elaborating upon and extending their organizing and protest strategies. Lastly, these women established new social, political, and technical networks that are vital to their present and future plans.

THEORETICAL IMPLICATIONS

Wentworth women residents' creation, improvement, and/or maintenance of the field house and laundromat, and their struggles to save their homes and their neighborhood from the threat of the impact of the new White Sox stadium are visible, material indicators of the appropriation of homeplace. With no monetary resources, little political clout, minimal technical assistance, and a generally obstructive CHA bureaucracy, Wentworth activists have managed to make small but significant improvements in the living conditions at their housing development and in the accountability of CHA.

Yet, Wentworth women activists provide more than just a service to their community. In transforming the spaces of Wentworth Gardens to meet their and their neighbors' daily needs they are transforming themselves. In their everyday, ongoing modest struggles and victories to appropriate homeplace, Wentworth women activists are empowering themselves.

APPROPRIATION OF HOMEPLACE AS EMPOWERMENT

The notion of empowerment has provided social scientists and activists with a new perspective to understand and support strategies by which people, in particular those who have limited access to economic and political resources, effect improved conditions in their communities (reviewed in Kieffer, 1984; Zimmerman, forthcoming; also see Rappaport, 1981). The idea of empowerment is grounded in the "social action" and "self-help" perspectives of the 1960s and 1970s, and the growing influence of community organizations that have functioned explicitly to counteract helplessness and disenfranchisement (Kieffer, 1984; Zimmerman, forthcoming). Empowerment research and activism is based on an ideology that seeks to shift the attention to social problems from deficits and needs to rights and abilities (Rappaport, 1981).

Empowerment, like space appropriation, generally has been conceived of as a multidimensional construct including both actions and psychological experiences to exert control and influence (reviewed in Zimmerman, forthcoming). Julian Rappaport has defined empowerment as

> both individual determination over one's own life, and democratic participation in the life of one's community. . . . Empowerment conveys both a psychological sense of personal control or influence, and a concern with actual social influence, political power and legal rights. (1986, p. 3)

Moreover, Rappaport notes that empowerment is not a fixed resource, but rather a process that tends to expand. Empowerment is earned, developed, and ongoing (Zimmerman, forthcoming).

Charles Kieffer (1984) further elaborates on this conceptualization to explicate the developmental process of empowerment. He describes empowerment as a "building up" of skills through repetitive cycles of action and reflection that evoke new skills and understandings, which in turn provoke new and more effective actions. Kieffer further describes empowerment as the attainment of commitment and capabilities that include the development of a more positive self-concept and self-confidence; a more critical world view; and the cultivation of individual and collective skills and resources for social and political action.

This case study of Wentworth women's resident activism uncovers the central contribution of the appropriation of homeplace to the ongoing development of their empowerment. Wentworth residents' actions to control and influence the use and maintenance of the field house served to initiate what Kieffer (1984, p. 18) has called the "era of entry," an initial "empowering response" that marks the onset of the long-term and on-going process of empowerment. Kieffer (1984, p. 19) observed that initial provocations that lead to empowerment are a result of an "immediate and physical violation of the sense of integrity" and a "personally experienced sense of outrage or confrontation." And indeed, Wentworth residents were provoked and outraged by a perceived immediate and tangible impact on the quality of the youths' lives in their development. And their ongoing acts to develop the laundromat as well as maintain the field house fostered and reflected processes of their empowerment.

We have shown how resident activists' ongoing appropriation of the physical settings of their housing development mediated the satisfaction of everyday material needs for safe and decent shelter; facilitated the processes of community building within sited social spaces; provided for economic development opportunities; and served as visible signs of their modest victories. Furthermore, what began as a loosely structured core of concerned residents, today is a not-for-profit organization with attendant greater organizational structure and maintenance activities, and with some political legitimacy in the local and municipal arenas.

Appropriation of homeplace contributed to nurturing individual residents' positive self-concept and self-confidence, local leadership, and collective skills and resources for further social and political action. Through such actions and experiences, Wentworth women gained a sense of self-efficacy and a critical world view necessary for their effective negotiations with powerful actors such as those involved in the White Sox Stadium negotiations. They came to recognize that the obstacles they confront are shared and the result of social, economic, and political barriers rather than individual in nature (also see Wolfe, 1990).

Appropriation of Homeplace as Resistance

Currently, there is considerable scholarly interest in the role that places serve in the expression and imposition of both power and resistance, for instance in the well-known work of Foucault (1979). He argues that cultural discourses about power are transformed into actual power relations in bounded space and architectural forms (reported from an interview with Foucault, Wright, & Rabinow, 1982). Manzo and Wolfe (1990), in interpreting Foucault's work, propose that places are not only the site of power, of the assertion of dominance, they are also the site of resistance: "as power reveals itself it creates the possibility of resistance" (Manzo & Wolfe, 1990, p. 4). They extended Foucault's theories of the social production of people/environment relations to interpret the ways in which environments both reflect "the desires of some groups of people to reproduce the social order in which they are dominant" and also "the attempts by those without such power to resist and survive in a way that is meaningful in their lives" (Wolfe, 1990, p. 3).

Stoecker (1992) reviews recent literature on the role of women's places—retreats and self-development centers, coffee shops, bars, and communities—as sites of recruitment in the latest women's movement. These sites serve as "safe" places where women not only gain a shared understanding of the social, economic, and political sources of oppression in their lives, but where women can act independently of this oppression. The appropriation of these places by and for women is a critical source of resistance in their lives (see Briet, Klandermans, & Kroon, 1987; Hartsock, 1979; also see Wolfe, 1990).

Our work at Wentworth Gardens illustrates the importance of considering the homeplaces in which, and over which, the everyday power struggles to maintain households and communities are manifest. It suggests that homeplace is an accessible and central site for groups of limited resources to engage in social change.

Bell Hooks (1990; also see Davis, 1981), in her book chapter titled "Homeplace: A Site of Resistance" notes the historic importance of homeplace in African-Americans' lives, in particular as a site where they obtained social validation of the existence of dominance and its transformation into resistance. Hooks argues:

> Despite the brutal reality of racial apartheid, of domination, one's homeplace was the one site where one could freely confront the issue of humanization, where one could resist. (p. 42)

Furthermore, Hooks argues that historically, African-Americans' struggles to make and sustain a home and community provided more than a domestic service; it has had a "subversive value" as a source of political action.

At Wentworth Gardens, the ongoing struggle for the appropriation of homeplace not only has provided a site for resistance, it is an act of resistance. To take control of the physical settings of their housing development, Wentworth women have had to defy conventional conceptions of their capabilities and institutional regulations of their rights to control these settings. In the spaces they have appropriated as their own, Wentworth women activists not only have obtained social validation of shared structural and institutional barriers to their access to safe and decent shelter, they have acted to resist this dominance by continuing their struggles to improve their housing conditions. Despite the modesty of their struggles and victories to appropriate homeplace, they are not inconsequential. They contain the transformative potential for Wentworth residents to create both the reality of their resistance and the possibilities for their future resistance.

THE PROSPECTS FOR WENTWORTH WOMEN

For Wentworth women resident activists, their charge is clear. Despite their recent setbacks with their sports stadium battle, Wentworth women are ready to take on new challenges and to take advantage of any opportunity that presents itself to exert control over their housing development. They do not see their efforts as extraordinary; rather they see their collective actions as a means to effect immediate necessary changes in their lives and the lives of other community residents. They have aspirations for a future in which they can make their public housing as nice a place to live as it was in the past.

The obstacles to Wentworth resident activists' ongoing appropriation of the spaces of their housing development are formidable. Their economic and political power over the spaces of their housing development remain tenuous, and their housing conditions are neither entirely safe nor decent. Yet, they are committed to the long-term goal of tenant management. In December, 1989, Wentworth Gardens Residents United for Survival amended their incorporation to officially change their name to Wentworth Gardens Resident Management Corporation (RMC).[9] The CHA has been pressured to recognize and endorse the RMC and provide them with office space. Within the last 2 years, the Wentworth RMC was awarded $100,000 from the U.S. Department of Housing and

---

[9]The Federal Public Housing Resident Management Act was signed into law on February 5, 1988. Under contract with a local public housing agency, a resident management corporation (RMC) may manage their own housing development. Currently one CHA development, LeClair Courts, and one high-rise building in Cabrini Green are established as fully resident managed. Two CHA developments, Dearborn Homes and one high-rise at Wells, have dual-management contracts. Nine other Chicago developments, including Wentworth, have received HUD grants toward the development of resident management.

Urban Development for resident development and training and office equipment. In addition, the RMC has received technical assistance from CHA, nearly $35,000 in private foundation grants for RMC staffing, training, and tenant operations, and organizing assistance from the Lindeman Center, the Nathalie P. Voorhees Center, and Women United for a Better Chicago. Without this monetary and technical assistance the RMC could not move ahead.

There is much left to be accomplished, but the Wentworth residents we spoke to believe that they have established the core group of experienced volunteers that will in the not-too-distant future make resident management a reality at Wentworth Gardens. Mrs. Marcella Bryant, a Wentworth activist and on-site VISTA youth worker, described the strengths of Wentworth women in their struggles for resident management:

> We don't give up . . . we're willing to fight for what we need here and what we want here, and I think that's the strength we have; and [we are] learning to pull people together to fight for what is needed.

And Mrs. Maggie Mahon, Chair of the Security Committee of Wentworth Gardens RMC challenged, "It can be done. Don't give up. Keep on fighting!"

FUTURE RESEARCH DIRECTIONS

Patricia Hill Collins argues that research has contributed to the invisibility of low income, and in particular African-American women's political activism:

> Social science research has ignored Black women's actions in both the struggle for group survival and institutional transformation. . . . White male conceptualizations of the political process produce definitions of power, activism, and resistance that fail to capture the meaning of these concepts in Black women's lives. (1991, p. 141)

Social science and dominant cultural portrayals of politics typically focus on the public, official actors and workings of government rather than everyday social resistance. Moreover, the social science literature generally disregards and devalues community-based struggles of people to gain control over their lives, struggles in which women traditionally have played major roles (e.g., Bourque & Grossholtz, 1974; Delamont, 1980; Bookman & Morgen, 1988; Collins, 1991; Haywoode, 1991; McCourt, 1977; Naples, 1988; Shanley & Schuck, 1974; Siefer, 1973; Stoecker, 1992; Susser, 1982; West & Blumberg, 1990). Feminist scholars are challenging this conventional conceptualization of politics.

The feminist and social-science empowerment literature elaborates the ways in which people's race, class, and gender not only account for their community-based needs but for the nature of their involvement in grassroots politics (e.g., Bookman & Morgen, 1988; Collins, 1991; Feldman & Stall, 1990; Gilkes, 1979; Haywoode, 1991; Krauss 1983; Leavitt & Saegert, 1990; Naples, 1988; Rappaport, 1986; Stoecker, 1992). Poor and working-class women and in particular women of color cannot rely on culturally normative routes of electoral politics nor financial resources to work in their best interests. Rather, they achieve their power from the bottom up, through their involvement in collective community-based action.

Feminist studies of grassroots community activism among low-income and working-class women reveal the ways these women bring critical skills to collective actions, skills that are cultivated through every-day routine activities of maintaining households and communities—tasks necessary to the "social reproduction" of individual households as well as the social arrangements they make to protect, enhance, and preserve the cultural experiences of all members of the community (Stoecker, 1992). Yet, feminist scholars (reviewed in Morgen & Bookman, 1988; also see Naples, 1988; Stoecker, 1992) note that low-income women's participation is not motivated solely by their concerns as wives and mothers. These scholars do not deny that women's domestic responsibilities contribute to their political consciousness and actions; rather, they advocate an approach that gives due recognition to the ways in which race and class specify women's housing and support service needs and the nature of their involvement in grassroots activism.

Despite the attention to the political dimensions of social reproduction in feminist scholarship, the *homeplaces* in which, and often over which, power struggles are manifest are largely overlooked. Although grassroots activism is implicitly place-bound, the physical setting of grassroots activism is presumed to be a background to power struggles.

Our observations of Wentworth residents' appropriation of homeplace and its relationship to empowerment processes are not unique. For instance, John Turner (1977; also see Turner & Fichter's edited volume, 1972) describes several examples of squatter settlements, self-help and tenant-management housing, and homesteading in underdeveloped and developed countries. He notes the individual and community pride, capabilities, and commitments that are developed in the process of gaining "dweller control" of their housing.

Jacqueline Leavitt and Susan Saegert (1990), in their recent study of what they call the "community household," describe low-income

African-Americans' and Hispanics' collaborative households' actions in "staking a claim to their buildings" (p. 11) to transform abandoned buildings in Harlem into co-op housing. In fact, they note:

> The people we talked with provided better models of coping with adversity than their building did of housing. We saw that the huge reservoir of unused human energy and talent lying in waste in many poor communities will come to the surface when conditions allow for its emergence, even when physical circumstances are difficult. (1990, p. 167)

Turner's, Leavitt and Saegert's, and our research findings add to the growing evidence and convictions of participatory researchers and grassroots activists that improvements in low-income people's housing conditions as well as the general quality of their lives must be grounded in local initiatives with the infusion of public and private technical support (see Birch, 1985; Sprague, 1991; Weisman, 1992). Rappaport (1981) charts a course that gives clear precedence to examining and supporting the bottom-up political efforts of people to gain control over their lives:

> On the one hand it [a social policy of empowerment] demands that we look to many diverse local settings where people are already handling their own problems in living, in order to learn more about how they do it . . . it demands that we find ways to take what we learn from these diverse settings and solutions and make it more public, so as to help foster social programs that make it more rather than less, that others not now handling their own problems in living or shut out from current solutions, gain control over their lives. (1981, pp. 1, 15)

We urge the continued investigation of the everyday, ongoing, and yet often invisible struggles of poor women of color to appropriate homeplace in low-income communities. As safe and decent shelter becomes increasingly difficult to obtain, the empowering experiences of appropriating homeplace provide a central, crucial means for low-income women of color to develop resources for collective power to improve their housing conditions.

To further this investigation, there are many research questions that need to be addressed: How is appropriation of homeplace supported or discouraged in other public housing developments? In other low-income neighborhoods? What are the physical characteristics of the existing housing and neighborhood that may promote and/or inhibit appropriation of homeplace; for instance, the condition of the dwellings and other built structures, landscaping, and infrastructure, dwelling, housing and neighborhood density, and land use mix?

We have found that appropriation of homeplace does not exist apart from other community-building activities. We need to know more about how space-appropriation efforts are facilitated by and facilitate other informal and organized means of developing community? How does participation in traditional community organizations (e.g., Parent Teachers Association, church groups, Girl Scouts) provide social resources and skill building for grassroots actions? What is beneficial and/or problematic when informal community-building processes become formalized?

Wentworth women's modest victories in appropriating homeplace received considerable assistance from outside resources. Further research needs to uncover and elaborate the ways in which partnerships with housing management, technical assistants, community organizers, and public and private funders function to foster and/or inhibit residents' activism. Furthermore, research needs to elaborate the ways in which public policies and bureaucratically supported political actions enhance or block ongoing appropriation processes.

In order to address these research questions and objectives, we recommend an historical perspective and interdisciplinary approach. Many decades of activism precede researchers' entry into the field. An in-depth understanding of these earlier efforts is integral to both to understand and appreciate current organizing efforts and entrenched structural constraints (including racism, classism, and sexism) that challenge these efforts. In a related way, we believe that an interdisciplinary approach both informs and broadens data-gathering processes and the development of theoretical frameworks. For example, our research observations and interpretations are dependent on insights from sociology, women's studies, and environmental psychology. Without the development of this multidisciplinary lens, we would have missed the complexity of Wentworth women's everyday resistance.

Finally, we believe that a participatory research paradigm is crucial to the success of these research efforts. Participatory research has interdisciplinary roots in environmental and ethnic studies, applied sociology, and women's studies. Also referred to as "advocacy research," "action research," "participatory action research," and "proactive community-based research," participatory research seeks to develop understandings of social relations and social change by fostering dialogue and social respect between the researcher and those researched (as reviewed in Petras & Porpora, 1992; see also Bonavich & Stoecker, 1992, 1993). Furthermore, this research paradigm necessitates the use of these understandings to uncover and improve inequitable societal conditions. Those who utilize a participatory research model are rewarded by both the depth and breadth of their research findings and by their contributions to efforts to transform unjust social relations.

Wentworth Gardens resident activists' appropriation of homeplace attests to the strength and resourcefulness of low-income women to gain control over their lives despite most oppressive conditions. An understanding of these and other acts of resistance is necessary to make visible the nature of political action in poor communities. If we do not develop an appreciation for these bottom-up efforts we cannot truly comprehend and support the roots of social change.

Acknowledgments

We want to thank the Wentworth residents for their generous support of our research efforts. These busy activists have welcomed us into their community and into their lives. We also would like to thank Stephan Klein for his suggestion that we examine the usefulness of the concept of space appropriation in interpreting our data; and again Stephan Klein, David Chapin, Marc Fried, Diane Haslett, Martha Thompson, and Maxine Wolfe for their comments on earlier drafts of this chapter.

REFERENCES

Acklesberg, M. A. (1988). Communities, resistance and women's activism: Some implications for a democratic polity. In A. Bookman & S. Morgen (Eds.), *Women and the politics of empowerment* (pp. 297–313). Philadelphia: Temple University Press.

Becker, H. S. (1966). Introduction. In C. F. Shaw, *The jackroller: A delinquent boy's own story.* Chicago: University of Chicago Press.

Birch, E. L. (1978). Woman-made housing: The case of early public housing policy. *Journal of the American Institute of Planners, 44,* 130–143.

Birch, E. L. (Ed.). (1985). *The unsheltered woman: Women and housing in the 80's.* New Brunswick, NJ: Center for Urban Policy Research.

Bonavich, E., & Stoecker, R. (Guest Eds.). (1992). Participatory research (Part 1). *American Sociologist, 23*(4).

Bonavich, E., & Stoecker, R. (Guest Eds.). (1993). Participatory research (Part 2). *American Sociologist, 24*(1).

Bookman, A., & Morgen, S. (Eds.). (1988). *Women and the politics of empowerment.* Philadelphia: Temple University Press.

Bourque, S. C., & Grossholtz, J. (1974). Politics an unnatural practice: Political science looks at female participation. *Politics and Society 4*(2), 225–264.

Bowley, Jr., D. (1978). *The poorhouse: Subsidized housing in Chicago, 1895–1976.* Carbondale: Southern Illinois University Press.

Briet, M., Klandermans, B., & Kroon, F. (1987). How women become involved in the women's movement of The Netherlands. In M. F. Katzenstein & C. M. Mueller (Eds.), *The women's movements of the United States and Western Europe: Consciousness, political opportunity, and public policy.* Philadelphia: Temple University Press.

Buttimer, A. (1980). Home, reach, and the sense of place. In A. Buttimer & D. Seamon (Eds.), *The human experience of space and place* (pp. 166–187). New York: St. Martin's Press.

Chicago Housing Authority. (1991). Department of Research and Program Development.

Chicago Tribune. (1986). The Chicago Wall, Special Report.

Chombart de Lauwe, P. (1976). Appropriation of space and social change. In P. Korosec-Serfaty (Ed.), *Appropriation of space.* (Proceedings of the 3rd International Architectural Psychology Conference, pp. 23–30). Strasbourg, France.

Clark, D. (1973). The concept of community: A re-examination. *Sociological Review, 21*(3), 397–416.

Collins, P. H. (1991). *Black feminist thought: Knowledge, consciousness, and the politics of empowerment.* New York: Routledge.

Cooper, C. (1974). *The house a symbol of self.* Reprint No. 122. Berkeley: Institute of Urban and Regional Development, University of California, Berkeley.

Csikszentmihalyi, M., & Rochberg-Halton, E. (1981). *The meaning of things: Domestic symbols and the self.* Cambridge: Cambridge University Press.

Davis, A. (1981). *Women, race, and class.* New York: Random House.

Delamont, S. (1980). *The sociology of women.* London: George Allen & Unwin.

Despres, C. (1989). The meaning of home: Literature review and directions for future research and theoretical development. Paper presented at the International Housing Symposium, Gavle, Sweden, August.

Duncan, N. G. (1981). Home ownership and social theory. In J. S. Duncan (Ed.), *Housing and identity: Cross-cultural perspectives* (pp. 98–134). London: Croom Helm.

Evans, S. M., & Boyte, H. C. (1981). Schools for social action: Radical uses of social space. *Democracy,* Summer, 55–65.

Evans, S. M., & Boyte, H. C. (1986). *Free spaces: The sources of democratic change in America.* New York: Harper & Row.

Feldman, R. M., & Stall, S. (1989). Women in public housing: "There just comes a point. . ." *The Neighborhood Works,* June–July, 4–6.

Feldman, R. M., & Stall, S. (1990). Resident activism in public housing: A case study of women's invisible work of building community. In R. I. Selby, K. H. Anthony, J. Choi, & B. Orland (Eds.), *Coming of age* (Proceedings of the Environmental Design Research Association Annual Conference, pp. 111–119). Urbana-Champaign, Illinois.

Fischer, R. (1959). *Twenty years of public housing.* New York: Harper & Brothers.

Foucault, M. (1979). *Discipline and punish: The birth of the prison.* Trans. Alan Sheridan. New York: Vintage.

Fried, M. (1963). Grieving for a lost home. In L. Duhl (Ed.), *The urban condition* (pp. 151–171). New York: Basic Books.

Fried, M., & Gleicher, P. (1970). Some sources of residential satisfaction in an urban slum. In H. M. Proshansky, W. H. Ittelson, & L. G. Rivlin (Eds.), *Environmental psychology: Man and his physical setting* (pp. 333–346). New York: Holt, Rinehart & Winston.

Gans, H. (1962). *The urban villagers.* New York: Free Press.

Gilkes, C. L. T. (1979). *Living and working in a world of trouble: The emergent career of the Black women community workers* (Doctoral dissertation, Northwestern University, 1982).

Graumann, C. F. (1976). The concept of appropriation (aneignung) and modes of appropriation of space. In P. Korosec-Serfaty (Ed.), *Appropriation of space* (Proceedings of the 3rd International Architectural Psychology Conference, pp. 113–123). Strasbourg, France.

Hartsock, N. C. M. (1979). Feminism, power, and change: A theoretical analysis. In B. Cummings & V. Schuck (Eds.), *Women organizing: An anthology* (pp. 2–24). Metuchen, NJ: Scarecrow Press.

Hayden, D. (1984). *Redesigning the American dream: The future of housing, work, and family life.* New York: Norton.

Haywoode, T. (1991). *Working class feminism: Creating a politics of community, connection, and concern* (Doctoral dissertation, City University of New York, 1991).

Hirsch, A. (1985). *Making of the second ghetto: Race & housing in Chicago: 1940–1960.* Cambridge: Cambridge University Press.

Hooks, B. (1990). *Yearning: Race, gender, and cultural politics.* Boston: South End Books.

Keys, L. D. (1991). *The effects of resident empowerment in community planning for African American underclass populations* (Doctoral dissertation, University of Illinois at Chicago, 1991).

Kieffer, C. H. (1984). Citizen empowerment: A developmental perspective. In J. Rappaport, C. Swift, & R. Hess (Eds.), *Studies in empowerment: Steps toward understanding action* (pp. 9–36). New York: Haworth.

Korosec-Serfaty, P. (Ed.). (1976). *Appropriation of space* (Proceedings of the 3rd International Architectural Psychology Conference). Strasbourg, France.

Kotlowitz, A. (1991). *There are no children here: The story of growing up in the other America.* New York: Doubleday.

Krauss, C. (1983). The elusive process of citizen activism. *Social Policy,* Fall, 50–55.

Lawson, R., & Barton, S. E. (1980). Sex roles in social movements: A case study of the tenant movement in New York City. *Signs: A Journal of Women in Culture and Society, 6,* 230–247.

Leavitt, J., & Saegert, S. (1984). Women and abandoned buildings: A feminist approach to housing. *Social Policy,* Summer, 32–39.

Leavitt, J., & Saegert, S. (1990). *From abandonment to hope: The community-household in Harlem.* New York: Columbia University Press.

McClain, J. (1979–1980). Access, security, and power: Women are still second-class citizens in the housing market. *Status of Women News, 6*(1), 15.

McCourt, K. (1977). *Working-class women and grass-roots politics.* Bloomington: Indiana University Press.

Manzo, L. C., & Wolfe, M. (1990). *The social production of built forms, environmental settings and person/environment relationships.* Paper presented at the International Association of People and Environment Studies, Ankara, Turkey.

Metropolitan Planning Council. (1986). *Untapped potentials: The capacities, needs and views of Chicago's highrise public housing residents.* September.

Metropolitan Planning Council. (1988). *Our homes, our neighborhoods: The case for rehabilitating Chicago's public housing.* April.

Morgen, S., & Bookman, A. (1988). Rethinking women and politics: An introductory essay. In A. Bookman & S. Morgen (Eds.), *Women and the politics of empowerment* (pp. 3–29). Philadelphia: Temple University Press.

Naples, N. A. (1988). *Women against poverty: Community workers in anti-poverty programs, 1964–1984* (Doctoral dissertation, City University of New York, 1988). *University Microfilms International.* Ann Arbor, Michigan.

National Council of Negro Women. (1975). *Women and housing: A report on sex discrimination in five American cities.* Commissioned by the U.S. Department of Housing and Urban Development, Office of the Assistant Secretary for Fair Housing and Equal Opportunity. (Washington, DC: U.S. Government Printing Office, June, 33.

Newman, O. (1972). *Defensible space.* New York: Macmillan.

Ollman, B. (1971). *Alienation: Marx's conception of man in capitalist society.* Cambridge, London: Cambridge at the University Press.

Pearce, C. (1978). The feminization of poverty: Women, work, and welfare. *Urban and Social Change Review, 11,* 28–36.

Pearce, C. (1983). The feminization of ghetto poverty. *Transaction: Social Science and Modern Society, 21*(1).

Petras, E. M., & Porpora, D. V. (1992). *Role, responsibility and reciprocity: Participatory research with grass roots and community organizations.* Paper presented at the American Sociological Association Annual Meeting, Pittsburgh, Pennsylvania, August.

Platt, J. (1984). *The meanings of case-study methods in the inter-war period.* Paper presented at the American Sociological Association Annual Meetings, San Antonio, Texas.

Proshansky, H. M. (1976). The appropriation and misappropriation of space. In P. Korosec-Serfaty (Ed.), *Appropriation of space* (Proceedings of the 3rd International Architectural Psychology Conference, pp. 31–69). Strasbourg, France.

Pynoos, J. (1986). *Breaking the rules: Bureaucracy and reform in public housing.* New York: Plenum Press.

Rainwater, L. (1966). Fear and the house-as-haven in the lower class. *American Institute of Planners Journal,* January, 23–31.

Rappaport, J. (1981). In praise of paradox: A social policy of empowerment over prevention. *American Journal of Community Psychology, 9*(1), 1–26.

Rappaport, J. (1986). *Terms of empowerment/exemplars of prevention: Toward a theory for community psychology.* An address delivered at the Annual Meeting of the American Psychological Association, Washington, DC, August.

Reinharz, S. (1984). Women as competent community builders. In A. U. Rickel, M. Gerrard, & I. Iscoe (Eds.), *Social and psychological problems of women* (pp. 19–43). Washington: Hemisphere Publishing Corporation.

Relph, E. (1976). *Place and placelessness.* London: Pion.

Sacks, K. B. (1988). *Caring by the hour: Women, work, and organizing at Duke Medical Center.* Chicago: University of Illinois Press.

Scobie, R. (1975). *Problem tenants in public housing: Who, where and why are they.* New York: Praeger.

Seamon, D. A. (1979). *A geography of the lifeworld.* New York: St. Martin's Press.

Shanley, M. L., & Schuck, V. (1974). In search of political women. *Social Science Quarterly* (December), 632–644.

Siefer, N. (1973). *Absent from the majority: Working class women in America.* New York: National Project on Ethnic America of the American Jewish Committee.

Slayton, R. A. (1988). *Chicago's public housing crisis: Causes and solutions.* Report for the Chicago Urban League, June.

Sprague, J. F. (1991). *More than housing: Lifeboats for women and children.* Boston: Butterworth.

Stoecker, R. (1991). Evaluating and rethinking the case study. *Sociological Review, 39,* 88–112.

Stoecker, R. (1992). Who takes out the garbage? Social reproduction and social movement research. In G. Miller & J. A. Holstein (Eds.), *Perspectives on social problems* (pp. 239–264). Greenwich, CT: JAI Press.

Susser, I. (1982). *Norman Street.* New York: Oxford University Press.

Suttles, G. D. (1968). *The social order of the slum: Ethnicity and territory in the inner city.* Chicago: University of Chicago Press.

Tuan, Y. (1977). *Space and place: The perspective of experience.* Minneapolis: University of Minnesota Press.

Turner, J. F. C. (1977). *Housing by people: Towards autonomy in building environments.* New York: Pantheon.

Turner, J. F. C., & Fichter, R. (Eds.). (1972). *Freedom to build.* New York: Macmillan.

Wacquant, L. J. A., & Wilson, W. J. (1989). The cost of racial and class exclusion in the inner city. *Annals of the American Academy of Political and Social Science, 501,* 32–39.

Weisman, L. K. (1992). *Discrimination by design: A feminist critique of the man-made environment.* Urbana: University of Illinois Press.

Wekerle, G. R. (1980). Women in the urban environment. *Signs: A Journal of Women in Culture and Society,* Special Issue, Women and the American City, Supplement, 5(3), S188–S214.

Werner, K. (Ed.). (1992). Group appropriation of space. *Architecture and Behavior, 8*(1), 1–79.

West, G., & Blumberg, R. L. (Eds.). (1990). *Women and social protest.* New York: Oxford University Press.

Wolfe, M. (1990). *Whose culture? Whose space? Whose history?: Learning from lesbian bars.* Keynote address at the 11th Conference of the International Association for the Study of People and Their Surroundings (IAPS), Ankara, Turkey, July.

Wright, G. (1981). *Building the dream: A social history of housing in America.* New York: Pantheon.

Wright, G., & Rabinow, P. (1982). Spatialization of power: Discussion of the work of Michel Foucault. *Skyline,* March, 14–15.

Wright, P. (1988). *The South Armour Square strategy plan.* Report for the Nathalie P. Voorhees Center for Neighborhood and Community Improvement. University of Illinois at Chicago.

Zhang, T. W., & Wright, P. (1992). *The Impact of the construction of the new Comiskey Park on local residents.* Report for the Nathalie P. Voorhees Center for Neighborhood and Community Improvement. University of Illinois at Chicago.

Zimmerman, M. A. (forthcoming). Psychological, organizational and community empowerment: Directions for future research. Working draft of chapter to appear in J. Rappaport & E. Seidman (Eds.), *The handbook of community psychology.* New York: Plenum Press.

—————————— 8 ——————————

In Search of Supportive
Structures for Everyday Life

LIISA HORELLI AND KIRSTI VEPSÄ

During the past decade, Scandinavian women have been active participants in a movement and have been action researchers in the issues of
building and housing on women's conditions. This chapter describes (1)
the history of the movement and its vision of supportive structures for a
"New Everyday Life"; (2) the theoretical perspective and practical examples of the Scandinavian women's action research project; and (3) two
case studies illustrating the application of the New Everyday Life concept in the Finnish context. The chapter also discusses critical issues in
this kind of action research and the implications for future research.

ENVIRONMENTAL AWAKENINGS OF SCANDINAVIAN WOMEN

More than 100 women from Denmark, Finland, Iceland, Norway,
and Sweden with different backgrounds, experiences, and political interests gathered for the first Nordic conference on Housing and Building
on Women's Conditions at Kungälv (Sweden) in 1979. Discussions fo-

LIISA HORELLI • Department of Psychology, University of Helsinki, 00570 Helsinki, Fin-
land.   KIRSTI VEPSÄ • Planning and Building Department, Ministry of Environment,
Korkeavuorenkatu 21, 00230 Helsinki, Finland.
Women and the Environment, edited by Irwin Altman and Arza Churchman. Plenum Press,
New York, 1994.

cused on problems resulting from the nonsupportive environmental structures of everyday life. The same issues are still on the feminist agenda today.

The Scandinavian women's situation differs from other industrialized countries in the Organization for Economic Cooperation and Development (OECD) in at least two ways: in the implicit gender contract of the welfare state and in the number of employed women. More than 70% of Nordic women were active in the labor force at the end of the 1970s, whereas the corresponding figure for the rest of Europe and even for North America was 37% to 66% (Tilastokeskus, 1990). In contrast to the Scandinavian welfare model, which includes a kind of gender contract aiming at equality in the form of promoting women's employment and economic independence, social security, and social services, the gender contract within the rest of Europe is hidden and based either on the concept of a homemaker wife, as in Germany, or on a strong domestic sector with women networks, as in Southern Europe. The Anglo-Saxon liberal model seems to vacillate regarding women's role in society (Julkunen, 1991).

Scandinavian women of the twentieth century have entered political arenas, introduced new themes into political discourse, and started many processes to increase their rights as well as their societal influence. In Scandinavian Parliaments, women representatives presently form a "critical mass" (30%), and the number of women in municipal political arenas is steadily rising. There is, however, a pattern of representation by women on boards of culture, education, social and health care, whereas the fiscal, technical, building, and planning boards have very few women representatives. Thus the slogan, "Where there are women, there is little money and little power. Where there is money and power, there are no women," seems to hold true.

The most important legal basis for equality in Nordic countries since universal suffrage is the Equal Status Act passed in the 1970s and 1980s in the various Scandinavian countries. The aim of the act is to promote equal status between the sexes by ensuring equality of treatment in most areas. The act is administered by official Equal Status Ombuds and municipal Committees of Equality. For example, this act has compelled the Ministry of Environment in Finland to admit that women are unrepresented on all three planning levels—regional planning, municipal master planning, and municipal detail planning. The corresponding ministry in Norway has promoted a series of experiments with women as planners (Saeterdal & Takle, 1991).

The Scandinavian welfare states have not been able to stop women's double load of managing both work and home nor resolve the structural fragmentation of society resulting in frustrating daily experiences. The separation between different aspects of everyday life is partly concrete and physical, resulting from the functionalist way of urban planning. Thus there is the home, the day-care center, the workplace, and the hospital where grandmother lies—all in often separate and distant locations from one another. All of them may be excellent institutions that solve the problems of dwelling, baby-sitting, and care, but their services must be patched together in a complicated way. Thus the separation goes deeper than mere physical distance. The welfare society is built on the fact that "somebody" automatically takes care of the work needed to tie together all the previously mentioned elements: homes, markets, public institutions. All have their special rules and logic that have to be learned. A great deal of women's time and energy goes into the process of transforming the segmentation of these settings to yield something that resembles a coherent whole. This "shadow work" brings about, however, the classic vicious circle. By compelling women to find individual solutions to collective problems, a situation is created where the women themselves assist in making the causes of the problem invisible and therefore unresolved. The fragmentation continues because women spend enormous energy developing informal solutions, thereby perpetuating the problem.

These experiences of frustration and the critique of the separations of everyday life led the first conference in 1979 to come up with a vision of housing and building on women's conditions. It was a vision of a society based on the needs of children and of daily life organized in another way in the neighborhoods. This initiated a dialogue between the women's movement and a Scandinavian interdisciplinary women's research group, which led to the forming of a project called the New Everyday Life. The group has worked on the concepts formulated in 1979 and presented them for criticism at five successive conferences and to the Council of Europe's seminar on Women in Regional Planning (Forskargruppen för det nya vardagslivet, 1984, 1987, 1991; Horelli & Vepsä, 1990).[1] This work has focused on the evaluation of various experiments, especially in the field of planning and housing. The critical question is "Will this kind of active social construction by women lead to the creation of material and sociocultural support structures for daily life?"

[1]The Research Group consists of the following members: Birte Bech-Joergensen, Tarja Cronberg, Hedvig Vestergaard (Denmark), Liisa Horelli, Kirsti Vepsä (Finland), Sigrun Kaul, Anne Saeterdal (Norway), Ingela Blomberg, Birgit Krantz, and Inga-Lisa Sangregorio (Sweden).

THE NEW EVERYDAY LIFE: THEORETICAL PERSPECTIVES AND PRACTICAL EXPERIMENTS

THE NEW EVERYDAY LIFE AS A VISION

The New Everyday Life project is not just a critique of present conditions but is also a vision of a harmonious, creative, and just society where the most central motives of action are children's and women's needs, as well as the social reproduction of all people and nature. The goal is for wholeness and integration, both as a personal experience and for the organization of daily activities. The vision is inspired by the early utopians and American material feminists (Kanter, 1972; Hayden, 1982) as well as by the critical texts of Gortz (1980) and Lefebvre (1971).

The vision of the New Everyday Life is in fact a concrete utopia of a postindustrial mosaiclike society consisting of varying self-governing units responsible for the use of local resources. Important elements are work, care, and housing, the separation of which is to be replaced by their integration in the living environment on the intermediary level (see later discussion).

An essential part of the vision is the expansion of the concept of work. Both paid and unpaid work are seen as equal, and the process of work is shared and organized in a different way. The aim is to convert the production-centered mode of thinking and acting, that is, the technocratic rationality, into a rationality of responsibility. The latter implies an ethic in which the care of people and nature really matters. This means that production and economics serve the reproduction of human beings, nature, and culture and not vice versa. Thus the aim is to restore the optimum balance in the dialectics of production (work) and reproduction (care) (Altman & Chemers, 1980). Reproduction here is not used in the Marxist sense as reproduction of the work force but refers to the direct nurturing and caring for children and elderly, as well as that of social and cultural relations.

THE NEW EVERYDAY LIFE AS A THEORETICAL APPROACH

The New Everyday Life is also a theoretical way of thinking about the possibilities of constructing the surrounding reality in another way. From the very beginning of the project, it was clear that the problems caused by the separation of the daily activities of work, care, and housing, as well as the scant possibilities of women to control their own lives, are phenomenal, functional, and structural. In other words, the problems are personally experienced; they are closely tied to daily activities, and they result from the separated spatial, temporal, organizational, economic, and political structures of society.

The theories of everyday life developed by the philosopher Agnes Heller (1984) and the cultural sociologist Birte Bech-Joergensen (1988) allow for the integration of both humanistic and structural approaches, as well as for micro-, meso-, and macrosociological perspectives. Everyday life is above all a paradigm for the understanding of subjectively and intersubjectively caused interventions in a structural context.

Everyday Life as a Process

Everyday life as a theoretical concept brings to focus the meaning of the "natural" and invisible activities (of women) often defined by the dominant culture as trivial. "Everydayness" or ordinariness is a fiction that hides drama and magic, conflicts and change. Everyday life—the culturally natural, symbolically "right," and common way of living—is a process rather than a substantive concept (Bech-Joergensen, 1988). It evades sociological definitions, but it can be described by means of concepts denoting the activities, relations, and processes by which it is created. Both Heller and Beck-Joergensen stress that the root of everyday life lies in the reproductive actions forming the psychosocial forces with which people transform societal and cultural conditions into phenomenal experiences. In the appropriation of everyday life, it is important to analyze both the level of institutions reproducing the structural conditions of that life and the ways in which these conditions are handled psychosocially and culturally. The latter not only reproduce and transform the very same institutions that make them possible but also create everyday life (cf. Giddens, 1984).

Everyday life also has a material dimension. The material aspects of everyday life consist above all of the built environment. The physical environment can be seen, on the one hand, as the objectification of the social order and rationality, and on the other hand as the bodily and sensory context of individual activity and thereby as part of psychic self-regulation (Horelli, 1993). The physical environment is also closely woven into the repetitions that form the spine of the routines of everyday life.

Through our own actions we maintain the normative orders of material surroundings and simultaneously create the normative social reality. Therefore, the physical environment of a society is a basic condition and/or a straitjacket for everyday activities. Material surroundings, along with politics, economics, and law, are important factors influencing culture and society (Foucault, 1979). The physical environment is thus both a social construction and a social constructor.

The physical environment limits everyday activities in certain ways, but on the other hand the mode with which people manipulate the material environment can also be the beginning of change. Everyday life contains within it an aspect of potential change on different levels. It is based on the assumption that the inherent goal of the individual is to construct and maintain an adequate sense of self and the world. Correspondingly, the "goal" of a culture and a society is the maintenance of a self-evident reality, or at least an image of it. This requires constant struggling because the dominating self-evidence consists of a series of continuities and changes. This process is characterized by cracks or even breaks that, in the form of social movements, may lead to changes in societal structures.

Change in everyday life is connected with the issue of subjectivity and intersubjectivity. For subjective individual longings to cause change, there must be arenas where intersubjective reality can be produced and the "psychosocial powers of everyday life" be released (Beck-Joergensen, 1988). The intermediary spaces of everyday life are the "free living spaces" that are characterized by digressions from the generally accepted ways of orientation. It is these intersubjective arenas that the New Everyday Life project deals with, as it strives for wholeness in life via integration of housing, work, and care on the intermediary level.

The Intermediary Level as a Mediating Structure

The idea of the intermediary level bridging individual private lives and the formal public world is closely tied to the discourse on community and neighborhoods (Hillery, 1955; Beck, 1986; Altman & Wandersman, 1987; Noro, 1989). The intermediary level as a concept was introduced at the first conference on Housing and Building on Women's Terms in 1979. The women chose this concept because it implied both the longings for a more communal way of life and the practical possibilities to readjust the presently missing supportive structures in the near environment. The research group developed the intermediary level further as a concept referring to the structural and functional basis for the reorganization and integration of housing, work, and care in the neighborhoods or local areas (Forskargruppen, 1987).

Figure 1 illustrates how the presently separated elements of daily life can be temporally and spatially integrated on the intermediary level, resulting in local activities. The intermediary level is also a structure

Separated organization of everyday life

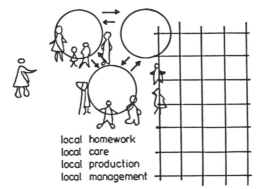

Integrated organization of everyday life

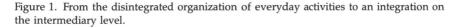

local homework
local care
local production
local management

Figure 1. From the disintegrated organization of everyday activities to an integration on the intermediary level.

between the state, the market, and the household (see Figure 2). It is a presently missing structure mediating between the private and the public, and the formal and informal spheres of life. It also makes visible the relationship between work (production) and care (reproduction), as well as its division between the genders.

Figure 2 illustrates a model for the creation of the functional basis of the intermediary level, which is done by integrating dwelling, care, and work in space and time. It takes place by transferring to the neighborhood some of the daily tasks presently located in different sectors and places. Care of domestic chores and children can be transferred from

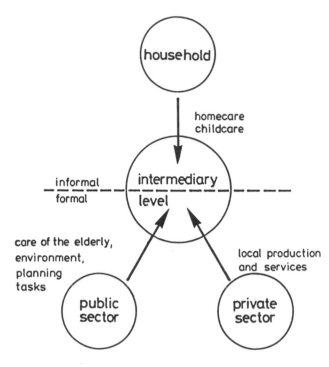

Figure 2. The scheme for the development of the intermediary level based on the transfer of activities from households to the public and private sectors.

private homes to the communal grounds, as in the examples of cohousing. Environmental planning and management, as well as care of the elderly, can be transferred to the neighborhood from the centralized institutions of the public sector. Even "the market" finds it occasionally interesting to create some production that serves the local community. These transactions result in new activities called local housework, care, and production, as well as local planning and management.

The intermediary level has a functional, organizational, sociocultural, geographical, economic, and political dimension. The intermediary level does not exist as a ready phenomenon, and it does not "look" like something definite. It is not necessarily as fixed as a behavior setting (Barker, 1968). In some ways, it resembles Bronfenbrenner's (1979) micro- and mesosystems. As a geographical phenomenon, the intermediary level is a locally limited territorial whole varying in size from a group of dwellings or a block to a neighborhood, village, or part of a town. As a physical phenomenon, the intermediary level is supported by shared arenas and spaces of communication. Its architecture supports different modes of housing and the identity of the local culture.

The intermediary level is also an economic phenomenon. It furthers the development of the informal or "third" economy, which lies between the private households, on one hand, and the formal market and the state, on the other hand. This kind of economy is also called life cycle or ecological economy because it enhances the possibilities of the residents to collectively organize the recycling of materials and the exchange of goods and services without money.

As a formal organization, the intermediary level is one in which the organizational unit is larger than the family but smaller than the municipality. The intermediary level is expressed as various kinds of interest associations, resident organizations, and forms of cohousing. Politically the intermediary level can mean a new structuring of the political institutions that enhances participation and self-government.

As a cultural concept the intermediary level involves a mediating structure, which comes about as the result of daily activities and common experiences in a sphere that lies between the private (individual or family) and the public (society). It is a culture of varying degrees of communality comprising both local and translocal networks.

The New Everyday Life as Action and Change

The publication called *Ways to the New Everyday Life* (1987) illustrates how aspects of the vision have been realized in various parts of Scandinavia. Most of the experiments described in the following sections have been arranged around a key activity of the "New Everyday Life," for example, local housework, care, production, or planning.

Local Housework

Unpaid housework has always been one of the key issues in women's striving for equality and for economic independence. Domestic work doesn't necessarily have to be done at home, as has been shown by the American material feminists in the late 1800s (Hayden, 1981) as well as by the movement toward communal service houses with central kitchens in Vienna, Berlin, Copenhagen, Stockholm, and Helsinki at the beginning of this century. This first generation of cohousing in Europe functioned on the principle that residents had their individual flats, and they paid for the domestic services. The service house replaced the private servants that the bourgeois class could no longer afford.

The second movement of cohousing began in the early 1970s not among "hippies" but among academically educated and socially conscious people. It was based on the idea of shared housework. The leading country was Denmark, where approximately 200,000 inhabitants now live in different types of cohousing communities, including detached, row, or apartment houses. There are no official statistics on alternative housing as yet because it is more a question of different styles of living. The official housing policy in Denmark has supported alternative housing, and in some places this kind of living has become part of the social service system. In Sweden, Norway, and Finland, alternative forms of housing are spreading but have not yet reached the level of those in Denmark.

The starting point in the second stage of cohousing was not so much in the freeing of women or men from housework but the socially dreary situation of children with no adult contacts besides their parents. The critique of the industrial society was expressed in the slogan, "Every child should have a hundred parents." New forms of cohousing were created to break the isolation of the nuclear family, singles, and children.

Because domestic work is controlled by individual households and especially by women, it can be reorganized without too many legal changes. As shared housework is closely tied to housing, it is described here in connection with different modes of (co)housing. The following classification in Figure 3 of the different modes is arranged according to the aspired communality in housing, in which the different levels or modes relate both to local activities and to the formal and informal economy (Cronberg & Vepsä, 1983; Forskargruppen för det nya vardagslivet, 1987, p. 161):

1. *A well-functioning housing area.* This is a neighborhood or a village with spaces for different kinds of municipal services and shared activities, especially for leisure. Although the residents mainly live in traditional housing, communal eating may be arranged at neighborhood clubs. There are active resident organizations, which take part in the maintenance and management of the area.

2. *A cohousing community.* This form of housing ranges in size from 8 to 30 households with individual houses in a group or flats in an apartment house. The shared spaces for eating, leisure, and for child care comprise 5% to 20% of the building. The residents may choose whether to take meals with the community daily or only during the weekends. In spite of the possibilities of choice, there usually is the principle that everyone participates in the domestic chores as an individual, not as a family. The norm is that both men and women take part in cooking on equal terms. The exchange of services is not paid for.

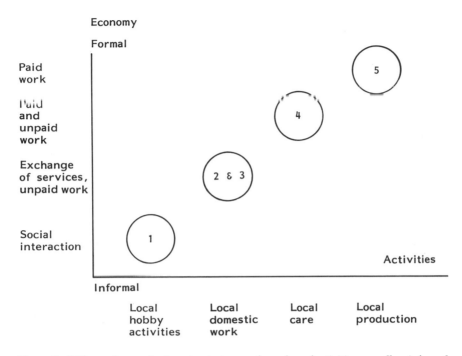

Figure 3. Different forms of cohousing in terms of number of activities as well as informal and formal economy.

3. *A dwelling collective or "big family."* The collective comprises 5 to 20 persons living in the same house. Each individual, both adults and children, usually has a room of her/his own, and the rest of the spaces are communal. Cooking, cleaning up, and maintenance of the building are tasks shared by women, men, and children over 10 years old. The cooking turns usually come up once a week, in addition to one weekend in a season. The cleaning of the house is often done according to fixed territories. Each member of the collective pays for his or her share in the budget for food and maintenance.

4. *A service house community.* This form of housing is an improvement on the first-generation cohousing because it is a combination of both cohousing and exchange of unpaid and paid services. The housing form is usually an apartment house with approximately a hundred flats with common leisure and dining rooms. The municipality provides services for the elderly and the handicapped as well as supports the day-care center for children, in which the residents may work part time. The

residents may use the spaces for unpaid exchange of services such as collective cooking and dining.

5. *A working community.* This is a form of cohousing in which the members also work in the same residence or outside but bring the money into the community. This form of living, which is not very widespread in Scandinavia, resembles that of the kibbutzim in Israel. In addition, there are work communities in which members do not reside.

The housework in these different modes of cohousing has been made visible by bringing the work to the intermediary level and by sharing it between men and women. There are conflicts, but learning to deal with them is part of the ideology of cohousing. This kind of mode of living is a voluntary choice. There are, however, different kinds of cohousing communities, based on shared interests.

The sharing of housework in the cohousing experiments seems to expand the roles of women and men. Women learn to take care of technical matters such as the central heating system, and men learn to cook and to do domestic chores. Both men and women learn to cooperate with neighbors and to find out what local democracy is in practice (Forskargruppen, 1987; Anttonen, 1989; Horelli, 1993).

Local Care

There is a recent trend in Scandinavian countries toward a welfare pluralism, where the public, the market, and the user groups produce, organize, and finance the social and health-care services. The state or public is still responsible for the universal social security system, but the tailoring of services depends on local initiatives and contexts. Denmark —a forerunner in this field, too—has systematically experimented with the welfare mix since the beginning of the 1980s. The state has directed public resources not only to the municipalities but also to resident groups willing to take responsibility for local services.

Local care means cooperation between the public, formal, and the private, informal caregivers. It takes place either as a top-down or as a bottom-up initiative. On the one hand, the municipality may localize its resources and arrange care of children, the handicapped, or the elderly in existing shared spaces in the neighborhood. Presently, there are also more and more resident or user groups who come up with their own solutions and apply for public support. For instance, in Sweden there are over 100 cooperative child-care centers run and managed by the parents and subsidized by municipalities.

Kossan, one of the first cooperative day-care centers in Sweden, was founded by parents who were without child care in their neighborhood (Forskargruppen, 1987). Presently, there are 15 children and three nurses or teachers in Kossan. The parents work in the center 10 to 15 days a year, bringing new knowhow into the activities. Thus the relationship between the children, the personnel, and the parents is qualitatively different from that of a traditional institution. The cost of day care is far less than the average in Sweden, and the parents pay only two thirds of the normal fee in addition to their own contribution of work. The most important advantage, however, is not economic, but social. The social network among parents also functions outside the day-care center and improves both the children's situation and that of the personnel. The children always have a baby-sitting place, and the staff of the center can always rely on parents to help out when needed.

Local care in the intermediary level allows one to conceptualize social service in terms of "social and material support networks." These are not merely natural networks, but they include both professionals and nonprofessionals in the local infrastructure. This conceptualization encourages the perception of child care in terms of a partnership between people with different skills (Walker, 1989, p. 203). So far the gender of the partners is mostly female, but in some cooperative day-care centers there are many fathers who do their share of child care.

Local Production

Local production implies that the products satisfy the needs of local inhabitants (food, clothing, buildings, technical equipment), the production uses local resources (materials, people, buildings, etc.), or production strengthens local traditions or creates new social innovations (forms of cooperation, etc.). In contemporary industrial societies, local production is more often the exception than the rule. Nevertheless, there are a few community or village cooperatives in the Scandinavian countries that aim at the development of the whole village (Mårtenson et al., 1988). Sometimes the cooperatives are centered around a telecottage. Telecottage means that information technology is freely available for the residents in common facilities of the local communities such as libraries, local schools, neighborhood centers, or other facilities. Telecottages, as a collective alternative for distant work at home, have succeeded in developing some local workplaces in rural and smaller urban communities in Finland, Sweden, and Denmark.

The adoption of new technology seems to strengthen the existing societal structures, unless it is connected with a new way of thinking and organizing (Cronberg, 1991). The new technology may, in the form of telecottages, support the intermediary level, which in turn helps the residents to control technology and to apply it in a socially innovative way. Cronberg et al. (1991) conducted an extensive study of 16 social experiments in different parts of Denmark, concerning the consequences of information technology and its potential for new social organizations, local development, and local mobilization. Participants were assessed according to Roger's (1983) typology based on speed of adoption of new technology. Community members were grouped according to the time it took for them to adopt the innovation. The first ones to adopt (2% to 3% of potential users) were called "innovators." The second group consists of "early users" (13% to 14% of potential users), followed by the "early majority" (34% of potential users), and the "late majority" (about 34% of potential users). The last ones to adopt were called "laggards" (16% of potential users). Men dominated in the first groups. Women and men were equal in numbers only in the "late majority" or "laggards" groups.

According to Cronberg (1991), women were not curious about the technology and did not identify their needs in terms of technology. Women only came to telecottages when they had a reason to use the technology, for example, for word processing or bookkeeping. The male framework for the social construction of technology is one of play and extension of self. The corresponding framework for women is "I will use it only if I know beforehand that I have something to use it for." The differing frameworks of men and women have meant in this Danish context that when the local development or the future of society are seen only in technological perspective, women's visions are doomed to be invisible (Cronberg, 1991, pp. 21–22). These results have to be further tested in other contexts.

Local Planning

The Congress on Building and Housing on Women's Conditions in 1990 at Örebro, Sweden defined a women's perspective in environmental planning, as requiring a conscious priority of care, sustainable economy, ecology, and a conscious mode of participatory action (Norrby & Paavonen, 1990). Thus, a women's perspective implies an effort to integrate both the social and ecological domains in planning (Kaul, 1990). This perspective continues the radical tradition of planning begun in the early 1800s (Owen, Fourier, Morris, Howard, Geddes, Freeman, Turner, Kennedy), by creating alternatives to the rationalistic industrial and market-oriented urban development still dominant today (Choay, 1983).

The requirement for participatory action means that planning is a locally anchored dialogue between the residents and different officials and specialists. Planning that expresses the interests of inhabitants and that develops through ongoing participatory experiments can be called emancipatory (Kaul, 1990). Emancipatory planning releases the unused forces of women, children, youth, and the elderly, aiming at a material structure that supports the relevant contents of everyday life. The intermediary level makes it possible to integrate the social and ecological domains, if the care of nature becomes a normal everyday action. Thus, the creation and maintenance of the intermediary level, which may become a space of emancipation for nature, women, and men, is an important aim of planning (Kaul, 1990).

In Norway, where the women's movement was particularly vigorous in the 1970s, women have begun to take an active role in community development and planning. In the middle of the 1980s, an experimental program was initiated in six municipalities by five ministries (Environment, Agriculture, Fisheries, Industry, and Local Governments) in cooperation with the Norwegian Association of Local Authorities. The objectives of the program were to try out alternative models for integrating women's needs and values into the local planning process and to do so in preparing local plans for long- and short-range development of the municipality (Saeterdal & Takle, 1991).

The population in the six municipalities ranged from 1,700 to 7,000 inhabitants. Each municipality appointed a project group, all with a majority of women. There were several hundred women of different ages participating. Some women were politicians and administrators; others were housewives.

It was important to organize the participation as a learning experience for women. Besides traditional seminars, there were futuristic workshops with time for dreaming because "dreams about the future, when shared and discussed, become visions. Visions for the future become goals for the community. Goals for the community become action for the people in the planning process" (Saeterdal & Takle, 1991, p. 27).

The experiment showed that mobilizing the total human potential for development—men, women, children, youth, and the elderly—is an "all-win" situation, both individually and locally. The main results were described in terms of the process of participation, the planning document, and the content of the plan. The planning process was changed from an enterprise with a few technical professionals into a process of participation on a broad basis. Women were mobilized in new ways of collaboration and working methods. The short- and midterm (3-to-5-year perspective) plans were prepared simultaneously. The participatory process seems to be continuing, in the form of new ways of cooperation between private and public sectors, genders, and ages. Thus the project has contributed to a new planning praxis.

The participatory planning produced a document that was more concise and more to the point than before. It dealt with the most important issues, not just general activities of the municipality. The women's perspective was reflected in the content of the plan regarding issues of environment (new ways of solving environmental problems) and everyday life, such as health and social matters, job-creating activities, leisure, and cultural affairs. Thus the content of the new plan was more congruent with women's needs than was the former plan.

The Norwegian experiment mobilized women into the planning process and thereby succeeded in breaking down barriers between the perspectives of men and women. The experiential knowledge of women was approved and applied in planning. The issues of care of human beings and nature were accentuated to the point that they started to become part of a new planning culture defining sustainable development from both a technocratic–ecological perspective and from a socio-cultural perspective. The participatory mode of planning and producing services in partnership is a structural change that may bring about a new consciousness and a new rationality.

These examples of the "New Everyday Life" in terms of local housework, care, production, and planning indicate that the new everyday life around the intermediary level is not based on a static model but rather on a web of many different endavors sharing a common interest. It implies a way of thinking and acting in which the surrounding reality is seen as a culturally and structurally bound process of construction with a value-laden basis and goals. The strategies of change in the preceding examples represented "top-down" and "bottom-up" strategies. The "top-down" strategy means that the decision-making process and urban planning is influenced via political and public institutions. This means that women have to participate and be represented in public planning and political boards. The "bottom-up" strategy emphasizes a step-by-step approach with many different alternatives for breaking old ways of thinking and finding suitable "islands" for development. It enables social innovations and local initiatives. Thus the "New Everyday Life" has developed into an approach consisting of a strategy that is both "inside" and "outside" of politics. Every locality and country has to find, however, their own tailor-made applications.

THE NEW EVERYDAY LIFE APPROACH
IN THE FINNISH CONTEXT

Finland is the fourth largest country in Europe in terms of territory, but one of the smallest in population, with about 5 million inhabitants. Finland has experienced a rapid transition from an agricultural to an industrial and even postindustrial society during the past 40 years. Therefore, the separation of environmental structures is a problem for a smooth daily life in Finland.

The authors of this chapter have been involved in a 3-year action research project, the goal of which was to create and evaluate supportive local structures with women and children (Horelli & Vepsä, 1993). The project took place in three neighborhoods in different parts of Finland. One neighborhood reflects the planning ideology of the 1970s, another symbolizes that of the 1980s, and the third was expected to become a 1990s version of the "New Everyday Life." Two of the cases are described in the following sections of the chapter.

A "Living Room" for Local Inhabitants

The first case is a small-scale prototype of what might be applied in other communities. It deals with Malminkartano, a suburb of Helsinki built in the early 1980s for approximately 10,000 inhabitants. Malminkartano is a low-income neighborhood with many social problems. Its successful architecture and relatively good supply of services have prevented its stigmatization. In the spring of 1989, the social workers of the area arranged a workshop with the residents' organization to improve the situation of women and young families in Malminkartano. The workshop was financed by the WHO Healthy City Project and stimulated by one of the members of our research team. The workshop ended up with a plan for a meeting place of different ages—a public "living room" for Malminkartano.

The following autumn different institutions—schools, child-care centers, play parks, and youth clubs that all lie within 400 meters from one another—took part in the development work along with local women. There were also about a hundred children between the ages of 5 and 15 who participated in an extensive environmental analysis of their neighborhood, the results of which were presented in an exhibition in May, 1990, in the youth house—the future "living room" of Malminkartano.

In the fall of 1990, the community "living room" was opened in the former youth house. It was a wooden building of two stories and a basement, with four rooms and a kitchen on the main floor. Its program consisted of a resident cafe, open from 9 in the morning till 9 in the evening 5 days a week. There were two women (a hostess and her assistant) in charge of daytime activities and two youth leaders in the evening. In the morning, there were handicrafts for women and children, and at midday, lunch could be obtained for an inexpensive price. In the afternoon, the place was filled with young teenagers playing pool and computer games. In addition, the resident association as well as local officials used the "living room" as a regular meeting place. The evenings were mostly occupied by older teenagers. Twice a month there were club evenings for all ages. Gradually, the mixing of different generations became more and more usual. The most popular activity was the luncheon meal, with 40 to 60 persons—from babies to grandpas—taking a meal.

Following is an excerpt from the field notes describing a typical afternoon in the "living room":

> Mothers were dressing or undressing their children in the front room. The project group had a meeting in the main room around a big table, close to which one of the mothers was breastfeeding her baby. A couple of youngsters went in and out of the pool room, interfering now and then with our discussions about the plans for the neighborhood. The hostess peeped out from the kitchen and said that the buns had just come out of the oven.

In the spring of 1990 the schools, day-care centers, and the church came more actively into the "living room" network, and weeks of common action were arranged. The resident association planned to start a job-creation program for the unemployed and the handicapped. In spite of the success of the project, the municipality wanted to eliminate the job of the hostess in the fall of 1990. This resulted in a stormy protest from the users, most of whom were women. They expressed their feelings in the diary of the "living room" in the following ways:

> As a mother of small children I see the activities of the "living room" as very important for children, and it is a breathing place for mothers.

> This is the only place in Malminkartano where you can have normal interaction with different ages. I, a former problem youth and single mother of small children, have a strong need to keep in contact with others. Visiting the "living room" is the social highlight of the day.

> When in the darkness of winter one arrives at this warm cafe which smells of fresh buns and where motherly "Mumin trolls" bustle about, the day is saved.

The protest succeeded in guaranteeing the financing for the living room for 1992. The results of the project are fourfold:

1. The project was successful in producing unusual, but important local care, such as social support for single mothers, for neglected children, for lonely old people and men, a job creation program for unemployed, and a "Gentlemen-preferred club" twice a week for a group of 12-year-old boys who were vandalizing the neighborhood.

2. The hierarchical and sectorized municipal administration was a major constraint in the development of joint projects with the residents and local officials and hindered new forms of praxis.

3. The physical environment—the resident house—had an important role as an integrator of different ages, interest groups, administrative sectors, formal and informal activities, and even genders to a certain degree. Thus it contributed to the creation and maintenance of a culture of communality.

4. Communality in this project turned out to be a psychological, practical, and political strategy of survival for women. The "living room" became a collective restorative space and thus a protective factor of health (Rutter, 1987; Kaplan & Kaplan, 1989). The "powers of everyday life" (Beck-Joergensen, 1988) helped not only to solve practical daily problems such as baby-sitting, but also raised the consciousness of women to try political action for the first time in their lives. For the officials, most of them women, too, it meant a learning process in which they had to transcend their narrow sector and adopt new techniques of communality. The latter implied material and psychosocial networking on the individual, group, and community levels.

Planning as a Struggle between Different Rationalities

Urban planning systems in the Scandinavian countries resemble one another, but Finland has been the last country to decentralize the decision-making process from the state to the municipalities. The following case describes an effort to apply the "New Everyday Life" approach to the planning of a new neighborhood (Kekkola) of 1,500 inhabitants at Jyväskylä—a town of 60,000 inhabitants in the center of Finland.

The planning of Kekkola was a top-down project initiated in the fall of 1989 by municipal officials and the Ministries of Environment, Housing, and Health. The aim was to make a town plan from the perspective of the "weak ones," namely children, the elderly, the handicapped, and the caregivers. Although women were not mentioned as a special group, they implicitly also belonged to the "weak" citizens class. The responsible planning group consisted of six women and nine men. The group represented, besides the usual technical sectors, even specialists of social services and health care, youth, culture, and environment. A group of children and youth were included in the planning process to represent this user group.

The first version of the town plan was ready in autumn of 1991. The reproductive aim of the project was to be satisfied by an "activity oasis" in the center of the neighborhood. This "oasis" was to be a combination of local school, day-care center, and activity space for residents of all ages. In addition, there were spaces for small day-care centers on the first floors of multiunit houses. The scale of the plan was "human" in the sense that the houses ranged from one to four stories. Also, the children's wishes for a free play area and the safeguarding of wild nature were partly taken into account by the architect.

The women participants pointed out, however, that the most prominent "planner" had been the car. The area was split by a highway, making the "activity oasis" almost inaccessible to children and handicapped. Many of the yards of the houses were too small because parking took the space intended for play or cultivation. Another hidden principle had been cost cutting. The rigid plan had yards that were too small and left too little of the nearby forest. In addition, some of the hills were planned, not from a natural or ecological perspective, but from that of formalist urban esthetics. This critique started a struggle between the technocrats and the "softies." The architect elaborated two alternative plans for the dangerous Kekkola highway, one with a cosmetic improvement and another in which the highway was blocked by a big square. The engineers retorted: "The latter alternative is out of the question, because there are these realities of traffic flow . . . , you have to take the realities into consideration." The researcher's comment "Isn't the safety of children and the handicapped a reality?" was met with silence.

The results of the project show, among other things, that the key issues in the planning rhetoric were dominated by "technorationality" associated with cars, traffic, building rights, planning as a product (the document), and an emphasis on professional knowledge. In contrast, the planning rhetoric reflecting a rationality of responsibility emphasized the material structures of care, safety in traffic, conditions for ecological housing (recycling and cultivation of land), alternative modes of cohousing, and an organic architecture.

The differences in rationality were, however, not gender-specific. People working on everyday problems and in the protection of nature have internalized more often a rationality of responsibility than those working in the technical and building sector. The 2-year planning process began, however, to influence the structures of consciousness of most participants, both men and women. The "polyphonic dialogue" of the planning was slowly accepted, and space was found for an ecological block at the end. Also, the material structure of care in Kekkola will support the ease of everyday life for women. Thus the messages and modes of action from the context of daily life have been transformed into structural elements. These may enhance the "powers of everyday life" to influence society from beneath.

Methodologically the use of the New Everyday Life as a theoretical and practical approach in the preceeding cases has meant the application of the tenets of feminist research. Ahrentzen (1990, p. 11) has described these tenets as the social grounds of knowledge, empathy and care, emancipatory interest, a contextualist imagination, and a move from synthesis to pluralism.

Research, where the aim is both to analyze and change existing realities, requires a large frame of reference and a multiplicity of methods. We have relied in practice on the so-called "VETA methodology" of the participatory future studies (Friberg, 1986). In this methodology "V" means a vision of the desired or possible future, "T" means theory by which the probable changes are explained and predicted, "E" means the evaluation of the empirical data, and "A" means action with which the desired future is realized. This kind of action research, where intentional development work is central, relies on three types of methods: (1) methods for producing different situations or possibilities for change, such as futuristic workshops, exhibitions of children's evaluations, provocative panel discussions, planning simulations, and techniques of community development; (2) methods for data gathering, such as observation and interviewing; and (3) methods for analysis and interpretation, such as content analysis (Miles & Huberman, 1984).

The results of the study are not causal explanations, but rather descriptions of both the process and new models, concepts or forms of praxis. Thus the results raise epistemological and methodological questions, which are dealt with in the last section of this chapter.

IMPLICATIONS FOR FUTURE POLICY, PLANNING, AND RESEARCH

We will conclude by discussing three critical issues relevant to the development and evaluation of material and sociocultural support structures for everyday life. First, the Scandinavian examples described in this chapter show that it is possible to create specific settings of a "New

Everyday Life," resulting in new forms and modes of production of care, new ways of organizing domestic work collectively, and new praxis in environmental planning. The development work, however, is a time-consuming and strenuous effort and involves a conscious struggle to frame issues from the perspective of users and their needs. Because a lot of the development work comprises the production of support networks in partnership with the municipal officials, there is always the danger of being exploited by the public sector. Therefore, a balanced interplay between the formal organization and informal processes is of utmost importance (Walker, 1989, p. 204). When successful, it is reflected in a creative planning process and in material structures that are supportive of everyday life, as in the Norwegian cases. Thus the Scandinavian women's construction of supportive structures is closely tied to the crisis of the welfare state. The New Everyday Life approach does not eliminate basic municipal services but offers an alternative solution to the growing privatization of services and a new vision for the development of the welfare mix.

Second, mainstream sociology has emphasized the disintegration of communities and communality (Beck, 1986), but there are also some oppositional voices (Schiefloe, 1990). The concept of the intermediary level as a material, functional, economic, political, cultural, and emancipatory structure is a contribution to this debate. The intermediary level in the Scandinavian experiences described in this chapter seems to have potential for being a supportive structure for everyday life. Postmodern communality is, however, a matter of choice, unlike the forced communality of traditional societies. Men and mobile women seem to prefer less intensive communality offered, for instance, by communities of leisure or hobbies (Noro, 1991), but many local women and children have a longing for social togetherness in the living environment.

It is also important to remember that the development of communality with varying levels of aspired intimacy is based on material structures. The infrastructure of the service system in Kekkola (the "Activity Oasis" and dispersed day-care spaces), as well as the house for the "living room" at Malminkartano, were conscious choices of material and social investment in the aspired communality of everyday culture (cf. Saeterdal & Takle, 1990). The "living room" at Malminkartano turned out to be a restorative environment for women and their children (Kaplan & Kaplan, 1989). Therefore, the question of investment in the material infrastructure also becomes a question of whose options for joy and communality are to be supported.

Third, the intermediary level of the "New Everyday Life" raises questions of what kind of women it serves and whether it is a new trap for women instead of being a promoter of gender integration? Interests of women vary in social class, age, and ethnicity, as well as in the potentialities of the living area. Women's interests come out indirectly via activities, tasks, places, and other significant issues of daily life. The Scandinavian women interested in building and housing have taken a stand for both work and care as basic activities in their lives. It is also a choice of a rationality of responsibility, which does not mean that it is a trap but rather a springboard, even for mobile women and men with emancipatory interests.

The mere representation of women in public life does not guarantee that the environment will become ecologically and socially more sustainable, as long as the technocratic, externally imposed mode of planning dominates. Although women have, due to their everyday experiences, a feeling for the meaningful aspects of local environments, the competence to contribute to a sustainable development only rises from women's opportunities to learn from local experiences in participation in planning (Saeterdal & Takle, 1991). Without these learning experiences, which allow them to try out new ways of integrating informal and formal action, women are not able to question and overcome the technorational, bureaucratic ways of decision making current in the fora of representative democracy.

The examples of intermediary-level applications described above give hints about the expansion of the roles of both women and men. Especially important are the examples of cohousing that show a slow change toward integration in the spatial and temporal division of activities between ages and genders (Horelli, 1993). We believe that the intermediary level will not really become generally attractive unless it acquires economic or political power in the form of direct local democracy and a new distribution of public funding.

As the application of the New Everyday Life approach is still at a preliminary stage, the implications for future research are discussed here in terms of highlighting a few philosophical and methodological issues. First, the commitment to the feminist tenets of methodology (Ahrentzen, 1990) means that the research questions are not concerned with "truth" as such, but how to change the conditions of the "truth" (Harding, 1987, p. 8). Thus we question the adequacy of traditional research and opt for the combination of both intentional change (development work) and scientific evaluation. Methods for producing new situations and possibilities for change have received little attention in the literature on methods or on action research. There is a great need for experimentation with and evaluation of nontraditional methods such as futuristic workshops, sociodrama, planning simulations, and the like.

The central concept of the New Everyday Life—the intermediary level—is also a methodological structure in which theory and praxis meet. More experiments are needed that simultaneously develop different kinds of intermediary levels in housing and work environments and evaluate their consequences for gender integration and environmental sustainability. An important question is also whether the intermediary level will enhance sustainable development from both ecological and sociocultural perspectives.

One must also be prepared to answer, "What is changed?", "From whose perspective?", and "With what consequences for women, other groups, and nature?" Change from the women's perspective is closely tied to an ethic of care, which is embedded in a contextual moral theory. The characteristics of an ethic or rationality of care is that moral situations are not defined in terms of rights and responsibilities but in terms of relationships of care for the self and others. But Tronto (1987, pp. 646, 658) points out that "the equation of 'care' with 'female' is questionable." In the context of planning, the rationality of care is, however, not enough because the construction of supportive structures for everyday life is also a hard struggle for another type of infrastructure (cf. the example of Kekkola). Therefore, we have chosen to call the rationality in question that of "responsibility." The latter requires the expansion of both conventional understanding of the boundaries of care as well as the willingness to fight for the appropriate material and social institutions. The conditions for the adoption of this kind of rationality by women and men and how it affects the content, process, and document of planning as well as the management of the living area are some of the empirical research questions for the future. An important issue is also the role and consequences of the intermediary level for the socialization of children.

This chapter has dealt with the issue of women and environment in a broad frame of reference. The natural and built environment has been viewed as embedded both in the vision of the welfare state and its societal structures, as well as in the intersubjective and subjective experiences of women. Material structures affect all these levels, which in turn affect the physical environment. A more holistic approach comprising many environmental levels is a challenge not only for feminist research in the future, but is also a challenge for environment and behavior studies in general.

REFERENCES

Altman, I., & Chemers, M. (1980). *Culture and environment*. Monterey, CA: Brooks/Cole.
Altman, I., & Wandersman, A. (Eds.). (1987). *Neighborhood and community environments*. Human behavior and environment. *Advances in Theory and Research. Volume 9*. New York: Plenum Press.
Ahrentzen, S. B. (1990). Rejuvenating a field that is either "Coming of age" or "Aging in

place": Feminist research contributions to environmental design research. In R. I. Selby, K. H. Anthony, J. Choi, & B. Orland (Eds.), *Coming of age: Proceedings of EDRA Annual Conference* (pp. 11–18). Oklahoma City: EDRA.

Anttonen, A. (1989) *Tarina Tuulenkylästä* [The story of Tuulenkylä]. Helsinki: Asuntohallitus, asuntotutkimuksia 3.

Barker, R. (1968). *Ecological psychology.* Stanford: Stanford University Press.

Bech-Joergensen (1988) "Hvorfor gör de ikke noget"? In C. Bloch, L. Höjgaard, B. Bech-Joergensen, & B. Lindeskov Nautrup, *Hverdagsliv, kultur og subjektivitet* [Everyday life, culture and subjectivity] (pp. 56–82). Köbenhavn: Akademisk Forlag.

Beck, U. (1986). *Risikogesellschaft.* [The risk society] Frankfurt am Main.

Bronfenbrenner, U. (1979). *The ecology of human development: Experiments by nature and design.* Cambridge: Harvard University Press.

Choay, F. (1983). *The modern city: Planning in the 19th century.* New York: Brazilier.

Cronberg, T. (1991). *Gender and the diffusion of information technology: The case of the Danish telecottages.* A paper to the GRANITE seminar, Amsterdam, November 1.

Cronberg, T., & Vepsä, K. (1983). *Asumisen uusi suunta* [The new direction in housing]. Helsinki: Tammi.

Cronberg, T., Duelund, P., Jensen, O. M., & Qvortrup, L. (Eds.). (1991). *Danish experiments—Social constructions of technology.* Copenhagen: New Social Science Monographs.

Forskargruppen för det nya vardagslivet. (1984). *Det nya vardagslivet* [The New Everyday Life]. Oslo: Nord.

Forskargruppen för det nya vardagslivet. (1987). *Veier till det nye verdagslivet* [The ways to the New Everyday Life]. Oslo: Nord.

Foucault, M. (1979). *Surveiller et punir.* Paris: Gallimard.

Franck, K. A. (1985). Social construction of the physical environment: The case of gender. *Sociological Focus, 2,* 143–158.

Friberg, M. (1986). Deltagande framtidsstudier—om VETA-metodologin. In *Att studera framtiden* [To study the future]. Stockholm: SOU, 34.

Giddens, A. (1984). *The constitution of society.* Cambridge: Polity Press.

Gortz, A, (1980). *Adieu au prolétariat. Au delà du socialisme.* Paris: Galilée.

Harding. S. (1987). Introduction: Is there a feminist methodology? In S. Harding (Ed.), *Feminist methodology* (pp. 1–14). Bloomington and Indianapolis: Indiana University Press.

Hayden, D. (1981). *The grand domestic revolution.* Cambridge: MIT Press.

Heller, A. (1984). *The New Everyday Life.* London: Routledge & Kegan Paul.

Hillery, G. A. (1955). Definitions of communitiy: Areas of agreement. *Rural Sociology, 20,* 111–123.

Horelli, L. (1993). *Asunto psytologisena ympäristonä lineenä* [The dwelling as a psychological environment]. Doctoral dissertation, Helsinki, University of Technology.

Horelli, L., & Vepsä, K. (1990). *The New Everyday Life.* A memorandum for the Council of Europe's seminar on participation by women in decisions concerning regional and environmental planning, Athens, 25–27.10.

Horelli, L., & Vepsä, K. (1993). *Ympäriston lapsipuolet* [The stepchildren of environment]. Helsinki.

Julkunen, R. (1991). Hyvinvointivaltion ja ja hyvinvointi pluralismin ristiriidat [conflicts of the welfare state and welfare pluralism]. In A. Mathies (Ed.), *Valtion varjossa, katsaus epävirallisen sektorin tutkimukseen* [In the shadow of the State] (pp. 51–68). Helsinki: Sosiaaliturvan Keskusliitto.

Kanter, R. M. (1972/1977). *Commitment and community: Communes and utopias in sociological perspective.* Cambridge: Harvard University Press.

Kaplan, R., & Kaplan, S. (1989). *The experience of nature: A psychological perspective*. Cambridge: Cambridge University Press.

Kaul, S. (1990). Fysisk planlegging mellom natur-struktur-hverdagsliv. In S. Kaul (Ed.), *Fysisk planlegging i forvandling, natur-struktur-hverdagsliv* [Physical planning in transition, nature-structure-everyday life] (pp. 193–224). Stockholm: Nordplan.

Lefebvre, H. (1971). *Everyday life in the modern world*. New York: Harper & Row.

Miles, M. B., & Huberman, A. M. (1984). *Qualitative data analysis: Sourcebook of new methods*. London: Sage.

Mårtensson, B., Alfredsson, B., Dahlgren, L., & Grahm, L. (1988). *Det hotade lokalsamhället. Om sårbarhet, strategier och självtillit* [The threatened local community]. Stockholm: Byggforskningsrådet.

Noro, A. (1989). Yksilöllistävä palkkatyötäisyhteiskunta Kyllä, entä posttraditionaalit yhteisöt? [About post-traditional communities]. *Sosiologia, 1*, 1–5.

Norrby, C., & Paavonen, H. (Eds.). (1990). *Bygga och bo—en fråga om människosyn*. [Build and dwell—A question of concept of the human being]. Rapport från kvinnoseminarium. Örebro: Sverige.

The Research Group for the New Everyday Life. (1991). *The New Everyday Life—Ways and means*. Copenhagen: Nord.

Rogers, E. (1983). *Diffusions of innovations*. New York: Free Press.

Rutter, M. (1987). Psychosocial resilience and protective mechanisms. *American Journal of Orthopediatrics, 3*, 316–331.

Saeterdal, A., & Takle, E. L. (1991). *Mobilizing women in local planning and decision-making: A guide to why and how*. Oslo: The Ministry of Foreign Affairs.

Schiefloe, P. M. (1990). Networks in urban neighborhoods: Lost, saved or liberated communities? *Scandinavian Housing and Planning Research, 7*, 93–103.

Tilastokeskus. (1990). *Tilastonainen* [The statistical woman]. Helsinki: Tilastokeskus.

Tronto, J. (1987). Beyond gender difference to a theory of care. *Signs, 4*, 644–663.

Walker, A. (1989). Clients, consumers, or partners? In *Clients or co-producers? The changing role of citizens in social services*. Helsinki: The National Board of Social Welfare in Finland and European Centre for Social Welfare Training and Research.

—————— 9 ——————

Women, Work, and Metropolitan Environments

SUSAN HANSON, GERALDINE PRATT, DOREEN MATTINGLY, AND MELISSA GILBERT

Women work. They work at home without pay and, increasingly, they also work outside of home for wages. In the United States in 1990, women comprised 45.5% of the labor force, and fully 57.5% of working-aged women worked for pay (U.S. Bureau of Labor Statistics). Combining paid work with the unpaid work of domestic labor now describes the daily life of the majority of women in the United States and elsewhere, and the nature of the local environment certainly affects the ease with which women are able to carry out their diverse activities (Dyck, 1990; Pratt, 1990). Because of the different settings within which women link domestic work and paid employment (as well as the other activities of daily life), it is important to look at women's lives in the context of their local environment.

With an eye to understanding how the local environment shapes and is in turn shaped by women's strategies for combining home work

SUSAN HANSON AND DOREEN MATTINGLY • Graduate School of Geography, Clark University, Worcester, Massachusetts 01610.   GERALDINE PRATT • Department of Geography, University of British Columbia, Vancouver V6T 1Z2, British Columbia, Canada.   MELISSA GILBERT • Department of Geography, Georgia State University, Atlanta, Georgia 30303.

Women and the Environment, edited by Irwin Altman and Arza Churchman. Plenum Press, New York, 1994.

and paid work, we first briefly review the nature of women's paid employment and the role of the local environment in women's working lives. We then draw upon our study of women and work in Worcester, Massachusetts, to illustrate the importance of local context in understanding women's lives. The empirical portion of the chapter compares two different suburban parts of the Worcester metropolitan area, showing how different local contexts affect and are affected by the ways women and their families manage home and work. We find that despite substantial differences between the two areas in local employment opportunities, women's wages are essentially the same in both places. The role of women's employment in household strategies does, however, differ dramatically between the two communities, emphasizing the role of local context in defining the meaning of women's work.

THE NATURE OF WOMEN'S EMPLOYMENT

The growth of women's participation in the paid labor force is well known. Although women have always been a presence in the work force, the proportion of women in the United States who work outside the home has more than doubled since 1940, when only 25.8% of working-age women held jobs outside the home. Moreover, women with young children, traditionally the group of women least likely to hold paid jobs, have been entering the labor force in record numbers so that in 1988 57.7% of mothers with children under 6 years of age were in the labor force (Hayghe, 1990).

Although women are well represented in the paid labor force, most are still confined to certain jobs that are considered appropriate for women. This gender-based occupational segregation means that in 1987, 46% of all employed women were employed in just four occupations: clerical workers, saleswomen, waitresses, and hairdressers (Women Employed Institute, 1988). Occupational segregation is one of the main reasons why women's earnings are still well below men's; in 1987, a college-educated woman could expect to earn less than a man with only a high-school degree (Women Employed Institute, 1988). Women's lower wages reflect not only their concentration in stereotypical "women's jobs" that are undervalued and therefore underpaid but also their inability to climb the job ladder via promotions as easily as men have been able to do.

Gender-based occupational segregation has proven to be remarkably persistent. A vast literature in economics and sociology outlines explanations for this (e.g., Reskin & Roos, 1990), including employer discrimination, sex-typed educational opportunities, and women's domestic responsibilities. Although these factors are undoubtedly important, our understanding of occupational segregation is enriched when these processes are placed in geographic context, within people's concrete experiences of living in places

Geographic context is important to understanding occupational segregation for two reasons. First, women's lives are more rooted than are men's to the immediate local area. Second, the ways in which home and work are intertwined and consequently the construction of gender relations varies from place to place, depending upon what is available locally in terms of jobs, public services, informal resources, and local traditions of gender relations and of combining domestic and paid work. We briefly review the links between occupational segregation and women's spatial constraints before turning, in the next section, to a discussion of how the local environment affects women's employment.

Journey-to-work studies comparing women's and men's work trips have documented repeatedly that women consistently work significantly closer to home than do men (see Hanson & Johnston, 1985, for a review). In Worcester, for example, men on average travel about 20 minutes to work, whereas the average work trip for women is only about 15 minutes (Hanson & Pratt, 1990). These averages conceal considerable variability in women's and men's work trip lengths, a point that researchers are increasingly sensitive to as they pay closer attention to differences among women (McDowell, 1991). Worcester women in professional and managerial positions, for example, travel significantly longer (20 minutes) than women in unskilled jobs (12 minutes). Many women work part time and for that reason curtail their work trips; someone who spends 4 hours a day at work is generally less willing to commute an hour each way than is someone who spends eight hours at work.

In Worcester, women who work part time commute an average of 14.6 minutes daily, compared to the 16.9-minute commute of full-time working women (Hanson & Pratt, 1990). Race and class also complicate generalizations about women's and men's commuting times. In some contexts, such as New York City, low-income Black women must commute long distances to paid employment (McLafferty & Preston, 1990); in others (e.g., New York City and Worcester), Hispanic women have been found to work especially close to home (Pratt & Hanson, 1991). The general point, however, is that women's work trips are shorter than men's, which means that women's labor markets are smaller in their geographic scale than men's are.

The spatial constraints on women's labor markets seem to be related in part to the fact that women bear heavier domestic responsibilities than do men. Johnston-Anumonwo (1992) found that sex differences in commuting are significantly larger between married men and married women than they are between single men and single women, and sex differences in commuting are greatest in two-earner households. Hanson and Pratt (1990) have traced out the links among women's domestic workload, their labor-market status, and their journey-to-work times. Women who work in female-dominated occupations (defined as those occupations in which at least 70% of the workers were women) are more likely than are other employed women to work part time, to bear primary responsibility within the household for a number of household chores (e.g., house-cleaning, cooking, and meal cleanup), to place a great deal of importance on having a job that is close to home and that fits with the schedules of other household members, and in fact to have short journeys to work. The fact that women choose jobs that are easily accessible from home, in part so that they can more readily combine paid work with domestic responsibilities, points to the importance of local context for understanding women's employment.

We turn now to unravel more carefully the ways in which the local context can affect women's employment and the meaning that this employment holds.

THE ROLE OF THE LOCAL ENVIRONMENT IN WOMEN'S EMPLOYMENT

The role that local context plays in shaping gender relations and what is defined as women's work has been explored most extensively at a regional scale. (In geography, this is associated with the "localities" tradition: see Bowlby, Lewis, McDowell, & Foord, 1989.) For example, Parr (1990) explores the construction of gendered work practices in two Ontario towns, Paris and Hanover, from 1880 to 1950. She contrasts the gendering of particular occupations and skills in Paris to the gendering of the same occupations in the East Midlands of England, the region from which many of the Ontario women had emigrated. Tasks defined as men's work in the East Midlands were redefined as women's work in Paris, reflecting local labor availability and union organization.

Local traditions of occupational segregation can also influence local levels of service provision that, in turn, affect women's opportunities to work outside the home. Mark-Lawson, Savage, and Warde (1985) make this argument through a close study of three towns in the English midlands between the first and second world wars. They argue that in the town in which there was little occupational segregation, where women and men had traditionally worked side by side on the same jobs, women also had more effective political power and were able to instigate a range of social services such as institutionalized child care. This service provision presumably reinforced the tradition of gender integration in work places within this town.

Contexts also vary at a finer geographic scale, *within* urban areas. A distinction is frequently made between city and suburb, with suburbs seen as particularly problematic environments for women who wish to work outside of the home (Popenoe, 1977; Wekerle, 1984). In her article, "A Woman's Place Is in the City," Wekerle summarizes this viewpoint, arguing that suburban locations are often isolated and inaccessible to paid employment, public transportation, and social services.

One dimension of difference between women living in suburbs and those in the central city can be attributed to variations in the geography of job opportunities. Hanson and Pratt (1988) have documented for the Worcester metropolitan area that male and female jobs are clustered in different areas. In certain areas (for example, a regional shopping center in a suburban area), a high proportion of employment is in female-typed jobs. In others, such as an isolated industrial park, almost all locally available employment opportunities take the form of male-dominated jobs. This spatial variation in employment opportunities indicates that residential location, whether it be in city or suburb, is crucial in defining a person's access to particular types of work, but this may be truer in the suburbs where the overall density of employment options tends to be lower.

The nature of employment opportunities in the immediate vicinity of home is likely to play an particularly crucial role in the type of work found by people unwilling or unable to undertake long commutes, most often women. In addition, formal service provision, particularly day care, may be less accessible in dispersed suburban areas. Studies such as Dyck's (1989, 1990) ethnography of women living in Coquitlam, an outer suburb of Vancouver, point to the intricate webs of informal networks that suburban women must construct in order to juggle paid employment with domestic responsibilities. Inner-city residence may allow women access to a wider range of jobs, including professional and service-sector ones, as well as to urban amenities and formal and informal services, such as institutionalized child care (Rose, 1990). Some see the decision to live in the gentrifying inner city as part of a strategy on the part of women and men to remake gender relations so as to allow a more equitable distribution of paid and domestic work (Mills, 1989).

Though the dichotomous regionalization, city/suburb, no doubt describes general patterns of accessibility and strategy, it also veils a great deal of variability in both city and suburb. Whether an inner-city area is rich in employment opportunities and public services undoubtedly depends on national context. It is noteworthy that much of the literature extolling the virtues of the inner city as an environment rich in formal and informal resources emerges out of the Canadian context; according to Goldberg and Mercer (1986), one of the distinctive characteristics of Canadian as opposed to American cities is the "health" of the inner cities, in terms of average household incomes and public service provision.

Even within a particular inner city, resources vary across neighborhoods. In the case of Montreal, Rose (1990, p. 370) notes that the highest density of day-care centers is found in the inner-city area that was "the cradle of many of the popular struggles of the 1970s, and which has since undergone considerable gentrification [by former activists and newcomers]." The "historical legacy of a 'local dynamic' of organizing for services" (p. 370), as well as the high educational levels attained by current residents, provide the necessary resources to navigate bureaucratic rules governing the organization of cooperative and after-school day care.

Suburban environments are no less diverse. Scholarly treatments of the suburbs have been criticized for the tendency to overgeneralize the middle-class suburban experience; in fact, suburban environments come in many forms, including working-class ones (O'Connor, 1985; Lehmann, 1989). But even less attention has been given to variability in the construction of gender relations and in the local resources that enable or constrain women's employment options in different suburban areas.

As an example of variability within suburbs, Wekerle and Rutherford (1989) found a considerable range of commuting and employment patterns within a single suburban municipality in metropolitan Toronto. They identified four types of "zones" in terms of the median commuting distance and average income of residents. In one type, the residents traveled a short distance to work (an average of 3 miles), and employed women living within it earned quite low wages (an average of only $Can16,300 per year). In another type of zone, residents traveled the same distance, but women earned an average of $3,000 more per annum. Residents in yet another zone category, had to travel long distances to work (5.6 miles) but were rewarded with low wages (women earned on average $15,100 per annum). The geography of employment opportunities and willingness or necessity to travel long distances to work clearly varies within this suburban municipality.

One shortcoming to some characterizations of the suburban environment is that one model—a post–World War II middle-class community created from scratch on redeveloped agricultural land—is overgeneralized, and consequently the diversity of suburban places is flattened. Some of this diversity emerges from the fact that many suburbs carry a history, having evolved from small towns or rural communities with local traditions of work and gender relations. This history, as well as the characteristics of present residents, becomes part of the process that leads to the continuing diversification of suburban environments.

Nelson (1986), for example, has argued that back offices, which employ women as routine clerical workers, are being moved to middle-class suburbs in the San Francisco region because managers are attracted to the middle-class, well-educated, female labor force residents within them. She argues that these women are particularly attractive employees because they perceive their primary role as one of family caregiver, they desire part-time employment to supplement mortgage payments, but are a relatively docile labor force, undemanding in terms of wages and benefits in comparison to inner-city, often single-parent, female employees. Nelson's work suggests that the caricature of the suburban environment as one that is isolated from all employment opportunities is now outdated. It also suggests that as employers move to varying types of suburban areas to capture different types of female labor, the diversification of these environments, in terms of locally available employment opportunities, will continue.

We turn now to explore our claims about the diversity of experiences within suburban environments through a case study of two suburban areas within the Worcester, Massachusetts, metropolitan area. These areas have different histories that structure the contemporary context, and they vary in terms of class characteristics and local employment opportunities. Despite the fact that women in both areas tend to be segregated to female-typed jobs and earn low wages, they combine paid and unpaid work in varying ways and draw upon different community resources in doing so.

The essence of traditional urban social geography is that residential areas within metropolitan areas vary by class, family status, and ethnicity. The differences go beyond this, and women's roles within the household, family, and community also vary in response to local differences in gender relations, economic structure, and local service provisions. The strategies women develop in leading their daily lives, particularly for combining home and paid employment, are embedded in, and actively shape, their local cultural and economic context.

A CASE STUDY: TWO WORCESTER SUBURBAN AREAS

In this section we draw on our research in Worcester, Massachusetts, to explore the relationship between local context and women's strategies for combining paid and unpaid work. Through a comparison of two very different communities within the Worcester metropolitan area, we seek to shed light on the different ways in which women and their families weave the connections between work and home. Conducted at a fine spatial scale, our study aims to show how gender relations are constructed in place through the stitching together of home and work and to illuminate how the structuring of gender relations is related to the location of economic activity.

Our study compares the strategies women and their families develop around home and work in two suburban communities adjacent to Worcester: the town of Westboro and a collection of towns along the Blackstone River Valley (Figure 1). After describing the interview data that provide us with insights about ways of structuring the home–work

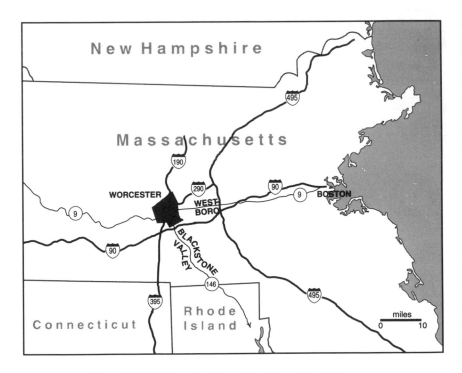

Figure 1. The Worcester, Massachusetts, metropolitan area.

link, we provide a brief historical overview of the economic and social geography of these two communities. We then examine how the economic role of women within the household differs in these two areas and explore the causes and consequences of this difference.

DATA

The case study draws upon two large survey data sets. The first, collected in 1987, involved lengthy in-home interviews with the men and women in some 620 households living throughout the Worcester area. These interviews were aimed at learning about how people make decisions about where to live and where to work, how people find their jobs, and how they evaluate various job attributes (for more details about this survey, see Hanson & Pratt, 1990, 1991). The second survey, carried out in 1989, focused on the owners and managers of manufacturing and producer services firms located within four small areas in the Worcester region. In these interviews we were interested in learning about how firms make location decisions, what is the role of perceived labor-force characteristics in those location decisions, how the labor process within the firm affects location decisions, and how employers search for workers (for more details, see Hanson & Pratt, 1992, and Pratt & Hanson, 1992).

The case study developed here relies primarily on the 1987 data, which is based on a representative sample of Worcester-area households. Because the 1987 survey was not aimed specifically at collecting a minimum number of cases from the two particular areas we focus on here, the sample sizes in the case study are relatively small.[1] The sample individuals were, however, selected in a way that makes them representative of the populations resident in each of the two areas.

CONTEXT: WESTBORO AND THE BLACKSTONE VALLEY

Westboro, a town of 15,000 people, is located to the east of Worcester, 26 miles west of Boston. Immediately adjacent to the junction of Route 9, Route 495, and the Massachusetts Turnpike (Route 90), Westboro is within easy reach of the towns along the Route 128 corridor. Like many other towns along Routes 128 and 495, Westboro's economy has changed with the recent development of technology-intensive industry. Data General, a large manufacturer of microcomputers, located in West-

[1]They are as follows: 33 Westboro women, 14 Westboro men, 76 Blackstone Valley women, and 22 Blackstone Valley men.

boro in 1977. Since that time dozens of other high-technology facilities have moved to the town's several industrial parks.

Prior to the recent wave of development, Westboro was socially and spatially defined as a "small town," with a local employment base centered on an abrasives plant and a residential population that included many professionals who commuted to Boston and Worcester. The ideals of middle-class, small-town life influenced the way the town of Westboro has responded to the most recent round of economic change. When construction of homes and apartments boomed in the 1970s, the town passed a zoning bylaw, effectively banning all further apartment construction. The combination of "snob zoning," the high quality of the housing stock, and the town's proximity to high-paying jobs in high-technology industries have made Westboro one of the most expensive and elite towns in the Worcester area. Because the town is located at a major crossroads, residents of Westboro find a wide variety of employment opportunities within reasonable commute times, a factor that contributes to the town's attraction and economic health.

Westboro's status has been reinforced through a series of local government decisions to encourage industrial and retail development rather than housing construction, producing the attractive combination of a well-funded town government and low residential property taxes. Westboro's public schools are considered to be among the best in central Massachusetts; in the early 1980s, approximately 75% of Westboro's high-school graduates went on to college (Allen, 1984). In addition, the town's public library, senior center, recreation program, and fire and police protection have continued to expand through the 1970s and 1980s, despite the fiscal crises faced by most municipalities.

Six towns in the Blackstone River Valley, south of Worcester, provide a stark contrast to Westboro.[2] Since 1790, when Samuel Slater introduced mechanized spinning production in a Pawtucket Falls mill, the economy of the Blackstone Valley has been dominated by textile mills, and the social and political life of the region has been shaped by the community-based paternalism of mill owners.[3] Through the Depression of the 1930s, Blackstone Valley mill workers in Massachusetts were

---

[2]Blackstone Valley stretches 46 miles from Worcester to Pawtucket, Rhode Island. There are a total of 11 towns in the Massachusetts Blackstone Valley, but we have limited our focus to the six towns that are within the Worcester SMSA: Grafton, Millbury, Northbridge, Sutton, Upton, and Uxbridge. In 1990 the six towns had a combined population of close to 60,000. The five other towns in the Massachusetts Blackstone Valley are Blackstone, Douglas, Hopedale, Mendon, and Millville.

[3]For recent historical treatments of labor in the Blackstone Valley, see Lamphere (1987) and Gerstle (1989).

largely nonunion and earned wages that were roughly one-half to three-fourths of the wages of other textile workers in New England (Reynolds, 1990, p. 179). The textile industry of the Blackstone Valley had its last major growth spurt during World War II, when plant expansion and market demand reached all time highs. During wartime, unionization efforts broke the traditional patriarchal control of the mill towns but did little to boost the economic security of workers as the movement of the textile industry to the South was already underway.

Since the 1950s, the textile industry and the communities along the Blackstone River have continued to decline. Once "the cradle of the industrial revolution," the Blackstone Valley has recently been called "the cradle of deindustrialization" (Reynolds, 1990, p. 177). One mill owner estimated that 90% of the woolen and worsted mills operating in the Blackstone Valley at the end of World War II were closed by 1989 (Reynolds, 1991, p. 183). Between 1970 and 1980 the net outmigration from the Blackstone Valley was almost 2,000 adults (Cravins, 1988, p. 206), 4.5% of the adult population.[4] Many of the workers who stayed were forced to seek work outside the valley; in 1988 the Blackstone Valley Chamber of Commerce estimated that 60% of the employed residents of Massachusetts Blackstone Valley towns worked outside of the valley.

The commuting patterns of residents surveyed in 1987 reveal the influence of the flight of manufacturing jobs from the Blackstone Valley. Table 1 shows the average journey-to-work times and distances for women and men in Westboro and the Blackstone Valley. Blackstone Valley men, over 50% of whom travel more than 30 minutes to work, have longer commutes on average than do members of any other group. The long commutes of men living in the Blackstone Valley are likely due to necessity created by deindustrialization: Despite their long commute times, many Blackstone Valley men actually expressed a preference for working close to home; 33.3% of the Blackstone Valley men surveyed compared to only 7.1% of Westboro men reported that working close to home is one of the three things they value most in a job.[5]

The inaccessibility of the Blackstone Valley also shapes the commuting patterns of the people living there. Traffic between the Blackstone Valley communities flows largely along Route 146, which runs from along the Blackstone River between Worcester and Providence but is not connected to the Massachusetts Turnpike, the state's major east–west route into Boston (Figure 1). Plans are underway to build an interchange

[4]These figures do not include outmigration from Sutton.
[5]See Table 4 for the job attributes most valued by women and men in the two areas.

TABLE 1. A COMPARISON OF DAILY
JOURNEY-TO-WORK TIMES AND DISTANCES
OF MEN AND WOMEN LIVING IN
WESTBORO AND THE BLACKSTONE VALLEY

	Women	Men
Average commute times in minutes (standard deviation)		
Westboro	24.2	24.5
	(22.5)	(17.0)
	$n = 24$	$n = 13$
Blackstone Valley	17.5	34.5
	(14.5)	(14.8)
	$n = 42$	$n = 17$

Difference between two groups of men significant at $p = 0.15$.

	Women	Men
Average commute distance in miles (standard deviation)		
Westboro	13.5	15.0
	(13.4)	(11.8)
Blackstone Valley	7.8	15.4
	(12.5)	(13.2)

Difference between two groups of women significant at $p = 0.10$.

Source: 1987 Worcester Survey (for details of the survey, see Hanson & Pratt, 1991).

at Route 146 and the Massachusetts Turnpike, but until it is built, the valley towns will remain relatively isolated, requiring long commutes for those who seek work elsewhere. In the last few years, a few Blackstone Valley communities have shown signs of renewed growth. The valley's relatively low-priced housing and proximity (despite low connectivity) to growing high-technology areas have attracted new residents, in what has been called the "shift from mill-town to bedroom community" (*Worcester Telegram and Gazette*, May 18, 1988).

Westboro and the Blackstone Valley, then, have strikingly different histories and geographies despite being located just a few miles apart within the same SMSA. One consequence of these differences lies in the remarkably different employment landscapes of these two places today; the kinds of jobs that are available in Westboro differ markedly from those available in the Blackstone Valley. The occupation profiles of the

TABLE 2. PERCENTAGE OF OCCUPATIONS OF ALL WOMEN AND MEN
IN WESTBORO AND THE BLACKSTONE VALLEY IN 1980

	Women		Men	
	Westboro	Blackstone Valley	Westboro	Blackstone Valley
Professional/managerial	40.4	28.0	44.3	23.7
Service, sales, and clerical	51.4	55.5	24.2	20.8
Production workers	10.2	20.0	30.8	52.3

Source: U.S. Census of Population and Housing.

two areas show that a substantially larger concentration of Westboro residents work as professionals, managers, and engineers, whereas more Blackstone Valley residents are employed in manufacturing jobs (Table 2).

The contrast is particularly noticeable for men: 44.3% of Westboro men are employed in either professional–technical or managerial–administrative jobs, whereas Blackstone Valley men are far more concentrated in production occupations. In 1980, 52.3% of the men living in the Blackstone Valley were employed as skilled or unskilled laborers (the categories of laborer/operative and craft/repair/precision production) compared to only 30.8% of Westboro men. For women the differences are less dramatic but still apparent. Women living in Westboro are more likely to hold professional and technical jobs than are women in the Blackstone Valley (26% compared to 19.2%), whereas a larger percentage of women in the Blackstone Valley (17.4%) than of women working in Westboro (8.4%) are employed as laborers and operatives.

Differences in the employment landscapes of the two places are especially apparent from the 1989 survey of employers in manufacturing and producer services firms, which are the types of employers most likely to locate with labor needs in mind (Table 3). Among employees of Blackstone Valley firms, 44.3% of the women and 36% of the men worked in unskilled or routine production jobs, compared to 14.2% of the women and 9.4% of the men employed in jobs like these in Westboro firms. As with the census data, which include jobs in all sectors, both men and women in Westboro are more likely to be employed as engineers and professionals than in Blackstone Valley. Although consumer services, such as retail stores and medical offices, locate with respect to consumer demand, production-oriented firms are more likely to select locations that provide access to particular forms of labor; such firms are

TABLE 3. PERCENTAGE OF OCCUPATIONS OF ALL MEN AND WOMEN
IN PRODUCER SERVICES AND MANUFACTURING FIRMS IN WESTBORO
AND THE BLACKSTONE VALLEY IN 1989

	Women		Men	
	Westboro (n = 718)	Blackstone Valley (n = 415)	Westboro (n = 1,443)	Blackstone Valley (n = 583)
Professional/managerial	23.0	10.2	67.8	19.9
Service, sales, and clerical	50.1	36.3	14.2	14.8
Production workers	26.9	53.3	18.0	65.3

Source: Information collected from 42 firms in Westboro and 31 firms in the Blackstone Valley (for details of survey design, see Hanson & Pratt, 1992).

therefore more likely to be sensitive to and to play an active role in reproducing differentiated residential landscapes (Nelson, 1986; Storper & Walker, 1989; Hanson & Pratt, 1992).

What is the impact of these differences on the lives of women in the two areas? Here the social geography becomes less clear-cut and more interesting. Traditional economic theory and common sense suggest that differences in employment, like those shown in Tables 2 and 3, should lead to differences in income. This expectation is borne out if we focus on household income. In 1980, Westboro households had substantially higher average incomes ($23,000) than did Blackstone Valley households ($20,000). The 1987 survey also found Westboro households to have significantly higher incomes than Blackstone Valley households; for example, 45% of the Westboro women, compared to only 13% of Blackstone Valley women, lived in households with annual incomes above $50,000.

When personal earnings, rather than household incomes are compared, the differences between women in Westboro and those in the Blackstone Valley disappear. Despite the differences in the nature of work women do in the two areas, the 1987 survey showed no significant differences in women's personal earnings between the two areas; in fact, the computed average hourly wage for women is identical in Westboro and the Blackstone Valley at $9.40/hour.[6] In each area, almost half of the employed women interviewed have annual incomes of less than $15,000.

[6]We computed average hourly wages from each person's reported annual income and weekly hours; the figure therefore includes salaried workers.

In addition to earning similar incomes, employed women living in the two areas were similar in many other respects as well. We found no significant differences between Westboro and Blackstone Valley women in the proportions employed part-time or full-time or not in the labor market; the proportions who are salaried or waged; or the proportions employed in female-dominated, male-dominated, or gender-integrated occupations.[7]

These similarities are surprising in light of the educational backgrounds of the two groups of women. A variety of comparisons reveal that Westboro women have significantly more years of formal education than their Blackstone Valley counterparts. In particular, Westboro women are more likely to have postsecondary education (74% of them do) than are Blackstone Valley women, only 35% of whom have education beyond high school. These dramatic differences in women's formal education suggest that their employment outcomes should be different, yet, as we have seen, their earnings and employment profiles are remarkably similar. Differences in the two communities' occupational and industrial structures indicate, however, that similarities in women's income probably mask substantial differences between the two places in the lives of working women.

THE SOCIAL CONTEXT

The local environment within which women weave the home–work link cannot be defined solely in terms of the nature of employment opportunities; local history, culture, and custom also shape the strategies used to connect home and work. Rootedness, or degree of attachment to the local area, can be a particularly important aspect of community life for women, who may rely heavily on social networks and bear the main responsibility for maintaining them. Westboro and the Blackstone Valley are strikingly different places in terms of the rootedness of the local populations and degree of connection people have to their local social environment.

In the Blackstone Valley a history of mill-town paternalism has contributed to a legacy of extreme rootedness. Mill families, who once provided the core labor force of the textile industry, tend to remain in the valley towns (Lamphere, 1987; Gerstle, 1989). Blackstone Valley residents have lived in the Worcester area an average of 25.3 years, signifi-

[7]We define female-dominated occupations as those in which at least 70% of the workers are women; male-dominated occupations are those occupations in which at least 70% of the workers are male. The remainder of occupational categories are defined as gender-integrated.

cantly longer than Westboro residents, whose residence in the area averages 17.3 years. More Blackstone Valley residents (44.6%) said that they grew up in the Worcester area than did Westboro residents (37.6%), reaffirming the greater rootedness of Blackstone Valley residents. In addition, men and women living in the Blackstone Valley have held their present jobs longer than have their Westboro counterparts. The growth of high-technology industry in Westboro has doubtlessly contributed to the mobility of that town's residents. Engineers and scientists are among the most mobile of workers, often operating in labor markets that are national or international in scale (Greenwood, 1975; Angel, 1989).

The local presence of extended families contributes to a tightly woven social fabric in the Blackstone Valley. Among the women we interviewed there, more than 50% have one or more relatives living in their neighborhood, and 23% have three or more, whereas only 12% of the Westboro women have any relatives living in their neighborhood. The place-based stability of valley residents is illustrated through people's job and residential histories. Typical of the Blackstone Valley is the story of a 41-year-old Uxbridge woman, who is a food service manager in a nearby nursing home. Both she and her husband are lifelong residents of the town, with a dense local network of friends and relatives. She and her husband found their home through his grandmother, and she found her present job through the father of one of the boys in her son's scout troop. Her family's connections have kept them rooted to the area despite hard economic times. Both her husband and father recently lost their jobs when local manufacturing plants closed down.

Another indicator of people's relative rootedness is the ordering of their workplace and residential location decisions. In the 1987 survey, respondents were asked whether they had chosen their job first and then found their place of residence or had found a residence first and then searched for a job from there. Table 4 shows the responses of employed men and women in both locations. Reflecting the greater rootedness in the Blackstone Valley, the majority of both men and women there have looked for jobs from an established residential location. In contrast, Westboro households are more likely to have chosen a home location near the husband's employment; 86% of Westboro women reported that their husband found his job before they found their residence, and then they (the women) searched for a job from that residence. Significantly fewer women in the Blackstone Valley (only 26%) reported this pattern of job and residential search. These findings suggest that men's jobs are a more important part of household strategies in Westboro than in Blackstone Valley households, no doubt reflecting the

TABLE 4. PERCENTAGE OF EMPLOYED
RESPONDENTS WHO SELECTED THEIR
CURRENT RESIDENCE BEFORE THEIR
CURRENT JOB

	Westboro	Blackstone Valley
Women[a]	91.7	96.2
Men[b]	35.7	75.0

[a]Differences between two groups of women not significant.
[b]Differences between two groups of men significant at $p = 0.03$.
Source: 1987 Worcester survey (for details of the survey, see Hanson & Pratt, 1991).

greater earnings of Westboro men, as well as the culture of middle-class and working-class gender relations.

WOMEN'S ECONOMIC ROLES WITHIN THE HOUSEHOLD

To grasp the influence of local social and economic environment on women's lives, we must expand the scope of inquiry to include not only women's positions in the workplace but their roles in their families and communities as well. To do this, we turn to the wealth of household data collected in the 1987 survey. A cursory glance reveals many similarities in the domestic situations of women in Westboro and the Blackstone Valley: They are essentially the same age, have similar household sizes, and numbers of children. In both places, roughly 80% of the women lived in dual-earner households. Women's marital status, however, differs in that more women in the Blackstone Valley (79%) than in Westboro (69%) are currently married. Furthermore, among unmarried women, a larger proportion of Westboro women (15%) than Blackstone Valley women (3%) lived with a partner, suggesting that couples in Westboro may be less traditional.

For women living with male partners, the man's employment status and income level have an impact on the choices women make in weaving together domestic life and paid employment. Despite being identical to the personal earnings of women in Westboro, the wages of women in the Blackstone Valley constitute a significantly larger proportion of family income than do the wages of Westboro women. Employed married women in the Blackstone Valley earn on average, 38% of their family's income, whereas Westboro women's earnings account on average for only 24% of family income. Another way of grasping the importance of a woman's economic contribution to the household is to compare the family income of married-couple households where the woman is in the paid labor force to that of such households where the woman does not have a job outside the home. In Westboro, the family incomes of the two groups did not differ significantly, indicating that women's employment there has had little impact on family income. In the Blackstone Valley, however, families where the woman worked had significantly higher incomes.

This local variability in the economic role of women within the household affects their crafting of home–work linkages in important ways. It is probably because Blackstone Valley women's incomes are crucial to the household's living standards that they are more likely to report feeling compelled to work full time. Although the percentage of women who actually worked full time does not differ between the two areas, a larger proportion of the full-time employed Blackstone Valley women (38%) than of the full-time employed Westboro women (14.3%) said they would prefer to work part time rather than full time if they could choose to do so.

Another way of assessing the meaning of paid employment in women's lives is to ask them to evaluate the relative importance of various job attributes. Such preferences do not necessarily correspond to the attributes of the jobs the women actually hold, but the preferences do reveal some interesting patterns in the way women think about paid employment.[8] A higher proportion of Blackstone Valley women than of Westboro women value proximity to home and child care, job benefits, and the fit of work times to household schedules (Table 5). In contrast, a higher percentage of Westboro women place importance on the type of work, the people with whom they work, the amount of independence on the job, and the prestige of the job. Also interesting is the fact that almost 9% of Westboro, compared to only 2% of Blackstone Valley, women list pay as something that was *least* important to them in choosing a job. (These small percentages in themselves attest to the importance of wages for the vast majority of working women.) In general, these differences in women's evaluation of job attributes are consistent with the differences between the two areas in women's economic role in the household. Many more Blackstone Valley women see their employment as an economic necessity because it is more likely to be one.

---

[8]Respondents were asked to say how important each of a number of job attributes were to them in their evaluation of jobs in general. They were also asked to identify which three of the attributes on our list were most important and which three were least important.

TABLE 5. GENDER AND LOCATION DIFFERENCES IN EVALUATION OF JOB
ATTRIBUTES IN GENERAL: PERCENTAGE OF EACH GROUP LISTING ATTRIBUTE
AMONG TOP THREE ATTRIBUTES

	Women		Men	
	Westboro	Blackstone Valley	Westboro	Blackstone Valley
Close to home	12.5	24.5	7.1	31.6
Easy to get to/low transportation expense	8.3	9.4	0.0	5.3
Proximity to child care and/or schools	8.3	13.2	0.0	0.0
The job hours when you have to be at work	8.3	13.2	0.0	0.0
Having flexible job hours	25.0	22.6	21.4	21.1
Possibilities for advancement	20.8	20.8	50.0	15.8
The people you work with	41.7	26.4	42.9	31.6
The type of work	45.8	26.4	57.1	42.1
Good pay	41.7	43.3	50.0	52.6
Good benefits	12.5	24.5	21.4	47.4
Amount of independence	12.5	7.5	28.6	21.1
Amount of prestige	8.3	3.8	7.1	5.3
Physical work environment	4.2	3.8	7.1	10.5
Hours fit with partner's work schedule	20.8	22.6	7.1	10.5
Hours fit with school schedule and/or child-care arrangements	25.0	37.7	0.0	0.0

Source: 1987 Worcester survey (for details of the survey, see Hanson & Pratt, 1991).

These differences between the two groups of women pale in comparison to the gender differences evident in Table 4 (see also Hanson &
Pratt, 1991). Men, for example, placed a higher value than did women
on the amount of pay and independence a job offers and were far less
concerned about the time/space dimensions of a job (e.g., that it be easy
to get to, have convenient hours, or be near schools and child care).

In comparing the economic geographies of Westboro and the Blackstone Valley, we have sought to trace the relationships between the local
economic environments and women's daily lives. Employment opportunities vary dramatically for both men and women between the two
places, in part because the residential populations of the two areas are
quite different. These differences are reflected in significantly higher
male incomes in Westboro than in the Blackstone Valley, whereas wom-
en's earnings are the same in both locations. The discrepancy between

Westboro and the Blackstone Valley household incomes reflects, then, the contrast in men's, not women's, employment outcomes. But this divergence between the two places in men's relationship to the labor market means that women's economic role within the family is quite different, with women in the Blackstone Valley contributing a greater proportion of family income and consequently viewing their jobs differently from Westboro women. Blackstone Valley women are also more likely to work as laborers and operatives, and this may lead them to view their job more instrumentally, in terms of wages, and to privilege fit with family circumstances over characteristics intrinsic to the job. Westboro women, given their educational standing and white-collar status, are more likely to view their jobs in terms of status and the opportunities they offer for independence and interpersonal satisfaction. Much of the variation may be accounted for by the class characteristics of resident women; it is also conditioned by local employment opportunities and other resources.

HOUSEHOLD STRATEGIES

In many respects, the typical Westboro household, where family income is largely based on male professional employment that women's work may supplement, fits economists' conceptions of the family (for a review, see Becker, 1981). But this model is not the norm for all households; the pattern found among Westboro households is one of many possible configurations, influenced by male and female wage-earning capabilities in specific economic and social situations. Because of the higher earning potential of educated white men relative to other groups in society, households that include educated white men are able to maximize their household income by maximizing the income of the male, which often involves moving the household's place of residence to accommodate a job location.

Recent research has emphasized the different types of strategies developed in response to economic and social change by families in different social and geographic contexts—strategies that may incorporate the paid and unpaid work of several members (Pahl & Wallace, 1985; Pratt & Hanson, 1988; Wheelock, 1990). In this light, the home–work link of Westboro men is part of a household economic strategy, one that privileges male employment over female. Women's home–work links in this scenario generally are negotiated around, and in response to, decisions that maximize male income. In the Blackstone Valley, household strategies tend to rely less on male wages, which are not as high, and to draw more heavily on both women's income and the family's dense local social networks.

One factor contributing to the greater rootedness among households in the Blackstone Valley is the importance of women's income to households. Studies of residential mobility have found that households where the wife is employed are less likely to migrate for the husband's employment. Mincer (1978) and Bartel (1979) both found local job change to be more common, and long-distance moves to be less frequent, among men with working wives than among married men whose wives did not work outside the home. In addition, Bartel (1979) found that as the relative contribution of the wife's wages to the household income increased, the average distance of residential moves decreased.

A community's rootedness affects the ways in which its people find housing, jobs, and child care; in other words, the social networks built up over time are important to the strategies women use to combine home and paid work. Hanson and Pratt (1991) have found interesting differences between women and men in their patterns of job search, particularly in the use of personal contacts: For instance, 60% of employed women had learned of their present job through a community or family contact, compared to 32% of men (pp. 240–241). Women in the Blackstone Valley were significantly more likely to have found a job through a friend, relative, or neighbor (82% of them had found their current job this way) than were women in Westboro, "only" 61% of whom had obtained their job through a personal contact. Much of this difference can be attributed to the strength of family networks in the Blackstone Valley. When asked, in an open-ended way, to list the three most important reasons for choosing their present job, 19% of Blackstone Valley women said they had "simply fallen" into the job through a relative, whereas only 8% of Westboro women cited family contacts.

The deep family and community connections in the Blackstone Valley also influence where women living there are likely to work. Table 1 showed that women in the Blackstone Valley have shorter average daily commutes than Westboro women (17.5 minutes vs. 24.2 minutes), a pattern that stands in especially marked contrast to the longer average commute times of the valley men (34.5 minutes). Although the long commutes of men living in the Blackstone Valley can be attributed to a combination of local job loss and inaccessibility, the short commutes of Blackstone Valley women probably reflect in large part their reliance on locally based personal contacts in finding work. Hanson and Pratt (1992) have documented for the Worcester area a link between finding a job through personal networks and working close to home. Because personal contacts tend to be local, using such contacts to find employment tends to limit the geographic range of possible jobs, exerting a sort of spatial inertia on local labor market processes. Respondents were also asked the maximum time they would be willing to spend traveling to work without a pay increase. Westboro women reported a willingness to travel a significantly longer time (average = 35.4 minutes) than did Blackstone Valley women (average = 29.1 minutes), further reflecting the importance placed on working close to home by Blackstone Valley residents.

The rootedness of Blackstone Valley residents has also influenced their housing choices. When asked if they found their present housing through informal means, 65% of Blackstone Valley residents, but only 35% of Westboro residents, said they had. In addition, a greater percentage of Blackstone Valley women than of Westboro women were renting or had bought their homes from a relative, suggesting that women in the Blackstone Valley are more likely to use their kinship networks to find housing as well as employment. In Westboro, on the other hand, where affordable housing is limited and the cost of average housing is quite high, it is the high (male) income of families that matters most in securing housing. This parallels Forrest and Murie's (1987) findings that among affluent professional workers in London, housing careers tended to be based on the employment careers of men.

In addition to finding employment and housing, securing child care is a crucial part of combining responsibilities at home with the demands of paid employment for women with young children. The type, amount, and location of child care available in a woman's neighborhood has substantial influence over her choices in combining home and work. The availability of child care is geographically uneven. In the Blackstone Valley, family day care (where children are taken care of in the provider's home) is much more widely available than formal day care (where children are brought to a day-care center). Family day care accounts for 52% of the total day care available in the Blackstone Valley, but only 26% of available care in Westboro.[9] Family day care usually costs far less than formal day care and can have more flexible hours. This is compatible with the household incomes and women's job characteristics (more shift work and earlier starting times) in the Blackstone Valley. The scheduling of institutionalized child care is more compatible with a "9-to-5" job. But informal child care can also be less reliable than formal care, possibly further restricting women to jobs close to home.

[9]These figures were compiled from data collected by Child Care Connection in Worcester, Massachusetts. Totals do not include baby-sitters who come into a family's home or relatives and friends who care for children informally.

We have shown how the rootedness of Blackstone Valley residents presents them with certain options for securing work, housing, and child care, whereas family strategies in Westboro are more likely to privilege male employment. In the Blackstone Valley, the home–work link of men and women can also be seen as part of a household economic strategy formed in response to specific local conditions. In a time and place dominated by job loss and plant closure, men in "blue-collar" occupations are less able to support households as single earners than are men in "white-collar" occupations. Therefore women's employment, as well as the social and familial networks that women maintain, become more important to the household. For households in the Blackstone Valley, their ability to negotiate other aspects of the home–work relationship, particularly low-cost housing and child care, has become crucial to their economic strategy.

Clearly, people's lives are complicated and cannot be grasped through simple categorizations. In our analysis we have attempted to conceptualize community, class, and gender, not as categories one belongs to but as processes that are constructed and negotiated through the practices of everyday life.

FUTURE DIRECTIONS OF RESEARCH AND POLICY

Our examination of home–work strategies in two Worcester suburbs demonstrates the extent to which occupational segregation is spatially variegated. Although there is a depressing consistency to women's low wages across middle- and working-class suburbs, we found geographic variability in the types of work that women do. We also see different traditions of searching for work and housing, and of arranging child care. Paid employment holds different meanings for women within different household economies. The wages of working-class Blackstone Valley women are more central to the family income, and these women are more committed to benefits and wages. Westboro women have the opportunity to value other attributes of jobs: the type of work and job status and interpersonal relations within the workplace.

Our findings are consistent with the claims that Pringle (1988) makes about middle- and working-class secretaries. She observes a greater degree of fluidity of home and work among working-class secretaries (those who are married to manual workers and employed in more routine clerical positions) insofar as they bring the concerns of home into the workplace and chat about family and home at work. Middle-class secretaries were more likely to partition home and work in their conversation and to retain the family as a private sphere. In our case study, the Blackstone Valley women were more likely to find their jobs through, and to value their jobs in terms of, their family obligations and linkages.

These class attributes emerge out of and within local and spatially grounded contexts. Westboro has attracted white-collar employment because of its class history, and it is now more likely to offer this type of employment to middle-class women living there than is the Blackstone Valley. The deindustrialization of the Blackstone Valley, even as it has seriously affected men's employment, is not unrelated to women's situations. Men's long work trips and job instability influence women's employment, making women's wages and benefits more important and perhaps tying women more closely to the home. The history of rootedness in the Blackstone Valley no doubt influences women's reliance on local networks for information about jobs, housing, and child care. The household incomes in Westboro are more likely to sustain institutionalized child care. Given Blackstone Valley household incomes, local culture, and scheduling of women's paid employment, it is not surprising that informal child care is more readily available there.

What are the implications of noting this geographical variability in employment profiles, local resources, and home–work strategies for future research and policy? An examination of the variability of women's experiences in different contexts highlights the importance of local resources and opens up our thinking about choices, constraints, and possible worlds. For example, through the comparative approach, the differences in child-care and job-search strategies became more obvious, and one is led to think more carefully about the meaning and impact of locally available resources. Does the reliance on family and informal child care in the Blackstone Valley reflect people's choices or the constraints of low household incomes and the inflexibility of existing institutional child-care arrangements? Do existing arrangements suggest the necessity of child-care subsidies and more flexible institutional care? Does the reliance on local networks for job information open up or close down opportunities? More generally, what are the processes by which women's networks link them to jobs, child care, and housing opportunities? Are these processes different for different groups of women? These are not questions that our case studies allow us to answer, but the discovery of differences leads us to pose such questions as directions for further research.

Our research suggests that policymakers need to assist both women and men in combining home and paid employment, thereby enabling women to deal more easily with the double burden and allowing men to participate more fully in child-care and household responsibilities. Seeing people's housing, child-care, and employment needs as separate problems sets up unnecessary barriers to their solution; only when housing, child care, and employment are seen as integrally related within the broader strategies of combining home and paid employment can innovative and effective policy solutions be found.

Many policies would improve the current situation. Paid maternity and paternity leaves, child-care subsidies as part of benefit plans, child care at the job site, longer school days, afterschool programs, and child-care providers' furnishing transportation—all would ease the double burden of paid work and domestic responsibilities for families with children. Such policies would probably also draw into the paid labor force many people (mostly women) who are kept out of it by child-care responsibilities. The availability of part-time jobs with benefits might also increase labor-force participation. Flexible work hours for *all* jobs, not just those in female-dominated occupations, as well as more part-time jobs in non-female-dominated occupations, would go a long way to attracting more women to jobs that are not traditionally female.

Finally, both researchers and policymakers need to be sensitive to the issue of scale in determining their research agendas and policy suggestions. The scale at which one chooses to address a problem affects the kinds of questions asked and the solutions that seem possible. Our case studies do suggest that urban politics must be sensitive to local context, delineated at a very fine spatial scale. By taking local context into account, urban policymakers are more likely to be responsive to individuals' and communities' needs. For example, a national or state-level child-care policy aimed to increase access to institutionalized child care may reflect and fulfill the needs of middle-class women in a community such as Westboro. Given the schedules and shifts of locally available jobs, as well as a local culture of relying on informal networks for information and other resources, Blackstone Valley women may have little interest in this type of child-care arrangement (at least in its present, relatively expensive and inflexible form). Policies that allow for such local geographic variation are likely to be more effective than those that do not.

REFERENCES

Allen, K. N. (1984). *On the beaten path: Westborough Massachusetts*. Westborough: Westborough Civic Club and Westborough Historical Society.

Angel, D. (1989). The labor market for engineers in the U.S. semi-conductor industry. *Economic Geography, 65*, 99–112.

Bartel, A. P. (1979). The migration decision: What role does job mobility play? *Journal of Economic Literature, 13,* 397–433.

Becker, G. S. (1981). *A treatise on the family.* Cambridge: Harvard University Press.

Bowlby, S., Lewis, J., McDowell, L., & Foord, J. (1989). The geography of gender. In R. Peet & N. Thrift (Eds.), *New models in geography* (pp. 157–175). London: Unwin Hyman.

Cravins, G. (1988). *Industrial restructuring and its impact on communities and populations of northern mature regions: A case study of Worcester County, Massachusetts, 1965–80.* PhD dissertation, Department of Geography, Clark University.

Dyck, I. (1989). Integrating home and wage workplace: Women's daily lives in a Canadian suburb. *The Canadian Geographer, 33,* 329–341.

Dyck, I. (1990). Space, time and renegotiating motherhood: An exploration of the domestic workplace. *Environment and Planning D: Society and Space, 8,* 457–483.

Forrest, R., & Murie, A. (1987). The affluent homeowner: Labour market processes and the shaping of housing histories. In N. Thrift & P. Williams (Eds.), *Class and space: The making of urban society* (pp. 330–359). London: Routledge & Keegan Paul.

Gerstle, G. (1989). *Working class Americanism: The politics of labor in a textile city, 1914–1960.* Cambridge: Cambridge University Press.

Goldberg, M. A., & Mercer, J. (1986). *The myth of the north American city: Continentalism revisited.* Vancouver: University of British Columbia Press.

Greenwood, M. (1975). Research on internal migration in the United States: A survey. *Journal of Economic Literature, 13,* 397–433.

Hanson, S., & Johnston, I. (1985). Gender differences in work-trip length: Explanations and implications. *Urban Geography, 6,* 193–219.

Hanson, S., & Pratt, G. (1988). Spatial dimensions of the gender division in a local labor market. *Urban Geography, 9,* 180–202.

Hanson, S., & Pratt, G. (1990). Geographic perspectives on the occupational segregation of women. *National Geographic Research, 6,* 376–399.

Hanson, S., & Pratt, G. (1991). Job search and the occupational segregation of women. *Annals of the Association of American Geographers, 81,* 229–253.

Hanson, S., & Pratt, G. (1992). Dynamic dependencies: Geographic perspectives on local labor markets. *Economic Geography,* forthcoming.

Hayghe, H. V. (1990). Family members in the workforce. *Monthly Labor Review, 113,* 14–19.

Johnston-Anumonwo, I. (1992). The influence of household type on gender differences in work trip distance. *The Professional Geographer, 44,* 161–169.

Lamphere, L. (1987). *From working daughters to working mothers: Immigrant women in a New England community.* Ithaca, NY: Cornell University Press.

Lehmann, P. (1989). Naperville: Stressed out in suburbia. *Atlantic Monthly, 264,* 34–48.

Madden, J. (1981). Why women work closer to home. *Urban Studies, 18,* 181–194.

Mark-Lawson, J., Savage, M., & Warde, A. (1985). Gender and local politics: Struggle over welfare policies, 1918–1939. In Lancaster Regionalism Group (Eds.), *Localities, class and gender* (pp. 195–215). London: Pion.

Massachusetts Division of Employment Security. (1985). *Southern Worcester delivery area: An analysis of employment and unemployment conditions.* Boston: DES.

McDowell, L. (1991). Life without father and Ford: The new gender order of post-Fordism. *Transactions of the Institute of British Geographers NS, 16,* 400–419.

McLafferty, S., & Preston, V. (1990). Gender, race, and commuting among service sector workers. *Professional Geographer, 43,* 1–15.

Mills, C. (1989). *Interpreting gentrification: Post industrial, post patriarchal, post modern?* PhD Dissertation, Department of Geography, University of British Columbia.

Mincer, J. (1978). Family migration decisions. *Journal of Political Economy, 86,* 749–773.

Nelson, K. (1986). Female labor supply characteristics and the suburbanization of low-wage office work. In M. Storper & A. Scott (Eds.), *Production, work, territory* (pp. 149–71). Boston: Allen Unwin.

O'Connor, C. A. (1985). Sorting out the suburbs: Patterns of land use, class and culture. *American Quarterly, 37,* 382–394.

Pahl, R. E., & Wallace, C. (1985). Household work strategies in economic recessions. In N. Redclift & E. Mingione (Eds.), *Beyond employment: Gender, household and subsistence* (pp. 189–227). Oxford: Blackwell.

Parr, J. (1990). *The gender of breadwinners: Women, men and change in two industrial towns, 1880–1950.* Toronto: University of Toronto Press.

Popenoe, D. (1977). *The suburban environment.* Chicago: University of Chicago Press.

Pratt, G. (1990). Feminist analyses of the restructuring of urban life. *Urban Geography, 11,* 594–605.

Pratt, G., & Hanson, S. (1988). On the links between home and work: Family-household strategies in a buoyant labour market. *International Journal of Urban and Regional Research, 15,* 55–74.

Pratt, G., & Hanson, S. (1991). Time, space and the occupational segregation of women: A critique of human capital theory. *Geoforum, 22,* 149–157.

Pratt, G., & Hanson, S. (1992). Feminist politics and the dangers of difference: Some notes from two geographers. Mimeo.

Pringle, R. (1988). *Secretaries talk.* New York: Verso.

Reskin, B., & Roos, P. (1990). *Job queues, gender queues: Explaining women's inroads into male occupations.* Philadelphia: Temple University Press.

Reynolds, D. (1990). Deindustrialization in the Blackstone Valley: 1920–1989. In D. Reynolds & M. Myers (Eds.), *Working in the Blackstone River Valley: Exploring the heritage of industrialization* (pp. 177–186). Woonsocket: Rhode Island Labor History Society.

Rose, D. (1990). "Collective consumption" revisited: Analysing modes of provision and access to childcare services in Montreal, Quebec. *Political Geography Quarterly, 9,* 353–380.

Siltanen, J. (1986). Domestic responsibilities and the structuring of employment. In R. Crompton & M. Mann (Eds.), *Gender and stratification* (pp. 97–118). Cambridge: Polity Press.

Storper, M., & Walker, R. (1989). *The capitalist imperative: Territory, technology, and industrial growth.* New York: Basil Blackwell.

U.S. Bureau of Labor Statistics. *Monthly Labor Review,* Current Labor Statistics. Various issues.

Wekerle, G. (1984). A woman's place is in the city. *Antipode, 6,* 11–20.

Wekerle, G., & Rutherford, B. (1989). The mobility of capital and the immobility of female labor: Responses to economic restructuring. In J. Wolch & M. Dear (Eds.), *The power of geography: How territory shapes social life* (pp. 139–172). Boston: Unwin Hyman.

Wheeler, J. O. (1969). Some effects of occupational status on work trips. *Journal of Regional Science 9,* 69–78.

Wheelock, J. (1990). Capital restructuring and the domestic economy: Family self-respect and the irrelevance of rational economic man. *Capital and Class, 39,* 103–141.

Women Employed Institute. (1988). *Occupational segregation: Understanding the economic crisis for women.* Chicago: Women Employed Institute.

Worcester Telegram and Gazette. (1988). "New Faces Are Changing the Blackstone Valley." May 18.

A Feminist Analysis of Gender and Residential Zoning in the United States

MARSHA RITZDORF

INTRODUCTION

Beginning in 1985, I published a series of articles addressing the relationship between land use and zoning issues and the changing demographics of American society. Implicit in all those pieces, and explicit in some, was the important relationship between changing gender roles and municipal land-use law. Specifically, I addressed the power of municipal zoning ordinances to spatially direct family lives, the location of support systems, and the very composition of intimate household arrangements.

In the 1970s and 1980s, literature about women and planning flourished. The edited volume *New Spaces for Women* was instrumental in helping define women and environments research (Wekerle et al., 1980). A special edition of *Signs*, the first feminist journal, devoted to women and the city, appeared the same year (Stimpson et al., 1980). These collections addressed women's activities in the urban environment. The authors acknowledged and examined women's different daily-life activ-

MARSHA RITZDORF • Department of Urban Affairs and Planning, Virginia Polytechnic Institute and State University, Blacksburg, Virginia 24061-0113.
Women and the Environment, edited by Irwin Altman and Arza Churchman. Plenum Press, New York, 1994.

ity patterns. They provided empirical evidence that the built environment is gendered and called for understanding of, and response to,
these differences in community planning and design.

However, even within the small cadre of writers and scholars who
concern themselves with the issues of women and the built environment, little is ever said about land-use planning and zoning. Although
there is a clear understanding that zoning and land-use planning have to
change to realize the redesign of the American dream, it is often dis-
missed as worthy of a sentence or two, as if by magic a new consciousness would automatically arise to wipe out 60-plus years of entrenched
behavior. Although ground-breaking work has been done in the relationship of women's lives to suburban development, housing form, and
community change, only this author has explored the regulatory aspects
of planning (most often played out as zoning ordinances) and their
linkage to women's lives.[1]

Zoning, simply defined, is the regulation of the use of land within
the community as well as the buildings and structures that may be
placed upon it. In theory, its purpose is to protect the health, safety, and
general welfare of the community by separating incompatible uses.
These "police powers" are reserved for the states under the U.S. Constitution and have been passed on to the individual communities (or coun-
ties in some states) by enabling legislation.

Much of what zoning proscribes has to do with laying out the compatible uses for any type of zone and the placement of buildings upon
parcels of land in that zone. In general, the typical American zoning
code regulates the major land-use categories for a zone (for example,
residential zones are usually categorized as single family, duplex, and
apartment), other land uses allowed in the zone (in residential this often
includes churches and schools), and several technical measures related
to lot coverage and the size of lots in a zone. Zoning was legitimated by
the Supreme Court in 1926 (*Village of Euclid v. Ambler Realty Corp.*) and
the right of American municipalities to enact ordinances regulating land
use is well established. The courts have strongly supported the suprem-
acy of local-level control.

However, zoning ordinances have reached beyond the simple regulations of density and use described above to enforce a social agenda in a
variety of ways. For example, current residential land policies in many
communities exclude the combining of home and work; they exclude the
location of child care, shopping, or services in residential neighborhoods; forbid the remodeling of large, expensive, older homes into more

---

[1]For example, see this author's articles in the References, especially Ritzdorf (1985, 1986, 1990).

than one unit and exclude other forms of affordable housing such as modular or manufactured units. In addition, family definitions dictate the composition of the family, limiting, or forbidding those who are unrelated by blood or marriage from living together.

Most of these policies have a direct impact on the lives of women, increasing the time they spend taking care of their families while holding down jobs outside of the home. In addition, these policies have a disproportionate impact on low-income working women, whether single or married, and on the many elderly women who live alone, often in oversized, underutilized homes.

The history of zoning over the past 60 years has largely been written in the suburbs, where zoning has created a strong exclusionary control mechanism for suburban residents who wish to have only others like themselves in their neighborhoods. However, zoning issues related to gender occur in both high-density cities and low-density rural areas as well. Many of the specific issues discussed in this chapter are endemic to all zoning ordinances. Some problems are unique to high-density, medium-density, or low-density environments. For example, in Oregon, home-based child care must be allowed by right within the state-established urban service boundaries (lines surrounding urban and suburban areas that have been state designated as the outermost boundaries of all but rural development in the state) but are not allowed by right outside those areas. This means that home-based child care for rural families can be forbidden by the local county if they wish to do so.

Zoning is a potent tool for directing the spatial distribution of wealth, prestige, and opportunity in American communities. It is the policeman of a certain, suburban (or suburbanlike) lifestyle. If a single-family detached home on its own piece of land, located in a quiet and tree-lined neighborhood far from the bustle of the city, is the metaphor for the American dream, zoning is the tool with which this spatial metaphor is bonded to the landscape.

Traditional arguments say zoning is a way to control the physical environment of a community. However, a long line of court decisions and commentators point out the profound social impacts of community land decisions. Constance Perin documented the moral regarding the value-laden base of American community zoning and concluded:

> What has been thought of as singularly technical concerns in land use matters I take to be value laden . . . American land use classifications, definitions and standards . . . name social and cultural categories and define what are believed to be the correct relationships among them. (Perin, 1977, p. 3)

It would be misleading to say that zoning has not received a significant amount of attention by scholars; it has. However, the existing scholarship primarily explores the legality of zoning and legal aspects of its application. After all, zoning is a legal tool, and it has been the province of lawyers and the courts to figure out the intricacies of its boundaries. Although a few authors have explored the cultural, social, and political meaning of zoning, none have explored gender roles. However, it is no surprise that the changing lives of women and their families as they relate to municipal land-use policies have not been the subject of much research. There is almost universal acceptance among both men and women, both planning professionals, academics, and community residents, that the nuclear family unit, living in a single-family detached dwelling unit, is the only acceptable lifestyle to which one should aspire. The collective identity of the American middle-class family is bound within this suburban ideal and impacts city, suburban, and rural zoning.

ZONING AND FAMILY VALUES

The family has always occupied a special niche in American culture. European settlement in the United States was heavily influenced by the expanding continental notion of a zone of private life and the conceptionalization of the family as a personal defense against society, "a place of refuge, free from outside control" (Jackson, 1985, p. 47). By the middle 1800s this "cult of domesticity" was fully entrenched in American society (Hayden, 1984). As the nation shifted from an agricultural to an industrial base, urban-living conditions became intolerable. Transportation systems improved, and living conditions deteriorated. Newly affluent urban businessmen began to remove their families to the suburbs (Hayden, 1984; Jackson, 1985).

As men commuted to work, wives became more and more responsible for everything connected with the domestic environment. Families became more isolated and the home came to be regarded as a superior sphere of the world (Jackson, 1985). By the late 1800s, single-family detached dwellings became "the paragon of middle class housing, the most visible symbol of having arrived at a fixed place in society, the goal to which every decent family aspired" (Jackson, 1985, p. 50).

By the end of the progressive era and the beginning of World War I the single-family suburban ideal was firmly established. Within and around American cities, the peripheral, more suburban areas became the haven of the middle class. However, the meaning of family for purposes of zoning was not clear even though the word was used repeatedly in even the earliest zoning ordinances (Bassett, 1936).

With a generous degree of help from the federal government by the late 1950s, good living conditions, schools, private space, and personal safety were inexorably connected to suburban living (Hayden, 1984; Jackson, 1985). Communities were concerned with preserving certain characteristics that were clearly based on segregated residential communities with rigid, socially created gender roles. "Post war propaganda told women that their place was in the home, as nurturers; men were told that their place was in the public realm, as earners and decision makers" (Hayden, 1984, p. 42). Federal Housing Authority rules, which encouraged housing schemes segregated by age, race, and class, created communities that were homogeneous, suspicious of outsiders, and ready to defend their turf against any groups that challenged "married suburban bliss" as the only acceptable lifestyle choice (Hayden, 1984; Wright, 1981; Jackson, 1985).

Although virtually ignored in the planning literature, an implicit meaning of the word *family* (working father, stay-at-home mother, and children) imbedded in "married suburban bliss" has shaped much of the municipal land-use planning agenda. Built into the exclusive single-family residential zoning district is the assumption that a parent, almost always the mother, will be at home all day and available to take care of her children.

Preoccupation with the nuclear family unit is not limited to the planning profession but permeates all public policymaking. The concept of "the family ethic" is advanced by Abramovitz (1988) to explain this historic pattern:

> As a dominant social norm, the family ethic articulates the terms of women's work and family roles. According to its rules, proper women marry and have children while being supported by and subordinated to a male breadwinner. Even through major changes in the political economy, the family ethic has persisted. . . . Since colonial times, social welfare policies have treated women differently based on the extent to which their lives conformed to the terms of the family ethic. (1988, p. 2)

The presence of a male to head the household is intrinsic to this Eurocentric model. However, cross-culturally, family form is so varied that it is impossible to argue for the existence of universal psychological, sociological, or biological relations. Therefore, the nuclear family, so important to white nineteenth- and twentieth-century European and American cultural norms, is not always the central point of reference for minority groups, even for those living within the Euro-American context.

Historically, in Western Europe, nuclear-family households were associated with high degrees of independence and the connected possibility of rapid economic mobility. It is no wonder that in nineteenth-century America, as home and workplace drew apart, the nuclear-family unit took on a more significant social meaning. In their classic study of middle America, the Lunds (1937, p. 410) wrote of the "monogamous family [as] the outcome of evolution from lower forms of life and [which] is the final divinely ordered form." It is also no wonder that Americans would embrace residential patterns that protected the nuclear family as the one socially legitimate family.

The separation of work and residence in the nineteenth century made it possible to physically separate social classes. The acceptance of the "cult of domesticity" made the home-based wife the middle-class ideal and the single-family detached home the American dream. Therefore, middle-class women of that era generally applauded land-use patterns that helped physically create these separate domains at a neighborhood scale. Historically, the best way to reinforce the values of "womanhood" was to be surrounded by those of similar classes and values. "Even in the absence of zoning regulations and the massive housing tracts of postwar conglomerate merchant builders, homogeneous residential neighborhoods evolved initially as the result of informal arrangements" (Rothblatt et al., 1979, p. 16).

The home in a suburban neighborhood allowed the nineteenth- and early-twentieth-century woman an opportunity to show that she had "made it" no less than it does today. Overall, Americans have been culturally conditioned to accept no alternative as being "as good as, as acceptable as" the single-family home in a neighborhood containing only other single-family homes, and most Americans seek this utopia often at significant economic costs. For women, there are considerable social costs as well.

Land-use patterns based on the traditional family ethic serve contemporary women poorly and do not reflect their changing needs or those of their families. They have never reflected the need of alternative families, and as more middle-class women find themselves downwardly mobile through divorce, they are hard-pressed to maintain their middle-class identity. Studies show that most divorced women (primarily for economic reasons) must relocate their family (Siedel, 1986).

In contemporary America, "the popular vision of the typical household of father, mother, and two or three children is fast assuming the proportions of folklore" (Houstoun, 1981, p. 73). Census statistics show, for example, that the most common American household form (29% of households) is a married couple with no children. Almost as many Americans live alone (25%), and only 12.9% of households contain a married couple with children with a mother who is not in the labor force (U.S. Bureau of the Census, 1990).

Nonnuclear families were, and are, more likely to occur among disenfranchised groups, the impoverished, and those from different races and cultures. For women who are both poor and of color, race becomes a "second axis of oppression" with rules that often benefit whites while exploiting or diminishing their life chances. This has been absolutely true of zoning that has consistently been used to prevent the spatial extension of people of color into white, middle-class America.

Today, female-headed households are more and more likely to be white, but they, too, are viewed as culturally deviant. Widows and divorcees as well as single mothers are "not like us," and an abundance of literature exists to support the claim that they are treated differently in our society (Perin, 1988).

All these stereotypes are played out in zoning regulations that attempt to separate these deviant living arrangements from the neighborhoods called "single-family" where the mythical nuclear family resides. Perin states in her newer study of the relationship between land use and social order in America that Americans find the very presence of those of different status in their neighborhood to be an unsettling experience and are especially discomforted by female-headed and minority-headed households (Perin, 1988).

FAMILY DEFINITIONS IN AMERICAN ZONING ORDINANCES

Zoning ordinances have the right (in all but three states—Michigan, New Jersey, and California) to determine household composition. The typical ordinance defines a family as an *unlimited* number of individuals related by blood, adoption, or marriage but only a *limited* number of unrelated individuals living together as a single housekeeping unit. They are a potent tool allowing municipalities to exclude residents from their communities. Family definitions should reconsider the notion that the traditional, nuclear family with one worker is the current social norm and recognize the needs of the elderly and of single-parent families to share housing for economic, social, and security reasons as well as accept the needs or desires of alternative families to be accepted and housed in the community.

For example, sharing a traditional single-family dwelling unit may allow two single-parent families to own or rent a home that they might otherwise be unable to afford. Most municipalities have effectively excluded the "elder commune" and other forms of contemporary living arrangements that are enhancing the lives of older women and women with disabilities. Indeed, in some communities, it is illegal for any unrelated people to live together at all. This has a significant impact on single parents (89% of whom are women) who may choose to share their homes with others, cohabitating couples, lesbian and gay partnerships, and families with foster children. A wide variety of reasons and rationalizations have been advanced by courts and communities for restricting household composition. These justifications have included preservation of property values, preservation of rent structures, prevention of parking or traffic problems, preservation of neighborhood safety, control of population density, prevention of noise and disturbance, and the control of immoral or antisocial behavior (Shilling, 1980).

Family definitions have been neglected in the scholarly literature on exclusionary zoning (which focuses only on the issue of large-lot, single-family-only zones as an exclusionary tool and only on race as the issue that prompts exclusionary behavior), yet they have a significant impact. Almost all American zoning ordinances contain a definition of family. These definitions have a history of use that is as old as zoning itself. Early definitions tended to use a simple standard, defining family as "one or more individuals sleeping, cooking, and eating on the premises as a single housekeeping unit" (Bassett, 1936, cited in Netter & Price, 1983, p. 173).

However, since the 1960s there has been a move in American communities toward more restrictive definitions containing limitations on the number of unrelated people who can live in a dwelling unit. Faced with changing lifestyles and a strong desire to preserve the existing small nuclear-family oasis, local governments began to incorporate strict family definitions into their ordinances. The regressive shift was prompted, in large part, by the move for deinstitutionalization in the mental-health community and the rise of "hippy" communal lifestyles both of which were regarded as threats to traditional neighborhoods (Ritzdorf, 1985b).

The new post-1960 definition of family most typically defines a family as all individuals related by blood, marriage, or adoption, but only a limited number (most typically, four or five) unrelated individuals living together as a single housekeeping unit (Ritzdorf, 1987). The new definitions provided the courts with a chance to clearly establish whether zoning's function was restricted to regulating land use or whether it could be extended to the regulation of household composition. Generally speaking, restrictive definitions have been rejected by those state courts that have considered them, especially in those cases where the definition was being used to restrict the location of a group home. However, the cases that have dealt more directly with the right of alternative families (such as a group of elderly women or a lesbian couple and their children) have often been decided in favor of the municipalities. Indeed, the landmark family definition case, decided by the Supreme Court in 1974, leaves no doubt that alternative family formation is suspect and legitimately controllable by municipal regulation.

The case, *Village of Belle Terre v. Boraas* (416 U.S.1.39LE2d797, 94S.Ct.1536) is well known. Belle Terre, a small village in Long Island, New York, imposes a family definition that allowed any number of related individuals to live together but only two unrelated individuals to occupy a single-family dwelling. The owners of a large home rented it to six college students from a nearby university. The matter wound up at the Supreme Court where Justice Douglas wrote a majority opinion that recognized the preservation of traditional family values as a legitimate state objective. In the nearly two decades since it was decided, the impact of the decision has increased significantly.

Oft-quoted, much-criticized, *Belle Terre* could have been a landmark case in resolving the fundamental relationship between zoning and various constitutionally protected rights. However, the court chose to ignore the constitutional questions and to see the fundamental question in the case as one involving the local power to protect residential areas from disruptive intrusion.

In sustaining a zoning ordinance that restricted all the land use in a village to single-family dwellings and defining a family as "one or more persons related by blood, marriage or adoption or two unrelated persons living and cooking together as a single housekeeping unit, exclusive of household servants" (*Village of Belle Terre v. Boraas*, 1974), the court refused to recognize the choice of one's intimate household companions as deserving of any constitutional protection.

Since *Belle Terre*, the court has gone on to carve out a set of zoning decisions that serve to support the contention made by Kenneth Perlman and others (Perlman, 1978; Tribe, 1978) that the use of the Constitution as a wedge to end residential exclusion has been severely limited. But *Belle Terre* remains extraordinary in its impact because it allows the local zoning authority to reach inside the household and regulate its composition. It gives single-family zoning, as a legitimate objective, the right to protect and encourage the institution of the traditional family. Restrictive ordinances are still supported in the 1990s. In a 1991 case (*Dinan v. Town of Stratford*), the Connecticut Supreme Court upheld a local restrictive family definition in Stratford that allowed only a maximum of two individuals unrelated to the family of the occupant to live in a single-family unit. Although an amicus curiae brief was filed by the American Planning Association (the first time they have ever taken an organizational stand against such restrictive definitions), the court praised traditional family districts and vacated the lower court decision that invalidated the regulation because it regulated the user (the people) and not the use.

Although it is often argued that family definitions are irrelevant because communities never enforce them, a 1984 survey found that not to be true. A national survey of 329 randomly selected communities conducted by the author revealed that 87% of the communities defined family in their ordinance. Nearly 60% established a numerical limit to the number of unrelated people who could live together as a family group. Forty percent of the communities had enforced their family definition and required nontraditional family groups to change their lifestyle or location (Ritzdorf, 1985b). An earlier study of all the communities in the Seattle–Everett Standard Metropolitan Statistical Area found one-third of the communities had family definitions that allowed no unrelated persons to live together (Ritzdorf, 1983). The right of communities to regulate the intimate composition of family groups should be a major concern for women as we move out of the traditional family and, whether by choice or necessity, begin to look at alternative living arrangements.

BARRIERS TO HOUSING INNOVATION
IN SINGLE-FAMILY NEIGHBORHOODS

For the vast majority of impoverished women, especially women of color, changes in family definitions will barely begin to address their housing problems. In newer, suburban areas they are simply zoned out of many single-family residential districts by more traditional exclusionary zoning tools such as large-lot zoning that creates communities where all home values are kept high by establishing minimum lot sizes of 1 acre or more of land. In older suburbs and in single-family zones in the city, serious restrictions on the division of a home into more than one living unit often limit their options to denser, less safe, and less "acceptable" neighborhoods. Elderly women are especially impacted as they are more likely to own a home that they are reluctant to leave but are ill equipped financially or physically to maintain. Yet, many are not interested in living with roommates. Accessory apartments within existing single-family houses are an optimum solution for many of them; however, they are not the only group that benefits from better use of large underutilized single-family homes.

Accessory apartments are defined as self-contained dwelling units created from existing space that include separate bath and kitchen facilities and have their own independent entrance. Many communities already contain innumerable illegal accessory apartments. Preliminary data from the 1980 census indicate that between 1970 and 1980, there may have been as many as 2.5 million conversions of single-family houses to create accessory apartments (Pollak, 1989).

The advantage to accessory units is that when they are properly regulated, they remain virtually invisible while enhancing and preserving residential neighborhoods. Although rules vary from community to community, in general accessory units are limited to 30% or less of the floor area of a home and may not have an exterior entrance on the front of the house. The owner of the home must occupy one of the units at all times (a rule that is usually strictly enforced).

There are many benefits of well-managed accessory apartments to communities. The provision of rental income from these units can make the difference between keeping or losing their home for many elderly and female-headed households. Also, it can offer a buyer of a home the means to meet the high payments prevalent in today's market. Accessory units can provide a source of inexpensive housing units in the community and can bring households at a variety of stages in their life cycle into the community, increasing diversity and reducing fluctuation in demand for certain services, such as education (Hare, Connor, & Merriam, 1985). Most important to many women, the tenant can provide much-needed security. To elected officials and community planners, accessory units represent both an opportunity and a problem. The opportunity is the ability to expand the available affordable housing. The problem is citizen concerns about property values and the decline of the neighborhood environment.

Although accessory apartments have received a lot of attention, research shows that most communities are not adopting ordinances to allow them (Ritzdorf, 1987; Pollak, 1989). Therefore it is difficult to assess their impact. The 1984 random sample survey of zoning referred to earlier, found that only 10 of the responding communities had ordinances allowing accessory units. The remaining 93% did not permit, define, or regulate accessory units. Yet a 1983 study by the Department of Housing and Urban Development found that accessory apartment could add to the stock of affordable housing, allow better use of existing housing, better maintenance of existing housing, achieve housing diversity while maintaining neighborhood quality, and improve the local tax base (Pollak, 1989).

Families with both young children and elderly parents to care for find a solution to parental independence and caregiving in intergenerational arrangements such as accessory apartments. According to the

Older Women's League, a majority of women are caregivers to aging parents at some time in their lives, often in addition to their child-rearing and other familial responsibilities (Sommers et al., 1987). In many cases, senior homeowners move into the small accessory unit and rent the larger space to younger families with children. Because the largest percentage of renters are women and the majority of female headed households are renters, women stand to gain housing opportunity from this housing option.

Elder cottages are another housing innovation that are controlled by zoning ordinances. They are small, often portable units that can be placed temporarily in someone's yard and can be made available to families to allow an ill or elderly relative to live on their property. These units, often referred to as Granny flats, are far more popuiar in other countries (Canada and Australia, for example) than they are in the United States. In most of the very few places that allow such a unit in the United States, the owner of the main home must build the cottage and then rip it down when it is no longer needed, which is an expensive proposition. The 1984 survey of zoning ordinances mentioned earlier found that not even one of the communities had or had considered such an ordinance (Ritzdorf, 1985a). Since that time, a major housing initiative in New York State has created a few revisions to town ordinances to allow such a use, and the state is making monies available to communities that will consider purchasing and renting out a portable unit (Pollak, 1989).

ACCESS TO CHILD CARE

Although affordable, safe, and accessible shelter is the need of women most often linked to zoning, it is an arbiter of the location of child care as well as shelter. The need for affordable, quality, and conveniently located child care is one of the pressing concerns of contemporary family life. Much has changed in the life patterns of today's families due in large part to the dramatic increase of working mothers.

In a major transformation of the American work force, half of all women who are old enough to work hold jobs. Over 75% of those women between 25 and 46 (the Baby Boomers) are in the work force. Approximately 60% of all women with children under the age of 15 worked outside the home (59% work and another 3% attend school) (U.S. Bureau of the Census, 1990). Nearly one-half of all mothers of children under the age of 1 worked outside the home during the same period.

Contrary to popular belief, most mothers work full time. In 1985,

82% of employed single mothers and 68% of employed married mothers held full-time jobs (National Commission on Working Women, 1985).

The number of children needing care greatly exceeds the number of licensed care spaces. Even when the estimated number of unregulated "underground" spaces are considered in estimating demand and supply, many more spaces are needed. In addition, recent real-estate-industry studies show that child care will be a major development issue in the next decade (Lachman & Martin, 1987).

Poor families have faced child-care problems for a long time. But, it has been the entry of middle-class mothers into the workplace in unprecedented numbers that has brought attention to the imbalance in the supply of and demand for child care. Their political sophistication, money, and power to demand change makes child care a high-profile issue. A February, 1989, CBS/NY *Times* poll indicated that 87% of adult Americans agreed that there needs to be a joint effort between employers and the government to meet peoples' caregiving needs (Child Care Action Campaign, 1987).

However, it is still the working poor who bear the heaviest burdens when zoning laws exclude or limit child-care services. In 1980, three-fourths of families using day-care centers earned under $15,000 a year, and most of the families' incomes hovered near the poverty line. Minority families are also disproportionately affected. Seventeen percent of American children under the age of 15 are minorities, yet they comprise 33% of all children in day care. Thirty-three percent of all children in child care are black (U.S. Bureau of the Census, 1987). In 1987, poor families spent 25% of their income on child care as compared to 6.9% percent of the income of nonpoor families (U.S. Bureau of the Census, 1990).

Zoning of child-care uses has a far-reaching impact on access to care, quality of care, and cost of care. In September of 1987, the American Planning Association Board of Directors ratified a policy statement on the Provision of Child Care in local planning and zoning. The statement advocates the inclusion of child-care policies as part of local comprehensive plans and encourages communities to amend their local ordinances to remove obstacles to the provision of child care in all zoning districts. In 1989 the American Society for Public Administration also adopted a resolution of child care that explicitly mentions the need to change land-use policy to be more child-care friendly and to allow family-based child care by right in residential zones as a "customary home occupation" (ASPA, 1986).

In spite of these policies, in many U.S. cities and suburbs, child care is limited to commercial zones, and the provision of small-family-based care is discouraged or prohibited. When zoning regulations restrict child-care facilities to a few areas of the community, are too rigid, do not conform to state licensing standards, or require excessive hearings processes or permit fees, there is a profound negative impact on child care that is already in short supply. According to the Child Care Action Campaign, approximately 35 million American children under the age of 14 have working mothers. However, there are only 5 million places in licensed or registered child-care facilities in the United States.

Where are American children being cared for? Nearly half are being cared for by nonrelatives in a place other than the child's home. However, the majority are cared for in unlicensed or unregulated homes. A few cities around the country now encourage the provision of child care through comprehensive programs. Some have created child-care coordinator positions. The role of the coordinators varies. Some are merely there to provide referral and coordination services, whereas others are involved in a range of planning and policymaking efforts to improve child-care resources. Other cities have created comprehensive programs aimed at creating a children's policy for the city. The two best-known examples are the Kidspace Program in Seattle, Washington, and Urban Planning for Children and Youth in Sacramento, California. Two planning agencies (Carlsbad, California, and the Maryland National Capital Park and Planning Commission) have adopted specific policy statements regarding child care (Cibulskis & Ritzdorf, 1989).

But in most communities around the country, little or nothing has been done to acknowledge the changing needs of child-rearing families in the land-use planning and zoning process. In a 1984 national random sample survey of 212 urban and suburban communities about their zoning policies toward child care, I found several major zoning issues related to day care needed attention. Only two-thirds of the responding communities even acknowledged the existence of child care in their ordinances. In two-thirds of these communities, there was no acknowledgment of the differences between large day-care centers and small day-care homes, even though all 50 states require day-care centers to be licensed and differentiate between family day-care homes and child-care centers for that purpose in the state legislation (Ritzdorf, 1987). In many states, family child-care homes are further broken down into small and large facilities according to the number of children being cared for in the home.

The biggest stumbling block to accessible neighborhood-based child care is zoning that forbids or severely limits family day-care homes. Family day-care homes in which a provider cares for a small (under 12) group of children in her own home is the most common out-of-home child-care arrangement selected by working parents. A survey commissioned by the National Commission on Working Women showed that 40% of children were being cared for in these settings (NCWW, 1985).

As stated earlier, the majority of children in the United States are cared for in unlicensed, unregulated child-care homes. These facilities and their operators remain underground for a number of reasons. Many providers are unaware that they need to license their facility. Others fear local regulations because they may need to pay exorbitant fees, face unreasonable inspections, or have to remodel their homes to an extent they cannot afford to satisfy local building inspectors. Unfortunately, their fears are not unfounded. According to the Child Care Law Centers records, many communities still totally prohibit family child-care homes in residential neighborhoods, lack definitions that distinguish small homes from large centers (which parallels my findings), have regulations that are inconsistent with the state licensing standards and have onerous permitting processes, public hearings, and high permit fees (Cohen, 1987).

Family day-care providers have legitimate reasons to fear extra costs in providing their services. Despite the importance of the service they provide, their average earnings are small. In 1984, 90% of private household child-care workers earned poverty-level wages (Child Care Action Campaign, 1987).

Despite the demand for regulated family day care, it remains in short supply. One frequently voiced complaint to family day care is that it is not "residential use of property." This is particularly ironic because no use is so connected to the function of the single-family residential zoning district as the rearing of children. Since the original decision establishing the constitutionality of zoning (*Euclid v. Ambler*) in 1926, the importance of this housing district for children is brought up in virtually all defenses of zoning.

Child care is an essential neighborhood and community service. Just as houses of worship, schools, and libraries are considered compatible with residential life because of the fundamental importance of the services they provide, so should be the provision of child-care services.

Women give myriad reasons why they prefer family child-care homes. These include small-group size and individualized attention, provisions for flexible and part-time care, affordability, the availability of care for very young children or more than one child from the same family, and greater adaptability to emergency situations than the traditional day-care center (Cohen et al., 1989).

In addition, the licensing laws for family child-care homes in most states require that the care be given by a provider in her/his own home putting zoning laws that restrict or forbid such activities in direct conflict with the necessary requirements for licensing/registration—a true Catch-22 situation.

In the face of local unwillingness to the overwhelming need for family child care, these small-home settings have been the focus of preemption legislation in 14 states to date, and laws are currently pending in two others. Preemption statutes are state laws that essentially lay out a statewide zoning rule for a particular issue. Although there are differences from state to state, the preemption statutes generally have three major objectives: the clarification of state policy regarding the location of family day care; the creation of an assurance that family day care is not prohibited in any residential zones (including single-family zones); and the setting of parameters regarding what localities can and cannot do in respect to zoning regulations of these homes. Powerful citizen lobbies, most frequently led by women, have led the successful campaigns for these statutes.

HOME-BASED WORK

Although there is still much debate on the costs and benefits of homework for women (see Christensen, 1988), there is evidence that many women (and men) want to work at home. A study by ATT found that approximately 23 million Americans do at least some work out of their home. Ten to 12 million (10.5% of the total work force) are estimated to work strictly at home (Butler & Getzels, 1985). In a major national survey of 14,000 women funded by HHS and conducted by Christensen with the cooperation of *Family Circle Magazine*, 53% indicated that they are currently conducting their work in their homes, and another 42% indicated that they would like to if it was possible. The opportunity to be one's own boss and create a job around a personal schedule is important as many women are overseeing the care of both children and elderly relatives while needing to contribute to their family's income. For single parents and/or rural women, working at home may be the only path toward any economic self-sufficiency. This is also true for the elderly and handicapped population.

However, working at home violates the most cherished norm of land-use planning: the separation of home and work environments. Home occupations are governed by ordinances that often put the pursuit of home work secondary to class interests. Although reasonable and well-written guidelines are needed to sensitively integrate home and work environments, many ordinances are neither reasonable nor sensitive. Concerns regarding traffic, parking, signs, noise, or toxic materials seem reasonable. Those that arbitrarily preclude "nonprofessional" occupations or only allow family members to be employed are not. Yet, in many communities professional occupations (doctors, lawyers, and accountants) are specifically permitted, whereas beauticians, barbers, and similar occupational workers are forbidden from working out of their home in the same town (Ritzdorf, 1985). Ironically, a survey that investigated home-occupation ordinance enforcement found that doctors were the worst abusers of rules regarding the use of their homes as businesses. They were the most likely to expand in physical size, cause neighborhood traffic problems, or stop living in the house and use it purely as an office (Butler & Getzels, 1985).

Limitations on nonfamily employers are common. Instead of limiting the number of employees to those whose parking needs can be accommodated on the property or directly in front, limiting it to relatives or dwelling residents can have serious impacts on women, especially in communities where dependent care provision is regulated as a home occupation. It often puts large child-care home providers in a Catch-22 situation. They must (in most states) have a second caregiver if they are caring for more than 5 to 6 children (or even fewer infants) in order to be licensed by the state. They also, in many states, must show they meet zoning requirements in order to be licensed—an irreconcilable position.

Lists of "permitted" or "prohibited" lists are common and are often not rationally based. In conversations, planners or town clerks often mentioned a bad experience with one person as the basis for forbidding a whole category of users in a community (Ritzdorf, 1983). A typical example of this irrationality is contained in the Long Beach, California, ordinance that permits architects, art restorers, and artists to work at home but forbids beauticians, barbers, and upholsterers. It allows gardening and interior design studios but forbids bed and breakfasts (Butler & Getzels, 1985).

Eighty percent of communities in a national survey already regulated home occupations. The regulations included parking requirements (38%), noise regulations (50%), and limitations on nonfamily employees (90%). Of special interest, however, was a follow-up survey of municipal planners to access their attitudes toward home work. The majority of the respondents (who were overwhelmingly male) were hostile to home work. They wanted even more stringent regulation of the right to work at home, even in those towns the study's author had identified as already having restrictive zoning treatment of home occupations.

A FEMINIST PERSPECTIVE ON ZONING

Because current land-use and zoning policies clearly inconvenience women's lives, why has there been no major public outcry? The use of physical space as a representation of the differences between classes is a critical component of the answer to why women support and encourage spatial segregation. Just as a home in a suburban neighborhood allowed the nineteenth- and early twentieth-century women an opportunity to show that she had "made it," in today's America a home in a neighborhood without services, purely residential and preferably suburban is no less potent a class indicator. Americans are culturally conditioned to accept no alternative as being "as good as, as acceptable as" the single-family home in a neighborhood containing only other single-family homes, and most Americans seek this utopia at significant economic and social costs.

The attainment and ownership of a single-family home are fundamental to the socialization of most middle- and upper-class American women. Her failure to achieve such a dwelling is tantamount to failing to achieve full womanhood (Perin, 1988). The main key to the attainment of the house, for most women, is the presence of a man. Because women earn, on the average, 64% of what men earn (and used to earn proportionately less), they are virtually assured that this dream is unattainable (or unkeepable in the experience of most divorced women) without a man to help them.

Renting, even a single-family home, does not confer the same familial status. Neither does ownership, if the unit is a condominium or townhouse. According to Perin's respondents, ownership of these units is seen as a transitional step—okay for a young family who can afford nothing else or for retirees as a transition from single-family home ownership to heaven (1977, 1988)!

Historically, women play-out larger portions of their daily lives in the suburban landscape that has and will dominate American land-use patterns for an indefinite future. "Journeys through the world of women criss-cross landscapes designed by men," wrote Mazey and Lee (1983, p. 8). This has not changed in the decade since they wrote it.

Traditional zoning histories give two main reasons for its rise and acceptance. The first is the sincere desire to do something about the continually disintegrating quality of urban life. The second is the growing realization that it was to the advantage of the burgeoning capitalist economy in the United States to spatially separate home and work life and to glorify that separation in order to create a consumer-oriented society. Recent revisionist history acknowledges the role of racism and ethnocentrism as well in the original planning of suburban communities (Ritzdorf, 1990).

I propose an additional interpretation of the historical suppositions behind municipal land-use and zoning policies. That the family ethic reinforced the growing industrial expansion and provided a way to translate the growing separation between middle-class and working-class lives into a spatial reality. Further, that the social importance of the separation of middle- and lower-class lifestyles was of keen significance to middle-class women and men who participated and still participate in its enforcement. The irony of this cultural conditioning is that it has created a landscape that now inconveniences the lives of middle-class women in myriad ways. Yet, the importance of living in a single-class, residential-only neighborhood so fundamentally defines the collective identity of the middle class that it supersedes gender-role considerations for the vast majority of women. Even though a body of environmental/behavioral research shows that contemporary women are less happy with the suburbs than their male counterparts, there is little evidence to show that any large number of them are doing anything to change their neighborhoods into more economically, socially, and physically mixed environments. Class consciousness and racism are not merely the province of men (Ritzdorf, 1990; Abramovitz, 1988; Perin, 1988).

In the historical development of municipal land-use and zoning policies, there is an emphasis on the family ethic as the benchmark of policy legitimacy. There is a clear denial of the lifestyle differences and needs of poorer women and women of color. There is little understanding or recognition of any other family or kinship form other than the nuclear-family unit, and there is an unspoken assumption that the comfort and welfare of middle-class men are the heart of municipal planning policies. The changing lives of middle-class women, including their entry into the workplace in massive numbers and their equal descent into poverty through divorce in significant numbers, have not yet resulted in any major changes in community attitudes toward land-use patterns.

As historians explore the everyday life of women and their families in America, the metaphor of separate spheres is used to describe the power relationships that proscribe the operating arenas of men and women. Women operate in the private, or domestic sphere, and men in the public sphere. However, it is important to note that men also control the operation of the private sphere. Even recent research shows that in the majority of American families, the father "holds the purse strings."

Although the ideas of separate domains was intrinsic to the development of family life in the eighteenth century, it is not always discussed in terms of physical space. Indeed, until the mid-nineteenth century, these domains were more social than spatial. As industrialization led to the emergence of large urban centers and eventually to metropolitan environments, the idea of separate spheres of activity for men and women became part of the physical environment itself. However, the division of space into a domestic domain, that is, the home for women, and the public domain, that is everything else for men, was treated as a natural evolution of the changing times. The physical environment was perceived as a benign and neutral setting in which activity took place, although it is neither.

Anthropological evidence supports this notion. In societies where the public and domestic spheres are closely integrated, women are more likely to share domestic obligations (Salem, 1986). Labor-force participation and a share in the control of the means of production and a role in the distribution of available surplus have been identified as integral to the achievement of gender equality by numerous scholars (Salem, 1986; Coontz, 1988).

The socialist feminist writers expand the concept of patriarchy (the personal and individual control of individual men over individual women) to include the male dominance that is built into a variety of social and political interests. This broader understanding of the terrain permits a discussion of both the individual and society, and both the private and public spheres.

The scholarship that addresses the life of women in the built environment to date primarily focuses on the larger issues inherent in the urban environment and on housing. As mentioned earlier, work exists on women and housing, the need for new urban and neighborhood design, transportation, and the metropolitan context. Scholars are slowly reconstructing the significant historical contributions of women housers and planners.

Although many of these scholars mention the need to change local land-use planning and zoning regulations in order to accomplish the reforms that they suggest, the exploration of those regulations in any detail has been ignored. This is not surprising as it parallels the subordinate treatment of the significance of zoning in traditional planning history.

However, it is municipal zoning and land-use regulation that regulates and enforces separate physical spheres at the community level in the built environment. If buildings, as Torres (1977) argues, are the symbolic form that embodies a cultural ideology about how people live and the kind and hierarchy of values that should be fostered by them, zoning ordinances are the rules that make sure that the forms are nurtured and created over and over again. This leads to a community where physical design is defined as the constant recreation of the status quo.

Inherent in the use of zoning ordinances in most American communities is the perpetuation of the lives and values of white, middle-class Americans. These values are based on the model provided by the family ethic, and inherent in them is the assumption that the separation of the domestic and public spheres is the morally correct lifestyle for everyone.

FUTURE DIRECTIONS OF PLANNING AND POLICY

From the middle of the nineteenth century to the present day and likely well into the future, Americans have sought an environment that they perceive as a safe and pleasant one in which to raise their families and seek the better life. Despite excellent critiques of this norm by feminist architects, planners, environmental psychologists, and historians, it is unlikely to change. Yet, it is possible to accept the eventuality of single-family detached family as an American societal norm and still restructure zoning. This can be done in ways that allow the changing lives of women to be met with changing neighborhood availability of needed goods and services. The relatively narrow range of choices found in suburban or suburbanlike developments can be expanded while the symbol of middle-class security—the single-family detached home—is protected. It is clear that middle-class Americans desire the reassurance that comes from conformity to shared standards.

One of the challenges of the twenty-first century is increasing the scope of the boundaries that shape suburban lifestyles, primarily because of the changing patterns of women's lives. Similarly, women from poor families and those who have been thrust into poverty by divorce are more and more aware of the impact that their exclusion from that suburban lifestyle has on their lives and the lives of their children.

> There is a lot of power expressed by the social structure of society as it is manifested in the spatial design of communities. These exert a strong influence on those who live and work within them. While for "those whose activities are facilitated may not be aware of the power inherent in the physical arrangements, it is clear to those whose options are limited by them." (Salem, 1986, p. 107)

Redesigning the "American dream" may not take the more optimist communal forms that are described and urged by contemporary feminist reformers such as Dolores Hayden, but there will be change. Like the feminists of the late nineteenth and early twentieth centuries, there are contemporary women leading an energetic charge for the academic and practical recognition of the needs of women in the design and planning of American communities. The work of Dolores Hayden, Gerde Werkele, Jacqueline Leavitt, Eugenie Birch, Sandra Rosenbloom, Leslie Weissman, Karen Franck, Sherri Ahrentzen, and many others adds to a historical understanding of and/or contemporary call for change in the planning and design professions. However, in the planning profession, where approximately 75% of the practitioners and 83% of the academicians are men, their work is not always discussed or implemented (Ritzdorf, 1993).

In addition, as stated earlier, many of the women engaged in the teaching and practice of planning do not see or acknowledge gender-related issues in planning, including municipal land use.

Writing about planning in 1986, Leavitt asserted that "planners assume a value set that is inherently and historically masculine . . . the overriding goals and objectives are more likely to be shaped by men than women politicians, male corporate heads rather than female" (p. 187). Although the issues of family life are significant to the majority of women, reproductive and domestic activities are not considered in the traditional economic and planning arenas (economic development and land-use regulation) where "accepted frameworks of analysis have inherent biases that isolate and denigrate women" (Fainstein, 1992, p. 14). Women are still presumed to operate in the private sphere of home and are begrudgingly accepted in the public arena.

Female planners and planning scholars have to make a conscious choice about their professional identity. If one chooses to approach planning from a feminist consciousness, she must be ready to be labeled and have her professional credibility, intelligence, and/or research methodology challenged by hostile, or at best, indifferent colleagues.

Although class consciousness muddies the waters of residential zoning reform, it is only one piece of the land-use pie. Other issues of concern to women as they go about their daily lives are also given little attention by planning and design professionals. A simple example of an issue that crosses race, gender, and class lines is the lack of attention to rape and personal safety. For women, a poorly lit street, an ill-designed or poorly placed parking lot, or even too much landscaping can be a life-or-death issue.

Land-use planners, including zoning administrators, need to take positive steps toward restructuring more "women-friendly" environments. Implicit in the granting of land-use and zoning powers to U.S. municipalities is a mandate to use those powers in a socially responsible way. Although municipalities, legislatures, and the courts have historically placed a great value on the family and its needs, now that the family is changing, zoning must change with it.

In order to change, municipal policy awareness must be established at the grassroots level of the ways in which zoning affects the daily lives of women. At present, I do not think most women (or men, for that matter) understand that there are institutional forms of land-use discrimination that impact their lives. They need to learn to question the validity of continued support of zoning that complicates their lives and think about ways to integrate their class consciousness and family needs. Both men and women's lives would be enhanced by residential neighborhoods that allow them the freedom to work at home, to have their children (or parents) watched at small neighborhood-based day-care centers, to share living spaces with the companions of their choice, and to use the spaces within their homes as they choose, within parameters that assure the safety and health of the entire community. Undue noise, inappropriate uses of property, disruptive neighbors, and other potential problems that may arise in any neighborhood are easily handled through nuisance laws that apply equally to all community residents, regardless of age, sex, or relationship to one another.

Creating true options for women in our society is not just an economic issue. Creating women-sensitive environments will take conscious political action on the part of women. Women-dominated movements have changed zoning regulations related to family child-care home placement in 13 states in the past decade. Women who are concerned about the current quality of life in their community and about the quality that will be available to women and their families in the next century must get involved in the local decision-making process.

Bringing about the changes that are necessary to "maintain" a lifestyle that is culturally comfortable for middle-class Americans as well as accommodating the changing life patterns of women of all ages, races, ethnicities, and sexual orientations is a collective responsibility. It will not be easy as conflicts between and among women of different backgrounds, classes, and life conditions will need to be addressed.

However, the community land-use issues that innovative zoning can address: More convenient child and elder care, safer, more innovative neighborhoods, and a better meshing of home and workplace responsibilities cross the lines of age, race, and class effectively enough that there is reason to be optimistic. We can work together, as professional planners and designers and as community activists, to help create more women-friendly land-use patterns.

REFERENCES

Abramovitz, M. (1988). *Regulating the lives of women: Social welfare policy from colonial times to the present*. Boston: South End Press.

American Planning Association. (1987). *Policy implementation statement on child care*. Chicago: American Planning Association.

American Society of Public Administration. (1986). *Policy statement on child care*. New York: American Society of Public Administration.

Bassett, E. (1936). *Zoning: The laws, administration and court decisions during the first twenty years*. New York: Russell Sage.

Butler, J., & Getzels, J. (1985). *Home occupation ordinances* (Planning Advisory Service Report No. 391). Chicago: American Planning Association.

Child Care Action Campaign. (1987). *Child Care Fact Sheet*. New York.

Christensen, K. (1988). *Women and home based work*. New York: Henry Holt and Co.

Cibulskis, A., & Ritzdorf, M. (1989). *Zoning for child care* (Planning Advisory Service Report No. 422). Chicago: American Planning Association.

Cohen, A. J. (1987). *Planning for child care: A compendium for child care advocates seeking the inclusion of child care in the land development process*. San Francisco: Child Care Law Center.

Cohen, A. J. (assisted by Ritzdorf, M., & Vasey, V). (1989). *A local officials guide to zoning for family day care*. Washington, D.C.: National League of Cities.

Coontz, S. (1988). *The social origins of private lives: A history of American families, 1600–1900*. New York: Verso Press.

Dinan v. Town of Stratford. (1991). CT. Sup. Ct. 14208.

Euclid v. Ambler Realty Corp. (1926). 272 Sup. Ct. 365.

Fainstein, S. (1992). Planning in a different voice. *Planning Theory Newsletter* (forthcoming).

Hare, P., Connor, S., & Merriam, D. (1985). *Accessory apartments: using surplus space in single family houses* (Planning Advisory Report No. 365). Chicago: American Planning Association.

Hayden, D. (1984). *Redesigning the American dream: The future of housing, work and family life*. New York: W. W. Norton.

Houstoun, L., Jr. (1981). Market trends reveal housing choices for the 1980's. *Journal of Housing, 38*, 73.

Jackson, K. (1985). *The crabgrass frontier: The suburbanization of America*. New York: Oxford University Press.

Leavitt, J. (1986). Feminist advocacy planning in the 1980's. In B. Checkoway (Ed.), *Strategic perspectives in planning practice*. Lexington: Lexington Books.

Lachman, L., & Martin, D. (1987). Changing demographics shape tomorrow's real estate market. *Urban Land*, November.

Lund, R. S., & Lund, H. M. (1937). *Middletown in transition: A study in cultural conflicts*. New York: Harcourt, Brace and World.

Mazey M. E., & Lee, R. L. (1983). *Her space, her place: A geography of women*. Washington, DC: Association of American Geographers.

National Commission on Working Women. (1985). *Fact sheet on working mothers*. Washington, DC.

Netter, E., & Price, R. (1983). Zoning and the nouveau poor. *Journal of the American Planning Association, 49*, 171–179.

Pearlman, K. (1978). The closing door: The Supreme Court and residential segregation. *American Institute of Planners Journal, 44*, 160–169.

Perin, C. (1977). *Everything in its place: Social order and land use in America*. Princeton: Princeton University Press.

Perin, C. (1988). *Belonging in America: Reading between the lines*. Madison: University of Wisconsin Press.

Pollak, P. (1989). *Community based housing for the elderly: A zoning guide for planners and local officials*. (Planning Advisory Service Report No. 420). Chicago: American Planning Association.

Ritzdorf, M. (1983). *The impact of family definitions in American municipal zoning ordinances*. Unpublished doctoral dissertation, University of Washington, Seattle.

Ritzdorf, M. (1985a). Zoning barriers to housing innovation. *Journal of Planning Education and Research, 4*(3), 177–183.

Ritzdorf, M. (1985b). Challenging the exclusionary impact of family definitions in American municipal zoning ordinances. *Journal of Urban Affairs, 7.*

Ritzdorf, M. (1986). Women and the city: Land use and zoning issues. *Journal of Urban Resources, 3*(2), 23–27.

Ritzdorf, M. (1987). Planning and the intergenerational community: Balancing the needs of the young and the old in American communities. *Journal of Urban Affairs, 9*(1), 79–89.

Ritzdorf, M. (1990). Whose American Dream? The Euclid legacy and cultural change. *Journal of the American Planning Association, 56*(3), 386–389.

Ritzdorf, M. (1993). Feminist contributions to the theory and practice of planning. In Sue Hendler (Ed.), *Planning ethics*. New Brunswick: Center for Urban Policy Research.

Rothblatt, D., Garr, D. J., & Sprague, J. (1979). *The suburban environment and women*. New York: Praeger.

Salem, G. (1986). Gender equity and the urban environment. In J. Boles (Ed.), *The egalitarian city: Issues of rights, distribution, access and power*. New York: Praeger Press.

Shilling, B. (1980). *Exclusionary zoning: Restrictive definitions of family: An annotated bibliography*. Monticello, NY: Council of Planning Librarians.

Siedel, R. (1986). *Women and children last*. New York: Viking.

Sommers, T., & Sheilds, L. Older Women's League Task Force on Caregiving. (1987). *Women take care: The consequences of caregiving in today's society*. Gainesville, FL: Triad.

Stimpson, C. R., Dixler, E., Nelson, M., & Yatrikis, K. (1980). *Women and the city*. Chicago: University of Chicago Press.

Torres, S. (1977). *Women in architecture: Historic and contemporary perspective*. New York: Whitney Library of Design.

Tribe, L. (1978). *American constitutional law*. Mineola, NY: Foundation Press.

U.S. Bureau of the Census. (1987). *Who's minding the kids? Child care arrangements* (Current Population Reports, Series P-70, No. 20). Washington, DC.

U.S. Bureau of the Census. (1990). *Household and family characteristics: March 1990* (Current Population Reports, Population Characteristics, Series P-20, No. 447). Washington, DC.

Village of Belle Terre v. Boraas (1974). 416 U.S. 1.

Werkele, G., Peterson, R., & Morley, D. (1980). *New space for women*. Boulder: Westview.

Wright, G. (1981). *Building the dream: A social history of housing*. New York: Pantheon.

Partial Utopian Visions

FEMINIST REFLECTIONS ON THE FIELD

LYNDA H. SCHNEEKLOTH

INTRODUCTION

The practice of environment and behavior[1] is distinguished by its aim to understand and improve the relationship between people and their places. Practice in this chapter describes collective human activities that share aims, locations, and methods of work. In this sense, the work of the academy, the activity of expert discourse, and the design, making, and maintaining of places all constitute the practice of environment and behavior.

Those of us engaged in the practice of environment and behavior are constantly and consciously reflective and critical of our work and methods in order that we may conduct our practice more effectively. It

---

[1]"Environment and behavior" is one of the names applied to our practice. Also used in the text is "environmental design research and practice" and "human–environment relations." None of the names is sufficiently inclusive nor explanatory but represents the best that we have to date.

LYNDA H. SCHNEEKLOTH • School of Architecture and Planning, State University of New York at Buffalo, Buffalo, New York 14222; and The Caucus Partnership, Buffalo, New York 14222.

Women and the Environment, edited by Irwin Altman and Arza Churchman. Plenum Press, New York, 1994.

is, nevertheless, occasionally useful to examine critically a practice from an outside perspective to question the boundaries of the field and the nature of work. This type of inquiry is useful in problematizing how the conceptualization and reproduction of a practice and its location within the larger human enterprise both enable and constrain.

Toward this end, I am using the ongoing discourse in feminist theory[2] to ask some questions about the nature of our own enterprise. The practice of feminist theory is to problematize the idea of gender, "how gender relations are constituted and experienced and how we think or, equally important, do not think about them" (Flax, 1987, p. 622). There has been a concerted attempt to extend and reinterpret various theoretical domains so that the life experiences of women are included, that is, women are made visible. What many feminists have come to believe, however, is that we cannot simply add women into the existing discourses without distorting either women's experiences or the discourses themselves.[3] Through the problematization of gender, feminist theorists have found themselves questioning the foundational assumptions of Western knowledge and culture.

> In the case of feminist theory, it is the discovery that from the vantage point of women this "absolute knowledge" is really a particularistic account developed largely by males and always in circles of discourse dominated by men who have generalized the basis of their own gender and power experiences. (Lengermann & Niebrugge-Brantly, 1990, p. 317)

In this chapter, I will be using the ways of working in feminist theory to question and reveal our own practice in environment and behavior. However, just as those who are doing science do not necessarily speak about science in their work, in doing feminist theory, I will not necessarily speak about women. Rather, I seek to question entrenched beliefs about the nature of knowledge and its relationship to power; where and who are knowers and their relationship to that which

---

[2]This exercise in no way suggests that there is *a* single feminist theory. People engaged in this practice diverge widely on many important and theoretical issues. See Harding (1986) for an overview of five feminist epistemologies.

[3]There was an assumption that masculinity and femininity were combinable expressions. "But femininity and masculinity are not so easily combined; central to the notion of masculinity is its rejection of everything that is defined by a culture as feminine and its legitimated control of whatever counts as feminine. Masculinity requires the conception of women as 'other,' as Simone de Beauvoir pointed out. Femininity is constructed to absorb everything defined as not masculine, and always to acquiesce in domination by the masculine. . . . Gender is an *asymmetrical* category of human thought, social organization and individual identity and behavior" (Harding, 1986, pp. 54–55).

is "known"; and how the language we use to describe the world and our work structures our practice.[4]

This critique is not meant to suggest that a feminist perspective is the only way in which to problematize the practice of our field.

> Feminists are certainly not alone in their critiques of positivist epistemology . . . but their work originates in response to an alienation from methods of research and definitions of knowledge that denigrate or ignore women's experiences and that refuse to consider the political content of knowledge creation. (Sandercock & Forsyth, 1992, p. 51)

My purpose is to engage in an exercise of "situated theorizing" (Fraser, 1989, p. 7) that attempts to demonstrate the intrinsic relationship between critical theorizing and political practice as we experience it in our daily work as practitioners, broadly defined, in the field of environment/behavior. The aims of our practice, our location within our culture, and our ways of working are based on specific forms of knowledge and privileged ways of working, and on our experience as political agents in the world. It is my hope that by doing feminist theory rather than writing about it that we might be provided with a fertile set of tools to deconstruct and reconstitute our work.

The intent of situated theorizing is not necessarily to make more clear, but to muddle and confuse boundaries that we have taken for granted. Such is the work of feminist practitioners who seek through the problematization of gender to deconstruct and reconstitute what it means to live in this world as a gendered person. I seek to engage in the tricky business of questioning the boundaries we place on our work in human/environment relations and to confuse the professional, personal, and political. A confounding guide to this type of work is the coyote,[5] an irreverent mythic commentator, who "is blamed and praised . . . for originating death, mixing up the stars, fornicating with birds, bringing fire, losing his eyes, freeing the buffalo" (Lopez, 1977, p. xi).

The coyote, trickster and teacher, wise one and fool, is a difficult being for our dualistic Western mind to get around—being both good and evil, wise and stupid, bestial and celestial. Like Hermes, the coyote

---

[4]I will not, in this feminist critique of human/environment relations, address the way in which women have been excluded from this environmental design and research domain, nor will I focus on the invisibility of women as subjects of inquiry. For other work, see Ahrentzen (1990); Berkeley and McQuaid (1989); Feldman and Stall (1990); Franck and Ahrentzen (1989); Hayden (1984); Peterson (1987); Stimpson, Dixler, Nelson, and Yatrakis (1981); Torre (1981).

[5]The coyote has served as a serious/humorous figure in many Native American stories. See Vizenor (1988); Lopez (1977); LeGuin (1987, 1989); Haraway (1988).

is a god of the in-between, messy boundaries, and humor. If we accept the gifts of coyote thinking for a short time, we might find ourselves responding to the questions about our practice by trotting sideways and backwards, sniffing around to see where we are and what we have been missing.

The chapter is organized into three sections. The first section addresses the question of the beginnings and intentions of the field of environment/behavior. This story sets the context for the argument of the inherent relationship between our epistemological and intellectual foundations and our political agenda, revealing the utopian vision that shapes our discourses and battles. Second, I address the issue of our location, within the university and the professions, to uncover the implications for our ways of working in science and as experts. And last, I explore how we may come to own our utopian project through mindful practices that we may be free to engage with passion and humor in a practice that both facilitates our work and creates more just and liberating places for people.

A UTOPIAN PROJECT

The field of environment and behavior emerged during the 1960s as a response to scientific and social concerns. Issues such as environmental deterioration, a housing crisis, and concerns about the quality of life emerged as urgent and in need of scientific study and social change. Innovative practitioners from psychology, architecture, geography, and many other fields "embraced the challenge of developing new scientific approaches for studying human behavior and well-being from an interdisciplinary and ecological perspective" (Stokols & Altman, 1987, p. xi).

Although the field of person/environment relations is older and broader than the Environmental Design Research Association (EDRA),[6] the origin story of this one organization is useful in considering the utopian nature of the project. EDRA originated in June 1968 with an unrelenting focus on the interdisciplinary nature of the field of inquiry. It was perceived from the very beginning to be a meeting ground for what Sanoff (1989, p. 15) called "the fringe dwellers" of various disciplines and professionals where they might find support for both their academic interest in human/environment relations *and* their social goal of better places for people to live.

---

[6]See Moore (1987) for overview of field in North America that places EDRA within the larger enterprise.

The "founding fathers" shared a sense of hope that people, working together, could transform the institutions and places that were oppressing them. When EDRA published *Environmental Design Research Directions* (Moore, Tuttle, & Howell, 1985) more than 15 years after the first EDRA meeting, the goals presented for the field contained the same utopian language.

> In order to respect the integrity of the transactions of people and events in everyday settings, environmental design research adopts a variety of scientific methods from the social and behavior sciences and relies heavily on the rigorous application of exploratory, descriptive, and field research methods. The bottom line is a respect for environmental justice and a call for the redress of injustices in the form of inaccessibility, exclusion, or unequal distribution of environmental resources and amenities. (Moore et al., 1985, pp. xvii–xviii)

Although the 1985 language was still utopian, the project was endangered. The 1970s and 1980s (and it appears 1990s) in the United States have been hostile to emancipatory idealism in the university and professional practice. Those involved in the practice of people/environment relations, including their organizations such as EDRA, could not help but be affected by the national climate. Presentations at the conferences more often used the language of science as evidence for assertions, and problems for inquiry were framed within traditional disciplinary boundaries. More recently, we have heard a different voice, phenomenological and poststructural, following the insertion of such languages into the university in the disciplinary and professional schools. Both science and philosophy are voices of the academy. And what has emerged within the field has been an uneasy coalition between those practicing environmental design as an academic inquiry within the framework of science and those whose practice has been structured primarily as a social movement.

These two approaches, science and reform, have their origin in different intellectual traditions. The one is based on the idea that the practice of environment/behavior rests in the generation and rational application of knowledge about people and places; the other believes that such a practice is a legitimate structure to change the existing power relations and social structures.[7] Saegert (1987) identifies two different strategies developed as a result of these traditions. One group calls for more multidisciplinary research/policy/design work and would have academic institutions develop programs to educate people able to work in

[7]For an interesting discussion on science and reform in planning, see Albrecht and Lim (1986).

cross-disciplinary ways and more opportunities for researchers from the social sciences to work with designers on "real-world" problems. The other group insists that citizen participation, actually involving users in changing their own environments, is the vehicle for environmental and social change. Both stress that their aim is to make better places for people to live.

These two different traditions do not hold equal position within our practice. To a large extent, those of us engaged in the practice of social reform have been unable to frame our practice within a theoretical discourse that is academically respected. We have failed to demonstrate the structure and purpose of our knowledge. For example, little has been written on how power distorts communication or how our position as professionals continues forms of oppression. Therefore, we have not been perceived as contributing to the body of knowledge in the field, but only as applying knowledge that is generated elsewhere. The vision and methods of science, and more recently theory and history, have been privileged.[8]

The difference in these perspectives rests on a belief in science as a way of knowing and being in the world, or a belief in the imperative of socially negotiated change, a democratic project, if you will. Nevertheless, it is important to stress that these traditions in environment/behavior are more the same than different. Their oppositional position shares a foundation in Western dualistic epistemology, one of the areas consistently problematized by feminist and other postmodern theorists. Further, both of these practices are utopian. They rest their ideological claims on a critique of current world structures, and they share the aim of the field's collective work—quality places for people.

To consider the field of environment and behavior a utopian project suggests that inherent in our collective practice is a vision of how people and places might be, and practices that struggle to produce and/or reproduce that vision.[9] Yet to acknowledge a utopian vision would open

[8]See, however, Canter et al. (1988); Francis et al. (1987); Lewin (1951); Schneekloth (1987); Schneekloth and Shibley (1981, 1987); Sommer (1984); Wandersman et al. (1978); Weisman (1983).

[9]The many disciplines and professions around which the field of environmental design emerged have been essentially utopian. "This double movement is a profound one: architecture is always dream and function, expression of a utopia and instrument of a convenience" (Barthes, 1979, p. 6). Architecture from the earliest interpretations of the garden/Paradise and city/Jerusalem (McClung, 1983) to the modern movement has been essentially utopia (Fishman, 1977). "In seeking a unity of aesthetic and social goals, theorists of the Modern Movement (like their radical predecessors, such as William Morris . . .) attacked established cultural symbols, they challenged the dominant cultural ideas of their time. . . . Their aesthetic, their utopian vision, embodied and simultaneously revealed an emancipatory potential" (Harries, Lipman, & Purden, 1988, p. 196). Also, social theorists from Marx and Engels to Benjamin worked with a utopian sensibility seeking to understand the implications of the modern industrial metropolis (Chorney, 1990).

our practice to the criticisms of utopianism; that is, utopia is a totalizing, patriarchal, dangerous, and oppressive idea. Utopia is "someone's vision" and doesn't necessarily include the vision of many "excluded others" such as women. And yet the denial of a vision of utopia enmeshes our practice into a dehistoricized and uncritical situation. To have no vision leaves humans impoverished; it kills the dream of a more just society and traps people in the status quo. And perhaps most importantly, it denies the power of hope and possibility of change.

The scary question about any utopian project is whose vision is it and where are the vision makers situated with respect to the critique that both generates a utopia vision and the struggle to achieve it. How do we, as practitioners of environment and behavior, address the tension inherent in the critique of utopia while recognizing its transformational power?

Perhaps it is time that we reclaim, rethink, and re-present the word and idea of utopia. We can accept ours and others' knowledge and experience that the world is not as it should be and that we share a vision of a more just, loving, and playful world, a place where coyotes are celebrated and not shot on sight. To recognize and affirm our vision facilitates understanding our actions in the world as individuals and as a group of people who share a way of working and seeing the world. The utopian consciousness "brings imaginative possibilities of what is not into the concrete realm of what could be" (Bartkowski, 1989, p. 10). But let's do this utopian work with critical self-reflection that acknowledges our location within the culture, that criticizes our ways of working, and that attempts to be passionate and inclusive.[10]

To place the possibilities of a utopian practice in environmental and behavior into the world of social relations, I would like to explore the location of our practice in the university with its legitimated forms of knowledge, and in the domain of expert discourses wherein we contribute our knowledge to the ongoing debates of our culture. In doing this critique, I am employing feminist theory as a point of view. I will then question how we might partially restructure and participate a utopian practice—not *the* utopian vision nor utopianism—but utopian work that empowers people and places.

THE PLACE OF OUR PRACTICE

Practices, such as environment and behavior, are located in particular places within cultures. This location acts as a lens, the position from

[10]After all, our beginning emerged as a struggle to include an "excluded other" from our world view, that is, the environment as an actor in human affairs, and the user as an important consideration in architecture and other design professions. So there is hope and possibility in a conscious struggle to confirm and interrogate our utopian vision.

which we see the world, interpret it, and take action. And although each individual in these cultural locations is different, the position itself frames what constitutes knowledge, whose construction is privileged, and how knowledge is socially and politically inserted and distributed.

Those engaged in the practice of environment and behavior have two primary locations—the university and the professions. These two places are intimate and overlapping. And however these two groups characterize themselves and elaborate on their differences, they share a privileged space within the culture.

THE UNIVERSITY AS A REPRODUCTIVE SYSTEM

Professionals and professors constitute a class of "experts" who share a similar status[11] and have passed through similar rites of passage. The academy reproduces not only its own workers but also professionals because their training has been appropriated within and transformed by the university.

> Throughout much of the world today, universities have replaced religious institutions as the conveyors of social values and prestige. They play a central role in molding cultural and social elites. Institutions of higher learning have become primary purveyors of status. (Harrison, 1985, p. 235)

In this position, we have the intellectual tools and the time to engage in a sustained critique of the culture, to resist the elitist claims of the university, and to transform the deformation resulting from participation in oppression. This work is one of our most emancipatory projects.

But in order to engage effectively in this critical work, we must be secure within the university system; we must have a place that is recognized as legitimate. The criteria for legitimization is made clear through mechanisms such as the educational process, tenure criteria, publication reviews, and professional accreditation. We speak the language of science and theory; construct and employ specific forms of knowledge; use understood and approved methods of inquiry; and contribute to the maintenance of the institution by acquiring reputation for the academy

---

[11]"The failure to see and name pervasive class dynamics in this society is robbing middle-strata people—especially men—of the critical insight needed to become aware of their subjugation or to act creatively and effectually against human oppression. White feminist women and racial and ethnically marginated women and men have entered into the sort of critical consciousness required for active resistance to oppression" (Harrison, 1985, p. 60). Winant (1987) calls this the "consolation prize" that comes with marginalization and "otherness." If you are fluent in more than one discursive practice, you are better able to decode and interpret your own culture and that of the dominant culture.

through scholarly work and publications, accessing "good students," and bringing in funded research.[12]

As the field of environment/behavior emerged in the 1960s, it simultaneously critiqued the existing practices within the disciplinary boundaries of the university and attempted to generate a legitimate location for itself within that same institution. This is tricky business, coyote business. The cost of achieving legitimacy can be absorption, annihilation, and/or the creation of another disciplinary boundary that further reifies and separates the interdependencies of bodies of knowledges. But to remain without voice gives us no position from which to speak for a different, transdisciplinary work within and outside the academy.

The university is positioned to arbitrate various knowledges and to claim as "truth" some forms of knowing embedded in class and gender structures. It sets the rules of evidence for the acceptance and rejection of knowledge; creates, maintains, and dominates the knowledge industry. We, who are located in the university and trained by the university as professionals, are implicated in the production and reproduction of the existing truths that marginalize and empower. How do we situate ourselves within the academy that simultaneously privileges us and excludes others and is therefore a form of oppression that subjugates other knowledges and peoples? The processes of exclusion and appropriation are subtle and real.

The coyote, a renowned narrator, tells it like this:

> The university is the best club in town, and is very selective in its membership. (No coyotes need apply.) Most of the decisions affecting the lives of the community-at-large are made within its walls. So of course, we (all who are systemically excluded) want to belong. We begin a serious campaign to be allowed to enter—first by demonstrating how women have supported and maintained the club in invisible ways. (You couldn't have spent all of your time solving the world's problems if we hadn't been taking care of the kids, washing your clothes, maintaining your car, cleaning your office, etc.) We found and celebrated those extraordinary few women (people of color, coyotes) who made significant contribution but who, because of their gender (race, class, species), were never given credit. We untangle and represent to you the ways in which your club has discriminated against all nonwhite male human beings. Surely you don't mean to discriminate, and if only you understand how your practices are exclusive, you would change your ways.

[12]The pressure to become legitimate within the academic enterprise (i.e., using faculty to create a surplus of reputational capital for the school and university as well as real subsidy capital through outside funds) arrived at architecture and landscape architecture schools later than the discipline-based departments of the university, such as psychology and sociology. The architectural enterprise was able to maintain a claim for the legitimacy of faculty work as art until the last 5 to 10 years. For an interesting discussion of the current pressures within architectural schools, see Mayo (1991).

> For many reasons, these forms of conversation become more accepted, and some of us actually are allowed to join. As members of the club we assume responsibility for the work of the club: We seek to achieve the aims even while inserting our experience. We also critique the work from our perspective, seeking to make it more responsive and inclusive. But once in the club, we begin to notice that we are starting to sound like one of the guys and wonder what is happening to us. We are beginning to see more clearly that the changes we had hoped to make may be impossible within the club itself: the very foundation, value assumptions, social structures, and ways of interpreting the world from the vantage point of the club are exclusive and deeply flawed. Being outside is beginning to look like a preferred place; perhaps we don't want to belong to the club anyway. The coyote says, "Give it back to the boys, we have much more important work to do!"

Feminism is not the only voice questioning the place of the university within the structure of systematic discrimination against women and marginalized groups in late capitalism. But it is a persistent and nagging one. From this critique, one of our tasks, surely, is to maintain a critical stance toward our own practices, their premises, and our ways of working. Science, as a privileged mode of inquiry in the academy, is and should be a focus of ongoing concern.

SCIENCE AS A SOCIAL PRACTICE

Science as a paradigm and mode of inquiry is about the business of healing itself from its repressive practices and captured world view aided by its own internal critique and the postmodern discourses including the feminist theory.[13] In no way can this chapter reconstruct the arguments of these theoreticians. But it is critical to the interpretation of our own work in human/environment relations to remember that the practice of science, the foundation of our way of working, has been the tool of preference to support the capitalist/industrial utopian (dystopian?) project of modernism.

"Better living through chemistry" reveals the vision of the modernist world; that we, through the rational application of knowledge gained through science and its servant, technology, will reach a state of happiness in this world. Science is not a separable, discrete function, but an integral and unremovable part of the modernist utopian project. We are

[13]Scholars in semiotics, deconstructionism, psychoanalysis, structuralism, postmodernism, and feminism have all addressed the question of science. All "share a profound skepticism regarding universal (or universalizing) claims about the existence, nature and powers of reason, progress, science, language and the 'subject/self'" (Harding, 1986, p. 28). For feminist critique, see Keller (1983, 1985); Harding (1986, 1991); Harding and O'Barr (1975); Code (1991); Haraway (1985, 1988); Lengermann and Niebrugge-Brantly (1990). See also Berry (1988); Griffin (1988); Thompson (1987, 1991).

only beginning to untangle the science/industrial/capitalist culture of domination to recognize that "their very realism was as pure a superstition as was ever professed by humans, their devotion to science a new mysticism, their technology a magical way to paradise" (Berry, 1988, p. 41).

The critique of science in the feminist discourse has mindfully explored the social practice of science, the enterprise itself, the organization of the club, its ways of working, and its relationship to the world. This work has situated science as one of many social practices that is used to maintain existing gender and class structures.

> Rather than standing as an impartial tribunal of truth, transcendent over the battle field of competing social forces, science is seen as one more interested participant, using its status to legitimate certain social, political, and economic forces and to delegitimate others. More than that, the scientific community's interest in its own social power relative to other professions and institutions is now seen to condition the picture of the world it sanctions as "scientific." (Griffin, 1988, p. 9)

Science, by claiming that the production of knowledge through science is distinct from the social/political/economic uses of that same knowledge, has failed to assume responsibility for its own practice. In other words, it has been irresponsible. The dualistic conception of basic versus applied science (the old theory/practice split) creates a space for science to claim that all knowledge seeking in the practice of science is "good" in itself. According to the duality of basic/applied, it is only after knowledge is generated that it falls into the political/ethical domain. The domain named "the applied" is assigned responsibility for the social use/abuse of science. And within the protected domain of basic science, scientists are seen as uninfluenced by their own social position, gender, or politics.

Feminists have worked hard at decoding and re-presenting ways in which the work of *science has maintained gender, class, and race inequalities in spite of its claim of being outside the socially constructed world*. The use of categories of men and women in research is an interesting case in point. Until very recently, gender distinctions themselves have been taken as "natural" descriptions of reality rather as unsymmetrical cultural constructs. Research conducted on men has been considered to reflect the human experience, rather than a particularistic perspective of men. And now that there is a much greater consciousness of the difference in the life experience of women, we have become a "special user group," whereas men are the norm against which this special user group is measured.

Bias is seen in categories such as the public/private domains with their gendered spheres, and concepts such as leisure/work dichotomy that reflects men's worlds in the twentieth century, leaving no space for activities such as "housework," other invisible (read unpaid) work by women, or "spillover activities" such as domestic laborers and baby-sitters (Harding, 1986; Smith, 1987).

Once engaged in a critique of the subjects of science and finding systematic incidences of "bad science" that exclude or misinterpret women's experience, the work of feminists expanded to include the basic assumptions and aims of science itself. Epistemology, the condition of knowing through the medium of constructed and structured interpretations and their relationship with the "known," has been problematized in many ways. Questions about what is knowledge, who knows, and where is knowledge have relocated the discourse on knowledge from an objective, Archimedean perspective into a discourse on the politics of knowledge. Who benefits from maintaining power over the production of knowledge? Untangling such social practices reveals the relationship between science and power.

Many forms of subjugated knowledges have been denied a legitimate place in the construction of meaning, and many purposes of knowing have not been given voice. Feminist epistemology suggests a much broader conception of the construction of knowledge to include such activities as talking and listening (Belenky, Clinchy, Goldberger, & Tarule, 1986), tacit knowing, perhaps even unspeakable knowing (Keller, 1982), and symbolic and aesthetic forms of communication as found in art and theater. Such research challenges the universal knower and science as the arbitrator of truth. Feminists have developed arguments for the plurality of knowledge and diverse forms of communication. However, when they construct theory and base their research on diverse and alternative modes of knowing, their work is suspect. Feminists are accused of not engaging in legitimate science because they have breached accepted ways of working and boundaries of legitimate knowledge.

However, if we accept the feminist critique of legitimate knowledge and assume that all knowledges are valid, we have to confront the confounding condition of a relativist perspective. Once the rules of evidence that privilege some forms of knowledge are challenged, once we assert that all knowers have equal claims to knowledge construction, once we recognize many different methods by which to construct and use knowledge, we are faced with a world in which knowledge is everywhere and everyone is a knower.

One of the earlier tenets of scientific faith was the belief that knowledge discovered through the methods of science was valid because it was "objective."[14] It was not an interpretation of a situated scientist about a phenomenon, but a fact that was replicable and general. The myth of objectivity has been critically challenged in all domains, including the "natural" science of physics, chemistry, and biology. It is acknowledged today, at least theoretically, that the knower is a part of the known. The fact that much research continues on the assumption that the two are distinct reveals that what we know and how we work may proceed at different paces. The coyote says this is a good reason not to take ourselves quite so seriously.

The dualism, objectivity and subjectivity, is one of the thorny questions within the paradigm of science. The aspiration for objectivity is itself diagnostic and, furthermore, it has been said that objectivity is a peculiar form of subjectivity.

> The objectivist illusion reflects back an image of self as autonomous and objectified; an image of individuals unto themselves, severed from the outside world of other objects (animate as well as inanimate) and simultaneously from their own subjectivity. (Keller, 1985, p. 70)

The claims of objectivity place the universal knower "nowhere"— outside and autonomous. How can we accept knowledge from no one from nowhere? But the dislocation of objectivity brings subjectivity into the center of the discourse as framed, with all of the criticism of relativity, of knowledge from everyone from everywhere. How do we know and take action on our knowing in such a slippery and relative world? We are offered a terrible choice—knowledge from nowhere or knowledge from everywhere. *We don't have to accept these terms.* The frame of the either/or choice reflects an inability to consider forms of relationship other than dualistic, oppositional, and hierarchical. Feminists[15] suggest that this is a gap, a "line of fault" that permits a reconceptualization.

Most postmodern feminists are calling for situated and embodied knowledges that acknowledge the *partial vision* of everyone's seeing and knowing, that is, to be from somewhere, to speak from a place (Haraway, 1988). Embodied and situated knowledge is always partial and

[14]"And on the banks of the San Juan River, the old poet told me that there is no fucking reason to pay attention to the fanatics of objectivity: 'Don't worry,' he said to me. 'That's how it should be. Those who make objectivity a religion are liars. They are scared of human pain. They don't want to be objective, it's a lie; they want to be objects, so as not to suffer'" (Galeano, 1991, p. 120).
[15]Haraway (1988); Harding (1986, 1987); Keller (1985); Lengermann and Niebrugge-Brantly (1990); Smith (1987).

incomplete. This liberates it to connect to other knowledges and ways of knowing—in fact, demands that we "stitch together" wholer knowledge based on many partial knowings.

Situated knowledge implicates the researcher in the subjects of research; there is no distance or position from which to claim objectivity. The involvement of the researchers in the political and personal accounts of their work attunes them more closely to the voices of the others; it demands that they become intimate and personal. The process of science in this endeavor is one that tries simultaneously to attend to and love the subject while disentangling oneself sufficiently to frame the questions of inquiry. In fact, it is the claim of located and positioned knowledge and not universality that is the condition of being heard in making knowledge claims.

Knowledge from someone from somewhere, situated knowledge, affirms the postmodern claim that the world is political and socially constructed. Yet this is not enough for science, a visionary and utopian project if there ever was one. We need good accounts of the world in all of its slippery and transforming conditions.

> I think my problem, "our" problem, is how to have *simultaneously* an account of radical historical contingency of all knowledge claims and knowing subjects, a critical practice for recognizing our own "semiotic technologies" for making meaning, *and* a no-nonsense commitment to faithful accounts of a "real" world, one that can be partially shared and that is friendly to earthwide projects of finite freedoms, adequate material abundance, modest meaning in suffering, and limited happiness. (Haraway, 1988, p. 579)

From the perspective of a situated, located knower, the work of a reclaimed science is a process of ongoing critical interpretation and invention. A reconstructed science becomes a social practice that is not irresponsible (no one from nowhere), but rather accepts responsibility for translations and partial knowings of ourselves and all forms of previously subjugated knowledges. "I don't think that in our wildest dreams we ever imagined that we would have to reinvent both science and theorizing itself in order to make sense of women's social experience" (Harding, 1986, p. 251).

EXPERT DISCOURSES AS INSERTION

The other place we find ourselves as practitioners of environment and behavior is in the world of "experts." We are called upon to insert our professional expertise by making comment on aspects of the social world and to do research in support of appropriate strategies for resolving social issues related to our field of inquiry.[16]

Because of the emancipatory aims of environment and behavior, we are often involved in issues of social justice such as handicapped accessibility, public housing, homelessness, enriching environments for children and the aged, and the like. In this location, we employ our theoretical constructs such as loci of control, freedom of choice, territoriality, and so forth to enlighten public discussion on the state's provision of needs. We use the practice and language of science to assert the veracity of our knowledge. But unlike the place of university that may, indeed, pretend to be a special place of neutrality, the world of expert discourses locates us in the middle of the politics of needs interpretation, a distinctive characteristic of late capitalist political culture (Fraser, 1989). This discourse is the terrain for contestation over what are legitimate needs, who gets to interpret them, and who gets to decide how they will be addressed. Our professional work in science in this domain is a political activity and to understand our role we will need to do critical work and some serious sniffing.

Before experts such as environment/behavior practitioners become involved, an issue must have been brought into the public domain as a critical area in need of action. How does an issue become a legitimate *public* question "appropriate" and/or fundable as a subject of academic inquiry?

This question frames a major activity of feminists, that is the challenge to the boundaries and meaning of the private and public as drawn in our times. "Public vs. private is a mapping of the psychological, social, and physical space of people's lives" (Lengermann & Niebrugge-Brantly, 1990, p. 333). The feminist oppositional voice claims that the personal is political and has maintained the struggle to redefine and redirect the current public/private spheres. The conceptualization of the private/public realms permeates our world. It is seen in the division between official economics ("the private sector") and politics (government)[17]; the division between the public and the domestic spheres; and

[16]"[E]xpert discourses tend to be restricted to specialized publics. Thus they are associated with professional class formation, institution building, and social 'problem solving'" (Fraser, 1989, p. 174). In some way, we have replaced the clergy and aristocracy in the process of needs identification, definition, and delivery.

[17]"The United States of America is distinct for virtually silencing the debate about democratizing economic life" (Harrison, 1991, p. 69). This silence makes it difficult for citizens to claim power over economic productive power and conceals the condition that the entire structure of the political economy in the United States is designed to support "the private sector." See also MacKinnon (1989).

the separation of public and private spaces into gendered urban and suburban worlds (Ackelsberg, 1988).

The feminist voice declares that many social acts and personal experiences are not private but public and political activities. And as aspects of the human condition in the late twentieth century become inscribed as "needs" and are thrust into the public domain for debate, experts are implicated to both define and refute such claims to the state's provision of services to alleviate the needs.

Fraser (1989) provides a fascinating discussion of the intersection of "needs discursive practices," that is, what happens when issues "break out" of the bounded domains of the domestic or official economic spheres and become identified as needs that must be addressed as communities of people embodied in the state. Activities or conditions that have always existed but that were not attended to in the public domain, issues such as universal design/handicap accessibility, domestic violence, day care, are identified by oppositional groups that give voice to the newly named "need." First, established conceptual boundaries of the "private" are contested, boundaries that had denied the issue a place in public discourse. Second, the groups who are struggling to bring this issue into the public domain develop activities and structures to meet the needs they have identified through informal networks such as community-based centers for battered women.

The attempts to redraw boundaries between public/private spheres are not without opposition and serious debate. Newly identified "needs" are challenged by those who wish to "reprivatize" the need, that is, take it back out of the public discourse and reaffirm its location within the private domain. The arguments are familiar—state intervention into homelife violates rights to privacy; or we have private institutions such as handicapped shelters to take care of people with disabilities; or the private sector can responsibly regulate its own affairs. Reprivatization arguments *must* be made when the boundary of public/private are disputed.

The social space within which these needs are now contested is moved closer to the domain of the political, wherein the state will be forced to take some kind of action because the boundaries of public and private have shifted. This is the space within which we, as academics and professionals, insert ourselves as "experts" to assist in defining the needs and developing programs to meet these needs. Much of our work on child-care centers, the elderly, group homes, and handicap access, and the like is a result of our position as a professional class of experts called in to frame the issue.

In this position, we, through the conduct of science and research, universalize and decontextualize the needs. In other words, we appropriate the needs, interpret them, and create social/institutional structures to address the satisfaction of the needs as we have defined them. This expert discourse acts as a bridge between popular social movements and the state by depoliticizing the discourse into administrative and managerial languages. Within this space, our activities serve to legitimize and/or delegitimize the various voices struggling for the right to interpret, define, satisfy, or deny the needs.

This is often the point when those engaged in the early social movement, the oppositional voice, strike out at "the experts" and call their/ our work inadequate. They claim that we have acquiesced to "the state" and appropriated their more "real" interpretation of the need. In our decontextualization of the need, in our academic generalization and categorization, we are accused of taking the passion, the world-as-lived dimension out of the experience. We become the voice of no one from nowhere. This is coyote business. Can we practice and speak from a situated place ourselves, acknowledging our role in expert discourses and the politics of knowledge in the interpretation and provision of needs? As the boundaries between what is public and what is private are continually redrawn, we find ourselves in a unique position to attend to the political nature of our actions or to ignore our position as both "inside and outside" the arenas in which we practice in the university and in expert discourses. The boundary between participation for understanding as a professional activity and participation to further the struggles for a better world is blurred, overlapping, and commingled.

OWNING OUR UTOPIAN WORK

A rethinking of our location in/through the university, engaged in the social practice of science and the insertion of our knowledge through expert discourses, calls us to be critical and mindful of our practice in environment/behavior. The critique of our practice as one of many human enterprises does not deny its gifts to construct and know the world but demands that we continually challenge its repressive tendencies. In other words, we are called not only to engage in a critical inquiry that deconstructs our situated work but also to reinvent science and other institutions of knowledge in which we participate. It is a project of hope; partial, transformative knowledges can be constructed that are more liberating, critical, and situated than we have known.

Mindful Practices

As in any practice, those of us in the field of environment and behavior structure our work by developing categories and types that facilitate research, making, and interpretation. Categories that name the subject of our research—names such as environment, office, users, clients, subjects, and "64-year-old Jewish Latina Lesbians" (Bradley & Wolfe, 1987)—are noninnocent ways of organizing our practice. They are not about semantic certainty but point to motivations and forces that include and exclude. Being mindful of our categories reveals the ways in which they both constrain our work and present opportunities for emancipatory projects.

The practice of creating a scientific subject reveals the dualism of "the knower" (us) and "the known" (them). Historically, the practice of science has neither problematized nor located the knower, one of the areas of critique discussed in the last section. In a similar way, research focused on the knower has not always problematized the known. We find ourselves in a world that "emphasize(s) the relationship of a sort of idealized individual to a place or environment" (Saegert, 1990, p. 11). Both foci are prevalent in environmental/behavior studies, but neither sufficiently problematizes the conduit by which the knower and the known know each other—the work of interpretation. This is the inserted and problematized space of postmodern theory including postmodern feminists.

Feminist theory has played an important role in demonstrating that the universal subject is a myth; "there are not now and never have been any generic 'men' at all—only gendered men and women" (Harding, 1987, p. 285). And within feminism, much of the recent writing speaks to the deconstruction of the universal category of "women" to reflect complex historical, racial, cultural, and class differences among women. This is the important work of contextualizing an abstraction, of recognizing real people in concrete social, cultural, and political contexts, living in real places.

The construction of "the user" in environment/behavior as a useful category in our practice demonstrates how classifications are produced, reproduced, employed, and finally, come to inhabit our thinking. Users appeared very early in our practice (Moore et al., 1985). Naming the subjects was an attempt to bring people back into the modernist discourse of architecture on the one hand, and the environment into the fields of psychology and sociology through a disciplined inquiry into relationship.

Categories such as users are dangerous in that they are often totalizing and universalizing; worlds and different experiences are subsumed under a norm that erases differences. A review of categories of people researched and reported on in EDRA proceedings revealed that descriptors of people were less specific than descriptors of environments. Differences were submerged into homogeneous categories, and certain groups of people do not appear at all. Sex/gender differences were absent in nearly one-half of the papers reviewed implying a universal nongendered person. Another critical aspect of the categories used in our practice was the specifying of nondominant groups and, conversely, not specifying dominant groups such as white, male, middle-class heterosexuals. "Without considering the particularity of *all* people's lives, we produce theory, design and policy recommendations which are inadequate and possibly oppressive" (Bradley & Wolfe, 1987, p. 180).

What does the construction of the category "user" tell us about our practice? The user is a specific type of research subject. User implies relationship—one who interacts with, acts upon, effects—some other. It speaks the language of capitalism. Users imply that the nature of the relationship between people and place rests in the rhetoric of consumption. People use environments; environments don't use people. Humans are in a position of dominance as if the world were present simply for our inscription.

And yet there is a curious passivity in the language of user that denies the possibility of acting upon place. To use a place is not to make a place. Much of our early research and some of our most developed conceptual models such as crowding, territoriality, proxemics, describe the effect of spaces on people. Likewise, our most developed methodologies of programming and postoccupancy evaluation often cast users as receivers, possibly inadequate to effect changes in their places. This is ironic in light of the theoretical work on loci of control and effectance as an indicator of quality relationships between people and place. Perhaps our historical reliance on empiricism without the accompanying reflective historical and critical work only permitted us to see people as they were affected by, not effecting places.

The category *user* creates a separate and distinct "them." As the voice of authority, the experts, we place our users within various material and conceptual domains. They and their needs will already be ascribed a space within the public/private domains, and this will be an official position reinforced by many social/culture norms. Our mindful problematization of this one aspect will place such discussions overtly in a political context—it will call into question the location and interpretation of what we/they have identified as needs.

Not only does a category such as user create a "them," it also creates an "us." Where does this place us? As discussed earlier, we occupy the privileged location reinforced by our sociopolitical position as professionals, "the experts." We are positioned to see and interpret the experience of others without being involved in their lives, essentially, voyeurs. We speak for others through our various discourses in teaching, publishing, consulting, and making. Users in various places become the field against which our work is framed. From one perspective, this can be conceived of as giving voice to those who are not heard. Or it can be read as appropriating the voice of others and producing their meanings for them.

The use of a category to describe the world-as-lived dislocates the experience of people-in-place. In other words, once we create and employ a category such as users (or elderly, or children), we actually replace the condition that captivated our interest in the first place. Our own categories then organize, inhabit, and colonize our thinking; we lose the people and places, their interpretations, and resistance. Our framing of the experience of people-in-place in the discursive practice of science or expert discourses represents their experiences within the language and meaning systems of *our* situations, and reframes our own thinking through the invention and reproduction of categories. In other words, by engaging the "problem" as we have framed it, we distance the world.

Does this mean we cannot, should not construct categories? How can we possibly proceed? Such a situation suggests that we accept a coyote attitude toward the ongoing restructuring of our work and accept that categories entangle, confound, and enlighten the work we would seek to do to better understand the relationship between people and the places they (we) inhabit.

We, historically located, gendered human beings, bring our knowledge and our categories into our practice. If we accept our own situated and partial knowing, then our engagement in the practice of environment and behavior might be structured somewhat differently. The idea of "interviewing" (Oakley, 1981) creates a space unlike the usual relationship between the researcher and the subjects of that research. This space is a place for mutual learning, a recognition that the power to construct meaning is a social, community activity, and not the territory of privileged academics or professionals. It is an acting-out of the premise of partial, situated knowledges that affirms that our knowing is always imperfectly formed, complex, contradictory, and needs the partially constructed, particular knowledge of specific others.

The attitude of mutual vulnerability and interrelating projects creates the opportunity to frame a dialectic between the meaning of the world as it appears to the various participants in any activity of place making and our academic/professional interest in the constructors of the reality, our users so to speak. We are responsible for an act of translation;

for enabling the various subjects to translate their own texts and experiences so that the accounts may be shared. We further are tasked with the translation of these texts of the world into the language of the academy so that different forms of knowing enter that discourse. In this location, we are confronted with the complexity of translating personal, particularistic texts of people's lives into sufficiently generalizable statements on which we join in creating acts of liberation (Lengermann & Niebrugge-Brantly, 1990, p. 325).

This comingling condition demands that we be less sure of our categories and the boundaries we draw around our subjects and our fields. In fact, it suggests that our aim of generating theory in the traditional academic sense may be getting in the way of our work of both generating knowledge and place making. We don't need a totality to work well, we don't even need to share a basic understanding of concepts. What we do need is the willingness to engage in the *conversation* about the construction and deconstruction of categories and knowledge. This is the position of many feminist theorists who initially attempted to create theories and analytical concepts free from patriarchal power. A critique of their own work has led many to suggest that the very creation of legitimate categories and theory prohibited the most useful and liberating work.

"[W]e can learn how to embrace the instability of the analytical categories; . . . to use these instabilities as a resource for our thinking and practices" (Harding, 1987, p. 286). To advocate instability makes a space to consider many different relationships and connections and to focus on the spaces between the categories, to bring forward formerly subjugated knowledge. Haraway demands even more as she argues "for *pleasure* in the confusion of boundaries and for *responsibility* in their construction" (Haraway, 1985, p. 66). This sounds like coyote work, demanding that we give up our position as knower and expert, creating the space to make mistakes, to be wrong, to make fools of ourselves, and to continue practicing.

How does the purpose of practice change if we dislocate objectivity and embrace situated knowledge? There is no question within the feminist discourse that there is an emancipatory aim for our work—academic, personal, professional living. Our aim is to create a more humane space within which all people may live. Once we remove the goal of objectivity in our reading and constructing of the world and recognize that our knowledge is partial and situated, we are free to be clear about the utopian wishes of human/environment relations.

If we use people for our ends—as users, as research subjects, as clients—we and they are impoverished. It is an not easy practice understanding the ways in which space, place, people, and the relationships between them have been structured to restrict personal and community power, and uncovering how we have been implicated in that process. But it is mindful, emancipatory work.

LIBERATING PROJECTS

> There is just one place where yesterday and today meet, recognize each other, and embrace, and that place is tomorrow. (Galeano, 1991, p. 135)

This chapter has been an exercise in situated theorizing in which I have attempted to problematize our location and its impact on the work we do as practitioners in the field of environment and behavior. Part of this exercise has been to untangle the webs and connections of the places in which we find ourselves—the university as an institution, science as a way of working, and expert discourses as a form of practice.

Our work as professionals in human/environment relations engages us daily in a social practice whether or not we are aware of the political dimensions of our activities. This is about us and our power relationships with the people with whom and for whom we work . . . users, clients, students, colleagues, friends, and institutions.

> Power is not only understood as something groups or individuals *have*; rather, it is a social relationship between groups that determines access to, use of, and control over the basic material and ideological resources in society. Fundamentally, then, empowerment is a *process* aimed at consolidating, maintaining, or changing the nature and distribution of power in a particular cultural context. (Morgen & Bookman, 1988, p. 4)

To acknowledge our political work requires that we reframe for ourselves a utopian vision so that we may be more mindful of our practice, and that by our articulation, enable connections to others. In many ways, this is not difficult for a field of inquiry rooted in a utopian project that aspires to social and ecological justice. To acknowledge our utopian vision(s) "establishes a standard, a goal; and by virtue of its existence alone it casts a critical light on society as presently constituted" (Elliott, 1970, p. 22).

Yet we must address the accusation that utopianism is totalizing and repressive, that is about no place, that can never be. One of the powerful insights of the feminist discourse on science is the gift of partial vision and therefore, situated knowledge. Perhaps we can accept a partial utopia, one that we recognize is ragged around the edges, whose boundaries shift and change, and one that requires the vision and knowing of others to patch together the web. *Utopia or no utopia? No thanks*, replies the coyote, *I have creative, visionary work to do, boundaries to confound, places to go, and people to see.* Our recognition of partial knowledge facilitates a different way of being and working in the world—one less precious, more playful, more willing to deconstruct and reconstitute boundaries, less truth to defend, and more conversations to engage.

> Feminist objectivity makes room for surprises and ironies at the heart of all knowledge production; we are not in charge of the world. We just live here and try to strike up noninnocent conversations by means of our prosthetic devices, including our visualization technologies. (Haraway, 1988, p. 594)

Our awareness of the political nature of our work does not demand that we all leave the university and march in the streets for various causes. We do political and utopian work in the academy. One of the emancipatory acts that all of us require is the disentanglement of the codependencies of oppression; we need located, partial, rigorous intellectual work.[18] Our position within the academy and as professionals places us in the position of doing situated theorizing—of unmasking debilitating structures such as the accepted boundaries of constructs as the public and the private drawn to exclude subjugated knowledges. Our location within expert discourses serves as a bridge between social movements and professional domains, and our critical intellectual work can both affirm and interrogate our own and oppositional voices struggling to empower themselves in the public domain. Our intellectual work can be radical, empowering, and utopian.

Yet there is an inherent tension in both speaking about and doing the intellectual work of the academy as a liberating social practice. As necessary as this work is, it smacks of a benevolent paternalistic attitude, that the social location of intellectuals "enables them to assume they have intellectual riches to give to the poor" (Harrison, 1985, p. 237). *This is coyote work—the tricky work of staying in-between, of being in more than one place.* We recognize our embodied lives in the ivory tower as professionals and experts, and our many connections with others.

Coyote business is never about doing work or not doing work—it is about how we choose to relate to our friends and the "real" places we share. I use the language of friend to name the others with whom we work that recognizes our codependencies in creating knowledge and in doing emancipatory work. The power of these relationships is awesome.

> (W)e have the power through acts of love or lovelessness literally to create one another . . . Because we do not understand love as the power to act-each-other-into-well-being we also do not understand the depth of our power to thwart life and to maim each other. (Harrison, 1985, p. 11)

The utopian vision I am describing, and which reflects ongoing work in feminist theory, is always partial, located, embodied, and proba-

[18]I thank Helen Liggett for clarifying the work of intellectuals as radical, political work. See also Fraser (1989), "Apologia for Academic Radicals."

bly already exists as long as we and others, coyotes included, continue to trot along.

Acknowledgments

I thank Sherry Ahrentzen, Louise Chawla, Karen Franck, Bonnie Ott, Robert Shibley, and the editors for their insightful comments and critique of this chapter.

REFERENCES

Ackelsberg, M. (1988). Communities, resistance and women's activism. In A. Bookman & S. Morgan (Eds.), *Women and the politics of empowerment* (pp. 297–313). Philadelphia: Temple University Press.

Ahrentzen, S. (1990). Rejuvenating a field that is either "Coming of age" or "Aging in place," Feminist research contributions to EDR. In R. Selby, K. Anthony, J. Choi, B. Orland (Eds.), *Coming of age* (pp. 11–18). Oklahoma City: Environmental Design Research Association.

Albrecht, J., & Lim, G. (1986). A search for alternative planning theory: Use of critical theory. *Journal of Architectural and Planning Research, 3,* 117–131.

Barthes, R. (1979). *The Eiffel Tower and other mythologies.* Trans. R. Howard. New York: Hill & Wang.

Bartowski, F. (1989). *Feminist utopias.* Lincoln: University of Nebraska Press.

Belenky, M., Clinchy, B., Goldberger, N., & Tarule, J. (1986). *Women's ways of knowing: The development of self, voice and mind.* New York: Basic Books.

Berkeley, E., & McQuaid, M. (Eds.). (1989). *Architecture: A place for women.* Washington DC: Smithsonian Press.

Berry, T. (1988). *The dream of the earth.* San Francisco: Sierra Club Books.

Bradley, E., & Wolfe, M. (1987). Where do the 64-year-old Jewish Latina lesbians live? Diversity of people as an environmental issue. In J. Harvey. & D. Henning (Eds.), *Public environments* (pp. 175–181). Washington DC: Environmental Design Research Association.

Canter, D., Krampden, M., & Stea, D. (Eds.). (1988). *New directions in environmental participation.* Brookfield: Avebury.

Chorney, H. (1990). *City of dreams: Social theory and the urban experience.* Scarborough: Nelson Canada.

Code, L. (1991). *What can she know? Feminist theory and the construction of knowledge.* Ithaca, NY: Cornell University Press.

Elliott, R. (1970). *The shape of utopia.* Chicago: University of Chicago Press.

Feldman, R., & Stall, S. (1990). Residents' activism in public housing: A case study of women's invisible work of building community. In R. Selby, K. Anthony, J. Choi, B. Orland (Eds.), *Coming of age* (pp. 111–119). Oklahoma City: Environmental Design Research Association.

Fishman, R. (1977). *Urban utopias in the twentieth century: Ebenezer Howard, Frank Lloyd Wright, Le Corbusier.* Cambridge, MIT Press.

Flax, J. (1987). Postmodernism and gender relations in feminist theory. *Signs, 12* (4) (Summer 1987), 621–643.

Franck, K., & Ahrentzen, S. (1989). *New households, new housing.* New York: Van Nostrand Reinhold.

Francis, M., Moore, R., Iacofano, D., Klein, S., & Paxson, L. (1987). Design and democracy. Special issue. *Journal of architectural and planning research*, 4(4).

Fraser N. (1989). *Unruly practices: Power, discourse and gender in contemporary social theory*. Minneapolis: University of Minnesota Press.

Galeano, E. (1991). *The book of embraces*. New York: W. W. Norton & Co.

Griffin, D. (Ed.). (1988). *The reenchantment of science*. New York: State University of New York Press.

Haraway, D. (1985). A manifesto for cyborgs: Science, technology and socialist feminist in the 1980's. *Socialist Review* (March/April 1985), 65–107.

Haraway, D. (1988). Situated knowledges: The science question in feminism and the privilege of partial perspective. *Feminist Studies, 14* (3) (Fall 1988), 575–600.

Harding, S. (1986). *The science question in feminism*. Ithaca: Cornell University Press.

Harding, S. (1987). The instabilities of the analytical categories of feminist theory. In S. Harding & J. O'Barr (Eds.), *Sex and scientific inquiry* (pp. 283–302). Chicago: University of Chicago Press.

Harding, S. (1991). *Whose science? Whose knowledge? Thinking from women's lives*. Ithaca: Cornell University Press.

Harding, S., & O'Barr, J. (Eds.). (1987). *Sex and scientific inquiry*. Chicago: University of Chicago Press.

Harries, P., Lipman, A., & Purden, S. (1988). Meaning in architecture: Post-modernism, hustling and the big sell. In D. Canter, M. Krampden, & D. Stea (Eds.), *Environmental perspectives* (pp. 188–199). Brookfield: Avebury.

Harrison, B. (1991). The fate of the "middle" class in late capitalism. In J. Thomas & V. Visick (Eds.), *God and capitalism* (pp. 53–71). Madison: A-R Editions, Inc.

Harrison, B., & Robb, C. (Eds.). (1985). *Making the connection*. Boston: Beacon Press.

Hayden, D. (1984). *Redesigning the American dream*. New York: Norton.

Keller, E. F. (1983). *A feeling for the organism: The life and work of Barbara McClintock*. San Francisco: Freeman.

Keller, E. F. (1985). *Reflections on gender and science*. New Haven: Yale University Press.

LeGuin, U. (1987). *Buffalo gals and other animal presences* (pp. 80–100). New York: New American Library.

LeGuin, U. (1989). A non-euclidean view of California as a cold place to be. *Dancing at the edge of the world*. New York: Harper & Row.

Lengermann, P., & Niebrugge-Brantly, J. (1990). Feminist sociological theory: The near future prospects. In G. Ritzer (Ed.), *Frontiers of social theory* (pp. 316–344). New York: Columbia University Press.

Lewin, K. (1951). *Field theory in social science*. New York: Harper & Row.

Lopez, B. (1977). *Giving birth to thunder, sleeping with his daughter*. New York: Avon Books.

MacKinnon, C. (1989). *Toward a feminist theory of state*. Cambridge: Harvard University Press.

Mayo, J. (1991). Dilemmas of architectural education in the academic political economy. *Journal of Architectural Education, 44*(2) (February 1991), 80–89.

McClung, W. (1983). *The architecture of paradise: Survivals of Eden and Jerusalem*. Berkeley: University of California Press.

Moore, G. (1987). Environment and behavior research in North America: History, developments and unresolved issues. In D. Stokols & I. Altman (Eds.), *Handbook of environmental psychology, Vol. 2* (pp. 1360–1410). New York: Wiley.

Moore, G., Tuttle, D., & Howell, S. (1985). *Environmental design research directions*. New York: Praeger.

Morgen, S., & Bookman, A. (1988). Rethinking women and politics. In A. Bookman & S.

Morgen (Eds.), *Women and the politics of empowerment* (pp. 3–27). Philadelphia: Temple University Press.

Oakley, A. (1981). Interviewing women: A contradiction in terms. In H. Roberts (Ed.), *Doing feminist research* (pp. 30–61). London: Routledge & Kegan Paul.

Peterson, R. (1987). Gender issues in the home and urban environment. In E. Zube & G. Moore (Eds.), *Advances in environment, behavior and design* (pp. 182–218). New York: Plenum Press.

Saegert, S. (1987). Environmental psychology and social change. In D. Stokols and I. Altman (Eds.), *Handbook of environmental psychology, Vol. 1* (pp. 99–128). New York: Wiley.

Saegert, S. (1990). Environmental design evaluation and the making of places. In M. Conan & C. Zimring (Eds.), *Critical approaches of environmental design evaluation proceedings, Vol. 2.* Paris: CSTB.

Sandercock, L., & Forsyth A. (1992). A gender agenda: New directions for planning theory. *Journal of the American Planning Association, 58*(1) (Winter 1992), 49–59.

Sanoff, H. (1989). Have we reached our vision of 1969? In G. Hardie, R. Moore, & H. Sanoff (Eds.), *Changing paradigms* (pp. 15–16). Oklahoma City: Environmental Design Research Association.

Schneekloth, L. (1987). Advances in practice in environment, behavior and design. In E. Zube & G. Moore (Eds.), *Advances in environment, behavior and design, Vol. 1* (pp. 307–334). New York: Plenum Press.

Schneekloth, L., & Shibley, R. (1981). On owning a piece of the rock. In A. Osterberg, C. Tiernan, & R. Findlay (Eds.), *Environmental design interactions* (pp. 183–196). Washington, DC: Environmental Design Research Association.

Schneekloth, L., & Shibley, R. (1987). Research/practice: Thoughts on an interactive paradigm. In R. Shibley (Ed.), *Proceedings of the American Institute of Architects/Association of Collegiate Schools of Architecture annual research conference* (pp. 27–36). Washington, DC: AIA/ACSA Research Council.

Shibley, R., & Schneekloth, L. (1988). Risking collaboration: Professional dilemmas in evaluation and design. In *The Journal of Architectural Planning and Research, 5*(4) (Winter 1988), 304–320.

Smith, D. (1987). *The everyday world as problematic.* Boston: Northeastern University Press.

Sommer, R. (1984). Action research is not business as usual. In D. Duerk & D. Campbell (Eds.), *The challenge of diversity* (pp. 3–8). Washington, DC: Environmental Design Research Association.

Stimpson, C., Dixler, E., Nelson, M., & Yatrakis, K. (Eds.). (1981). *Women and the American city.* Chicago: University of Chicago Press.

Stokols, D., & Altman, I. (Eds.), (1987). *Handbook of environmental psychology, Vols. 1 & 2.* New York: Wiley.

Thompson, W. (Ed.). (1987). *Gaia: A way of knowing.* New York: Lindisfarne Press.

Thompson, W. (Ed.). (1991). *Gaia 2—Emergence: The new science of becoming.* New York: Lindisfarne Press.

Torre, S. (1981). Space as matrix. *Heresies, 3,* 51–52.

Vizenor, G. (1988). *The trickster of liberty.* Minneapolis: University of Minnesota Press.

Wandersmann, A., Giamartino, G., & Peabody, G. (1978). Factors influencing participation. In W. Rogers & W. Ittelson (Eds.), *New direction in environmental design research* (pp. 453–453). Washington, DC: Environmental Design Research Association.

Weisman, G. (1983). Environmental programming and action research. *Environment and behavior, 15*(3) (May 1983), 381–408.

Winant, T. (1987). The feminist standpoint: A matter of language. In B. Stafford (Ed.), *Hypatia (special issue): Philosophy and Women Symposium, 2*(1) (Winter 1987), 123–148.

Index